THE TWO GEORGES

PARALLEL LIVES
IN AN AGE OF
REVOLUTION

Alexander Robertson, *Mount Vernon in Virginia*, 1800. Engraving by Francis Jukes. Colored aquatint.

Paul Sandby, *Windsor Castle from the West*, 1802. Pencil, bodycolor.

THE TWO GEORGES

PARALLEL LIVES
IN AN AGE OF
REVOLUTION

Edited by
Susan Reyburn and Zach Klitzman

LIBRARY
LIBRARY OF CONGRESS

Library of Congress Cataloging-in-Publication Data

Names: Reyburn, Susan, editor. | Klitzman, Zach, editor. | Library of Congress, issuing body.
Title: The two Georges : parallel lives in an age of revolution / edited by Susan Reyburn, and Zach Klitzman.
Other titles: Parallel lives in an age of revolution
Description: Washington, D.C. : Library of Congress, 2025. | Includes bibliographical references and index.
Identifiers: LCCN 2024042949 | ISBN 9780844495903 (paperback) | ISBN 9780844495927 (hardcover)
Subjects: LCSH: George III, King of Great Britain, 1738-1820--Exhibitions. | Washington, George, 1732-1799--Exhibitions. | Presidents--United States--Biography. | Generals--United States--Biography. | Great Britain--Kings and rulers--Biography. | United States--History--Colonial period, ca. 1600-1775--Exhibitions. | Great Britain--History--George III, 1760-1820--Exhibitions. | Library of Congress--Exhibitions. | CYAC: United States--History--Revolution, 1775-1783--Exhibitions. | BISAC: HISTORY / United States / Revolutionary Period (1775-1800) | HISTORY / Europe / Great Britain / Georgian Era (1714-1837)
Classification: LCC D107 .T896 2025 | DDC 321.00922--dc23/eng/20240927
LC record available at https://lccn.loc.gov/2024042949

Published in 2025

© Library of Congress
ISBN: 978-0-8444-9590-3
ISBN: 978-0-8444-9592-7

All rights reserved.

Director of Publishing, Library of Congress: Becky Brasington Clark
Editors: Susan Reyburn and Zach Klitzman
Designer: Marlena Rivera

Unsigned text by Susan Reyburn, Zach Klitzman, Julie Miller, and Colleen Shogan

Front cover images:
Benjamin West, *George III*, 1779.
Oil on canvas. Detail.
Charles Willson Peale, *George Washington at Princeton*, 1779.
Oil on canvas. Detail.

Back cover images:
Tim St. Onge, Maps showing travel areas for George Washington and George III, 2024.
George Washington and George III, ca. 1780. Etching.

The Two Georges exhibition was made possible by support from an anonymous donor, Beverly Lannquist Hamilton, HISTORY®, the estate of Leonard and Elaine Silverstein, and FTS International, LLC.

Printed in Canada

Table of Contents

Foreword, Carla Hayden, Librarian of Congress — ix

Introduction — xii

Chapter 1: Two Georges in a Georgian World — 1

Chapter 2: British Beginnings — 34

Chapter 3: Parallel Lives — 56

Chapter 4: Rupture: America Revolts — 116

Chapter 5: A King, a President, a Republic, and Executive Power — 146

Chapter 6: The Apotheosis Perplex — 190

Portrait Gallery — 206

Acknowledgments — 216

Contributors — 217

Selected Sources and Notes — 220

Image Credits — 229

Index — 232

Foreword

The two Georges were born six years and 3,700 miles apart; each was one of nine children who lost his father at an early age, and each was the eldest son of a widowed mother. Each worked from an early age to take his place on the public stage, George Washington in colonial Virginia, the young prince as future king of the British Empire. While George III followed a dynastic path, Washington could not have anticipated how influential his role would be. They would clash as commanders-in-chief of their respective armed forces in the American War for Independence (1775–1783) and are now best known by myths and images that began to accumulate even during their lifetimes.

The Two Georges: Parallel Lives in an Age of Revolution compares their characters, their interests, their leadership, and the roles of myth and imagery in their legacies. They were touched by and participated in revolutions of all sorts, including the political, scientific, and cultural. Both men were, in part, responsible for the creation of the images that they projected in the public sphere. As king, George III pursued an Enlightenment model of virtuous family life, using portraits and public appearances to display his commitment to benevolent fatherhood and fidelity in marriage. The king was also careful to model a balance between "private economy and public magnificence," as he expressed it himself in an early essay. George Washington, well aware of his commanding physical presence, carefully crafted his public image to project leadership and emotional control. He and his wife Martha commissioned likenesses steeped in the tradition of formal European portraiture and imbued with American symbolism. As Washington's fame grew, so did the popularity of his image.

In addition to their widely distributed images, the two Georges left behind troves of letters, household accounts, notes, and other items that chronicle their official and private lives. The Library of Congress purchased Washington's papers from the Washington family in 1834 and 1849. Through gifts, exchanges, transfers, and subsequent purchases, the George Washington Papers have grown to include his correspondence, diaries, financial and military records, and schoolbooks. The Library also has in its collection dozens of maps Washington created.

This publication and the accompanying exhibition, part of the Library's America 250 celebration, grew out of a partnership inspired by the Georgian Papers Programme that includes the Library of Congress, the Royal Collection Trust, King's College London, the College of William & Mary, and the Omohundro Institute for Early American History and Culture. See page 219 for information on these and other institutions, where readers can access robust collections of manuscripts, maps, images, and additional resources on the two Georges and their shared transatlantic world.

I invite you to experience the depth and breadth of what the Library of Congress collects, preserves, and makes available, whether in person in Washington, DC, or online at loc.gov.

Carla Hayden
Librarian of Congress

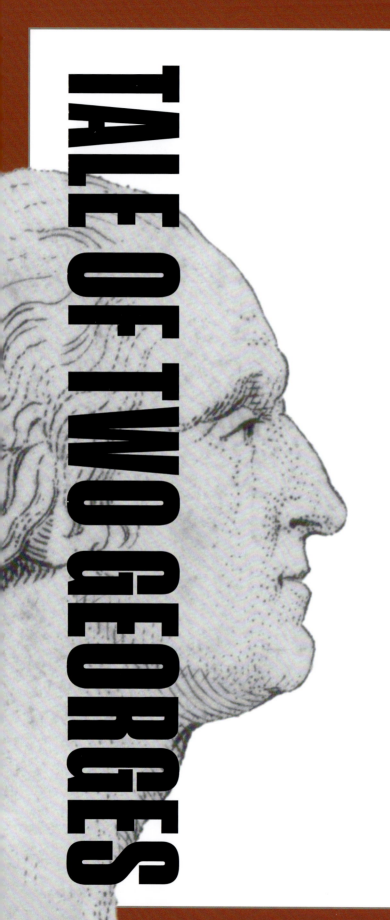

TALE OF TWO GEORGES

- Birthdate
- Birth location

- Height
- Wife
- Number of children
- Time as head of state
- Office(s) held

- Titles

- Education

- Religion
- Favorite drink
- Military experience
- Languages spoken
- Musical instruments played
- Favorite animal or pet
- Assassination attempts and plots

- Played baseball
- Lived in the "White House"

- Death date

George Washington	George William Frederick
February 22, 1732	June 4, 1738
Westmoreland County, Virginia, Colony of Great Britain	Norfolk House, London
6 feet, 2 inches	5 feet, 10 inches
Martha Dandridge Custis	Princess Charlotte of Mecklenburg-Strelitz
0	15
1789-1797	1760-1820
Burgess (Virginia legislator) President of the United States	King of Great Britain King of Hanover
Mr. President His Exellency	George the Third, by the Grace of God, King of Great Britain, France, and Ireland, Defender of the Faith, and so forth, Duke of Brunswick and Lüneburg, Arch-Treasurer and Prince-elector of the Holy Roman Empire
Private tutors and possibly some grammar school	Private tutors; he could read and write in English and German by age eight
Anglican Church	Anglican Church
Madeira wine	Borage and white wine
Served in the field for two wars	Never served in the field
English	English, German, and French
None	Violin, flute, harpsichord, pianoforte
His horse, Nelson	Dogs
1 (1776, plot included Thomas Hickey of the Life Guard)	6 (August 2, 1786, January 21, 1790, October 29, 1795, May 15, 1800 twice), 1802 plot was foiled.
No	Yes
Yes, but not the executive mansion: White House was Martha's plantation house	Yes occasionally, a mansion of that name at Kew Gardens
December 14, 1799	January 29, 1820

Introduction

Although American president George Washington and British king George III never met in person, at times they were very much on each other's minds. They knew and met people in common, appeared together in popular and pointed political cartoons, and faced off in war. They shared similar interests and responsibilities, and, as leaders, grappled with the upheaval of revolutions—political, economic, social, and scientific—that characterized the eighteenth-century Atlantic world.

From the beginning of his life, as an eldest son and an heir to the British throne, the king knew his destiny. Washington, with older brothers and far less to inherit, had to make the most of his opportunities. Both Georges had long happy marriages to women on whom they relied, and had those wives lived in a less oppressive era, might well have pursued their own interests to even greater effect. The king, born into a large family, famously produced an even larger one. Washington, who had no children of his own, became a stepfather and father figure to a slew of relatives, soldiers, and neighbors, not to mention his popular role as father of his country. The king was a devout Anglican and a sworn defender of the Church of England; Washington was a member in good standing, serving as a vestryman and churchwarden. The generally sober and stoic Washington appreciated a good joke but seldom made one, while George III regularly displayed a sense of humor and cheerful nature.

Each man was frugal, conscientious, and hyperaware of his behavior, reputation, and legacy. Each took his position seriously, the king as Britain's constitutional monarch and head of state overseeing an ancient kingdom and established global empire, Washington as the American colonies' commander-in-chief and later as first president of the United States, managing a new and experimental work in progress. And each, notably, respected and adhered to the limits of his constitutional authority.

Perhaps surprisingly, given their elevated positions, the two Georges thought of themselves as farmers, an occupation to which most ordinary people at the time were connected. Both were deeply involved in improving agriculture, and each was interested in ongoing scientific and technical advances, the king out of intellectual curiosity and the colonist out of practicality. Despite living on a global stage, Washington left the North American mainland only once, going no further than Barbados, though he was well traveled in America, and King George saw strikingly little of Britain. Both men were implicated in the institution of slavery, though in different ways: Washington held hundreds of people in bondage to work his plantation; the king did not enslave anyone himself, but enslaved labor enriched his kingdom. The tall and imposing Washington, who conscientiously projected strength, survived several severe physical illnesses, and as a robust individual, his death came as a shock. Meanwhile, the king wrestled with several overwhelming bouts of physical and mental illness that he fought to overcome and that later unfairly defined him.

The two Georges were not only curious and informed about each other, but together they experienced an extraordinary level of international recognition. Major developments in communication, including the rapid growth of media (newspapers, pamphlets, magazines, broadsheets, and prints), speedy clipper ships, and the infrastructure of the British Empire spread their images, words, and actions worldwide. This visibility and presence in public and among widespread populations ratcheted up the profound and personal effect of their great confrontation, the American War for Independence, in which each had compelling, defensible reasons for spearheading his respective cause. In the end, Washington was the celebrated victor and a devastated George III pondered abdication. They are forever linked by a schism that, while resulting in two separate and distinct nations, was eventually followed by reconciliation as close allies with a shared language, culture, and history.

In considering these men, *The Two Georges: Parallel Lives in an Age of Revolution* contextualizes, compares, and contrasts their experiences in youth, as family men, as men of the Enlightenment, as adversaries in war, as king and president, and as figures of national myth and memory. Short essays from scholars open each chapter and examine the commonalities and differences between the two Georges as well as the forces and circumstances that informed their lives and leadership. We have complemented these essays with features on specific areas of overlap and contrast, such as their military backgrounds, food preferences, and love of science, agriculture, and books; short biographies of their parents, wives, and extended families; and a variety of historic documents, maps, prints, and artwork in the Library of Congress collections and from around the world. These supplemental pieces underscore the myriad changes the two Georges participated in and witnessed during an age of revolution.

In the terminology used here, the terms "Whig" and "Tory" refer to political sentiments and loose groupings (rather than formally organized parties) during the reign of George III. Tories were conservative and in opposition to Whigs, who favored the political primacy of Parliament. The American Revolutionary War and the American War for Independence are used interchangeably in referring to the colonies' rebellion against Britain. The Anglican Church and the Church of England are also used interchangeably, though after the Revolution, the church was reorganized in the United States as the Episcopal Church, and Anglicans became known as Episcopalians. In quoting the two Georges and their contemporaries, we have kept original spelling, punctuation, and capitalization in quotations, modernizing when necessary for clarity.

Our hope is that readers will find new and surprising connections between two men who led opposing forces with tremendous consequences for their respective countries, and who as influential leaders helped shape the modern world: one beloved by many, and even apotheosized in the American mythos, the other conscientious of duty yet wrongly characterized as a mad tyrant. Both men were much more nuanced and complex than popular memory recalls. The technical advancements they explored and the ideas they embraced were as much a part of the age of revolution as the war that separated them.

Susan Reyburn and Zach Klitzman
Library of Congress

The WESTERN or ATLANTIC OCEAN, with part of EURO[PE]

A New Map, or Chart in Mercators Projection, of

The Atlantic World

John Senex, *The Western or Atlantic Ocean, with Part of Europe, Africa and America,* **1739.**

This map, published the year after Prince George's birth and when George Washington was seven years old, depicts the Atlantic world the two Georges grew up in and European claims in the Americas north of the equator. Yellow represents Britain and its colonies, stretching from Newfoundland to Georgia, as well as some Caribbean islands, including Jamaica, the Bahamas, and Barbados. Red signifies Spain and the Spanish Empire, most prominently in Mexico, Central America, and northern South America, as well as Cuba. France, in green, claims much of the North America interior as well as the western part of Hispaniola.

Chapter 1

George Washington and George III, ca. 1780. Etching.

Two Georges in a Georgian World

George Washington (1732–1799) was the first president of the United States of America. George III (1738–1820) was king of Great Britain and Ireland. Two Georges of the Anglo-American eighteenth century, the latter born to rule, the former coming to preside, together reveal new insights into a complex and consequential historical era—certainly for the United States and the United Kingdom, but also for the wider world. As we seek new windows on this wider world through a deliberate, focused pairing of the two Georges, we need to understand that world to comprehend their respective places in it.

The Georgian era, named after the four British monarchs reigning between 1714 and 1830, is often associated with an aesthetic style. It was also a time of important and interrelated changes in the economy, politics, and the reach of the British Empire. It was a period of new knowledge, published in the intense fury of a print culture that threw up broadsides, newspapers, pamphlets, satires, and novels. The era was also significant for the extended continuity of Hanoverian rule, following the tempestuous age of the Stuart dynasty (including the English Civil War and the Glorious Revolution).

All of these developments, by turn astonishing and influential, were profoundly important domestically in Britain, but what of the Georgian world? During the Georgian era, the British consolidated and expanded their empire in the Caribbean and North America, and deepened imperial claims in Asia, the Pacific, and then Africa. The consequences of empire reverberated throughout the Georgian world, as goods and people—and culture and language—moved with the compulsory rhythm and call of economic and military power. The trade in enslaved African people powered the sugar plantations of the Caribbean colonies and shaped the North American continent. A shared Anglo-American Protestantism meant that the diverse religious commitments of the empire's people were often defined against that standard—whether they were from a Judeo-Christian tradition, including Catholics and Jews, or from utterly different religions.

By comparing the two Georges we observe the full sweep and implications of this complex, dynamic era in which so much was determined by circumstance, and in which there were new opportunities for individual agency. Both Georges, competent, even talented in their own way, came to power and prominence through hierarchy and privilege. The monarchy that empowered George III was represented throughout the empire in material and visual iconography that conveyed the deep importance of this very British system. Almanacs, the most widely circulated texts in the American colonies other than Bibles, routinely noted the monarch's birth and other anniversaries. In every building of note the monarch's coat of arms distinguished British claimed spaces; gifts to Native American allies were stamped with the king's arms. Although the Hanoverians were a recent continental import from a German principality, their lineage through Sophia of Hanover (a granddaughter of James I) successfully harnessed the long tradition of the British monarchy.

For George Washington, the British system of hierarchy meant that he could and did expect to inherit property, pursue more, and include enslaved people among his holdings. Ever a diligent man, by his late teens Washington was an accomplished surveyor, soon to be commissioned in His Majesty's military service. His abilities and work ethic, one might like to think, would have been recognized and rewarded anywhere, but in truth had they been displayed by a person of color, or a woman of any color, they would not have been. Among his contemporaries, Alexander Hamilton stood as an extraordinary example of a white man not born to wealth who nonetheless worked his way to it.

If change and continuity are the foundations of historical assessment, the eighteenth-century world of the two Georges, the local context of George III's England and Washington's Virginia, the more expansive settings of the United Kingdom and the British Colonies, and more inclusively the Anglo-Atlantic, just part of the British Empire, were all characterized by both. This was a time and these were places of both extraordinary continuity and extraordinary—even revolutionary—change. Each of these two men experienced, advocated, and fought for both, and each was shaped by both. They have been remembered differently in their respective nations: Washington has long been considered an American hero, while George III is, after years of being caricatured as the mad king who lost America, coming to be better appreciated. As individuals with some decidedly unheroic qualities, and leaders who shouldered extraordinary responsibilities, we see each better for understanding their context and through them, we better perceive a richly complex world so vital to shaping our own.

George III's Britain

In Britain, the Georgian era has often been presented as the site of profound transformations, even the birth of "the modern." The notion of an "age of revolutions" associated with the latter part of the period incorporates not merely rapid political change but social and cultural developments. Historians have identified an "agricultural revolution," in which new methods of husbandry transformed farming and productivity; this facilitated an "industrial revolution" in which factory production, technical innovation and new labor practices bolstered output. In turn this, alongside increased trade, contributed to a "consumer revolution," as more, cheaper commodities flooded on to the market. Central to such historical narratives of the eighteenth century's foundational influence on subsequent eras is a "rise of the middle class" on the back of the expansion of market capitalism, and, in E. P. Thompson's famous interpretation, the first steps in the making of the English working class. Had another (and highly loaded) term not already been coined for an "intellectual revolution"—"Enlightenment"—this might be added to the list, contributing its own energy to the other transformations. New economic and demographic data, for example, has prompted reassessments of the reach, speed, and significance of each transformation, and questions as to whether the term "revolution" adequately encapsulates more complex and patchy developments marked as much by continuities as change. It would not be until the mid-nineteenth century that more of the English population dwelt in town than country; factories remained the exception rather than the rule; economic growth rates were weaker than once claimed; class formation was less clearly defined (both "middle" and "working" identities being less monolithic and distinct than formerly assumed); the progress of "enlightenment", especially if equated with secularization, liberalization, or even gradual "improvement," was less benign, dramatic, or irreversible.

Identifying these continuities does not imply the Georgian period in Britain was static. If Georgian Britain did not undergo revolutionary change, neither was it an *ancien régime* characterized by endemic "old corruption," irrationality, cruelty to man and beast, and archaic modes of operation. Victorian reformers looking back from the nineteenth century saw the earlier period swept away in the wake of landmark legislation. The repeal of the Test and Corporation Acts (1828) and Catholic Emancipation (1829) together transformed the relationship of church and state by removing membership in the Church of England as a requirement for public office. Above all the "Great" Reform Act of 1832 reshaped the British parliamentary system in ways that changed politics and rendered the crown a subordinate player. This account of major change sweeping away the Georgian era, however, was rooted in the self-congratulation of the Victorian reformers themselves. Subsequent scholars view Georgian England more as a site of continual experimentation, and of excited and ever more-inclusive discussion among not only its governors both local and national, but an increasing if still small proportion of its inhabitants. Both benefited from relatively easy access to sources of information and news, rendering even local and limited innovation in political, social, or cultural spheres the subject of debate and discussion, which perhaps disguised from contemporaries fascinated by each novelty the extent of the continuities.

One key continuity which became a platform

for change was the strength and clear purpose of the Georgian state. Primarily an engine for financing and conducting warfare, this "fiscal-military state" transformed both its capacities and ambition, and the demands it imposed on society. There is no better place to look for an "industrial revolution" in Britain than naval dockyards. The search for additional military personnel and wartime security drove tentative steps to increased religious toleration. Military needs too shaped the evolution of the fiscal system, whether that be the introduction of taxes on the North American colonies or the introduction of income tax in Britain. The increased demands on the resources

Isaac Cruikshank, *The Abolition of the Slave Trade, or the Inhumanity of Dealers in Human Flesh Exemplified in Captn. Kimber's Treatment of a Young Negro Girl of 15 for Her Virjen Modesty,* **April 10, 1792. Hand-colored etching. London, published by S. W. Fores.**

Isaac Cruikshank's highly charged abolitionist cartoon is based on a reported atrocity aboard the British slave ship *Recovery*, whose captain, John Kimber, whip in hand, is shown having an African girl hoisted up to be flogged. In September 1791 she was one of some three hundred people sold into slavery in New Calabar, on the west coast of modern-day Nigeria, and destined for Grenada in the West Indies. During the barbaric "middle passage" across the Atlantic, the captives, otherwise manacled in cramped, filthy conditions below deck, were regularly forced to dance for exercise, as well as the prurient amusement of the ship's crew. William Wilberforce, a member of Parliament, accused Kimber of whipping her to death for refusing to dance. In a case that received wide press coverage, Kimber was acquitted of murder —under shady circumstances—at London's Old Bailey, but its importance was twofold: the trial demonstrated that slave ship crews could be tried for the deaths of their human cargo, and along with Cruikshank's cartoon, it further galvanized the British public's growing opposition to the slave trade.

Two Georges in a Georgian World

of middling citizens stimulated the emergence of a politically salient "middle class" as much as changes in the British economy, while their purchase of government stock then gave them a vested interest in the status quo.

The exigencies of war also promoted a new thirst for information which could inform policy initiatives in areas hitherto seen as outside the purview of national government, from welfare to new forms of trade regulation. This inaugurated an "information state" necessitating novel approaches to statesmanship to oversee its workings, and which in its inquiries and investigations enabled voices beyond the elite to be heard in new ways. Aspects of this development are visible in King George himself, as this remarkably untraveled monarch buried himself in maps, tables, books, and communications, seeking to fit himself for governance of Britain and its extensive, complex empire.

George III's Empire

These maps and other instruments took the monarch to the distant lands he never visited in person. George III travelled only as far south as Plymouth and as far north as Worcester. "George's England" was thus confined to a region some 110 miles north to south and 170 miles west to east, yet Britain extended west to Wales and Ireland and north to Scotland, while the British Empire stretched around the globe. During the reign of George III and the life of George Washington, this full "Georgian Globe" was a matter of enormous consequence for all Britons, including Americans, and for people in Europe, Africa, and Asia. Its expansion, administration, and economic and military policies shaped the experiences and the opportunities of millions.

Britain's empire had become fiscally and militarily mighty in the late seventeenth century. Through several critical developments by financiers, merchants, and politicians, by the middle of the eighteenth century Britain was competitive with the most powerful European empires, including France and Spain. They fought a series of wars in Europe with key theaters of operation in North America, reflecting its economic and geopolitical importance. By the time George III ascended to the throne, the Seven Years' War (1756–63) was underway, the largest and most consequential of these global conflicts. It saw Britain and France come to blows across the Georgian globe, involving allies which in North America included Native Americans on both sides.

The British Empire started not with full throated, government-backed efforts, like those of France and Spain, but with private enterprise. And until the 1750s, official boots on the ground in North America were not those of soldiers, but of royal officials. From governors to customs officers at ports, these eighteenth-century enforcers of British law and imperial policy lived side-by-side with colonial subjects, both free colonists and enslaved people, and Native Americans. They carried out the will of the king, Parliament, and the Board of Trade, enforcing conformity with imperial regulations. When the infamous Stamp Act was passed in 1765, threatening to impose taxes on a host of everyday items, urban colonials up and down the coast resisted the tax collectors, their opposition taking the form of protest poetry and prose, and threats of violence. But plenty of colonists held offices: Benjamin Franklin, for example, was appointed one of two postmasters general for North America, a post he held for more than twenty years until he was dismissed in 1774 in the wake of prerevolutionary political unrest.

From an eighteenth-century imperial perspective, however, the most valuable colonies were not in North America, but the Caribbean. The island of Jamaica was the British Empire's largest sugar producer. The sugar plantations in the British Caribbean, in Jamaica as well as smaller islands including Barbados, Barbuda, Dominica, and St. Kitts and Nevis, produced tremendous wealth for their owners, and tremendous wealth for the British government through regulated commerce. Sugar also helped power a global consumer culture that reached beyond food (confections) and drink (tea and spirits) to furniture (the tea table), fashion (umbrellas), and architecture (tea gardens).

The consumer world of sugar and its profits was sustained by enslaved laborers. The Royal African Company held a monopoly on trade in West Africa and enslaved and shipped to the Americas approximately a quarter of a million African people in the late seventeenth and early eighteenth centuries. Private British merchants invested heavily in the slave trade, too. The Trans-Atlantic Slave Trade database documents more than 3.2 million African people enslaved and shipped out of Africa under the British flag before legislation ended the slave trade in 1807. Enslaved people were traded and sold to the British Caribbean, and then into North America. By the middle of the eighteenth century, enslaved African-descended people dominated the population of the Carolinas, were at least half the population of the mid-Atlantic colonies, and were present in all of the colonies.

George Washington's North America

Britain's North American colonies were knitted into the empire through the slave trade, and more broadly through economics, politics, and the military. Increasingly regulated and robust trade made North America a critical market for Britain's exports. Likewise, by the time of the two Georges, Britain was the most important customer for

William Woollett, *To the King's Most Excellent Majesty, This View of the Royal Dock Yard at Deptford*, painted by R. Paton, the figures by J. Mortimer; 1775. Engraving.

The Royal Navy was essential to maintaining a global empire, and as commander-in-chief, George III had a keen interest in the institution. It played a key role not just in warfare, but also in transportation and in communication. Fast clipper ships could travel between Britain and the American mainland colonies in as little as six weeks, delivering news and military orders. For example, the Declaration of Independence ratified in Philadelphia on July 4, 1776, was first printed in British newspapers around mid-August. Some historians argue that control of the sea was more instrumental to British imperial endeavors than control of colonial territory.

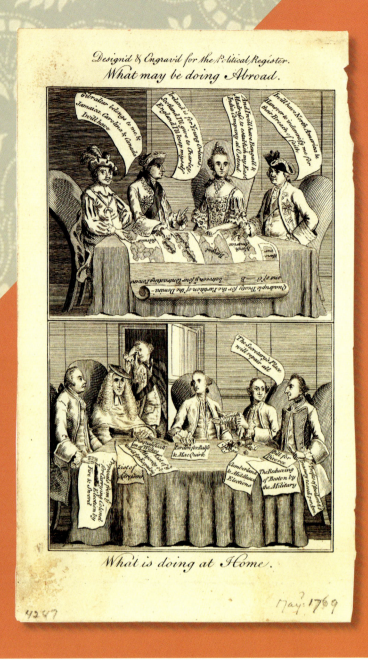

What May Be Doing Abroad—What Is Doing at Home, April 16, 1769. Etching and Engraving. Designed and engraved for the *Political Register*, London.

Juxtaposing possible external and existing internal threats to the empire, an anonymous artist envisions European monarchs pointing to a world map, top, and plotting to seize British possessions. From left, Charles III of Spain claims Gibraltar and covets Jamaica, the Carolinas, and Canada; Louis XV of France plans to take Ireland and England and pass Scotland off to Bonnie Prince Charlie, pretender to the British throne; Theresa Maria of the Habsburg dominions stakes out India; and Frederick II of Prussia aims for North America and Hanover. Meanwhile, George III's cabinet, bottom, is distracted with its own schemes, including a proposal for the "Reducing of Boston by the Military." The distressed king, standing behind his ministers, raises a handkerchief to wipe his tears.

North American exports, whether flour grown and milled in Pennsylvania, tobacco harvested in Virginia, or rice cultivated in South Carolina. The goods that Britain sent to the colonies included items that would be famously taxed: cloth, glass, paper products. They also included things that colonial elites desired to make themselves and their homes fashionable. In 1757, for example, Washington ordered a carved cartouche of his family's coat of arms to crown the overmantel in the front parlor at Mount Vernon. When Martha Custis married Washington two years later, she ordered embroidered purple silk heels to wear with her wedding gown.

Britain's importance to the colonies extended beyond the cultural and economic significance of

 Chapter 1

consumer goods and fashions. Politically, governance of the colonies was both becoming more centralized through the hands of royally appointed governors, and more self-governing as colonial legislatures flexed their capacities and expressed their desire for control over, for example, internal taxes. But to be clear, most British colonials saw themselves as importantly connected to England. In addition to various cultural examples of Britishness, they might not all be Anglicans (in fact, most were not) but they identified with a British Protestantism. Colonial political leaders regularly referenced the importance of the British form of government and constitution, though they disagreed about whether the king or Parliament was better upholding it.

What historian Joyce Chaplin called the "paradox" of the colonial political relationship with the empire was plainest in the ways that colonial legislatures created new statute law to recognize slavery. Making descent from the mother determinative of one's status, the doctrine of *partus sequitor ventrem* was an astonishing departure from English law. In legalizing slavery, the colonial authorities innovated in ways that countered longstanding English practice and ultimately law. These contradictions came to a head in the famous *Somerset* case of 1772, which found against chattel slavery as inconsistent with common law.

Colonists' constant push to expand territory rested on a desire for more settlements, more commerce, and scotching other European claims, especially those of the French. So when twenty-one-year-old Washington went to war, as a freshly commissioned major in the Virginia Regiment, it was in defense of the British Empire. As part of forces meant to secure British interests in territory along the Ohio River valley, he set out to challenge French incursions there. A key context was the power of Native Americans, who were the dominant population across North America until the later eighteenth century (European and African-descended people made up fewer than half of the remainder of the population and were mostly gathered on the Atlantic Seaboard). In Washington's first foray on behalf of his king's government, he tried to persuade the Iroquois Confederacy to change their alliances from French to British. The way he understood his task, to make claims on behalf of one European power against those of another, illustrated how a series of "treaties," often overlapping, and misunderstood on all sides, gave Europeans a false sense of ownership of lands occupied and largely in the power of Native Americans. The first salvos of the Seven Years' War in North America, in fact, included those in early 1754 under Washington's command.

From Unrest to Revolution

George III's early years as monarch in Britain, beginning in the midst of the Seven Years' War, also present a paradox. His accession as a young man skipping a generation from his cragged grandfather George II seemed rich in opportunity for his realm, something which contributed to the genuine celebration which accompanied his coronation. In his first years, three longstanding sources of threat and instability to the kingdom appeared suddenly to evaporate. First, on the global stage, victory in the Seven Years' War blunted the French and Spanish challenge to Britain's imperial enterprises. Secondly, in 1766, Pope Clement XIII declined to acknowledge the (no longer) "Bonnie" Prince Charlie as the rightful monarch of Britain, signaling the end of a serious Jacobite challenge which in the previous half century had seen two armed conflicts on British soil and significant sections of the political elite excluded from both local and national governance. Thirdly, the new king's youth ensured that there was no maturing but frustrated Prince of Wales in place as a rallying point for disaffected politicians, as George himself had been while awaiting his accession at Leicester House. George arrived on the throne after considerable reflection (and parental and gubernatorial counsel) on what constituted good monarchical rule and determined to apply it, an intention captured in his famous speech from the throne when he "gloried in the name of Briton."

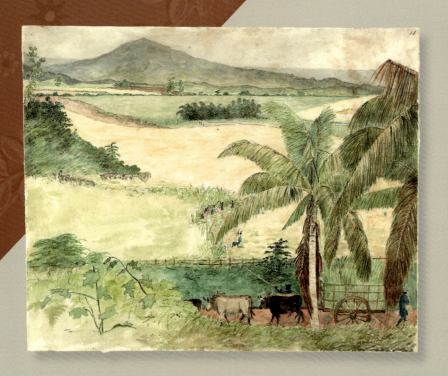

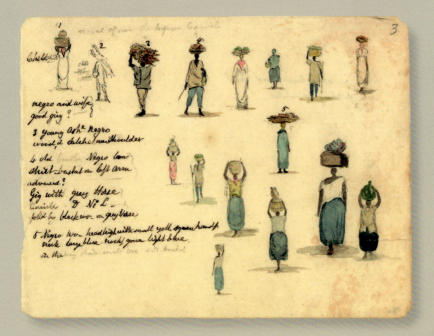

William Berryman, *Sugar estate - Negros cutting cane*, ca. 1808-1816. Watercolor, black ink.

William Berryman, *Negro portraits, 16 small drawings with notations*, ca. 1808-1816. Brown and grey ink, pencil, watercolor.

English artist William Berryman created three hundred pencil and watercolor studies of Jamaica's people, flora, landscape, and buildings while living there from 1808 to 1815. He envisioned selling engravings of the drawings, but he died around 1816 before the project came to fruition. Many of them, such as the examples here, depict the enslaved population of the island, Britain's largest Caribbean colony. In 1800, there were approximately 300,000 enslaved people in Jamaica. Sugar plantations created high demand for sugar in Europe and were hugely profitable, but the enslaved work force toiled under brutal conditions: on average, imported laborers died after only seven years. Although Britain outlawed the slave trade just before Berryman arrived in Jamaica, emancipation did not occur until August 1, 1834.

Despite all this, the first twenty-five years of George's reign proved politically tumultuous. New developments in both parliamentary and extra-parliamentary politics baffled and frustrated all concerned as they sought to explain why things had taken this turn. From a distance we might recognize how the sudden change of longstanding dynamics not only made it difficult to assess new developments, but also challenged contemporary understanding of the previous era. Just as the end of the Cold War allowed previously suppressed sources of conflict to emerge, which could only be understood by trying to reframe understanding of the Cold War itself, so from the 1760s contemporaries struggled to make sense of their disordered world; they only too frequently resorted to conspiracy theory or notions of corruption to do so. With the king among those contemporaries trying to make sense out of chaos, his every move served to entangle himself even more in the toxic web of accusation and counter-accusation that characterized these years. When the king suffered his earliest known profound episode of mental illness in 1788–89 (it would return both in 1801 and 1804, before finally settling in for the remainder of his life in 1810), it helped distance him from suspicion of covert intervention in affairs. Through the frame of conspiracy and suspicion of corruption were interpreted the motives and intentions of political actors not just in England, but from Scotland and Ireland too, even as, and partly because, the integration of those kingdoms into the British polity proceeded apace not only in constitutional terms but through the involvement of their peoples in the joint enterprise of the British Empire. And it was in such frames that the actions of the king's American subjects were also liable to be interpreted in Britain.

Then came Revolution.

In retrospect it might seem obvious that the British colonies in North America would revolt, but it was anything but obvious at the time. Attachment to Britain was strong and, as historian Andrew O'Shaughnessy has argued in an analysis of the British Caribbean, the independence of the North American colonies as a collective would not have seemed logical to any contemporary— right up until the very moment that it seemed the only reasonable course. The colonies were individual units, with individual relationships with Britain and one another. Early efforts at co-operation, most famously in the Albany Congress of 1754 that brought together seven colonies at the behest of British officials to urge a unified approach to French aggressions, did not leave a significant legacy.

But the legacy of the Seven Years' War was a key prelude to the American Revolution in several ways. Britain had been working to tighten administration of the colonies for decades, and the deployment of British regular troops to North America for that war was part and parcel of a growing recognition of the colonies' economic and strategic value. What began as disputes over taxation imposed in the wake of the war, to offset enormous costs Britain incurred in fighting across the globe, merged with increasing restlessness about the constraints on colonial legislatures. Colonial politicians, many from wealthy families but others with comfortable professional and other backgrounds, began to articulate a sense of their right to impose—or resist—types of taxation. Popular unrest around the same issues, particularly in port cities such as Boston and Philadelphia, burst into public view. Similarly, British officials' use of what seemed arbitrary searches undertaken without due process provoked a series of court cases and published protest. By the late 1760s, crowd action and pamphlets such as James Otis's *Rights of the British Colonies Asserted and Proved* including the sentiment—although without the precise and catchy phrase—"taxation without representation is tyranny," set the stage for intensifying conflict in the next decade.

George Washington represented Virginia at the First and Second Continental Congresses, formal meetings convened first to discuss boycotting British goods, and then to manage the increasingly obvious and violent confrontations between colonists and British officials and soldiers. In June 1775 Washington was appointed commander of the new Continental Army. The progress of the war was uneven, from early indications

Cityscapes

Thomas Bowles, *A General View of the City of London and the River Thames*, 1757. Colored Engraving. Published in *Views of London* (London: Laurie and Whittle, 1794).

When this print was originally produced in the mid-eighteenth century, London was the largest city in the Western world. Its population of 740,000 was roughly twenty times that of Boston and New York, or even British towns such as Liverpool and Bristol. The capital of a vast empire, it was the center of government, the military, commerce, the arts, and publishing. As such it attracted visitors from all over the British Empire, who went to see Westminster Abbey, on the horizon at left; tall, domed St. Paul's cathedral, center; and the imposing square fortress, the Tower of London, at right. In 1759, George Washington wrote that "The longing desire, which for many years I have had of visiting the great Matrapolis of that Kingdom is not in the least abated." Although Washington never saw London, people born in North America certainly did live there. At least 5,000 white men who hailed from the colonies resided in "the great metropolis" in the 1770s, as many colonial Americans who could afford it often sent their sons to study in London.

In the foreground of this print are ships in the Pool of London, the main port area of the period. Tobacco, sugar, rice, rum, and animal furs were unloaded here. It also was an embarkation point for indentured servants and other laborers heading to the colonies; on the eve of the American Revolution approximately two thousand migrants departed for the colonies each year.

John Carwitham, *A South East View of the Great Town of Boston in New England in America*, originally engraved ca. 1736. Hand-colored etching. London: Printed for Carington Bowles, ca. 1760–1764.

This print of Boston shows the seaport, with Fort Hill on the left, Long Wharf in the center, and Hancock's Wharf to the right. First settled in 1625 and incorporated in 1630, Boston had approximately 15,500 people in 1765. Just a few years earlier in 1760, the Great Boston Fire destroyed nearly 350 buildings.

A hotbed of rebellious fervor in the decade leading up to the Revolutionary War, Boston was the namesake location of critical events such as the Boston Massacre in 1770 and the Boston Tea Party in 1773. By the time the war started on the outskirts of the town, in the twin battles at Lexington and Concord, Boston was America's third largest city. George Washington arrived in nearby Cambridge, Massachusetts, in July 1775, besieging the British for the better part of a year. The king's troops finally evacuated the city about eleven months into the war on March 17, 1776.

Two Georges in a Georgian World   11

Henry R. Robinson, *A View of the Federal Hall of the City of New York, as appeared in the year 1797*, 1847. Color lithograph.

In 1776, New York City was second only to Philadelphia in population size, with approximately 25,000 residents. The British landed on Long Island in August of that year, and by the end of November—after defeating General Washington's forces in a series of battles—they controlled the important commercial and political city. In 1779, British general Henry Clinton issued the Philipsburg Proclamation from nearby Westchester County, decreeing that any enslaved person "who shall desert the Rebel Standard" would receive "full security" from the British Army. As a result, some 10,000 people escaped, pouring into New York City during the war. It remained a Loyalist hub until the British evacuated in 1783 following the Treaty of Paris.

This nineteenth-century print depicts New York in 1797, specifically Federal Hall, located in the present-day Financial District. First built on Wall Street in 1703 as New York's city hall, the building served as the home of the Stamp Act Congress in 1765, an outpost of the Sons of Liberty during the Revolution, and the site of the First Congress, which hosted George Washington's inauguration in 1789. It was torn down in 1812 and later replaced with a Greek Revival structure that serves as a national memorial to Washington and the early republic.

Thomas Jefferys, *An East Prospect of the City of Philadelphia*, 1768. Etching. Published in London.

Founded in 1682 by the Quaker William Penn, Philadelphia was a bustling colonial port town when this engraving was made nearly a century later. In the lengthy description underneath the main image, Philadelphia is described as a "flourishing city" "very full of inhabitants" with "the Trade so extensive" that one month saw 117 ships in the harbor at the same time. Thomas Jeffreys also included a street plan, landmarks of the city, and a closeup of the State House, which became known as Independence Hall in the early nineteenth century.

The 1760s saw rapid growth in Philadelphia. The population reached 33,000 on the eve of the Revolution, making it America's largest city. Both the First and Second Continental Congress met in the State House; it was there, in June 1775, that George Washington received his commission as general of the Continental Army, and in 1776, where the Declaration of Independence was debated and signed. During the winter of 1777-1778, British forces under General William Howe occupied the city while General Washington and his troops camped at Valley Forge about twenty miles up the Schuylkill River from Philadelphia.

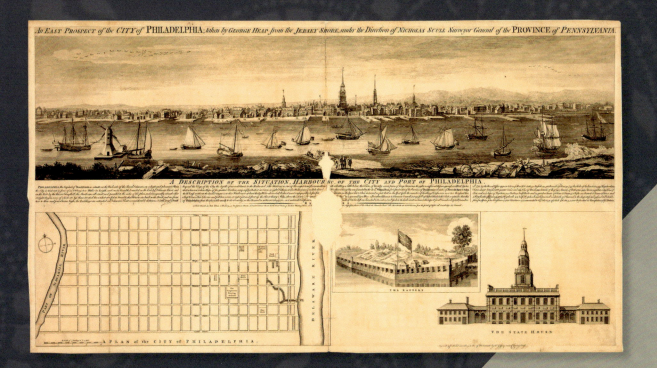

that the British army would surely and quickly overwhelm the Americans, to their occupation of key cities such as New York (1776–83) and Philadelphia (1777–78), the complex war in the southern colonies, the crucial American victory at Saratoga, and the decisive, final victory at Yorktown. George III was disinclined to recognize the "independence" of the United States in the Treaty of Paris ending the war, scribbling in the word "separation" instead.

For Washington, the Revolution resolved some issues, and created others. The struggle to craft a coherent and lasting national government concluded with the adoption of the Federal Constitution in 1789. For decades the political parties argued over whether their opponents were Francophile or Anglophile, with resonances not only of the British colonial past, but of the crucial French alliance in the American Revolution and then the complex and violent French Revolutionary era. Renewed war with Britain in 1812 was only one sign of the continuation of eighteenth-century conflicts into the nineteenth century.

It is the French Revolution and the Napoleonic Wars, rather than the American Revolution, that have long been the subject of British public attention. Students are frequently challenged to assess the "impact of the French Revolution" for example, and to disentangle this from the consequences of the ensuing French/Napoleonic Wars. The Battles of Trafalgar and Waterloo, and their victors Horatio Nelson and Arthur Wellesley, Duke of Wellington, inspired the naming of people, places and things across the British Empire: think only of the towns called Wellington in New Zealand, Australia, Canada, India, and indeed the United States; or of the tourist map of London which features Trafalgar Square, Waterloo Station, and the English response to Napoleon's last resting place at Les Invalides in Paris, the interment of Wellington's and Nelson's remains beneath the dome of St. Paul's Cathedral. Between them, the French Revolution and Wars were credited with inspiring a new popular radicalism and a countervailing and novel popular loyalism to reinforce an equally novel reaction among elites, a massive expansion of the state and its military and civil capacities, and new approaches to state expenditure and fiscal policy that would fuel much national and local history for the next half century. The French Revolution and its aftermath also provided Britons with grounds for self-congratulation over the absence of a similar constitutional conflagration within Britain itself.

Yet the significance of the *absence* of a British revolution for arguments advancing the idea of British exceptionalism may also explain why the importance of the *American* Revolution to British history was for so long so little explored. Since the 1970s, however, the American Revolution has finally re-emerged from under the shadow of the French as having its own distinctive—and equally enduring—impact on the domestic history of Britain (one, for obvious reasons, however, that left little footprint in British public spaces: there are no commemorative Yorktowns or Lexingtons on British soil).

In political terms, divisions over eighteenth-century American policy had generated realignments that contributed significantly to the later striking resurgence of a "Tory" tradition focused on defending existing arrangements in church and state. This ended a period in which patriotism had been an oppositional and often radical rather than loyalist position (hence Samuel Johnson's often misunderstood axiom of 1775 that "patriotism is the last refuge of a scoundrel"). The American Revolution also equipped British radicals with new universalist understandings of the basis on which "rights" might be claimed. At the same time, the crisis so sufficiently dented elite confidence in British institutions that it sparked a novel program of institutional reform, both progressive and defensive, that would set much of

Art in Warfare

Powder horn with hand-drawn map of the Hudson River (above Albany), Mohawk River, Niagara region, and Lake Ontario in New York Province, ca. 1757-1760. Map on bovine horn, pewter.

Before cartridge boxes were common, frontiersmen, hunters, and soldiers carried powder horns slung over their shoulders to store and access gunpowder. Lightweight hollow cow or ox horns were fixed with water-tight caps and a carrying strap, and their curved shape made transferring powder into a musket a tidy process. Owners often carved or engraved maps, scenery, designs, and their names on the surface—or had an artist do so—making the horns a personalized piece of equipment, a source of historical documentation, and works of art. Powder horns were widely used during the French and Indian War and the American Revolution, and the one shown here, shellacked, with a pewter spout and hinged pewter cap, features elegant script and extensive renderings, including the British coat of arms, ships, windmills, forts, and local skylines, making it an especially notable example of the craft.

References to one or the other of the two Georges appear on some surviving horns. A horn made in Cambridge, Massachusetts, in June 1775 and used by Henry Wilcoks reads "Come all ye sons of Liberty/Let us arise and take our arms/And then with curridge let us go/Against the troups which Gorge [sic] did send." A horn depicting the 1776 Battle of Long Island is inscribed "Success to Washington;" others illustrate the general in action as he takes command of American forces, chases hounds, and rides his horse in victory.

Two Lumps of Sugar

James Gillray, *Anti-saccharrites, or John Bull and His Family Leaving off the Use of Sugar*, March 27, 1792. Hand-colored etching.

Isaac Cruikshank, *The Gradual Abolition off the Slave Trade or Leaving of Sugar by Degrees*, April 15, 1792. Hand-colored etching.

In April 1791, Parliament rejected a bill to abolish the slave trade. Responding to that blow, British abolitionist William Fox published a pamphlet in August calling for a boycott of sugar to protest the horrific treatment and living conditions of enslaved people on Caribbean sugar plantations. The pamphlet was a huge success, going through twenty-six editions, and approximately three to four hundred thousand Britons gave up sugar, becoming, per the title of James Gillray's etching, "Anti-Saccharrites."

Although the royal family did not actually participate, these two cartoons published just weeks apart both satirize what a hypothetical sugar boycott might look like if they had. Published first, Gillray's more famous version questions this "noble" protest, per the subtitle (the king was not in fact an abolitionist). While drinking tea without sugar, the king (who is depicted as "John Bull," the archetypal Englishman) says "O delicious! delicious" while the queen (shown with missing teeth) tells her six daughters to "consider how much Work you'll save the poor Blackeemoors by leaving off the use of it! - and above all, remember how much expence it will save your poor Papa!" However, Princesses Amelia, Sophia, Mary, Elizabeth, Augusta, and Charlotte don't seem to agree. Meanwhile, in Cruikshank's version, George, wearing a plain night cap, says "leave it off at once, you know I have never Drank any since I was married."

According to historian Vincent Carretta, in creating cartoons that poke fun at the king's abstemious behavior, Gillray and Cruikshank perhaps were echoing economist Adam Smith's view that "We naturally expect more splendor in the court of a king, than in the mansion-house of a doge or burgo-master." Thus, in a nation like Great Britain, the king should not be seen as abstentious, but instead should be proportionally luxurious in clothes, housing, and food, and to avoid such luxuries was unbecoming of one's duty.

the political agenda for the next century or more. Nor was the impact confined to politics narrowly conceived. A public accustomed to understanding its successes and overseas expansion within a providential Protestant frame discovered in the loss of America a divine verdict on its current condition and policies. This provoked a concern that the nation had lost its way more generally, resulting in initiatives in moral reformation to accompany or animate institutional reforms in a determined effort to cleanse the Augean stables of corruption in all its forms. It would be too much to say that Victorian Britain was the child of the American Revolution; but the moralizing ethics that spurred it on owed much to the legacy of the events fifty years before and the self-examination it prompted, whether of slavery, vice, cruelty, or moral probity.

The Georges' World

In this essay we have sought to keep our eyes on the broad sweep of the Georgian era as a crucial context for understanding the world in which the two Georges passed their lives, and which they influenced in significant ways. In doing so, we have deliberately avoided foregrounding these two individuals as "great men," instead exploring the context in which they exercised their considerable personal power. This is not to deny the significance of biography as a lens through which to understand history. If George III is far less important to historical versions of British identity than Washington is to American self-understanding (and indeed American understandings of Britain), the bicentenary of his death in 2020 no doubt reinforced the significance he already has as a point of access to Hanoverian Britain thanks to his memorable appearances on stage and screen—most importantly in Alan Bennett's play and film *The Madness of George III/King George* (1991) and when he joins Washington in Lin-Manuel Miranda's *Hamilton: An American Musical* (2015). George III has never been seen as a "great man" in the way Washington has been. As less heroic aspects of Washington's life gain greater attention, and as a more sympathetic appraisal of George III makes him less of a pantomime villain in America, both notions perhaps suggest the potential for a more complex understanding—a "flawed (wo)man" approach via prominent figures.

The dual biographical approach offers a valuable opportunity to follow a clearly defined pathway through the complex and ever-changing temporal settings in which historical actors find themselves. As important, however, it facilitates the work of bringing together extraordinarily rich insights into the Georgian era across the globe being offered by an ever more diverse community of scholars exploring the past from a plethora of perspectives, and with an equally wide range of interests: from traditional subjects such as statecraft and politics, to intellectual, economic, and social history, to newer cultural and material histories of the home, science, emotion, dress, craft, self-fashioning, and space. In addition, one cannot understand the two Georges without a full appreciation of the physical spaces and material realities of their lives as both public and private individuals: their bodily disorders, the rooms in which they transacted their business and fashioned as statements of self, the labor that produced and supported their highly privileged existences. Their families also lived that privilege, though the well-documented domestic and household affairs of the two Georges ensures that their lives also shed particularly intense light on the operation of male and paternal privilege and responsibility in the Georgian era. They also illustrate the ways that wives and children, servants, and enslaved people managed romantic and marital relations, illness, education, wealth, and dependency within the structure of expectations and burdens particular to their gender, race, and status.

This volume arrives at a moment when the ambition of bringing together traditional approaches to studying the past with an ever-widening range of historical perspectives is also powered by new technologies for sharing the textual and material archives of these men and their world. Online platforms are breaking down barriers between the academy and a wider community interested in local and familial pasts. Through the process of digitizing archives and museum collections, we can also share and rearrange these collections into new and sometimes unexpected configurations.

Even the preparations required for making documents accessible online ensuring logical arrangement and searchability prompt new and fruitful questions about how archives or collections came to be assembled and what that collecting itself shows us about how we have apprehended the past. Why were so many of George Washington's papers preserved? He was very conscious of their preservation, and he directed his secretaries to catalogue his papers carefully, numbering the pages and volumes of his letter-books, for example. In contrast, relatively few letters or other documents from Martha Washington's hand survive. And for the many hundreds of enslaved people who worked at Mount Vernon or Washington's other farms, the lack of literacy, access to pen and paper, and someone who would work to preserve their materials means that the textual record is almost always simply limited to their names recorded in Washington's ledgers.

For George III, different institutional and individual imperatives, including the changing requirements of Parliament and other national agencies, as well as the desires of his extensive family, meant that his papers were preserved in several centralized locations. Many of his papers also were distributed across a wide expanse of people and geography in ways that we are only beginning to understand as we attempt to describe the archive before us. Like Washington, however, he was a conscious archiver, sometimes arranging his own letters as if in an exhibit to which he could refer to reassure himself that he acted honorably and rationally.

As documents appear online in the Georgian Papers Programme or the Washington Papers, the availability of word-searches and new textual analyses will reveal the underlying assumptions embodied in vocabularies and excisions—at times we can even literally read between the lines as well as under the scratchings out. And just as *The Two Georges* brings together documents and materials associated with these two prominent individuals who never stood on the same continent, online platforms allow us to reunite theirs and other correspondences which are distributed across the oceans or to juxtapose responses to events as articulated in different hemispheres and in very different cultural forms. Not only their words, but objects, representations, narratives and spaces can be brought into newly fruitful dialogue.

Even lists, inventories, and accounts can be rendered fresh and articulate. In a curious way, partly because they have been comparatively neglected by researchers, these may be the most immediately illuminating sources for the connections between the lived experience of the two Georges and the Georgian world, for they chart the way that the Georges consumed their world. In the Georgian papers the mensil and menu books chart the produce that found its way to the royal tables, the account books the furniture, fabrics, and objects that adorned the royal residences and personages (not least in the form of jewels). Here we see not just the notoriously extravagant Prince Regent, but also his equally notoriously restrained parents, in action as part of the consumer revolution that transformed the diets and living conditions of many of their contemporaries. But not all. Such documents also underline the exceptional privilege and purchasing power of those positioned at the apex of the social hierarchy.

As we align these records with the growing body of data available for tracking the production, passage, and consumption of commodities and persons across the globe, and position these alongside the records of the labor, both free and forced that powered the British empire, we find yet another way of examining the two Georges within the contexts that shaped their lives. We hope that in doing so, this volume, and the scholarship and engagement on which it draws, contributes to a remarkably new and fuller view of the Georgian world.

George Washington died in the last month of the last year of the eighteenth century. George III would live for another two decades, though for much of that time he was ill, and in the final ten years his son, the future George IV, ruled as Prince Regent. The critical overlap in our two Georges' lives and careers, their deep commitment to a British colonial North America, formally diverged with the declarations of rebellion and independence in 1775 and 1776 respectively. In the years before the Revolution, the colonies looked east to Britain, and Britain looked west to the colonies, but as they governed separated nations, the United States would turn its attention to the west and to the North American continent, and Britain would be increasingly consumed by its empire in India. Metaphorically and geographically, they turned their backs on one another. The foundational relationship between the two, however, would reverberate in important ways, not least in military alliances in the twentieth century, a "special relationship" which would no doubt alternately please and confound the two Georges.

— **Arthur Burns and Karin Wulf**

Clashing Colonial Claims

Beginning in the sixteenth century, European powers established, with varying success, outposts and settlements in North America, jostling each other for more territory and greater control in a series of armed conflicts. Spain, France, England, the Netherlands, and Sweden all founded colonies in the eastern regions of what would become Canada and the United States. In the mid-eighteenth century, despite diplomatic gestures between the British and the French, another colonial war appeared inevitable.

As a twenty-two-year-old lieutenant colonel in the Virginia Regiment and deeply loyal to the British crown, George Washington played a significant part in the unfolding confrontation. According to an eyewitness, Washington fired the first shot sparking hostilities on May 28, 1754, when he led his men and some Iroquois allies in a fifteen-minute skirmish that routed a small French force at the Battle of Jumonville Glen. The map-altering French and Indian War (1754–1763) was soon under way.

Shortly after the Jumonville episode, in 1755, the maps shown on pages 21 and 22 were published in London. They illustrate the same North American geography, but convey different messages, in part because one draws the eye vertically, the other emphasizes the horizontal. The landmark map by John Mitchell simultaneously celebrates Britain's vision of its territory, both real and embellished, and warns against French encroachment on its colonies. In depicting land that was claimed, but not necessarily held, the map visually reinforced the idea of Britain's stake in America and served as an effective form of propaganda and sense of ownership. Emanuel Bowen's map, however, distinctly delineates long-held French claims that uncomfortably overlapped and abutted British claims, primarily in the Ohio River Valley and west of the Appalachians down to Louisiana. The lands in question are cited on the Bowen map "as great a Prize as has ever been contended for between two nations," and that if George II (grandfather of George III) had known how valuable the territory was, he would not have permitted French encroachment or sacrificed "one of the best Gems in his Crown to their Usurpation and boundless Ambition!"

Both George Washington and George III knew the Mitchell map well, and both maps, among others, were available for sale to the public. Maps such as these were sold both in black and white and with hand-applied watercolors to indicate territorial claims and the viewpoints of their creators. ☀

John Mitchell, *A map of the British and French dominions in North America*, **1755. Second impression of 1st ed. Hand colored. Published in London.**

Lord Halifax, president of the Board of Trade, commissioned John Mitchell (1711-1768), a native Virginian living in London, to produce this aspirational map of British claims as the French and Indian War got under way. Based on information drawn from various crown charters, treaties, and colonial reports—including maps prepared by Major George Washington and Thomas Jefferson's father, Peter—the Mitchell map shows French Louisiana in yellow and New France in green north of the wishfully elongated British colonies. Mitchell depicted Virginia, North Carolina, and Georgia extending west beyond Appalachia and the Mississippi River, overrunning Indian-held lands and conveniently overlooking a longstanding French presence in the Ohio region (a couple of sites are labeled "usurped by the French"). Instead, the French are relegated to the green territory north and west of the Great Lakes, surrounded by bright British pink.

Mitchell included references to charters and treaties on the map to make his case for British claims. Throughout, detailed measurements, historical tidbits, Indian nation and village locations, and colorful notations abound ("dangerous rocks," "Wandering Indians," "Countrey full of Mines," "Extensive Meadows full of Buffaloes"). In the far left, a note indicates that "the Head of the Mississippi [River] is not yet known." An inset in the top left shows Hudson's Bay and environs, and a note regarding a much-hoped-for waterway to the Pacific suggests that "If there is a N. West Passage it appears to be through one of these inlets." The Mitchell map was repeatedly reprinted, with and without attribution, and officials consulted copies after the French and Indian War in drafting the Treaty of Paris (1763), in which France ceded virtually all its North American mainland territories to Britain and Spain, and the Treaty of Paris (1783), which formally ended the American Revolutionary War. Regarded as the most important map ever made of North America, it continued to be cited in legal and diplomatic cases throughout the twentieth century.

Two Georges in a Georgian World

Emanuel Bowen, *An Accurate map of North America...,* **1755. Hand colored. Published in London, printed for Robert Sayer.**

Emanuel Bowen, an Englishman, served as mapmaker to George II of Britain as well as Louis XV of France. Contrary to the Mitchell map, Bowen's "accurate" map presents significant French claims and includes the Caribbean, a small portion of California, and the top of South America. French Louisiana (in green), immediately west of the Mississippi River, is shown where British territory appears on the Mitchell map. Numerous indigenous tribes are identified, despite the map's reference to the land being "almost destitute of Inhabitants." The varying shades of yellow indicate that boundaries between some of the British colonies are not yet fixed, and the section in pink signifies disputed territory between the Appalachians and the Mississippi River. New Mexico, a province of Spain, is shown in beige stretching halfway across the continent to the Pacific Ocean, and Spanish Florida is in orange.

Allies, Enemies, and Indian Land

The British and, later, American need for Indian allies and the colonists' insatiable demand for Indian land led to policies and practices that were contradictory and unsustainable in the latter half of the eighteenth century. Both Georges would struggle with a calculus that had no satisfactory resolution for all concerned.

Since the first permanent British settlement at Jamestown in 1607, the Native American population along the Atlantic Seaboard met colonists armed with guns and paperwork claiming endless swaths of territory. Some individuals or entire tribes, such as the Cherokee, successfully traded with the newcomers and came to embrace aspects of colonial culture. They learned English, adopted forms of English dress, used British manufactured goods, and some even owned enslaved Africans. In 1712 the Cherokee aligned themselves with the British against the Tuscarora, and like other tribes, made alliances with European powers against their native rivals. Other tribes resisted Europeanization, but realistically understood that colonial settlers would never limit themselves to the land they already occupied.

George Washington first mentioned encountering Indians in his journal when he was sixteen and on a surveying trip in the Virginia back country. Although his family lived on the fringe of Indian territory, his plunge into negotiating with Native Americans began in 1753, when he met and traveled with Tanacharison (known to the British as "Half King") on a mission to Fort LeBoeuf, in modern-day Pennsylvania. They were together again the following year at the Battle of Jumonville Glen, after the Seneca leader tipped him off about a small French force positioned there. Tanacharison's diplomatic skill was instructive and sharpened young Major Washington's own negotiating abilities.

In addition to transactions between tribes and colonial officials, traders, Christian missionaries, and other settlers, Indian leaders and their delegations periodically traveled to London, meeting with Queen Anne, George II, and George III, who was well versed in American matters. He met with a wide range of Native Americans, showing great interest in these visitors, as did the public. Samson Occom, a Mohegan and a Christian convert, met George III on February 19, 1766, during a fundraising tour for an Indian school in New England. "We were Conducted to See the Kings horses Carriages and horsemen etc.," he wrote in his journal, "and then went to the Parliament House and went in the Robing Room and Saw the Crown first, and Saw the King, had the pleasure of seeing him put on his Royal Robes and Crown, — He is quite a comely man — his Crown is Richly adorned with Diamonds. How grand and dazzling is it to our Eyes."

Occom's reaction was precisely the effect British hosts hoped to have in strengthening ties with Native American communities. Maintaining good relations was crucial to keeping the peace and fending off French encroachment, but it was made more difficult by English settlers moving onto Indian land and sparking hostilities. Beyond any diamond dazzlement, though, Indian diplomats tried to secure fair trade, just treatment, and recompense for their people. In 1762, George III met with Otacity Ostenaco, a Cherokee leader and diplomat, which may have contributed to the royal proclamation the British government issued the following year. It would have a profound and dramatic effect on the fate of Native Americans and the British Empire in America.

In the 1763 peace treaty following the French and Indian War, defeated France ceded its North American territorial claims to Britain. France's Indian allies were outraged, given that it was their land. The royal proclamation of 1763 issued in George III's name publicly established how Britain would manage its newly acquired territory west of the Appalachians, declared Native peoples under the king's protection, and set a boundary line. Colonists could not occupy that land, which was now reserved for Native tribes, and squatters were ordered out. Having just concluded a major war in the area, the British government did not want the added expense of defending settlements from the inevitable conflicts their presence would cause. If tribes later opted to sell their land, the crown and its representatives would handle those transactions. It was now the land-hungry colonists' turn to be outraged, and one of them was George Washington.

In recruiting militiamen for the French and Indian War, Lieutenant Governor Robert Dinwiddie of the Virginia colony had announced that 200,000 acres west of the Appalachians would be distributed to its enlisted soldiers as a reward for their service. After the war, Washington, who had been promoted

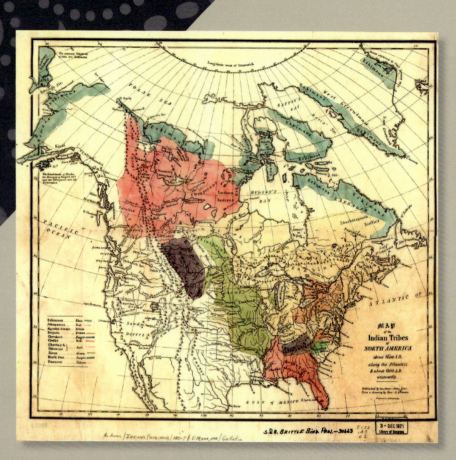

Albert Gallatin, *Map of the Indian tribes of North America, about 1600 A.D. along the Atlantic, & about 1800 A.D. westwardly*, 1836. Hand-colored map. Published by American Antiquarian Society, Washington D.C.

Major American Indian nations at the time of the Revolutionary era included the Algonquin (their territory in yellow), the Iroquois (brown), and the Cherokee (purple, at right). Previously rivals, the Cayuga, Mohawk, Oneida, Onondaga, and Seneca had formed the Iroquois Confederacy, or Haudenosaunee, before European settlement. The addition of the Tuscarora in 1722 resulted in the Six Nations, which continued to share a constitution known as the Great Law of Peace and controlled territory from the northeast to Virginia and from the Atlantic to the Mississippi Valley. After the colonists declared their independence from Britain in 1776, the confederacy broke up as nations and tribes took sides in what they viewed as a British civil war whose outcome would dictate their future prosperity.

from major to colonel during the conflict, demanded that officers also be included as land recipients and went to great lengths to ensure that this was done. He then sent his friend and business partner William Crawford to secretly scout out the best land for themselves, telling him that "I can never look upon the Proclamation in any other light (but this I say between ourselves) than as a temporary expedient to quiet the minds of the Indians. It must fall, of course, in a few years, especially when those Indians consent to our occupying those lands." (Tribes despised Crawford as a land speculator. In June 1782, responding to Wyandot and Delaware raids on western Pennsylvania, Crawford was captured on the Sandusky River in Ohio. He was executed in retaliation for the massacre of neutral, pacifist Delawares by American militiamen several months earlier in Gnadenhutten, Pennsylvania.)

Over time and through petitions, relentless lobbying, pushiness, and other machinations—often ruthless, some underhanded—Washington purchased or otherwise obtained property claims both for and

Chapter 1

from fellow officers as well as land in other locales. Eventually, he acquired more than 60,000 acres for himself in Indian country. But as long as the royal decree remained in force, Washington could not gain legal title to the land he claimed beyond the 1763 Proclamation line. It would be one of many grievances Washington and others would hold against the British government, and one more reason to separate themselves from Britain. In the Declaration of Independence, the founders referenced it as an example of the king "raising the conditions of new Appropriations of Lands" and concluded their list of complaints against George III stating that:

> He has excited domestic insurrections amongst us, and has endeavoured to bring on the inhabitants of our frontiers, the merciless Indian Savages whose known rule of warfare, is an undistinguished destruction of all ages, sexes and conditions.

When the American Revolutionary War broke out, the Cherokee quickly sided with the British; other Indian nations tried to remain neutral, but as the war spread, it became impossible, and most allied themselves with Britain. The Oneida, Mohican, Stockbridge-Munsee, and Tuscarora were among those that joined the American war effort, primarily because of grievances against the British, and Washington was open in his admiration of their military prowess.

During the peace negotiations that concluded in 1783, neither the British nor the Americans allowed Indian participation, infuriating their erstwhile allies. On becoming president of the United States in 1789, Washington attempted to change the dynamic, announcing that August that "The Government of the United States are determined that their Administration of Indian Affairs shall be directed entirely by the great principles of Justice and humanity." There was, however, no just and humane way for Washington and the US government to acquire Indian land while forcing Indians off it.

Washington's administration considered tribes or their confederations as nations separate from each other and that existed within, but were not of, the United States. Indian nations held that they were not under US jurisdiction. The president's goal, and that of so many Americans, was to extend the country westward, taking advantage of its resources, and becoming a powerful, wealthy republic and a successful model of self-governance. This could be accomplished by government purchase of Indian land that was then sold to American settlers and the revenue used to pay off Revolutionary War debts. But Washington was troubled by the question of how to accommodate Indian people, whose disappearance he saw as inevitable unless they adopted white American culture and became part of the predominant society. His solution was to pay Indians "fair prices" for their land, teach them farming, and grant them American citizenship, which he regarded as the greatest asset the US government could offer.

Despite numerous meetings, meals, and travel with American Indians over the years, Washington had little interest in, or appreciation for, their cultures. He did not understand the spiritual connection and communal approach to their homelands. Thus, Washington did not grasp why so few found his plan to "civilize" them and establish reservations for their use as beneficial as he did, or why separating them from their homelands would be so tragic. Nor as president could he prevent other land speculators or white settlers from interfering with government oversight of Indian country. As he wrote in 1796 to Timothy Pickering, the secretary of state, "I believe scarcely any thing short of a Chinese Wall, or a line of Troops will restrain Land Jobbers, and the Incroachment of Settlers, upon the Indian Territory."

In taking stock of the president's policies, historian Colin Calloway wrote that "Washington, more than most . . . was instrumental in the dispossession, defeat, exploitation, and marginalization of Indian peoples. . . . Neither his life nor that of his nation would have developed the way it did without his involvement and experiences in Indian Country. . . . [His] dealings with Indian people and their land do him little credit, but on the other hand his achievement in creating a nation from a fragile union of states is more impressive when we appreciate the power and challenges the Indian world presented."

Ultimately, the Indian land that Washington had worked so tirelessly to acquire for himself, "the cream of the crop" as he referred to it, let him down. He sold off portions for less than he believed it was worth when he needed cash, held out for better offers that never came, had tax problems due to delinquent renters on his property, and he must have been taken aback when he learned the year before he died that land superior to his lay further west. ☼

Two Georges in a Georgian World 25

The Cartographic Impulse

Both George III and George Washington were avid map collectors, and Washington was also a mapmaker. For the king, maps were vivid portraits of his realm. This was especially important since he never left southern England, despite ruling an empire that stretched across six continents. Viewing political, military, topographical, and maritime maps, prints, drawings, and charts allowed him to understand far-flung parts of his empire, including the American colonies. As a young man, Washington was trained as a surveyor, laying out the land that members of his elite planter class controlled. During the American Revolution, he used maps on battlefields, and later as president ordered the first map of the future capital city that would bear his name.

George III collected more than 55,000 maps, ranging from the mid-sixteenth century to contemporary maps of his era. The central part of this collection were his military maps, including several hundred related to the American Revolution. During the Revolution, the king pored over naval charts, and his topographic maps covered major fortifications, military campaigns, harbors, and ports. The eighteenth century was a time of great imperial expansion in North America, and to better understand their domains, the British Board of Trade led a campaign to systematically map their colonial holdings. Many of these maps were presented directly to the king, who, in addition to appreciating their military applications, also valued them for their scientific information. These maps covered areas from the St. Lawrence River in Canada to Florida. Later, in 1807, George III bought the five-volume *Life of George Washington* by chief justice of the United States John Marshall, which included maps of battlefields where Washington had led troops.

The king's fondness for maps was not lost on his subjects. The Seal of Quebec—created in 1763 after Britain gained control of the territory following the French and Indian War—depicted the king in all his majestic geographic control. Appearing in his coronation robes, the young king points his royal scepter at a map of America. The Latin inscription on the seal, *Extensæ gaudent agnoscere metæ*, indicated that the territory contained in the extended boundaries rejoiced to acknowledge the king, their legal protector.

George Washington is credited with creating nearly two hundred maps. Most of these were related to land surveys on the Virginia frontier, military operations in Pennsylvania, and surveys of his property near Mount Vernon. His survey maps often were cadastral maps, depicting the ownership boundaries of various properties, whether city plots, such as his 1749 map of Alexandria (see page 52), or vast country land holdings for the gentry of colonial Virginia, including land Washington himself had inherited from his father and half-brother.

In August 1776, while outlining Congress's plan to create a map collection to aid the Revolutionary War effort, John Adams wrote to his wife Abigail that "Geography is a Branch of Knowledge, not only very usefull, but absolutely necessary, to every Person of public Character whether in civil or military Life." Adams also wrote to Judge Advocate General William Tudor that "Geography is of great Importance to a General." However, Washington found his access to maps in the field lacking. He bemoaned in a January 1777 letter to John Hancock that "The want of accurate Maps of the Country which has hitherto been the Scene of War, has been of great dis-advantage to me. I have in vain endeavoured to procure them." As a result, he felt "obliged" to make his own "Sketches as I could trace out from my own Observations, and that of Gentlemen around me."

After Washington insisted that "a good geographer to survey the roads and take sketches of the country where the army is to act would be extremely useful," Congress appointed Robert Erskine the first geographer and surveyor general of the Continental Army in July 1777. Erskine and his team created more than two hundred maps; the surprise attack at the Battle of Stony Point, a key victory in the 1779 Hudson Campaign, was one instance where Erskine's expert mapmaking played a decisive role in a battle. ☀

Obverse side of the George III Seal of the Province of Quebec, ca. 1760s.

Two Georges in a Georgian World

An Inhuman Custom and Getting Clear: The Two Georges' Views on Slavery

In the 1730s, when George Washington and George III were born, Britain dominated the transatlantic slave trade, maximizing its honed "triangular" trade: ships loaded with manufactured goods sailed west from London, Bristol, Liverpool, and Glasgow to North America. They also went south from Britain to West Africa, trading or selling their wares and buying or trading for captured men, women, and children. Crammed with their chained captives, slave ships then made the infamous middle passage to the Americas, where the survivors were sold into slavery. From the Caribbean and North America, merchant ships headed east to Britain weighed down with sugar, tobacco, cotton, and other items produced by enslaved labor.

Slavery's tentacles wrapped around all major British institutions, leaving almost nothing untouched, from Tudor, Stuart, and Hanoverian monarchs, the aristocracy, the Anglican Church, and the army and navy to the nation's increasingly prosperous port towns, factories, merchants, and ordinary consumers. Demand for sugar from the West Indies and tobacco from southern American colonies fueled further expansion of the slave trade. Government policies and a strong military presence ensured that British companies and individual citizens that owned land and people in the Americas were protected and free to pursue extraordinary wealth. Eventually even those with modest incomes—widows, vicars, butchers, carpenters, and domestic servants in Britain—financially benefitted from slavery through investments and inheritances. The economy and early industrialization of eighteenth-century Britain could not have flourished as it did without slavery, and by the end of the 1700s, the United Kingdom was the wealthiest nation in the world.

For the young Georges, slavery was an inherent and integral part of the British Empire's economy and culture. Both grew to believe that enslavers' rights deserved protection, and neither thought that enslaved people were entitled to full human rights. To Washington, African slavery was a natural feature of life in the American colonies. It had evolved during the seventeenth century from treatment similar to indentured servitude to racially based lifelong enslavement, increasingly harsh slave codes, and enslaved people considered as "chattel," or property. Virginians spearheaded this transformation as American and European demand for tobacco required enormous workforces.

Whereas Washington initially accepted slavery without question, the prince expressed abhorrence. As an older teenager in the 1750s, Prince George penned his first thoughts on slavery. He took his cue from Montesquieu's landmark work, *The Spirit of the Laws* (1748), translating, paraphrasing, and adding his own thoughts in English in a series of notes and private essays. He wondered "what shall we say to the European traffic of black slaves, the very reasons urged for it will be perhaps sufficient to make us hold this practice in execration." He concluded that although racially based slavery was "an inhuman custom wantonly practiced by the most enlightened polite nations of the world, there is no occasion to answer them, for they stand self-condemned."

Although both Georges lived in societies that benefitted from slavery, their experiences with the practice could not have been more different. George III relied on others for eyewitness accounts. Princes William and Edward, his two sons who had spent time in the Americas and reported to him, held opposing views: William, friendly with British planters in the Caribbean, spoke at length in the House of Lords against a bill in 1799 to limit the slave trade, claiming of enslavers that "I may bear witness to their good conduct, to their humanity, and to the care and attention of their slaves." Edward, on the other hand, supported abolition societies. Even though some enslaved people were in Britain, to the king, as with most of the public, slavery existed out of sight, in the far-off Caribbean and American colonies.

Meanwhile, Washington ran his Mount Vernon plantation knowing hundreds of people he enslaved by name, family ties, and labor assignments. He bought, sold, and was daily in the presence of enslaved people; in his business and travels, Washington was thoroughly versed and enmeshed in the system. And in his own complex, paradoxical way, he referred to them as "a species of property" but most commonly as "my people" and "my negroes." He thought of them as part of his larger, extended Mount Vernon household, to whom he would send his own doctor to treat when

ill yet not permit to stand on the landscaped lawns he made them create for his immediate family.

Over time, each George came to change his mind about slavery. The seeds for Washington's growing discomfort were planted during the American War for Independence. Initially, Washington had disapproved of Black soldiers in the Continental Army, but impressed by their service and petitions to remain, he allowed them to stay; eventually, they constituted up to 15 percent of his troops. He also associated with men far removed from Virginia society—such as former enslaver-turned-abolitionist Benjamin Franklin and the young Alexander Hamilton, whose fresh and optimistic hopes for a new nation did not include slavery. And Washington's valet, William Lee—whom he had purchased for £61.15s in 1768 and was very fond of—was a constant reminder of enslaved people's humanity. In 1779, midway through the war, the general told a cousin that he hoped "more and more to get clear" of holding slaves. He pledged that after the war, he would no longer buy or sell them, with some exceptions—and then made exceptions.

Washington wrestled with how to "get clear" for the rest of his life, passing up pleas from abolitionists to again lead a cause for liberty, most notably in the case of the Marquis de Lafayette. He and the wealthy young French ally, a staunch abolitionist, became close friends during the war. In 1783 the marquis wrote the general about his "wild scheme" to buy a plantation in French Guiana. He would educate and pay the enslaved workforce, whose improved conditions and gradual emancipation would provide a stable and healthy labor pool, eliminating the need to continue the slave trade.

Lafayette ardently hoped that Washington, the most famous person in America, would join him in the effort since "such an example as yours might render it a general practice, and if we succeed in America, I will cheerfully devote a part of my time to render the method fashionable in the West Indies." Washington replied, "I shall be happy to join you in so laudable a work." Lafayette undertook his plan, but Washington did not join him in the laudable work, though he later

Am I Not a Man and a Brother? 1837. Woodcut on wove paper. Published by American Anti-Slavery Society.

Founded on May 15, 1787, the Society for the Abolition of the Slave Trade asked famed English potter Josiah Wedgwood to create a seal for the society that would promote the cause of abolition. The result, based on a design by Henry Webber and made by William Hackwood, was this image of an enslaved man on bended knee, imploring viewers to consider his humanity with the phrase "Am I not a man and a brother?" Wedgwood manufactured medallions and cameos featuring the stirring image; these were distributed by the Society and other antislavery groups. The design also proliferated in publications, ceramics, snuffboxes, and accessories, serving as a precursor to modern protest buttons, posters, and T-shirts. Wedgwood—who in addition to being an abolitionist also was a fervent supporter of American independence—shipped a packet of medallions across the Atlantic to Benjamin Franklin to support antislavery efforts in America. Franklin replied that the image "may have an Effect equal to that of the best written Pamphlet in procuring favour to those oppressed people."

told the marquis that the project "is a generous and noble proof of your humanity. Would to God a like spirit would diffuse itself generally into the minds of the people of this country."

Within a few years of noting that "slavery is equally repugnant to the Civil Law as to the Law of Nature," Prince George became King George III. What he had once found "a bad and obnoxious" situation "both to the master and to the servant" became tolerable. During his long reign over the British Empire, he made no effort to abolish the "inhuman custom" even though no one else in the world had a greater platform from which to attempt it. He had not forgotten in his study of Montesquieu his own handwritten note observing that "Sugar would be too dear if the plants which produce it were cultivated by other than slaves." As king, he felt an obligation to promote and maintain British prosperity, despite the tragic price others paid for it. For the devout Christian king, biblical approval of slavery might also have gone some way in offsetting his earlier concerns. Ultimately, the prince's humanitarian ideals succumbed to the king's national economic interests.

Both George III and Washington thought it best not to publicly share their views on the abolition movement, which each disliked and found irritating. The king was comfortable staying silent; Washington, for his part, was not about to upset the still-delicate balance of national unity. As president of the Constitutional Convention in 1787, Washington hovered above the fray as deeply divided delegates eventually agreed to permit the slave trade until 1808; count enslaved people as three-fifths of a person for purposes of Congressional representation and taxation; and require that fugitive slaves be returned to their owners. He accepted these concessions to ensure that pro-slavery delegates would ratify the new Constitution. His own preference was that abolition occur in a gradual, orderly manner through the legislative process rather than a hodge-podge of individual actions. In a letter to Robert Morris in 1786 regarding a Society of Quakers in Philadelphia that assisted enslaved people in escaping while temporarily in the city with their owners, Washington insisted that "there is not a man living who wishes more sincerely than I do to see a plan adopted for the abolition of [slavery]." Yet freeing them illegally, as the Quakers were doing, was unacceptable and unfair to the enslavers, he argued; there was "only one proper and effectual mode by which [ending slavery] can be accomplished, and that is by Legislative authority."

Increasingly, Washington found slavery inefficient, expensive, and troublesome, and toward the end of his life commented that "Negros are growing more & more insolent & difficult to govern." Even so, in those later years, he still made efforts to recover those who had escaped from Mount Vernon and the president's house in Philadelphia rather than accept their freedom. He felt further encumbered by the natural growth of enslaved families that subsequently created a surplus of labor, yet he was determined not to sell off unneeded people and break up their families. He investigated selling some of his land to fund emancipation, and he proposed selling his people to others who would pay them for their labor, but none of these plans came to fruition. Each time he ran the numbers, he concluded that emancipation would likely end in his ruination.

George Washington did not find a way to free the people he enslaved in his lifetime. In his will, he freed only his valet, William Lee, immediately after his death, the rest under his ownership to be manumitted after Martha Washington died. George III, who left little tangible evidence of his thinking on the matter later in life, was said to privately oppose abolishing the slave trade—perhaps believing it a slippery slope toward other progressive reforms, such as Catholic emancipation—as bills repeatedly introduced in Parliament gained traction. Finally, in 1807, more than 240 years after Queen Elizabeth I first shared in the profits of a slave ship voyage, Parliament passed the Abolition of the Slave Trade Act and King George III quietly gave his royal assent, ending Britain's role in the slave trade.

Both Georges chose treasure over emancipation, and in this they were no different than so many of their contemporaries, even as slave revolts and abolitionists edged the cause forward. In 1833, Parliament passed the Slavery Abolition Act, which King William IV, who as a prince had fervently defended African enslavement, was obligated to sign. George Washington and his fellow founders punted on the great issue at hand, believing it was for later generations to resolve. In 1797, Washington wrote his nephew Lawrence Lewis, "I wish from my Soul that the Legislature of this State could see the policy of a gradual abolition of Slavery; It might prevent much future mischief." It was not just future mischief, though, but rather a devastating Civil War—hinged on slavery and heavily fought in his Virginia homeland—that was to come. ☀

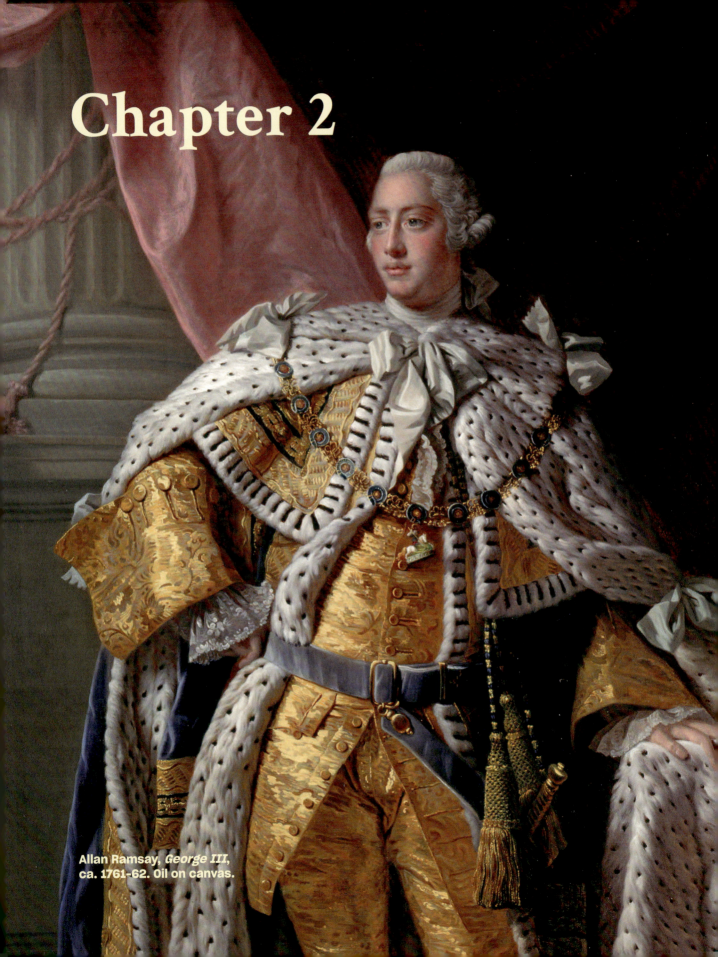

Chapter 2

Allan Ramsay, *George III*, ca. 1761–62. Oil on canvas.

British Beginnings

Charles Willson Peale, *George Washington as First Colonel in the Virginia Regiment*, 1772. Oil on canvas.

Inside London's National Portrait Gallery hangs a painting of Frederick, Prince of Wales, father of King George III. It was made around 1732, the year George Washington was born in Virginia, six years before the birth of the other George, Prince Frederick's son. The painter was Bartholomew Dandridge, a London portraitist whose brother, John, had emigrated to Virginia and had a daughter, Martha, born there in 1731. The painter's infant niece was the same Martha Dandridge Custis who would marry George Washington as her second husband in 1759.[1]

Dandridge's portrait, with its startling link to George and Martha Washington, shows how the same ties of family and common culture that connected Britain to colonial Virginia also linked the early lives of George Washington and George III. It is also a reminder that Washington, the embodiment of the American republic, spent more than half his life as a British subject. The two Georges (who never met) were also personally similar in surprising ways, with interests, values, experiences, and even traits in common. Their similarities persisted even after the American Revolution ripped their shared world apart.

Washington's ties to Britain were both distant and close at hand. He was the great-grandson of John Washington, who emigrated from England to America in 1657, but his British roots were nearer than that.[2] His mother, Mary Ball Washington, both of whose parents were born in England, kept in touch with her brother, Joseph Ball Jr., who lived near London.[3] Washington's father, Augustine, went to school in England and then, in common with other white Virginians of means, sent his two older sons, Lawrence and Augustine, there.[4]

George III also had an active connection to an ancestral land. He was the great-grandson of George I, who came from Hanover to take over the British throne in 1714. But nearer to him were his father, Prince Frederick, and mother, Princess Augusta of Saxe-Gotha, both of whom were born and spent their early years in Germany. His brothers and sons studied there, his sisters and daughters married into German and other European royal courts, and his queen was originally Princess Charlotte of Mecklenburg-Strelitz.[5]

In contrast to their well-traveled families, both Georges were homebodies. George III never left Britain, and George Washington left the American mainland only once, to go to Barbados with his brother in 1751.[6] News of their doings, however, traveled across the Atlantic. In 1755 Joseph Ball Jr. wrote his twenty-three-year-old nephew to express his "Sensible Pleasure" on learning that Washington had "behaved yourself with such a Martial Spirit" fighting alongside British officers in the French and Indian War. Ball, in turn, sent his Virginia nephew news of George II, George III's grandfather: "The King is not Returned from Hanover yet; but is lookt for very soon: The yachts are gone for him."[7]

George II learned about Washington's military exploits when they were published in a London magazine—establishing his reputation there more than two decades before the Revolutionary War. On reading Washington's boast: "I heard Bulletts whistle and believe me there was something charming in the sound," George II commented: "He would not say so, if he had been used to hear many."[8]

George II might scoff, but Washington's part in wresting the Ohio Valley from the French contributed to British imperial goals on the American continent. His first career as a surveyor had the same result: as Washington laid out boundaries for Virginia landholders, he helped to expand English settlement. As a surveyor, and later as a land speculator, Washington was able to accumulate land for himself and, with it, wealth, social position, and political power.[9]

Washington started on this upward path as a recipient of the patronage of the largest landholder in the neighborhood, Lord Thomas Fairfax, who had once served at the court of King George I.[10] Washington enjoyed fox hunting with this local representative of the British aristocracy, and he showed that he understood how to climb the ladder of power in British America when

Chapter 2

he reminded a younger brother to nurture the connection with the Fairfaxes since they had it "in their power to be very serviceable upon many occasion's to us as young beginner's."[11]

He was also eager to absorb British ideas, acquire British goods, and follow British fashions. Like other Virginia planters before the American Revolution, Washington shipped his tobacco to merchants in England, who sold it for him. With the proceeds, they filled his orders for a wide array of goods manufactured in Britain and imported from every part of the world touched by Britain's networks of colonization and trade. Washington bought sugar that, like the tobacco he sold to pay for it, was produced by the coerced labor of enslaved people. He indulged in exotic delicacies like almonds, anchovies, and capers. He bought himself a set of surveying instruments from the same London shop, the "Golden Spectacles and Quadrant," where George III bought a telescope. He ordered "all the numbers of the *Covent Garden Magazine*." He wanted "the newest and most approved treatise of agriculture" along with many other works on agriculture, an enthusiasm he shared with George III.

Soon after his marriage in 1759, he and Martha Washington bought a flurry of household goods and clothing, including a garnet necklace for Martha and a toy "coach and 6 in a box" for her children. Ordering a carriage for himself, he specified that it be made in "the newest taste" and, although he preferred green, would accept "any other colour more in vogue."[12] He yearned to go to London himself: "The longing desire, which for many years I have had of visiting the great Matrapolis of that Kingdom is not in the least abated," he wrote an English acquaintance.[13]

George III grew up in and around the metropolis of Washington's dreams. But despite the grandeur of his surroundings, he had some experiences in common with his Virginia counterpart. Each George lost his father before he reached his teens, and both were raised by their widowed mothers. Mary Ball Washington and Princess Augusta have both been judged harshly by contemporaries and historians who believed their assertions of independence and power were illegitimate, and that they controlled their sons too closely. Layers of judgement have obscured the characters of these two influential figures.[14]

Bartholomew Dandridge, *Thomas Bloodworth; Frederick Louis, Prince of Wales*, ca. 1732. Oil on canvas.

Martha Washington's uncle, Bartholomew Dandridge, was a portrait painter with a busy practice in London. Prince Frederick is shown with his groom of the bedchamber, Thomas Bloodworth, at left.

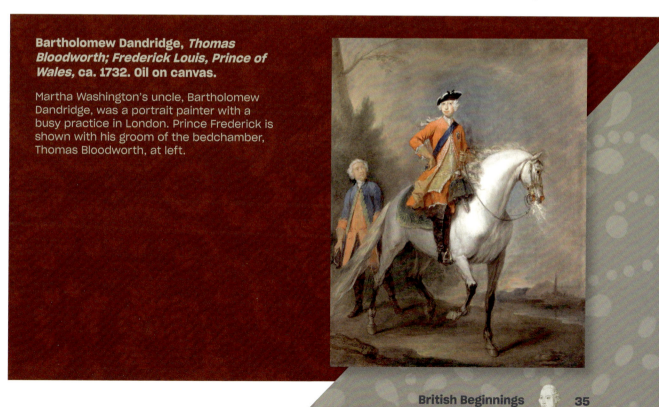

British Beginnings 35

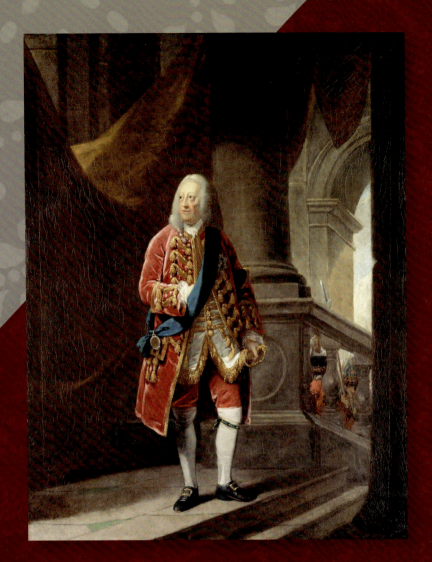

William Dickinson, *George II, after Robert Edge Pine*, 1759. Oil on canvas.

George II was the father of Frederick, Prince of Wales, and grandfather of the future George III. The king is shown here at Kensington Palace wearing the blue ribbon and the jeweled star accessory of the elite medieval Order of the Garter on his chest. On the recommendation of his counselors, the king invested eleven-year-old Prince George as a knight in the order in 1749. The military-minded George II took little interest in his grandson until the young man suddenly became his heir following his father's death. For the prince's eighteenth birthday, he gifted him a £40,000 annual allowance and apartments at Kensington and St. James's Palaces, so the young man could be at court. The prince took the allowance, but as a natural homebody, and to keep his mother happy, he chose to stay next door to her at Leicester Square. The prince, always humble and flattering in his correspondence with the crotchety monarch, grew increasingly resentful of his grandfather for denying him a place in the army; leaving his mother, Princess Augusta, saddled with her late husband's debts; and remaining more devoted to Hanover than to Britain.

What is clear is that each provided her son with an up-close look at a woman wielding power. Both Georges later formed marriages according to an Enlightenment model of virtuous family life in which women were granted an increasingly respectful, if still not equal, place.[15]

As they emerged into public life, both Georges engaged with the Seven Years' War (the American portion of which was the French and Indian War), though differently. The twenty-one-year-old prince futilely beseeched his grandfather, George II, for a military role as France threatened England during the war. "Now that every part of the Nation is arming for its defence, I cannot bear the thoughts of continuing in this inactive state," he wrote in 1759.[16] When less than a year earlier Washington, twenty-six, had retired from fighting in the American portion of the same war his officers offered him a tribute his royal counterpart would have loved for himself, commending him for, among other things, his "Love to your King and Country."[17]

In 1765, the year of the Stamp Act, almost five years into George III's reign, George Washington's identification with the goals of the British Empire began to waver. In the same letterbook in which he recorded his British purchases he complained bitterly to Francis Dandridge, brother of the portraitist and another of Martha Washington's London uncles: "The Stamp Act Imposed on the Colonies by the Parliament of Great Britain engrosses the conversation of the Speculative part of the Colonists, who look upon this unconstitutional method of Taxation as a direful attack upon their Liberties, & loudly exclaim against the Violation."[18]

Loud enough, evidently, for George III to hear. Soon he too had doubts about the Stamp Act. Just a year after he signed it into law, Parliament repealed it under pressure from British merchants who feared the effect of American boycotts on themselves. The young king (in 1766 he was twenty-eight to Washington's thirty-four), who had no doubts about Britain's right to tax its American colonies, now agreed to repeal rather than continue to "widen the breach between this Country & America."[19] But the continuing defiance of the American colonists hardened his attitude toward them.[20] In September 1774 as delegates from each American colony met at the First Continental Congress in Philadelphia, their king wrote his prime minister: "the dye is now cast, the Colonies

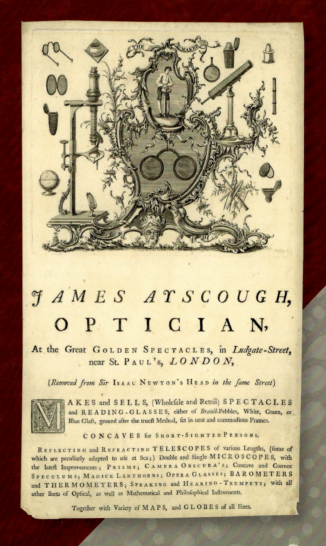

Trade card for James Ayscough, optician, London, ca. 1749-1750.

This trade card advertised the shop of optician James Ayscough, who worked as an optician and instrument maker not far from St. Paul's Cathedral on Ludgate Street. His shop was indicated by a sign with "Great Golden Spectacles." In addition to glasses, he also built telescopes, microscopes, and barometers, and sold globes and maps. George Washington bought surveying instruments from Ayscough while George III bought a "day and night" telescope with a fishskin-covered body.

British Beginnings

Garnet necklace, sold by Susanna Passavant, ca. 1759. Silver, gold, rhodolite garnet. Invoice from Robert Cary & Company, March 1759.

As a young man in colonial Virginia, George Washington bought almost everything he needed for his farm and household from England. Most of these goods were unavailable in Virginia because Washington, like his neighbors, concentrated on producing a single farm staple, tobacco. Washington shipped his tobacco to merchants in British port cities, who sold it, then used the proceeds to pay for his orders. The amazing array of goods Washington purchased show how the products of Britain's empire and global trade filtered into its American colonies. They also show how Washington, well before the American Revolution, chose to identify with fashionable London.

Washington carefully kept copies of his orders. To London merchant Robert Cary in the year of his marriage to Martha Dandridge Custis, he recorded: "1 sword belt, red morocco or buff"; "1 dozn most fash-[ionable] Cambrick Pockt Hand[kerchie]fs"; "6 lb. perfumd Powder"; pickled anchovies, capers, and olives; "1 bottle India mangoes"; strong, coarse fabric out of which to make clothing for enslaved workers and finer fabric for clothing for himself and his family; tools, including spades, sickles, and axes; medicines for people and animals, including ipecac, laudanum, and "tincture of myrrh," and more. At the end of his order, Washington included a request for busts of Alexander the Great, Julius Caesar, and other notables, along with small statues of "2 wild beasts," all to be used as household ornaments.

Another order from Cary in 1759 included a mix of personal, farm, and household goods (gingerbread, fans, jewelry, pans, hoes) and services (dying a gown, making a suit). He also purchased toys for Martha's children, including a "coach and 6 in a box," and for herself, a garnet necklace from London jeweler Susannah Passavant.

When a decade later Virginia began boycotting British goods as a form of protest, record books listing Washington's pre-revolutionary purchases took on another meaning: they detailed the imported finery a colonial gentleman left behind when he began purchasing goods locally and became an American in homespun.

must either submit or triumph; I do not wish to come to severer measures but we must not retreat."[21]

Washington was one of those delegates, but even as he signed and helped draft a series of nonimportation agreements and petitions of protest, he remained loyal to his king.[22] On May 31, 1775, describing the Battle of Lexington and Concord in a letter to a member of the Fairfax family in England, he blamed the "ministerial troops," since "we do not, nor cannot yet prevail upon ourselves to call them the King's Troops."[23] Less than three weeks later Congress appointed him to head the Continental Army.

Washington's decisive break with his sovereign came in 1776. That summer Congress sent him a freshly printed copy of the Declaration of Independence, with its pointed list of accusations against the king, whose character, Congress asserted, is "marked by every act which may define a tyrant," and asked him to have it read to the troops assembled in New York. Washington did so on July 9, 1776.

But even here, as Washington stood in direct opposition to his royal counterpart, he demonstrated what he had in common with him. Sixteen years earlier, when George III inherited the throne, he used his first speech to Parliament to remind his subjects that like them, but unlike his Hanoverian predecessors on the British throne, he was born and educated in Britain. More than that, he chose to "glory in the name of Britain."[24] In 1776, Washington similarly made a deliberate choice of national identity. He assumed the greater risk, but in America's Revolutionary War, both would be tested.[25] ☀

— **Julie Miller**

Two Mothers

It is hard to imagine two women whose lives began more differently than the mothers of George III and George Washington. Princess Augusta of Saxe-Gotha, born to a German duke in 1719, came to England in 1736 at seventeen to marry Frederick, Prince of Wales, son of King George II. Mary Ball Washington, born in Virginia around 1708, was the daughter of an indentured servant and her second husband, a prosperous tobacco farmer. Orphaned as a child, in her twenties she became the second wife of Augustine Washington, a widower with three children. Princess Augusta's opulent life as a member of the British royal family is evidenced by the many portraits made of her and her children, including the one below by Jean-Baptiste Van Loo, which shows the future King George III as a toddler, seated at left. There are no authentic portraits of Mary Ball Washington, although the print shown here, made from a painting purportedly by Robert Edge Pine, is often used to represent her.

With their marriages, the lives of these two women became more similar. As a young mother of nine children, Princess Augusta was popular with the British public, but with the death of her husband when George, her eldest son, was twelve, public opinion and the vicious print culture of the era turned against her. Critics regarded Princess Augusta as asserting too much control over the future king, falsely accused her of carrying on an improper relationship with Lord Bute, her son's tutor, mentor, and prime minister, and suspected her of wielding independent political power herself. The print shown opposite epitomizes the scorn directed at the widowed princess.

Washington had a difficult relationship with his mother, who raised him and his siblings alone after the death of his father when he was eleven. His typical tone toward her was coldly polite, but sometimes angry, as in a letter from February 15, 1787, when he was fifty-five and she was nearing eighty. The subjects were money, which he believed she demanded too much of, and land, which he felt she occupied illegitimately. "It is really hard upon me when you have taken every thing you wanted from the Plantation by which money could be raised—When I have not received one farthing, directly nor indirectly from the place for more than twelve years if ever," he wrote. Because of her complaints, he noted that, "I am viewed as a delinquent. & considered perhaps by the world as [an]

Attributed to Robert Edge Pine, *Mary Ball Washington at the age of about four-score,* **ca. 1784-1788.**

Jean-Baptiste Van Loo, *Augusta, Princess of Wales with Members of Her Family and Household,* **1739. Oil on canvas.**

unjust and undutiful Son."

Starting in the twentieth century, biographers, taking their cue from Washington himself and then from each other, described Mary Washington as grasping, querulous, and vulgar, peevish, crude, and, in a term used multiple times by more than one biographer, a "termagant." One criticized her, tellingly, as "in control." This was the problem. Mary Ball Washington and Augusta, Princess of Wales, two eighteenth-century widows in very different circumstances, tried to act independently and claim power for themselves. In doing so they attracted the scorn of men who celebrated the very same qualities in their sons.

"You have got him Ma'am, in the right Kew," 1769. Etching.

Augusta, Princess of Wales, leads her son George III by the nose through Kew Gardens as Lord Bute, George's former tutor, standing behind a tree, and the princess gesture to each other out of sight of the blindfolded king. Many wrongly suspected that Augusta and Bute were lovers and ruled over George, who had ended his friendship with Bute several years earlier.

Fathers Dying Young

The two Georges both lost their fathers before turning thirteen, upon which they immediately inherited money, land, and power. When George Washington's father, Augustine, died, his will bequeathed the best parts of his estate to his sons by his first marriage. However, eleven-year-old George, as the eldest son of his second wife, received Ferry Farm—the family's home on the Rappahannock River—a portion of another property, and ten of Augustine's sixty-four enslaved workers. Five years later, the future George III lost his father, Frederick, Prince of Wales, when he was twelve. With Frederick's death, George became the heir to the British throne. He immediately received the title Duke of Edinburgh before officially being named Prince of Wales three weeks later.

Augustine Washington died at age forty-eight on April 12, 1743, from a chill not long after he was caught in a downpour while riding his horse (fifty-six years later, George Washington died from a throat infection caused by similar circumstances). Augustine had been tall, fair complexioned, and quite strong; the only contemporary description of him stated he could load a wagon with as much iron as "two ordinary men could barely raise from the ground." Washington, however, had few memories of his father. His step-grandson, George Washington Parke Custis, recalled him saying that "he knew little of his father, other than a remembrance of his person, and of his parental fondness."

Augustine's death continued a pattern of Washington men dying in middle age: Augustine's father had died at thirty-eight and his grandfather at forty-six. (In 1784, Washington remarked to the Marquis de Lafayette, "Tho' I was blessed with a good constitution, I was of a short-lived family.") When Augustine became ill, George was away visiting cousins in King George County, Virginia. He immediately returned to Ferry Farm, where the family gathered around his dying father.

With the hopes of studying in England like his brothers dashed upon his father's death, George stayed with his mother at Ferry Farm for the next four years, running the plantation and overseeing the enslaved workforce as a teenager. He was the eldest of six children Augustine had with his second wife, Mary (nee Ball), but he was fourteen years younger than his half-brother Lawrence Washington. Lawrence, who had inherited the property now known as Mount Vernon, served as a surrogate paternal figure to George until his death in 1752, at the age of thirty-four. George inherited Mount Vernon a decade later when Lawrence's widow, Anne, died. Reflecting years later on losing his father, Washington gave credit to his "revered Mother, by whose Maternal hand (early deprived of a Father) I was led to Manhood."

In Britain, Prince George's father Frederick died at age forty-four on March 31, 1751, of a pulmonary embolism, though a popular myth claimed that he was killed by a cricket or "royal tennis" ball. Frederick had had a poor relationship with his own father, George II, from whom he was practically estranged, in part due to his restlessness to obtain the throne. (Months after Frederick's death, the king remarked, "I have lost my eldest son but I was glad of it.")

However, Frederick loved his son. In 1749 he wrote him a letter with instructions on how to be a good king. Advice ranged from familial ("I know that you will have always the greatest respect for your good mother"); to martial ("If you can be without war, let not your ambition draw you into it. … At the same time, never give up your honour nor that of the nation"); to financial, both personal ("When ever the Crown comes into your hands employ all your hands, all your power, to live with economy") and national ("The sooner you have an opportunity to lower the interest, for Gods Sake, do it").

According to Horace Walpole, on hearing the news that his father had died Prince George "turned pale," "laid his hand on his breast," and said "I feel something here, just as I did when I saw the two workmen fall off the scaffold at Kew [Palace]." The prince soon came under the stiff wing of George II, who now had to groom his grandson for the throne. The start was ignominious; for three days the king neglected Frederick's rotting body, the stench of which drafted to Prince George's apartments. Yet the prince took to heart his father's advice, and in addition to continuing to show "the greatest respect" for his mother, he followed his father's instructions to "be a kind Father" to his numerous siblings.

John C. McRae, *"Father, I cannot tell a lie: I cut the tree,"* 1867. Engraving after George G. White. New York: Published by John C. McRae.

Created nearly 125 years after Augustine Washington died, this engraving depicts the fictious episode in which young George Washington admits to cutting down his father's cherry tree. The legend first appeared in 1806, in the fifth edition of Mason Locke Weems' *The Life of Washington the Great*.

However, no historical evidence supports Weems' anecdote, as much of Washington's early life and relationship with his father are undocumented. Indeed, no image from life of Washington's father is known to exist.

British Beginnings

Schoolboys

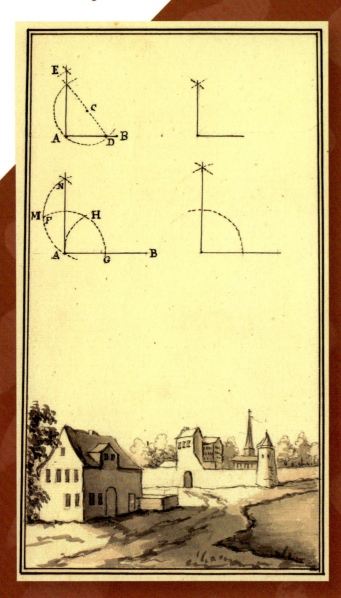

Prince George, "Geometric Study and a Landscape," ca. 1756. Pen and ink over pencil and wash.

The prince was about eighteen years old when he made a study with four right angles, above, and drew a house and walled town, below, as part of his studies in geometry and draftsmanship. His geometry assignments were modeled after those found in Sebastien le Clerc's textbook, *Pratique de la Geometrie* (1688). The prince especially enjoyed technical drawing, and he continued to sketch plans and ideas as king. Reverend Francis Ayscough handled the prince's early education and his religious studies; when George was eleven, he and his brother Edward, a year younger, progressed to an intense academic program under Ayscough and George Lewis Scott, a mathematician. The school day ran from 8 am until 8 pm, with breaks for meals and play; the boys studied Latin and modern languages, math (algebra, geometry, and trigonometry) and science (chemistry and physics), art and architecture, history and geography. A few years later their lessons extended to include fencing, dancing, riding, and other skills expected for their station. At seventeen, and for the next several years under Lord Bute, George buckled down and happily pursued the natural sciences and philosophy. As king, George III, the first British royal to receive a scientific education, was well prepared to meet the Age of Enlightenment.

Prince George of Wales, Playing at Soldiers, 1747. Pencil and ink drawing.

Nine-year-old George, having built a fort, sits with a book and the accoutrements of soldiery, including a sword, a dagger, and a gun. At twenty-one, during the Seven Years War (1756-1763), the young prince asked his grandfather, George II, the last British monarch to lead troops into battle, if he could serve in the army. "I really cannot remain immured at home like a girl whilst all my countrymen are preparing for the field and a brother younger than me allowed to go in quest of the enemy," he told Lord Bute. However, as Prince George was heir to the throne, the king denied his request. When he became king himself, George III was often depicted in military uniforms as the commander-in-chief, and his handwritten notes and correspondence show he was deeply involved in strategic discussions, read military intelligence, and tracked the whereabouts of army regiments and navy warships.

George Washington, "Surveying or Measuring of Land," George Washington's school copy book, Volume 2, page 46, 1745.

George Washington was a teenager when he filled this notebook with pages titled "Geometrical Definitions," "Geometrical Problems," "Extraction of the Square Root," "Plain Trigonometry Geometrical and Logarithmetical," and with survey lesson exercises such as the one shown here. He also had an old copy of William Leybourn's *The Compleat Surveyor* (1679) and reproduced lessons from that book into his school copy book. Whereas Washington's older half-brothers Lawrence and Augustine were given a formal, classical education in England, young George had lost his father before he could be sent away for a similar course of study. He had little formal elementary schooling as a youngster, but he did study with tutors at times, and Lawrence's in-laws, the Fairfax family, introduced him to literature and history. Bright, persistent, and ambitious, Washington was primarily self-taught, and he acquired a substantial library for his—or any other—era, which he used to his expand his knowledge, especially in the fields of agriculture, economics, politics, and law. In Washington's time, few boys even attended secondary school, but many of the men he later associated with during the Revolution and his presidency were among the rare breed of college graduates, which left him, as he wrote, "conscious of a defective education."

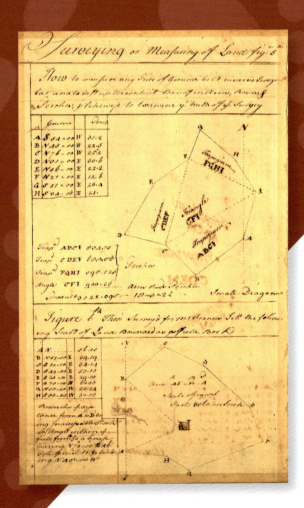

British Beginnings

Mentoring Men: Two Georges in the Houses of Lords

In their correspondence, George Washington addressed his mentor as "my lord." Prince George addressed his as "my dearest friend." Washington became acquainted with Lord Thomas Fairfax (1693–1781), sixth baron of Cameron, when his older half-brother Lawrence married into the powerful Fairfax family. Prince George got to know John Stuart, third Earl of Bute (1713–1792), after the Scotsman befriended his father over a game of cards during a rain delay at the Egham racecourse. Their lordships served as mentors and father figures, opening the world to the young Georges and leaving a lasting influence, though the two relationships were quite different.

Washington was in awe of Lord Fairfax: his status, his Oxford education, and his reliable common sense, and he hoped that through him he might acquire a cultured sensibility and the necessary connections to succeed in public life. With an obsessive interest in land acquisition, the ambitious Washington saw Fairfax in a position he aspired to, that of a wealthy, respected plantation owner and important public figure. Prince George, on the other hand, not only outranked Bute, whom his widowed mother, Princess Augusta, hired as his tutor in 1755, but reveled in his friendship, telling him that he was "the only man I shall ever meet with who . . . at all times, prefer[s] my interest to your own." Shy and lacking confidence, he thrived under Bute's inspired tutelage, and was eager to please him, promising in mid-1756 to make "such a progress in the summer, that shall give you hopes, that with the continuation of your advice, I may turn out as you wish."

Born in Leeds Castle, in Kent, England, to a prominent Yorkshire family, Thomas Fairfax was the only British lord to reside full-time in the American colonies. He inherited control of the five-million-acre Northern Neck Proprietary, a land grant King Charles II issued in 1649 to a handful of his supporters, including Fairfax's ancestor, John Culpeper. Located in the Virginia colony, the Proprietary lay between the Rappahannock and Potomac rivers, from the Chesapeake Bay to the Blue Ridge Mountains. Earning revenue from selling or renting proprietary tracts to English settlers, Lord Fairfax glided easily among the posh world of his aristocratic upbringing, elite Virginia society, and the frontier wilderness of the Shenandoah Valley, where he built Greenway Court, his rustic country estate.

The bachelor baron headed an extended family that welcomed Washington to Belvoir, the nearest plantation to Mount Vernon, home of Lawrence and Anne Washington. A regular visitor from the age of eleven, George spent what he later recalled as the "happiest" days of his life at Belvoir. His lordship's cousin and land agent, Colonel William Fairfax (Anne's father), also served as a mentor, unsuccessfully conspiring with Lawrence to get George into the Royal Navy but later nurturing his militia service and dispensing sage, fatherly advice.

Washington became close friends with the colonel's son, George William Fairfax, and he was besotted with George William's wife, Sally Cary Fairfax, whom he met in 1748. At Belvoir, the raw, unpolished Washington met, dined, and hunted with prominent figures, absorbed the social graces, learned to dance, borrowed books, and developed a taste for fashionable, cultured living at the peak of Virginia society. The Fairfaxes smoothed over his rough edges and made his steady advancement possible.

In 1748, Lord Fairfax hired sixteen-year-old Washington to help survey western parts of the Northern Neck Proprietary. He took an interest in the teenager's nascent career, and a few years later his influence helped Washington gain a commission in the Virginia Regiment of the colonial militia and soon win command of an expedition to Fort LeBoeuf. Throughout the 1750s, the young officer, stationed in nearby Winchester, spent time at Greenway Court, hunting with Fairfax and taking advantage of the well-stocked library there, a rarity in what the baron called "the back parts" of Virginia. During the French and Indian War, the two worked together in defending the area from persistent threats and attacks. Afterward, led by his lordship, the Fairfax family endorsed Washington's bid for a seat in the Virginia House of Burgesses, and his political career was successfully launched. As George wrote to his younger brother John of the Fairfaxes, "to that Family I am under many obligations."

In the tumultuous years leading up to the colonies' declaration of independence, even as his dissatisfaction

Chapter 2

with British policies increased, Washington maintained a good relationship with the Fairfax family. He handled business affairs and the rental of Belvoir after George William and Sally moved to England in 1773 on family business, never to return. During the Revolutionary War, Lord Fairfax, privately a Loyalist, lived quietly at Greenway Court and caused no trouble for his rebel protégé; that he was neither harmed nor had his property taken was likely owing to his relationship with Washington. He died in 1781, two months after General Washington accepted the British surrender at Yorktown. "Altho' the good old Lord. . . lived to an advanced age," remarked Washington wistfully, "I feel concern about his death."

As George Washington was waging war on behalf of George II and the British Empire during the French and Indian War, Prince George unexpectedly excelled as a student. By his own admission lazy and plodding in his schoolwork, the prince delved deep into his studies under the guidance of the intellectual and theatrical Lord Bute. The turnaround was stunning, and Princess Augusta was elated by the results. Although twenty-five years apart in age, Bute and George quickly became close friends and formed an intense partnership centered on a shared conservative political outlook and the prince mastering what he needed to know to be a good and effective king. Unlike previous instructors, Bute gave George a path for success: the prince read classic and serious contemporary works on history, law, finance, and economics, and wrote thousands of pages of essays on these and other topics—a method of study he would use for the rest of his life.

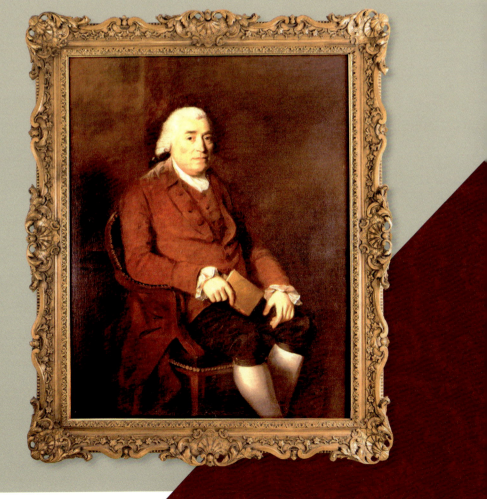

Joshua Reynolds, *Thomas, Sixth Lord Fairfax, Baron of Cameron*, ca. 1745. Oil on canvas.

Lord Fairfax, for whom a county and city in Virginia are named, was also one of the founders of Alexandria, Virginia.

British Beginnings

Joshua Reynolds, *John Stuart, 3rd Earl of Bute*, 1773. Oil on canvas.

Lord Bute, showing off his much commented upon legs, appears in his Order of the Garter robes and in a pose based on the classical Apollo Belvedere sculpture.

Educated at Eton and Leiden University in the Netherlands, the happily married Bute, who with his wealthy wife Mary Wortley Montagu had eleven children, left his eponymous Scottish isle in 1746 for better prospects in London. He was a serious botany scholar, and a skeptical Horace Walpole eventually regarded him as "a man of taste and science; and I do believe his intentions were good." Tall, handsome, famed for his well-shaped legs "of unrivaled symmetry," according to his biographer, Bute became a good friend of both the Prince and Princess of Wales before becoming their son's tutor and later the head of his household. As a member of Prince Frederick's inner circle, Bute shared many of his friend's ideas, including his desire to break the family link between the British crown and the German state of Hanover. Although the connection would remain for almost eighty more years, young George III's declaration that "I glory in the name of Britain" at the beginning of his reign reflected a new political direction.

The earl was a Tory, which raised red flags for a government long dominated by Whigs who were concerned about his influence on the future king. George had no doubts, though, telling his tutor "I will exactly follow your advice, without which I shall inevitably sink. I am young and inexperienc'd and want advice." Together, the prince and the earl came up with a plan for George's reign as king. It called for cleaning up rampant government corruption, reducing the national debt, and bringing Tories back into government service. The prince was grateful and energized by Bute's faith in him, and by another element of the plan: as king, he would appoint the earl as first lord of the treasury, an essential step in attacking debt and corruption.

George acceded to the throne in 1760, and Bute eventually connived the resignations of the Duke of Newcastle as prime minister and the powerful, popular William Pitt the Elder, secretary of state for the southern department. In 1762 Bute became prime minister and first lord of the treasury, infuriating Whigdom. Bishop of Gloucester William Warburton observed that "Lord Bute is a very unfit man to be Prime Minister of England. First, he is a Scotchman; secondly, he is the king's friend; and thirdly, he is an honest man."

Bute's greatest political success was in overseeing the 1763 Treaty of Paris that ended the Seven Years War (of which the French and Indian War had been a part), but the British public responded with rage and riots to his cider tax to help pay for that war and reduce the national debt. Violent threats against him forced the earl to travel at night or in disguise, and after three years in government, a fatigued Bute resigned in 1763, ending his political partnership with George.

For decades afterward, critics erroneously charged that Bute continued to control the king. Instead, George III was finding his own way as head of state, and his "dearest friend" was a declining influence. The end of their friendship came in the summer of 1766, when the king felt compelled to bring Pitt back into power. The earl viewed this as a betrayal and a sign of ingratitude for his efforts. Although Bute remained close friends with Princess Augusta, and he dedicated his nine-volume publication of botanical tables in 1784 to George's wife, Queen Charlotte, it was not until 1789 that the king and Bute saw each other again, when at the king's invitation the earl attended a ball at Windsor. Bute died three years later, the mentor and protégé having reconciled. ☀

Lawrence Washington

***Lawrence Washington* (likely by John Hesselius or his father Gustavus), ca. 1743. Oil on canvas.**

Lawrence Washington (1718-1752), George Washington's older half-brother, was born in Virginia but schooled in England, and the two did not meet until George was six years old. Fourteen years younger, George revered his ambitious brother, one of his mentors. Lawrence began his climb in Virginia society as a young planter, then fast-tracked his career in 1740 with a military commission from King George II, serving as a captain under British Admiral Edward Vernon in the Caribbean portion of the War of the Austrian Succession. After he returned home, Lawrence named his newly inherited estate Mount Vernon after his commander. He continued his ascent when he married fifteen-year-old heiress Anne Fairfax in 1743, aligning himself with one of the most prominent families in the colony.

Later, Lawrence represented Fairfax County in Virginia's House of Burgesses, introducing George to important and powerful figures, particularly Lord Fairfax, and he helped set up his brother as a professional land surveyor. In 1751, George accompanied Lawrence, suffering from tuberculosis, to Barbados, where it was hoped the climate would alleviate his condition. Eventually returning to Virginia, Lawrence succumbed to the disease at the age of thirty-four. George ultimately inherited Mount Vernon in 1761 from Lawrence's widow, and he kept this portrait of his brother—dressed as the adjutant general of the Virginia militia—in his study for the rest of his life.

Published Exploits

Isaac Kimber and Edward Kimber, *London Magazine: or, Gentleman's Monthly Intelligencer*, August, 1754.

In October 1753, George Washington volunteered to serve on a diplomatic mission as a major in the Virginia militia. Lt. Governor Robert Dinwiddie instructed him to deliver a message to the French to vacate the Ohio River Valley, which Britain claimed as its own. After the French rejected the overture, Washington returned to Virginia in January 1754 and wrote a detailed account of his trip. Dinwiddie was so impressed, he had the journal published in Williamsburg and then London, where it first appeared in June 1754.

Just weeks prior to his journal's publication in Britain, Washington had seen action with the colonial militia. In reaction to the French refusal to concede the territory the previous year, Dinwiddie ordered Washington, now a lieutenant colonel, to defend British claims by force. On May 28, 1754, he led his troops against a French contingent in southern Pennsylvania. Three days later, he wrote his brother John Augustine Washington of the skirmish: "I fortunately escaped without a wound, tho' the right Wing where I stood was exposed to & received all the Enemy's fire." He then boasted, "I heard Bulletts whistle and believe me there was something charming in the sound." With these "bullets," the French and Indian War began.

Hoping to leverage the interest in Washington's journal, his uncle Joseph Ball Jr. sought the publication of the letter, which appeared in this August 1754 issue of *London Magazine* (see section IX in the image). Combined with the publication of his journal, Washington became something of a minor celebrity in London. Even George II learned about Washington's military exploits, two decades before the Virginian would lead troops against his successor and grandson, George III.

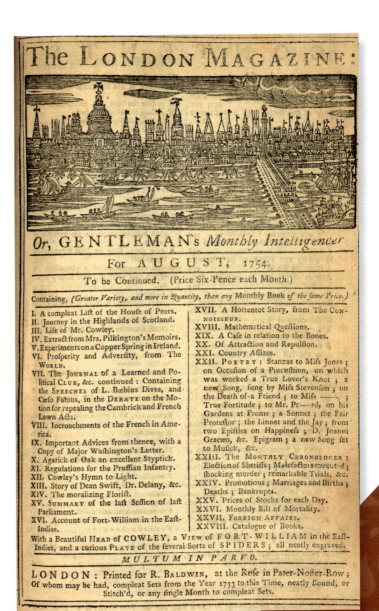

British Beginnings

Washington, Mapmaker

George Washington, *A Plan of Alexandria, Now Belhaven,* **1749. Manuscript map, pen and ink.**

The largest town near George Washington's Mount Vernon estate—eight miles away—was known in its early years as Alexandria or Belhaven, depending on whom one talked to. Some residents in the area used the names interchangeably. In his 1748 notes as a sixteen-year-old passing through, Washington mentioned "Alexandria," the earliest extant use of the name for the undeveloped riverside area. The following year, he helped survey lots, shown here, that were sold at public auction. Washington made this copy of John West's plat for his older half-brother Lawrence, the new owner of riverfront lot 51 on Water Street; another half-brother, Augustine, purchased nearby lots 64 and 65.

Washington's title for the map suggests Belhaven was the preferred name as the area transitioned from tenant farmland to merchant trade. However, the Virginia Assembly rejected a petition to change the town name, and the tribute to the Alexander family—Scottish immigrants and major landowners—won out. The Washington family remained deeply connected to the thriving town: George drilled his Virginia Regiment recruits at Market Square in 1754 and did so again twenty years later for the Fairfax Independent Company in preparation for a possible armed confrontation with Britain. Over the decades he banked, shopped, worshipped, and conducted plantation business in town, becoming a city trustee in 1763.

George Washington, *A Plan of My Farm on Little Hunting Creek & Potomack River*, 1766. Manuscript map, pen-and-ink and watercolor.

As a young man, Washington spent three years as a professional surveyor, working for Culpeper County. He produced this manuscript plat of his long-coveted 1,800-acre purchase that he would name River Farm and use as rental property. The map is a tangible representation of his profession and his personal interest in land speculation. The northernmost of his five farms that made up the Mount Vernon plantation, River Farm dwindled as sections were sold over time, but in a fitting happenstance for an estate with notable gardens, a twenty-seven-acre riverside portion of it became home to the National Horticultural Society in 1973.

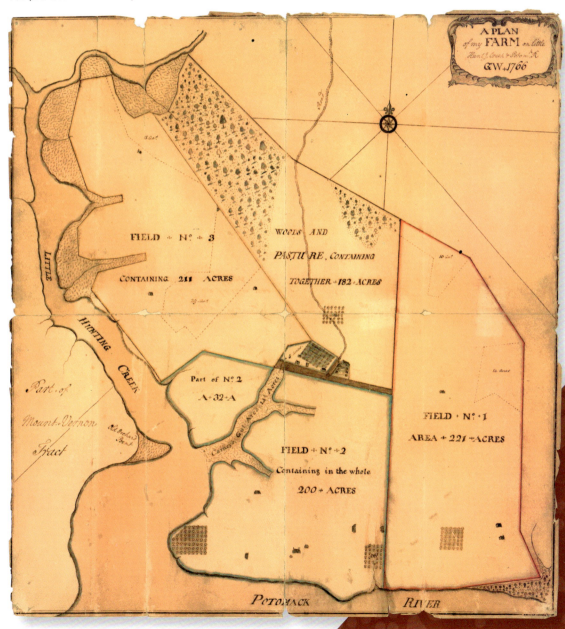

British Beginnings   53

Chapter 3

John Wollaston, *Martha Dandridge Custis*, 1757. Oil on canvas.

Parallel Lives

Thomas Gainsborough, *Queen Charlotte*, 1781. Oil on canvas.

George III, ruler of a great empire from a young age, and George Washington, revolutionary general and republican head of state, led very different lives. Both lived in an epoch, however, when there was much discourse of the laws of science so recently discovered by Isaac Newton and others, and of the relationship of man to God and the natural world. Some considered themselves "enlightened," after discarding any God in favor of the laws of science. Others, while considering themselves "enlightened" and allowing for the existence of God as creator of the universe, believed that He made no intervention in the workings of the natural world, which were entirely governed by scientific laws.[1]

Washington believed in God all his life. Tolerant of other faiths, as commander-in-chief and as president, he saw religious observance as a force for good in society.[2] George III, meanwhile, was a dedicated head of the Anglican Church and personally pious.[3] Both men, however, paid close attention to European and American scientific and technological advances which made rapid headway in this century. Both strained to "improve" their minds, their conduct, their homes, and their agricultural holdings. Patriots both, they were strongly attracted to innovations which could "improve" the fortunes of their respective countries.[4]

George III was born into wealth and royal privilege. Following the early death of his father, Frederick, Prince of Wales, efforts to make Prince George a fit successor to his grandfather, George II, redoubled.[5] The new Prince of Wales was a willing pupil when Lord Bute, a Scottish nobleman and politician, imparted to him the principles of statecraft.[6] He learned German, as well as Latin, French, history, geography, and mathematics, and he was also tutored in chemistry and physics.[7] These lessons were to be the foundation of his later passions for astronomy, architecture, experimental agriculture, and industrial production.[8]

Meanwhile, across the Atlantic in Virginia, George Washington had a rudimentary education following the death of his father.[9] The patronage of William Fairfax of Belvoir, a planter with aristocratic English connections, however, served to advance this American George's prospects.[10] As a county surveyor, as a colonial colonel, and as a member of the Virginia legislature, Washington served both monarch and mother country loyally.[11]

Retiring from military service, aged twenty-six, and marrying, in 1759, Martha Dandridge Custis, a rich young widow with two children, George welcomed the opportunity to pursue agricultural "improvements" at Mount Vernon, his plantation on the Potomac River, with his newfound wealth. Under British common law, Washington had the use, during his wife's lifetime, of her dower portion of her late husband's estate.[12] All the field work was done by enslaved families owned either by Washington or by the Custis estate.[13]

With Martha had come to Mount Vernon a superb library, comprising over four hundred and fifty volumes, acquired by her previous husband and his father.[14] Washington's systematic reading of these books on topics ranging from topography to husbandry, history ancient and modern, and foreign affairs did much to supplement his sketchy education. His ambitious plans for the schooling of John "Jacky" Parke Custis, his stepson, however, foundered on the rocks of the youth's indifference to learning.[15] Martha and George had no children together, but he grieved with her when her daughter, Martha "Patsy" Parke Custis, died at seventeen from epilepsy.[16]

Across the Atlantic, George III, who had succeeded his grandfather as king in 1760, had been fortunate in his choice of bride. Charlotte of Mecklenburg-Strelitz, a German Protestant princess, produced fifteen children over twenty-one years. She never voiced opposition to the king's wish to live a private and sedate existence when not at court.[17] In London, at Kew Palace, and, later, in apartments at Windsor Castle, the royal couple followed a rigid daily routine which made the livelier of their attendants groan with fatigue.[18]

Elegant in her dress, Queen Charlotte brought a Continental sensibility to her appreciation of the arts and sciences in her adopted country. She read widely in both French and German, learned to enjoy English novels, and cultivated friendships with intellectual men and women at court.[19] The king, meanwhile, encouraged scholars, including Dr. Samuel Johnson, to consult the library at the "Queen's House," the London home—now part of Buckingham Palace—which he had bought at the outset of his reign and which he stocked with works of art, scientific instruments, maps, and books.[20]

As his sons grew to manhood, unfortunately, the king found them no more biddable than Washington did his stepson. His heir, the Prince of Wales, launched a schoolroom rebellion in 1776, the very year in which America defied the "tyrant" king.[21] Incurring vast debts for Parliament to pay, he mocked his father during the regency crisis of 1788, when the king became, through illness, unfit to rule for six months, and courted opposition politicians.[22]

Meanwhile, in Virginia, Washington continued to uphold British rule from his marriage until the 1770s, living as a busy planter, burgess, spouse, and stepfather.[23] Few could have predicted that, in 1775, he would challenge the authority of George III, commander-in-chief of the British armed forces, with a newly minted American army.[24] General Washington had no high opinion of his untried troops at the outset of the war and yet, against all odds, they were victorious.[25]

In 1789, at the age of fifty-seven, George Washington became alike in dignity—if not in wealth—to his former king, when he was inaugurated as first head of state of the American republic.[26] Following Jacky's death during the Revolutionary War, Martha brought up two of his children in presidential mansions in New York and Philadelphia.[27] At Washington's death in 1799, there were outpourings of grief across America as well as in Europe.[28] This younger son of a colonial planter had surpassed all others in fame. He had one chief regret at the end of his life. While the gradual abolition of slavery had begun in several states, he had succeeded only in making provision in his will for the emancipation, after Martha's death, of the enslaved families he owned (representing fewer than half of those enslaved at Mount Vernon).[29]

The obdurate qualities of George III, Washington's former royal opponent, would later gain their possessor respect, when Britain successfully withstood the growing aggression of the Napoleonic Empire.[30] During that time anti-slavery agitation saw the abolition of the slave trade in the British Empire, although no enslaved persons in those territories were emancipated.[31] Penal laws affecting Catholics and members of other faiths remained in place during George III's reign, including the Regency, from 1810, when he remained, incapacitated, in seclusion at Windsor.[32] When the king died in January 1820, though it is doubtful if he knew it, he had faithfully followed, all his life, his coronation oath to "maintain … the Protestant reformed Religion."[33]

— **Flora Fraser**

Martha Washington
Martha Dandridge Custis Washington (1731-1802)

After Colonel John Custis IV, one of the wealthiest men in Virginia, learned that his thirty-eight-year-old bachelor son, Daniel, wished to marry eighteen-year-old Martha Dandridge, he threatened to disinherit him. Publicly badmouthing Martha and her respectable but less affluent family, he violently resisted entreaties from close friends and from the prospective groom to permit a union with the Dandridges. Fearful that her engagement was about to implode, Martha managed to meet privately with the cantankerous colonel, who was amazed and impressed that the petite, five-foot-tall young woman challenged him in making her case. To the surprise of all who knew him, Custis backpedaled and allowed the marriage to go forward. He would not be the last man of high rank to be taken by the resilient lady from rustic New Kent County.

The oldest of eight, Martha Dandridge grew up on Chestnut Grove plantation, midway between Richmond and Williamsburg in Virginia. Her father was a successful planter and an Anglican vestryman; her mother gave her what was considered a proper education for a daughter, covering housekeeping and the social graces, and she remained a well-informed, avid reader all her life. (Even so, and even though English spelling in America was not yet standard, Martha often deviated beyond the norm in her own writing.) She was devout, sociable, and a talented seamstress with a growing taste for the fashionable and the luxurious.

Martha married Daniel Custis in 1750, and the couple had four children, Daniel, Frances, John ("Jacky" or "Jack"), and Martha ("Patsy"). The two eldest died young, and she was only twenty-six years old when her husband died in July 1757, leaving her the wealthiest woman in Virginia, with two youngsters, several hundred slaves, and widespread tobacco plantations to manage. As Mrs. Custis, she might have crossed paths with George Washington, but they did not get to know each other until he called on her in March 1758. They got on well and were married in January 1759. What each perceived as a companionable marriage of convenience—great wealth, social advancement and pleasant company with an "agreeable" woman for him, security, and a dashing, dependable stepfather to the children for her—became a loving and devoted relationship. George described her as a "most worthy partner" and called her "Patsy"; she referred to him as her "Old Man" and later as "the General."

Martha's life primarily revolved around family, friends—she was a reliable and lively correspondent—and Mount Vernon, and the many visitors to the estate were uniform in their praise of her as a hostess and convivial personality. "Mrs. Washington is one of the most estimable persons that one could know, good, sweet, and extremely polite," wrote Polish visitor Julian Ursyn Niemcewicz. "She loves to talk and talks very well about times past. She told me she remembered the time when there was only one single carriage in all of Virginia." She doted on her children and grandchildren, sometimes to the annoyance of George, who worried about their being spoiled. An expert at knitting and needlework, she made quilts, clothing, and shortly before her death she completed a complex and regularly interrupted seat cushion project that had taken thirty-five years and more than a million stitches.

During the first year of the Revolutionary War, rumors were rife that Lord Dunmore, the royal governor of Virginia, intended to kidnap Martha from Mount Vernon while her husband was with the Continental Army. Later, at George's request, she joined him each year at his winter quarters, an abrupt change for someone used to comfortable, well-furnished living. "Some days we have a number of cannon and shells from Boston and Bunkers Hill," she wrote to a friend in late 1775, "but it does not seem to surprise any one but me; I confess I shudder every time I hear the sound of a gun." In camp, she was a sunny, welcome presence, visiting with soldiers, knitting them stockings, and handling administrative tasks for her husband. She threw herself into her work, having lost her youngest child, Martha, in 1773; her last surviving child, Jack, would die in 1781 of camp fever, after the siege of Yorktown.

The other part of the year, as the general was occupied with military campaigns, she returned to Virginia and helped estate managers run Mount Vernon. A skilled and experienced plantation administrator

 Chapter 3

with a natural flair for organization, she kept the account books, dealt with vendors in London, oversaw the overseers, and continued running the mansion household. Like George, she carefully tracked the output of the employed and the enslaved alike, right down to the number of socks produced each week. Unlike George, she seems not to have been troubled by slavery, only to the extent that idleness and carelessness inconvenienced her, and she was genuinely shocked when household slaves escaped, complaining that they had not "the least gratitude for the kindness that may be shewed to them."

When George was elected president of the United States in 1789, he was not enthused about it but felt obligated to take the position. Martha, on the other hand, resented this latest imposition on herself and her husband—their life of public service with the Continental Army and George's subsequent role presiding over the lengthy Constitutional Convention had required extensive personal and financial sacrifices. "I little thought when the war was finished, that any circumstances could possible have happened which would call the General into public life again," she told her friend Mercy Otis Warren in December 1789. "I had anticipated, that from this moment we should have been left to grow old in solitude and tranquility togather: that was, my Dear madam, the first and dearest wish of my heart; — but in that I have been disapointed; I will not, however, contemplate with too much regret disapointments that were inevitable."

As the first First Lady (a term not then in use; she was instead addressed as "Lady Washington") Martha managed the executive mansion household in New York and later Philadelphia as well as that of Mount Vernon from afar. Still, as she explained to her niece, Fanny Bassett, in 1789, "I live a very dull life hear and know nothing that passes in the town. I never go to any publick place—indeed I think I am more like a state prisoner than any thing else, there is certain bounds Set for me which I must not depart from—and as I cannot doe as I like I am obstinate and stay home a great deal." For one thing, she was occupied with planning for state dinners and Friday receptions, welcoming ordinary citizens to the latter, as long as they were properly dressed for the occasion. With guests, her friendliness and social ease made up for her husband's reserve and increasing aloofness. In 1796, Vice President John Adams wrote to his wife, Abigail, that "Mrs. Washington told me a story on Tuesday, before a Number of Gentlemen, so ineffably ridiculous that I dare not repeat it in Writing. The venerable Lady laughed as immoderately as all the rest of us did."

The "solitude and tranquility" Martha had hoped for after the war was even less likely after her husband left the presidency in 1797, as visitors both foreign and domestic made their way to Mount Vernon. Their shared retirement lasted only two years when George died in their bedroom after a short illness. Grief stricken, she burned their private letters and settled into an uncomfortable attic room for the quiet few remaining years of her life. In seeking to provide for her, George had bequeathed to Martha the enslaved people he owned, with the provision that after her death, they would be freed and given a basic education. However, as the sole obstacle between their continued enslavement and their promised freedom, Martha soon arranged for their emancipation, effective on January 1, 1801, terrified that they might murder her to hasten their release. A year and a half later, she died from a fever in the presence of her grandchildren and great-grandchildren.

From middle age on, Martha Dandridge Custis Washington was the most famous and well-regarded woman in America. She outlived her entire immediate family—siblings, husbands, children—while enduring the dangers of war and the strain of the presidency. "I am still determined to be cheerful and to be happy in whatever situation I may be," she once told a friend, "for I have also learnt from experience that the greater part of our happiness or misary depends upon our dispositions, and not upon our circumstances; we carry the seeds of the one, or the other about with us, in our minds, wherever we go."

On the Terrace and the Piazza

South-East View of Windsor Castle, 1783. Engraving after George Robertson.

At Windsor Castle, the royal family regularly gathered on the terraces, where they would promenade and meet with courtiers, friends, and be seen by the public. Early on the queen mentioned meeting "the *beau monde* on the terrace," but in later years she found it tiresome, writing the king in 1797 that "I will own fairly to your Majesty that my dislike to everything Public is greatly increased, and I have given full proof of that by appearing but three Times on the Terrace last year." The king enjoyed those afternoons, but not so the young princes and princesses, who were obliged to "walk the terrace," no matter the weather, a unique combination of fresh air, exercise, and display. So unpopular was this routine among them that one summer Princess Augusta wrote to her teacher that "We are now come to Windsor and for our sins forced of Sunday evenings to walk on the terrace."

Meanwhile, at Mount Vernon, the Washingtons and their ever-present multitude of family and guests were much more relaxed on the mansion's piazza overlooking a deer park and the Potomac River. In this watercolor by Benjamin Henry Latrobe, Martha and George sit at the table having coffee after dinner. Her granddaughter, Nelly, stands nearby as her dog Frisk approaches an unidentified seated child. The fellow with the spyglass examining the lush surroundings might be Latrobe himself. "It is from here that one looks out on perhaps the most beautiful view in the world," wrote Julian Ursyn Niemcewicz, a Polish writer who visited in 1798. He also noted a model of the infamous French prison displayed on the piazza, "wholly of a stone which was part of the Bastille; it is a foot and a half high, made with the greatest detail and exactness. It is a pity that the children have already damaged it a little."

Benjamin Henry Latrobe, *View of Mount Vernon with the Washington Family on the Piazza*, **1796, and detail. Ink, watercolor, graphite on paper.**

Queen Charlotte
Sophia Charlotte of Mecklenburg-Strelitz (1744-1818)

Historians have traditionally dismissed Charlotte as "dull," yet her correspondence, the observations of those who knew her, and the contents of her library reveal a personality that was intellectually curious, astute, and resourceful. The king's envoys sent to investigate the seventeen-year-old princess as a potential bride for George III had found the slender, brown-haired young woman healthy, good natured, and considerate, plain but acceptable in appearance, musical, educated "enough," and not likely to interfere in the business of state. She hailed from the small German duchy of Mecklenburg-Strelitz and married the king the day she met him—September 8, 1761. George was smitten.

From the outset, Charlotte understood her role: be a pleasant companion to the king, provide heirs, and learn English (she spoke German and French). She began each task immediately and quickly mastered them all. A faithful Lutheran, she seamlessly converted to her husband's Anglican denomination. After 1762, when children began arriving almost annually, and the royal household settled into its daily and seasonal rhythms, Charlotte cultivated her own interests, including needlework, gardening, and studying genealogy, paying particular attention to the lives of learned royal women.

At Buckingham House (which George bought for her use in London), she established her own substantial library, devouring a wide range of titles from history, theology, science, and law to literature, poetry, and the works of Jane Austen. She purchased leading treatises on education, using the latest recommended practices with her daughters. Her numerous philanthropic and charitable activities focused on widows, orphans, and the poor, a pursuit she passed on to her daughters, and she extended her support to less conventional causes in her patronage of female authors. As a patron of the arts and sciences, the queen met with leading Enlightenment figures, and she welcomed popular actors and musicians to perform at Buckingham House. Among them was eight-year-old prodigy Wolfgang Amadeus Mozart, from whom she commissioned a half-dozen sonatas in 1764.

At Kew and Buckingham House Charlotte tended to her gardens, renewing her studies in botany, cataloging plants, and acquiring a variety of unusual botanical specimens as well as animals from throughout the British Empire, including exotic birds, elephants, kangaroos, and a zebra. She kept her Pomeranians by her side or on her lap, but her tigers were housed at Richmond. Her rooms at Buckingham House were, as a visitor noted, "ornamented, as one expects a Queen's should be, with curiosities from every nation that can deserve her notice. The most capital pictures, the finest Dresden and other china, cabinets of more minute curiosities . . . one room panell'd with the finest Japan. The floors are all inlaid in a most expensive manner, and tho' but in March, every room was full of roses, carnations, hyacinths, &c., dispersed in the prettiest manner imaginable in jars and different flower-pots on stands . . . By the Queen's bed was an elegant case with twenty-five watches, all highly adorn'd with jewels." In time Charlotte became acclimated to the pleasures of refurbished Windsor Castle, her husband's preferred residence, writing in 1777 that there "the air is so good and so clear that we are all cheered up, above all when the young ones are with us, which is what I like best."

A vibrant but judicious conversationalist, Charlotte peppered her talk with literary references supported by a remarkable memory. Her close friend Lady Harcourt noted that the queen thrived on substantive discussions and those around her would be "stupid indeed that did not listen to her with pleasure; no one narrated better than she." Fanny Burney, an attendant, observed that "the King seems to admire as much as he enjoys her conversation, and to covet her participation in everything he either sees or hears." But at court, following her husband's directive, Charlotte was impartial and "civil to all" she told a friend, drawing a line between what she said as queen and as a friend. According to Lady Harcourt, "I remember once saying to her, 'I should like to tell you something, but pray promise never to let the Queen know it.' She laughed, and said, 'oh, no, *she* can have no business with what passes between us in our private, unreserved conversation.'" The queen's conversation was of such interest that in 1797 she complained to the king that "I found every word I spoke in the papers and thereby was convinced that spye's were sent to watch

me." On the other hand, and even worse, "So many untruths were reported last year" about her yet "there is no possibility to defend oneself."

The queen's correspondence with her adored brother Charles reveals that while she stayed out of politics at George's insistence—though occasionally exerting some discreet influence—she held strong and informed opinions on domestic and international affairs. She monitored news from the German states and followed the American rebellion and the French Revolution with intense interest (she even admitted to Charles that she was so preoccupied by these events, and their effect on her husband, that "I do believe that imperceptibly, I am becoming political, despite myself.") Charlotte also wrote to him of the monotony of court life and her misery in a continual state of pregnancy that led to fifteen children in twenty-one years: "I don't think a prisoner could wish more ardently for his liberty than I wish to be rid of my burden and see the end of my campaign."

As her children entered adulthood, the queen's relations with them were often difficult and strained over her worldly sons' indulgences and her sheltered daughters' discontent. A firm matriarch, she would occasionally bend as a mediator between her older sons and the king, urging that he be generous and lenient, but she, too, lost patience with them. Generally keeping her emotions to herself, Charlotte showed an increasingly quick temper in private. (A lifelong snuff user, she turned to the scented tobacco in treating her frequent headaches and stress, accumulating more than 450 ornate snuff bottles and boxes.) When the king was seriously ill in 1788, setting off the regency crisis, her brown hair turned white; she grew livid with the Prince of Wales for disrespecting his ailing father, and each suspected the other of seeking to be named regent. "I have only to add," she wrote the prince in February 1789, "that it was not owing to Lady Harcourt's presence that I said nothing particular to You and Your Brother, *but that I had Nothing to Say*. Which Confession must surprize You as it come[s] from a Woman." A painful rift ensued that was eventually but tenuously patched up. Later, the queen sided with her son in his disastrous marriage to Princess Caroline and oversaw the education of their daughter.

Charlotte and George enjoyed a successful marriage for several decades, but by 1797 their hectic schedules and family turmoil caused the queen to ask for some respite. "We live in a Constant Bustle either upon the Road or in Public," she told the king, "I may now begin to feel the consequences of that life. . . I distrust every Soul & every body that surrounds me & I trust that my Sincerity in telling Yr Majesty the Truth will lead You to acquiesce in my request." In 1804, another bout of his mental illness finally forced her to separate herself from him, a crushing blow to the king but a matter of safety to the queen. His frightening violent episodes, his insults and cruelty toward her when ill, and later the loss of a grown daughter took a tremendous toll on Charlotte, who at times withdrew from public engagements. When George's condition permanently left him unable to function as king, Parliament placed him in her custody, and the queen continued her royal duties alongside the Prince Regent.

In 1818, Richard Rush, American minister to the United Kingdom, met Queen Charlotte, who was suffering from dropsy (edema), seven months before her death, at the wedding of her daughter Elizabeth. "The bearing of the queen deserves special mention," he later wrote. "This venerable personage, the head of a large family—her children then clustering about her—the female head of a great empire. . .went the rounds of the company, speaking to all. There was a kindness in manner from which time had struck away useless forms." When she died of pneumonia, at age seventy-four, her husband was too ill to comprehend her passing. After her death, her daughter Mary wrote that she had been "the great link of the chain that brought us all together, which we must feel the want of, and the loss of, more and more every hour."

What's on the Table: Dining with the Two Georges

Despite the prestige that came with being the first American president, or the grandeur of life at Windsor Castle, both George Washington and King George III enjoyed simple pleasures at the dining table.

While living at Mount Vernon, Washington loved hoecakes for breakfast, especially ones "swimming in butter and honey." This type of soft cornmeal pancake likely appealed to him because of his dental issues. His step-grandson George Washington Parke Custis wrote that breakfast "was without change to him whose habits were regular, even to matters which others are so apt to indulge themselves in endless variety. Indian cakes, honey, and tea, formed this temperate repast." Hoecakes were labor intensive, and the enslaved cooks who made them had to be in the kitchen by 4:30am if not earlier. Other breakfast items included cold cuts or leftovers from the night before, and coffee and hot chocolate in addition to tea; Washington's youngest step-granddaughter, Eleanor "Nelly" Parke Custis Lewis, remarked that Washington routinely drank three cups of tea in the morning.

The main meal of the day was promptly served at 3pm. Many visitors noted that Washington's formal dinner table was well appointed but not overly luxurious. These meals might include a dozen separate dishes. For example, one visitor in 1799 recorded: a leg of boiled pork, goose, roast beef, boiled beef, mutton chops, hominy, cabbage, potatoes, pickles, fried tripe, and onions. Washington was particularly partial to fish. After dinner, Washington enjoyed a glass of madeira wine, which he bought in bulk, often a "pipe" (a cask that held 126 gallons). The last meal, served around sunset, usually consisted of tea, bread, butter, and cakes.

Washington's presidential table was often less lavish than at Mount Vernon. The only record of what was served on May 28, 1789, at the first state dinner of the new nation's inaugural administration came from guest Paine Wingate. The senator from New Hampshire was unimpressed, remarking "It was the least showy dinner that I ever [saw] at the President's.

As there was no clergyman present, Washington himself said grace on taking his seat. He dined on a boiled leg of mutton, as it was his custom to eat of only one dish. After the dessert a single glass of wine was offered to each of the guests, when the President rose, the guests following his example, and repaired to the drawing-room, each departing at his option, without ceremony." Pennsylvania Senator William Maclay mentioned a rumor in his diary that a dessert served at a presidential dinner was filled with rancid cream. Yet some meals were better provisioned. Maclay noted that the official dinner on August 27, 1789, included roasted fish, boiled meat, bacon, and poultry, as well as several desserts such as jellies, pies, puddings, and melons.

Although Martha Washington did not do any cooking herself, she did own several cookbooks, including a "Book of Cookery." This manuscript cookbook was given to her when she married Daniel Parke Custis in 1750. Passed down through the generations, it listed recipes of the Culpepper, Parke, and Custis families, some of which dated back to Elizabethan and Jacobean England, though these older recipes were rarely used; considered old fashioned, they were probably referred to only for inspiration. Recipes included stewed lamb, roast capon with oysters, fried pudding, and mushrooms in cream. Martha later gave this book to Nelly.

The constant flow of guests at Mount Vernon made it practically impossible for the Washingtons to share a meal without company. On July 31, 1797, George wrote to his secretary, Tobias Lear, that "unless someone pops in, unexpectedly, Mrs. Washington and myself will do what I believe has not been [done] within the last twenty years by us, that is to set down to dinner by ourselves."

The Washingtons' diet at Mount Vernon was paradoxically both hyperlocal and global. Enslaved people cultivated fruits and vegetables in the garden, grew and harvested wheat and corn, raised and slaughtered hogs, cows, and sheep, and caught fish in the Potomac River. At the same time, imported food from around the world appeared on Mount Vernon tables. According to Mount Vernon curator Jessie MacLeod, the Washingtons ordered "tea from China, coffee from Yemen and Suriname, chocolate from Mexico, Madeira wine from the Canary Islands, cheese from England, spices from the East Indies, sugar and molasses from the Caribbean, olives and raisins from the Mediterranean, and salt from Portugal."

As ruler of a vast British Empire, George III partook of a global diet as well. French, German, Dutch, and Italian dishes such as gateau a la duchesse (a type of cake), mettwurst (a type of sausage), and macaroni, regularly appeared at the king's table, even during war with France, evidence of Britain's extensive European trade networks. The colonies also provided new delicacies; foodstuffs from the Americas, Africa, and Asia increased from 18 percent at the turn of the eighteenth century to 40 percent of food imports by 1774. Thus, meals in Georgian Britain included a variety of spices, and even animals not native to Europe, such as turkeys or peacocks, became part of the royal diet.

When not attending large banquets, which were rare, the king preferred simple meals, even developing a reputation for abstemiousness. At breakfast, tea was preferred to coffee, though he sometimes drank cocoa. Dinner was served at 4pm and was often a simple affair usually including soup, mutton, occasionally fish, and rarely boiled chicken followed by pudding. George enjoyed pudding and had a royal chocolate maker, who was well paid—though not as highly as the wine steward. Other family members ate heartily, and a December 6, 1789, dinner menu at Kew, for example, included soup, chicken, lamb, mutton, veal, venison, duck, prawns, and pig trotters, along with asparagus, celery, and potatoes. Roast beef on Sundays was a rare indulgence. The king also sometimes ate "beef tea," a stew that was said to help with digestion. Tea was served at 7pm, and his last meal of the day, around 10pm, was usually cold meat, sometimes in sandwich form, or even just plain bread and butter. (The household steward's account books used the word "sandwich" as early as 1784, not long after the cabinet minister John Montagu, fourth Earl of Sandwich, popularized it.) The king preferred to eat quickly, with equerries complaining privately about the need to scarf down their portions rapidly, since etiquette required them to cease eating when the sovereign stopped.

Cooking with Glasse: The Bestselling Georgian Cookbook

Eighteenth-century Britain saw an increase in printed cookbooks, mostly aimed at women. By the 1740s, approximately half of women in London could read, and England was the most literate nation in Europe. Cookery books included recipes, cooking techniques, tips for being economical, and insights into how to emulate haute cuisine from France.

Hannah Glasse's *The Art of Cookery Made Plain and Easy* was one such book. As the title indicates, the recipes were geared toward a broad audience, not just royalty or the aristocracy. First published in 1747, it became a bestseller for the next century, eventually going through seventeen editions. The recipes were clear and written conversationally, but also had a flair for good presentation, a key element of fancy dining in Georgian Britain. Glasse—the illegitimate daughter of a lower member of the gentry—was also a dressmaker, and one of her clients was Princess Augusta, George III's mother.

The Art of Cookery was also popular in North America and was used in Benjamin Franklin's and Thomas Jefferson's households. Martha Washington owned a copy, likely the sixth edition from 1763. Decades after Martha's death, Nelly Custis Lewis wrote her son-in-law Charles M. Conrad: "I am very glad my lip salve pleases you. It was my beloved grandmother's recipe, & she found it I believe in Glass' Cookery."

Perhaps the best summation of the book's American success came from memoirist John Waters, who recalled post-Revolution culinary habits in 1844: "We had emancipated ourselves from the sceptre of King George, but that of Hannah Glasse was extended without challenge over our fire-sides and dinner-tables, with a sway far more imperative and absolute."

Frugal Fare

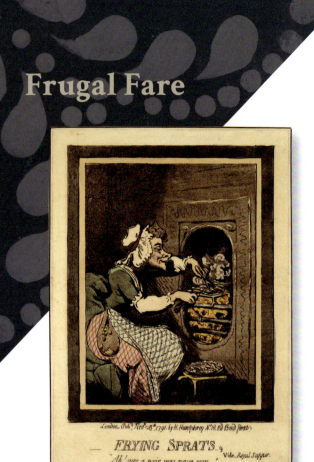

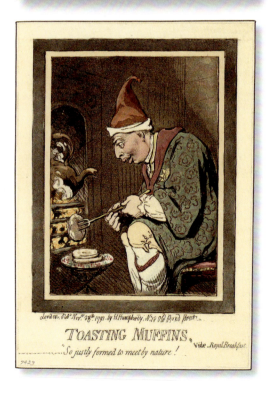

James Gillray, *Frying Sprats* and *Toasting Muffins* November 28, 1791. Color engravings.

King George and Queen Charlotte developed a reputation in the press for being miserly, although they gave generously to charities. However, the ever-expanding expenses associated with their children often forced the royals to try to better manage their funds, lest they be accused of not spending their allowances wisely.

Although some commentators appreciated the monarch's restraint and lack of pomposity at times, satirists especially harped on his perceived parsimony. While satirists often used luxurious foodstuffs to lampoon the wealthiest Britons, in George III's case, it was the lack of luxury that provided fodder for poking fun at his frugal diet and lifestyle.

James Gillray went back to this well several times. In November 1791, twin prints depicted Charlotte and George frying sprats and muffins, respectively, dressed like ordinary commoners.

The following July, in the most famous print to satirize George's austerity (opposite), he eats a boiled egg while Charlotte eats salad—possibly sauerkraut or cabbage, a dig at her Germanic roots. The rest of the room is full of symbols of miserliness: half-burned candles, empty picture frames, dustcovers on the chair, and a scale for weighing guineas.

George's favorite food and drinks also belied the stereotypical royal diet. In 1785, he stated "I prefer eating plain and little to growing diseased and infirm"—advice his eldest son did not take to heart. His favorite drink was a sort of lemonade, a concoction of borage (an herb) and white wine, which served as a general tonic. While it had some alcohol in it, a courtier remarked that a Trappist monk "might have drunk it without any infraction of his monastic vow." The king preferred barley water to wine, and never drank spirits; his minimal alcohol consumption even led to some speculation during his 1788 health crisis that the issue was caused by a lack of wine. He stipulated that brown bread should be eaten throughout the royal household, in the hopes of changing the popular belief that it was not fit for consumption. George also tried to avoid eating sugar, for health purposes, rather than the moral reasons put forth by opponents of slavery. In the 1790s, he responded to poor harvests by eating less, which did not go unnoticed; Fanny Burney, the queen's keeper of the robes, noted the king "accustoms himself to none of the indulgences which almost all his subjects regard as indispensable."

James Gillray, *Temperance Enjoying a Frugal Meal*, July 28, 1792. Color engraving.

Servants and the Enslaved

Operations as large as the king's household and Washington's Mount Vernon plantation required immense workforces. When George III came to the throne in 1760, he had nearly a thousand people at his immediate service under his many roofs, from lords- and-ladies-in-waiting to armed guards and kitchen scullery maids. His household included the Queen's House (later known as Buckingham Palace) in London and Kew Palace and Windsor Castle in the countryside, and servants moved with the royal family from place to place while others maintained the unoccupied residences. Meanwhile, at Mount Vernon in Virginia, George Washington's peak workforce numbered more than three hundred people, nearly all of them enslaved. During the American Revolution, his enslaved manservant William Lee traveled with him, and while president in New York City and Philadelphia, a small contingent of both free and enslaved people served him in the executive mansion.

At the beginning of his reign, in a spirit of reform and economizing, George III gave up revenue from crown lands in exchange for £800,000 in fixed annual funding from Parliament to cover his expenses and finance his household. It turned out to be a very costly decision, made before he had a wife and numerous children to support in addition to already providing for his younger siblings. As a result, he kept a close eye on spending and there were times when Parliament had to cover expenses that included delayed wages to his servants.

Three main divisions served the king and his family at home: the "upstairs" Lord Chamberlain's department oversaw the "ceremonial, artistic, and social" aspects of household and court life and was populated with administrative staff as well as housekeepers, grooms, ushers, cupbearers, and trumpeters. The "downstairs" Lord Steward's department was responsible for domestic tasks and household security; staff included clerks, yeomen, cooks, porters, maids and footmen, laundresses, gardeners and groundskeepers, and a water manager, known as a turncock and keeper of the buckets. Some menial servants were children. The Master of the Horse department provided transportation and comprised a gentleman of the horse, equerries, surveyors, grooms, and carriage staff. Household politics, overlapping responsibilities, and turf wars between the chamberlain's and steward's offices led to ongoing tension and inefficiency that impressively withstood occasional efforts at reform.

Royal employment offered the privilege of serving king and country, security, lodging, livery (clothing or uniforms for middling and lower-level servants, who received nominal pay), a comparatively excellent meal plan, and potential rewards and gratuities in exchange for long, taxing hours on one's feet, even for those in the highest positions. One also had to navigate complicated rules, unwritten customs, and rigid protocol. Fanny Burney, lady-in-waiting to Queen Charlotte, recorded that on formal occasions in the presence of their majesties, "You must not cough . . . if you find yourself choking with the forbearance, you must choke. But not cough," and if the violence of preventing a sneeze "breaks some blood vessel, you must break the blood vessel. But not sneeze." With no pensions at the time, many middle- and lower-ranking employees worked well into old age or until they died. "It's honor!" an equerry for George III said in explaining the appeal of royal service. "That's one comfort; it's all honor!"

The king appointed up to one hundred of the top household positions, a process involving nepotism and unseemly groveling from applicants, some of whom plotted for years to obtain choice roles. George and Charlotte also hired doctors, tutors, portrait painters, and others as needed. One area where the king was not as thrifty when it came to staffing was his bedchamber. Gentlemen and grooms helped him bathe and dress, joined him for meals, manned the door, and handled personal tasks as His Majesty required. (The king did save some money by not employing a secretary, as he tended to his own correspondence and kept his own notes during most of his reign.)

At the highest levels of royal service, lords- and ladies-in-waiting were part of an elite revolving set of courtiers—relatives and other titled nobility—who were privileged and honored to tend personally to the king and queen, usually in monthly shifts. Nannies, governesses, governors, and other atten-

Chapter 3

dants watched over the royal children. Honorifics and surnames were used for upper-level staff while those in the lowest ranks, who performed the most onerous or unpleasant drudgery—such as emptying chamber pots —wore uniforms and were addressed as Mr., Mrs., or Miss and their first name.

Both George and Charlotte treated the servants politely, and the queen regularly sent small gifts and notes of thanks to her ladies and attendants whose lives, entirely centered on their employers, were exhausting. In 1780, Miss Gouldsworthy (known as "Goulie"), an attendant to Charlotte, the Princess Royal, accompanied her from Windsor to Buckingham House three times in one week, dealing with logistics, long, uncomfortable travel, and near constant supervision of her thirteen-year-old charge. Back

James Gillray, *An Old English-Gentleman Pester'd by Servants Wanting Places,* **May 16, 1809. Color engraving. Published by Hannah Humphrey.**

From the moment he became king and throughout his active reign, George III faced an onslaught of job-seekers or those acting on behalf of friends and relatives. Here the king views through his spyglass groveling aristocratic applicants, some performing servants' tasks, as Lord Grey (middle right), leader of the Whigs and a future prime minister, in the guise of a dog, begs "Pray throw me a bone." Although the cartoon addresses events that occurred between the resignations of two prime ministers—bowing Lord Grenville (in bright gold breeches) and the Duke of Portland (smiling, to the right of the king)—Gillray's illustration is representative of the ongoing and frequently over-the-top efforts to win appointments from the king or positions in the royal household. On becoming president of the United States, George Washington experienced the same dreaded situation, calling it "an almost insupportable burden to me," and he was at great pains to politely reject requests from countless office seekers, many of whom he considered friends.

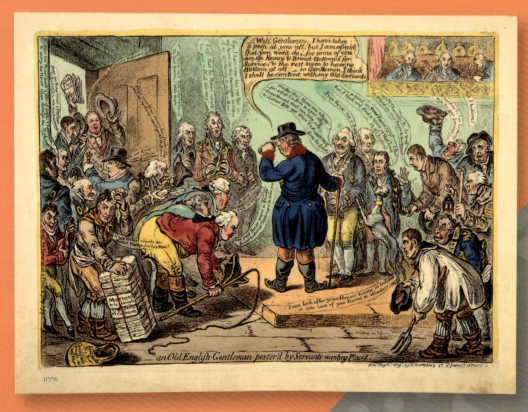

Parallel Lives

at Windsor Castle she wrote to a fellow attendant, "I return to this dungeon . . . heated to death and wishing . . . for the hour of going to bed." Their majesties' constant commuting, state occasions, regular activities, and both the many members of the royal family and the size of their residences kept servants in a near continuous flow of exertion.

Servants ate well and according to a repetitive weekly calendar: veal, beef, mutton, or pork was served with vegetables and bread; Sunday dinner came with a provision of plum pudding, and alcohol was freely available. Living quarters were plain; at Kew Palace, servants were stashed on the top floor in a series of small, dark, damp, and misshapen rooms. The Board of the Green Cloth, headed by the Lord Steward, dispensed discipline for employee offenses; traditionally, theft of royal property was punishable by death or imprisonment. In the Georgian era, punishment was not as drastic, and slow or poor work usually resulted in a reprimand or suspension rather than dismissal, which was usually reserved for repeated infractions, as in the case of a porter who was let go in 1786 for having "absented himself for upwards of two years without leave."

At Mount Vernon, Washington was at the top of his own workforce, a demanding and meticulous boss putting in long hours himself. He inspected his grounds daily; checked in with overseers and monitored progress in plantings, harvests, maintenance, and construction; purchased goods, sold crops, carefully maintained his accounts, and kept up with agricultural advances. Equipped with a ferocious work ethic, he also expected others to work diligently and conscientiously. As the many surviving letters to his estate managers and others show, the general was routinely disappointed in and frustrated with his workers, both hired and enslaved, complaining of drunkenness (the "ruin of half the workers in this Country"), indolence, "tricks", theft, and "roguery." Washington said of the frequently absent Thomas Green, whom he hired to manage his carpenters, "a more worthless one does not, I believe live."

Over four decades, Washington drew from several types of labor pools. He hired white men to manage his estate and oversee his farms; if they had wives, they, too, could be paid for their work. He used several hundred white indentured servants—mostly from Ireland, many of them former convicts—to teach skills to his largest workforce, enslaved Black men and women who fell into one of two categories: those Washington had inherited or purchased, whom he owned outright; and the Custis or "dower slaves" that he had use of through his marriage (children were classified as one or the other depending on which group their mother belonged to). He also rented and controlled more than forty workers held by a neighbor. In 1799, the year Washington died, Mount Vernon's pyramid of residents consisted of five members of the Washington family at the top; white employees and their families, numbering seventeen persons; and 317 enslaved workers.

Washington's plantation comprised five farms, each staffed with an overseer and anywhere from forty to eighty enslaved people. Originally, all overseers were white men, but eventually several were enslaved men who had earned promotions, which came with cash, better clothing, and extra food. His enslaved workforce included field hands, who were mostly women, tradesmen, craftsmen, unskilled laborers, and house servants. When away from Mount Vernon, Washington required his estate managers to provide weekly reports on what was accomplished. He instructed his overseers that "My people [must] be at their work as soon as it is light—work 'till it is dark—and be diligent while they are at it." To prevent the "misapplication of labor," Washington scheduled work projects a year or more in advance to ensure that everyone stayed busy even during natural lulls in the seasonal calendar. Not a moment was to be wasted.

At the mansion, Martha Washington oversaw the house servants, most of them enslaved, working as butlers, cooks, housemaids, waiters, and others who answered to a wired bell system at any hour of the day or night. She also supervised and worked closely with the seamstresses. Additionally, Martha had a personal maid and George had a valet. "The general's house servants are mulattoes," Louis-Philippe, later the king of France, noted following a visit in 1797, "some of whom have kinky hair but still skins as light as ours."

In 1762 Washington built a two-story "house for families," similar in style to army barracks, to house most of his enslaved workers on the Mansion House Farm. It was later replaced with brick bunkrooms for men and cramped log cabins for families, or what Julian Ursyn Niemcewicz, a visitor from Poland, described as "huts" when he visited in 1798, "for one cannot call them by the names of houses. They are more miserable than the most miserable of the cottages of our peasants. The husband and wife sleep on a mean pallet, the children on the ground; a very bad fireplace, some utensils for cooking, but in the middle of this poverty some cups and a teapot."

By the intrinsically low standards of eighteenth-century Virginia plantations, "Washington treat[ed] his slaves far more humanely than do his fellow citizens of Virginia," according to Niemcewicz. Enslaved children began their stolen lives with simple tasks, such as gathering kindling or fetching water, but they were expected to become full-time laborers no later than the age of fourteen. They received no education or training other than what was necessary to perform their work, although a handful of enslaved people at Mount Vernon acquired basic literacy skills. Washington allowed them to form their own families, which gave some measure of individual agency, and he recognized their marriages, which were not legal. They were given Sundays and holidays off, and on occasion permitted to attend horse races and other events offsite. Each year they received a new set of clothes and pair of shoes; those who worked in the mansion were well dressed, the men in suits, the women in simple gowns, while most others wore drab coarse linen. Washington offered no religious instruction and had virtually no interest in their spiritual practices, which for some were rooted in traditional African beliefs. As far as he was concerned, "If they are good workmen, they may be of Asia, Africa, or Europe. They may be Mahometans, Jews, or Christians of any Sect, or they may be Atheists."

Food provisions centered on cornmeal and salted fish; to flesh out their diets, enslaved people raised chickens, hunted (some men were permitted to use guns), and kept gardens, these personal chores being in addition to their work assignments. They earned money selling their surplus produce in Alexandria, and Washington himself was a regular customer. The general preferred to offer these perks and other rewards for good work, as well as "corrections," such as encouragement, reprimands, and demotions to field work, rather than physical punishments, finding that approach best in deterring indolence and sloppiness. Theft, fighting, ongoing insolence, refusal to work and other serious infractions, however, could be met with physical punishment, although it was not regular practice. Washington permitted his overseers to whip offenders if necessary, and he was known to have struck some in anger himself. Later in life Washington ordered overseers to withhold the whip and allowed time to review cases before determining physical punishments, if any.

As a last resort, Washington "disposed of" those he regarded as most troublesome, selling them into exile, never to see family and friends again. Perhaps the worst destination was the Caribbean, where death rates were staggeringly high and lifespans notably short. When estate manager Anthony Whitting reported problems with a teenage boy in February 1793, President Washington responded from Philadelphia, "I am very sorry to hear that so likely a young fellow as Matilda's Ben should addict himself to such courses as he is pursuing. . . . He, his father & mother may be told in explicit language that if a stop is not put to his rogueries, & other villainies by fair means & shortly; that I will ship him off (as I did Waggoner Jack) for the West Indias."

Ongoing theft, sabotage, slow work, feigned illnesses, and escape attempts, however, were not merely aggravations to Washington, which he was resigned to accounting for in calculating his expenses. They were clear statements that *his people* resisted their enslavement and the very premise of Mount Vernon.

George Washington, Slave Census, page four, July 1799.

Five months before his unexpected death, the former president prepared an eight-page list titled "Negroes Belonging to George Washington in his own right and by Marriage." The document includes each enslaved person's name (including children), age if known, occupation, family relationships, and where on the Mount Vernon estate they worked, providing insight into how Washington organized his labor force and the family networks enslaved individuals developed. In addition to the ten people Washington inherited from his father, he purchased fifteen more early in his career, and children born to women he enslaved became his property. On occasion, he hired workers enslaved by his neighbors for tasks that usually required a specialized skill. Through his wife, Martha Dandridge Custis Washington, he had the use of what were called "dower slaves," people belonging to the Custis family whom the Washingtons could not legally sell or emancipate. At his death, Washington held 317 people in bondage.

Planter George and Farmer George

"Agriculture being my favourite amusement I am always pleased with communications that relate to it," Washington wrote to Maryland planter John Beale Bordley in 1788, before discussing in detail varieties of wheat. Similarly, the king was so enthralled with his agricultural activities and royal farms that he was nationally known as Farmer George. And with their penchant for experimentation, precise recordkeeping, and hours spent out in the fields, the two men embodied the meaning of their shared first names, derived from the Greek word *geōrgos* (γεωργός), meaning "farmer."

The Georges' shared quest for agricultural advancement was part of the Enlightenment interest in scientific developments and the application of new knowledge. Each strove to improve crops, animal husbandry, farm management, efficiency, and quality. Both corresponded with Arthur Young, the leading British agronomist of the day, as well as with other planters and farmers in their respective realms, exchanging seeds, produce, and livestock.

Washington, a member of the Virginia planter class, owned a plantation of nearly 8,000 acres that included five farms. In 1766 he made a pivotal decision, swapping out labor intensive, soil-depleting tobacco in favor of grains, primarily wheat, as his main cash crop. During the 1780s, the retired general introduced a new seven-year crop rotation system at each of his farms, which led to greater output of higher quality. He designed a sixteen-sided barn and automated his gristmill using machinery he learned of from a patent he approved while president of the United States. Late in his career, at the suggestion of his Scottish farm manager, James Anderson, he built a distillery, and quickly became one of the nation's top whiskey producers. In the last year of Washington's life, Mount Vernon sold nearly 11,000 gallons, and whiskey became his biggest moneymaker.

The eighteenth century's scientific revolution was the one kind of revolution that suited George III, who established and operated model farms at Kew, Richmond, and Windsor. His farms were profitable commercial ventures, and he took over the role of ranger at both Richmond and Windsor Great Parks after the previous officeholders died, devoting himself to regular inspections of the farms and parkland there. Early on, he took a broad, national view. British food exports generated three times more revenue than manufactured goods and were the basis of national prosperity.

In his copious notes and essays on the topic, George III recorded that "Agriculture is the foundation of every other art, business, or profession, it is the chief attention of every wise Nation to see that this and Manufactures are proportionally encouraged but the preponderance ought to be in favour of the former." During his reign, the United Kingdom's population nearly doubled, from 8.1 million in 1760 to 15.3 million in 1820. To continue sustaining and employing such numbers, the king observed, better farming practices and new approaches were necessary, such as converting "waste" and "unimproved lands" into arable areas; using forage crops, such as cabbage and turnips, to replenish soil and feed cattle; and employing "old people and children" in the growing wool industry.

Both Georges experimented with different types of livestock and their uses, although Washington remarked in a letter that developing a better breed of cattle "will take more time than in the usual course of nature will be allowed me, to improve them much." He had greater success introducing mules to American farm life by way of his prized donkey, Royal Gift, whose breeding services he advertised annually for several years. A present from Charles III of Spain, Royal Gift and Washington's mares produced strong, hardworking mules that by the 1790s had taken over the drafting duties of his more expensive horses. Washington also gifted or exchanged animals with his correspondents, in part, to see how they fared in different environments. At

Parallel Lives

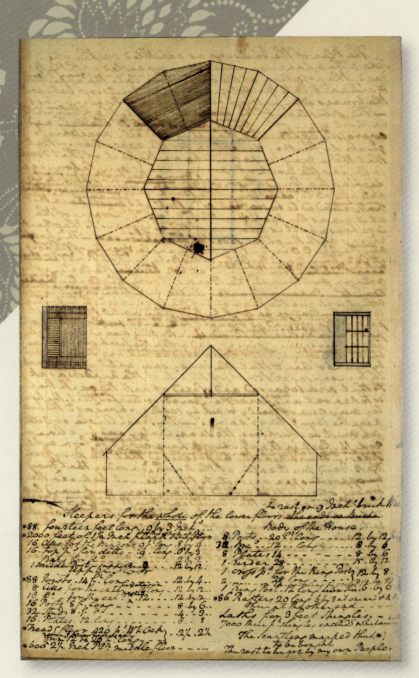

George Washington, Plan for a Sixteen-Sided Barn, October 28, 1792.

Combining his deep interest in agriculture and his passion for efficiency, Washington developed and sketched this innovative design for a new barn at his Dogue Run Farm at Mount Vernon during his first term as president. He even calculated the number of bricks required for the barn (30,820), which measured 52 feet in diameter, with each of the sixteen walls a little more than ten feet long. Below the drawing he listed the number and size of necessary construction materials, right down to the studs.

Enslaved carpenters Reuben, Nuclus, and Tom Davis were among those who constructed the decahexagonal structure—brick on the ground floor and wood on the second—to process and store grain. Horses entered the second story by a dirt ramp built up on one side, then trotted around the "treading floor," their hooves separating harvested grain from stalks. The grain fell through the deliberately spaced floorboards to the threshing floor below for collection. Washington regarded the barn as an experiment, asking Anthony Whitting, his estate manager, "What are the advantages and disadvantages, if any, of treading the grain out in this manner?"

Washington's innovations were the barred windows to prevent theft, the spaced floorboards, and an architectural design that facilitated the horses' circular route. By carrying out the operation indoors instead of outside, as was traditionally done, the extracted wheat berries were kept dry, clean, and safe. In the new barn, six or seven acres of harvested wheat could be processed in a day—much faster than before—and at a higher success rate. The project epitomized Washington's efforts to maximize available technology for greater output, less waste, and to wring out all possible profit. Completed in the spring of 1794, the barn remained standing into the 1870s, and in 1996 a full-size working replica was built at Mount Vernon.

Mount Vernon, he kept horses, goats, hogs, and chickens, and some three hundred head of cattle or more from the 1780s on. Sheep were his favorites, telling a friend that they were "that part of my Stock in which I most delight."

The king was very pro-sheep as well. George III's venture to improve British wool and revitalize the industry began with Merino sheep in the late 1780s, an endeavor the king called "a most national object." In seeking examples of the valuable breed that was tightly controlled by Charles III, George's men first purchased smuggled sheep from the Portuguese-Spanish border then later pursued legal channels to import more. King Charles diplomatically gave King George a small flock, which His Majesty settled at Kew. Renowned for their fine wool and mutton, but not accustomed to Britain's wet, cool climate, the sheep managed well enough to later draw high prices at auction and reproduce to the point that George sent hundreds of them to courtiers, gentleman farmers, and other recipients around the country. (Arthur Young was overwhelmed with gratitude when the king presented him with a ram, Don the Merino.) By 1805, some Merinos from the king's flocks had even landed in Australia.

The king's greatest challenge with these sheep was what to do with them all. Over the years, he repeatedly declined Spanish offers to accept more, as he had run out of space for them, even on his vast estates. That did not stop the Spanish; in July 1809, as Britain mobilized a naval campaign against the Dutch, the British foreign secretary reported to the king that 1,500 Merino sheep from Cadiz had unexpectedly arrived in Portsmouth "destined for Your Majesty, by the Supreme Junta." The king, taken aback, ordered the Admiralty to sail them up the Thames to the Deptford dockyards in whatever spare vessels were available, to be dealt with somehow. Nonetheless, that same year, Charles Henry Hunt wrote in his treatise on the breed that "I am persuaded the day will come, when the introduction of Merino sheep, and the care and anxiety [George III] has manifested to disseminate them through the kingdom, will not be considered as the least beneficial act of his reign."

The two eight-year stints Washington spent away from Mount Vernon during the Revolution and while serving as president, as well as his absence during the Constitutional Convention, had negative effects on agricultural production at his plantation and were part of the financial price he paid for his public service. He observed that his delightful sheep did not produce as much wool, there were work slowdowns, and greater carelessness among both the employed and enslaved. A dog owner himself, he was nonetheless irate about wild and stray dogs that preyed on his sheep and hogs, writing his farm manager from Philadelphia, "I not only approve of your killing those Dogs which have been the occasion of the late loss, & of thinning the Plantations of others, but give it as a positive order, that . . . if any negro presumes under any pretense whatsoever, to preserve, or bring one into the family, that he shall be severely punished, and the dog hanged."

When not engaged on their farms, the two Georges avidly read farm publications. Of particular interest to the king was Arthur Young's journal, *Annals of Agriculture and Other Useful Arts*. In 1787, under the pseudonym Ralph Robinson (a name taken from one of the king's shepherds at Windsor), George III contributed a piece, "On Mr. Ducket's Mode of Cultivation," to the journal. (Mr. Ducket was the king's bailiff at Windsor.) He described crop rotation, plowing methods and equipment, and the use of manure. In his article, "Robinson" explained to Young that as Ducket's "great modesty prevents his standing forth among your correspondents, I will attempt to describe his mode of cultivation, rather than it shall longer remain unnoticed in your *Annals*." Among the Annals' readers was George Washington, who likely read Robinson's piece with interest, whether or not he was ever aware of the author's true identity.

Initially focused on improvements to his own estate, Washington expanded his view of the need for greater dissemination of accurate agricultural information nationwide, a notion that had long preoccupied George III. Washington was incensed by "ignorant farmers" who kept moving west after ruining land with poor practices, telling his friend George William Fairfax in 1785 that "Our course of Husbandry in

Parallel Lives

Farmer George and His Wife, ca. 1780s. Hand-colored etching.

This unsigned satirical print of King George and Queen Charlotte depicts Their Majesties as ordinary English folk. Although the nickname "Farmer George" was first meant in ridicule, its use evolved into a friendlier, relatable meaning and connected the king to his people, most of whom lived in rural areas and worked in agricultural industries. George read deeply on the subject of farming, took extensive notes, and kept a close eye on developments in his own fields and pastures. When he visited the countryside, dressed in plain clothing and unaccompanied by courtiers, it was not unusual for him to strike up conversations with farmers and laborers about their work.

this Country, & more especially in this State, is not only exceedingly unprofitable, but so destructive to our Lands, that it is my earnest wish to adopt a better [course]."

Washington and the king both recognized that as wealthy landowners and public figures, their leadership in agricultural reform could have important effects, as they could afford to experiment and absorb losses that most farmers could not. King George saw to it that Young became the first secretary of the non-governmental Board of Agriculture, founded by royal charter in 1793—which two years later President Washington joined at its invitation as an honorary member. The board awarded sought-after medals as prizes for contributions, discoveries, and improvements "in the most important and leading points of husbandry." On the medals, George III appears in profile on the obverse, and on the reverse an allegorical female figure stands with a plough, spade, and other farming implements.

President Washington saw the value of establishing such a board in the United States, and in his final address to Congress, December 7, 1796, he declared that agriculture is "of primary importance. In proportion as nations advance in population and other circumstances of maturity this truth becomes more apparent, and renders the cultivation of the soil more and more an object of public patronage." He called for "the establishment of boards (composed of proper characters) charged with collecting and diffusing information. . . . Experience accordingly has shewn that they are very cheap instruments of immense national benefits." Despite Washington's strong endorsement, the United States would not establish an Agricultural Division until 1839; a year later George III's granddaughter, Queen Victoria, granted a charter to the Royal Agricultural Society of England, successor to the defunct Board of Agriculture.

Henry Kingsbury, *The Farm Yard*, 1786. Hand-colored engraving. Published by S. W. Fores.

Queen Charlotte, strewing bird feed, and King George face each other across an occupied pig trough with Windsor castle on a hill in the distance. A sign noting "Man Traps and Spring Guns" indicates the presence of devices to deter poachers. Well-known for his farming activities, the king was often portrayed in his "Farmer George" persona, a favorite characterization of Britain's irreverent cartoonists. George was more than a gentleman farmer or hobbyist, however. He pursued agricultural innovations (such as a mobile barn on wheels), and his farms were profitable commercial enterprises. Not everything was about profit, though. On one occasion, while showing a visitor around his farms at Windsor, the guest was critical of his German hogs, a gift from the queen. Do not find fault with the hogs, said the king, since "the value of the intention is better than a breed."

Farm Notes

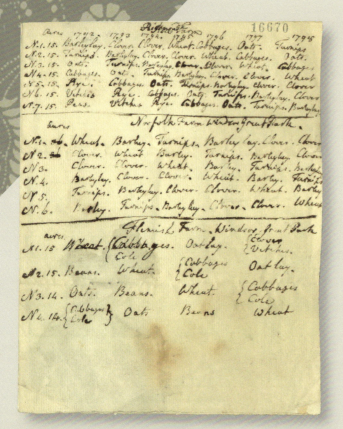

Crop Rotation Tables: George III, January 1793; George Washington, December 1793.

Both Georges kept crop rotation schedules as part of good farming practices, in which grains and vegetables were planted in different fields after a season or two to minimize soil depletion. The tables shown here indicate the king's and the president's handwritten plans for rotating their crops during the 1790s. The king's crops at his Richmond and Windsor farms include beans, barley, cabbages, clover, oats, turnips, and wheat; at Mount Vernon's Dogue Run Farm, Washington is planting clover or grass, corn, potatoes, and wheat.

A Map of General Washington's Farm of Mount Vernon from a Drawing Transmitted by the General. **Samuel John Neele, engraver. Printed in** ***Letters from His Excellency George Washington, to Arthur Young*** **(London, 1801).**

At the time of George Washington's death in 1799, Mount Vernon comprised farmland, a gristmill, a greenhouse, a distillery, a mansion, outbuildings, and woodlands on about 7,600 acres alongside the Potomac River in northeastern Virginia, fifteen miles south of Washington, DC. He inherited about 2,000 acres as a boy, and through near relentless land acquisition, assembled his plantation over several decades by purchasing adjacent and nearby property and combining numerous smaller tracts. The map is an amalgamation of drawings and descriptions Washington had sent English agricultural expert Arthur Young. It depicts his five Mount Vernon farms, from left, Union Farm, Dogue Run Farm, Muddy Hole Farm, Mansion House farm, and River Farm. The lettered key at the top, a facsimile of Washington's handwriting, describes areas suitable for future development.

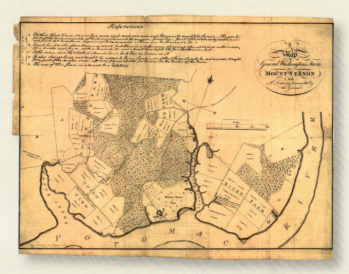

George Washington, notes on Henry Home, Lord Kames, ***The Gentleman Farmer*** **(1776), with drawing of drag harrow.**

George Washington and George III shared a strong interest in modern, experimental agriculture, and each owned a copy of *The Gentleman Farmer*. Washington took detailed notes and made sketches of the author's description of a drag harrow, which was used to smooth and level ground after plowing. In a diary entry for April 25, 1788, Washington wrote that he had ridden to all his farms that day and at one, "the Plows this Morng. began to cross the ground that had been broke up in the lower meadow. The drag harrow followed the Plows, and the Women (after they had spread the Dung there) followed the harrow, in order to knock the clods to pieces & remove the grass, to fit it for Oats—Clover, & orchard grass."

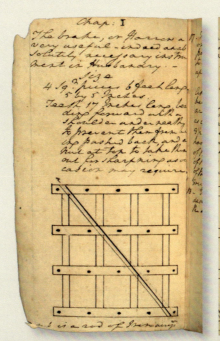
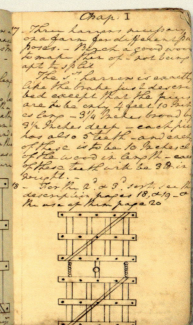

Parallel Lives

On the Cutting Edge of Science

Science went by the elegant name of "Natural Philosophy" in the eighteenth century, and both Georges were engaged in it, from conducting experiments and collecting scientific instruments to countering the scourge of a lethal virus. Each of them promoted scientific advances and used state-of-the-art technology, and neither saw a conflict between scientific progress and his religious beliefs. As Washington put it in a letter to the American Philosophical Society, which elected him a member in 1780, "The field of investigation is ample—the benefits which will result to Human Society from discoveries yet to be made, are indubetable—and the task of studying the works of the great Creator, inexpressibly delightful."

In the Georges' lifetimes, smallpox, horrifying in its putrid pustule manifestations and frequently fatal, was the most feared of diseases, leaving survivors pockmarked and scarred or even blind and infertile. Before a vaccine was produced in the 1790s, inoculation was the method of immunization in Britain and America beginning in the 1720s. It involved collecting a small amount of the virus from an infected person and inserting it into cuts or punctures in the arm of an uninfected person, who, after recovering from a milder case of smallpox over several weeks, usually remained immune to it. Inoculation was fraught with controversy, but both the king and Washington saw it as easily worth the risk and for the far greater public good. The king, inoculated as a child, had his children immunized; when Prince Alfred, age two, died from a fever after his procedure in 1782, it was thought that he might have been given too strong a dose. His devastated parents were not deterred, regarding the outcome as the will of Providence.

As a smallpox survivor, General Washington knew well the misery it caused. During the Revolutionary War, he ordered symptomatic soldiers to quarantine and suspected General William Howe, commander-in-chief of British land forces, of waging biological warfare by expelling diseased Bostonians to the American lines. In January 1777 he ordered that all American troops who had not had smallpox be inoculated; he had done so with his stepson five years earlier. An infected army, he wrote, would have "more to dread from it than the sword of the enemy." Later that year Martha Washington was inoculated, for her own sake, but doing so also served as an example to soldiers and their wives.

The two Georges were also of the same mind when it came to experimentation and new technology. The king amassed a collection of more than a thousand scientific instruments including microscopes, telescopes, globes, barometers, and models of the universe. Many of these items were acquired for demonstration purposes, such as his "philosophical table" (1762) by George Adams made of mahogany, ivory, and brass. Devices built into or attached to the table were used to show principles of mechanics and forces of motion, and the king was always keen to see scientific presentations.

Washington collected instruments on a smaller scale, but most of his were put to practical use in his early career as a surveyor and then on his farms at Mount Vernon. In addition to his many agricultural experiments, he was game to satisfy other curiosities. In September 1783, while in Rocky Hill, New Jersey, Washington and renowned pamphleteer Thomas Paine conducted an experiment to determine why some of the rivers and creeks in the area could be set on fire. Sitting in a boat with soldiers using poles to churn the creek bottom, the two men held lit cartridge paper over the water. "I saw the fire take from General Washington's light and descend from thence to the surface of the water . . ." wrote Paine. "This was demonstrative evidence that what was called setting the river on fire was setting on fire the inflammable air that arose out of the mud."

Given their workloads, schedules, and love of instruments, it was natural that both men were taken with timepieces. Washington carried plain gold pocket watches, including one made by Jean-Antoine Lepine, watchmaker to Louis XVI. Throughout his presidency, he habitually checked his watch against his Philadelphia watchmaker's regulator clock to maintain both accurate time and his reputation for punctuality. George III favored more ornate devices, and he was a driving force behind the growing British clockmaking industry, seeing its importance in military and business use. He commissioned a variety of timepieces and appointed Thomas Mudge as Royal Watchmaker in 1776. Mudge invented the lever escapement (to keep watch hands moving at a consistent rate, a landmark and rather necessary innovation) and included one in the watch that the king ordered for Queen Charlotte. Mudge claimed it was "the most perfect watch that can be worn in the pocket, that was ever made."

Both Georges were also drawn to what was happening in the skies. As a professional surveyor, Washington had learned how to make astronomical readings, and as a conscientious and scientific farmer at Mount Vernon, he recorded weather conditions, temperatures, and celestial activity daily. "A very remarkable Circle round the Moon—another Indication of falling Weather," he wrote on January 26, 1760. He tracked the phases of the moon with a keen eye, noting on May 18, 1768, that "the Horns of this Moon were also up as the two last were tho a little more declining." He could even be a touch poetic, as on November 16, 1785, mentioning "a large circle round the Moon last night—a red & angry looking sky at the Suns rising." During the Revolutionary War, he thanked the Pennsylvania Council of Safety on January 8, 1777, for alerting him to a forthcoming eclipse of the sun, so he could warn the troops, noting that "this event, without a previous knowledge of it, might affect the minds of the Soldiery, and be attended with some bad consequences."

George III provided pensions to amateur scientists, including brilliant astronomer William Herschel, and Queen Charlotte funded one for his equally brilliant sister, Caroline. According to William, "the king has very good eyes, and enjoys observations with the telescopes exceedingly." The king was thrilled when William discovered a new planet, and even more so when he named it "the Georgium Sidus"—the Georgian Planet, or George's Star. (In 1850 the name was changed to Uranus, in keeping with the planetary naming convention derived from classical mythology.) The king funded the four-year construction of William's £4,000 Great Forty-Foot Telescope, completed in 1789 and the largest in the world, located in the astronomer's backyard in Slough, near Windsor. On one occasion, the king brought the archbishop of Canterbury with him to see the huge iron telescope tube before it was set in place. According to Caroline Herschel, the king stepped inside it and turning to the archbishop said, "Come, my lord, I will show you the way to heaven." Although it would prove unwieldy and no better than smaller telescopes William had built, the great telescope was in use for decades, became a tourist attraction, and, as unmistakable as the moon in the night sky, was a sign of the king's commitment to a greater understanding of the cosmos. ☀

Jonathan Sisson, armillary sphere, 1731. Brass.

George III's collection of scientific instruments includes this armillary sphere that was made for his father, Frederick, the Prince of Wales. Sisson was a leading mathematical instrument maker, and this piece is an example of his precision and craftsmanship. It was made twenty years before Britain changed to the Gregorian calendar under George II, thus the calendar shown on the large horizontal ring is off by eleven days. An armillary sphere was used to demonstrate the rotation of planets around a model of the sun set in the middle of the device; it could also be used to determine hours of daylight and what time sunrise and sunset would occur. George III developed his interest in astronomy early on and might well have used this armillary sphere in his studies.

Dudley Adams, terrestrial floor globe, ca. 1789-1790. Paper mache.

In 1789, George Washington asked his London purchasing agents, Wakelin Welch & Son, "to send me by the first vessel, which sails for New York, a terrestrial globe of the largest dimensions and of the most accurate and approved kind now in use." The task fell to Dudley Adams (1762-1830), whose father George had made a pair of terrestrial globes for George III in 1766, inscribing one with the dedication "To the most august King of the Britons, George III, equally a devotee and protector of the sciences, this terrestrial globe, showing all the places on Earth thus far discovered." Washington's expensive new globe (£27), measuring twenty-eight inches in diameter, sits in a mahogany stand with brass fixtures and was used throughout his presidency. On retirement, he likely kept it in his study at Mount Vernon.

Samuel Whitford, George Washington's telescope, London, ca. 1765-1789.

George Washington regularly relied on scientific instruments, including compasses, pocket watches, and a thermometer, to help perform tasks as a surveyor, military commander, and farmer. He eventually owned a dozen handheld pocket "spye-glass" and field telescopes as well as this larger tripod-mounted brass scope. Washington kept it in his ground-floor study, overlooking the heavily trafficked Potomac River, but the telescope's folding legs would have allowed him to easily carry and use it anywhere in the house. Samuel Whitford advertised himself as a maker and seller of "Optical, Mathematical, and Philosophical Instruments, according to the latest Improvements, at the lowest Prices," which would have appealed to Washington's investigative and frugal sensibilities. He left the telescope in his will to Dr. David Stuart, who married into the family and earned the general's trust as a straight-talking advisor and a man of science.

Christopher Pinchbeck, King George's astronomical clock, London, 1768. Tortoiseshell, oak, gilt bronze, silver, brass, steel, and enamel.

Visitors to Buckingham House noted the presence of at least one clock, if not more, in virtually every room, one of the king's sensible and ornamental contributions to interior decorating. George III was drawn to the technical aspects of timekeeping and reveled in its practical effects, which made running both his household and his kingdom more efficient. He kept this, the second of his two astronomical clocks, in his apartment at Buckingham House.

More than a mere timekeeping device, the thirty-inch tall, four-sided table clock is both a work of art and a horological masterpiece. Commissioned by the king, its elaborate classical and baroque appearance, featuring bronze Corinthian columns, ornamental silver and brass traceries, enameled dials, and a tortoiseshell case, was designed by architect Sir William Chambers with input from the king. On the front face, seen here, the principal dial shows local time, with the looped end of the hour hand encircling a painted animated sun that moves across the sky during daytime hours. In the center is the time for twenty-four locations worldwide, including Boston, California, New Zealand, Japan, Constantinople, and Rome.

On the other sides of the device, dials indicate the temperature and planetary motions; the tides at British ports are given beneath a steel ball on which changing phases of the moon are shown in real time; and the current day and month above a planisphere (star chart) in which the constellations move according to time and date. The king's full support of the burgeoning watch and clockmaking industries prompted and encouraged greater innovations in horology, which in turn had innumerable applications for other scientific fields. In its coverage of local, global, and celestial data, its complex mechanisms, and its artistic craftsmanship, George's remarkable timepiece represented both enlightenment and empire.

Stephen Demainbray to King George III, Memorandum of the Transit of Venus, June 3, 1769.

In anticipation of a rare passage of Venus across the sun on June 3, 1769, the king's mother had given him a small observatory at Kew Palace gardens for his upcoming birthday. He also sent Captain James Cook to the other side of the world with astronomers to observe and document the phenomenon from Tahiti. His observatory superintendent, Stephen Demainbray, sent this memo to the king well in advance on what to expect (Venus would appear on the sun "as a black dot" and the transit would be visible at Richmond for about an hour and forty minutes). He also remarked that "Morally speaking, None now living will see the same Phenomenon again, which will only happen again in 1874 and 2004."

George, Charlotte, Demainbray, and twelve others witnessed the momentous occasion through the observatory's 170-magnification Shorts reflecting telescope. In an international effort, measurements taken during Venus' passage at locations around the world added to existing knowledge that would allow scientists to figure out the size of the sun, other features of the solar system, and determine the astronomical unit. George's observatory would contribute to other significant accomplishments in his lifetime, including the means for establishing longitude and the discovery of the planet Uranus.

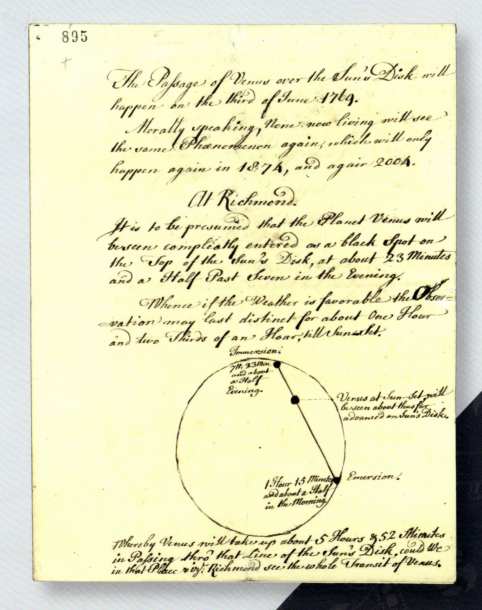

Fig. 13. Argand's aerostatic experiment at Windsor, Nov. 26, 1783.

James Basire, *The Royal Family Viewing a Balloon let off in the Garden of Windsor Castle*, 1784. Print.

On November 26, 1783, Swiss scientist Ami Argand demonstrated the first hot air balloon in Britain, with King George, Queen Charlotte, and other members of the royal family in attendance. Argand had arrived in London from Paris, where earlier that year he had assisted Etienne and Joseph Montgolfier with their pioneering balloon experiments. In September, the Montgolfier brothers had flown a sheep, duck, and rooster in the basket of a balloon in a presentation for Louis XVI at Versailles, the first occupied balloon flight.

George Washington, always enthralled with scientific advancements, was dumbfounded by the demonstrations, writing a French acquaintance in April 1784 that "I have only news paper Accts of the Air Balloons, to which I do not know what credence to give; as the tales related of them are marvelous, & lead us to expect that our friends at Paris, in a little time, will come flying thro' the air, instead [of] ploughing the Ocean to get to America."

In Residence and on the Road with the Washingtons

George and Martha Washington lived briefly in the White House, but it was not the executive mansion of the American president that would later be built in Washington, DC. Rather, on George's marriage to the widow Martha Dandridge Custis in 1759, the pair lived for a short time in her home of that name on the Pamunkey River, in New Kent County, Virginia. Within a few months the Washingtons and her two children, four-year-old John, known as Jacky and later Jack, and two-year-old Martha, known as Patsy, took up residence at Mount Vernon as a family. Through his marriage, George became the administrator of the Custis estate and the children's legal guardian; he also expected that he and his wife would have children of their own. The fact that they did not was of contemporary interest for what it meant to George personally and for its importance to the country in separating the early presidency from traditionally inherited power.

George and Martha called Mount Vernon home for four decades, with two significant stretches spent elsewhere during the Revolutionary War and his presidency. Perched on a hill in northeast Virginia, above a bend in the Potomac River, the estate had been in the Washington family since 1674. For George, it was imbued with childhood memories as his older brother Lawrence's home, but it was also a large business enterprise, a self-contained community, and a model of genteel Virginia society. For others it was an unrivaled source of hospitality, a refuge to homeless or unfortunate relatives, and a prison of sorts to hundreds of enslaved workers. In his own lifetime it was a national icon in the public mind. There was nowhere else on earth that George Washington would rather be than at Mount Vernon.

In the early years, the Washingtons were primarily occupied with their expanding plantation, their young family, and George's life as a political figure in Virginia's House of Burgesses. In setting up their household, the Washingtons, like other well-to-do families, ordered all manner of goods from Britain. Their orders usually ran for several pages, reflecting both the aspirational and the practical. George, who was using Daniel Custis' accounts for these purchases, sent his London agent a copy of his marriage certificate as proof of his right to do so as administrator of his predecessor's estate. In 1769, when colonists began demonstrating their opposition to Parliament's various taxes and impositions by boycotting British goods, the Washingtons turned to homespun wares, including more items made at Mount Vernon. This recalculation of financial costs and political considerations began to alter their sense of being truly British and facilitated their embrace of a new American identity.

A good example of their move toward greater self-sufficiency and profit was the Washingtons' decision in the late 1760s to increase, diversify, and closely monitor cloth production at Mount Vernon. The workshop grew from a few employed and enslaved workers—the men as weavers and the women as spinners—to ten or more. Using wool and flax produced on the estate, the workshop created textiles in a variety of fabrics and patterns for clothing, carpets, bedding, and other goods used on site or sold to neighbors. George carefully tracked workshop expenses and output as part of a cost-benefit analysis of homemade versus imported goods. About the same time, he expanded his fishing operations, when it occurred to him that the river could supply far more than food for his table and the main diet for his enslaved people. Selling locally and shipping internationally, Mount Vernon fish became a reliable and lifelong source of income. This experiment in greater self-sufficiency reinforced for him the concept that production and political autonomy were intertwined, and increased domestic manufacturing became a major goal of his presidential administration.

In their daily lives, the Washingtons maintained structured schedules to accomplish all that needed to be done. George was usually up between 4 and 5 am, spending quiet morning hours in his study reading or at his accounting books. After breakfast at 7 am he usually inspected his estate on horseback. In the late morning and early afternoon he dealt with his correspondence, characterized both by its volume and his penchant for thoughtful wordiness. "It's astonishing the packets of letters that daily come for him, from all parts of the world, which employ him most of the morning to answer," said Robert Hunter, a visitor in 1785. ". . . The General is remarked for writing a most elegant letter." Martha tended to the children, her handiwork, housekeeping, and guests. Dinner was at 3 pm, followed by tea or coffee later in the day. After a light supper in the evening, George often returned to his study. The Washingtons usually retired about 9 pm.

On Sundays, the family occasionally attended Anglican services at Pohick Church, Truro Parish, in Fairfax County or Christ Church in Alexandria and regularly did devotions at home. Martha held conventional Anglican views and schooled the children in the Bible, but less is known about George's spiritual life, which he was not inclined to discuss. Like many others of his time, George referred to God as "Providence" and "the Creator" but in certain instances he used "the Great Architect," invoking Masonic language. (He had joined the Masons as a young man, in 1752, drawn to the brotherhood's efforts to "enlarge the sphere of social happiness" as well the opportunity for social networking.) An active vestryman for Truro Parish from 1762 to 1775, George handled administrative and budget matters and was closely involved in the construction and furnishing of the new church at Pohick.

Although the Washingtons regarded the 1760s and early 1770s, before the Revolution, as an especially happy period for the family, raising Patsy and Jacky came with challenges, even with all the extended family help and enslaved labor that was on hand. Jacky was incorrigible while Patsy increasingly suffered from "fitts & fevours," as her mother put it, and she regularly experienced epileptic seizures by the time she was a teenager. Inseparable from her mother, Patsy was a "sweet innocent girl" in George's words. The Washingtons spared no effort or expense in getting her medical treatment—powders, pills, purging, and a month-long trip to a mineral spring—but little could be done to alleviate her condition.

The children had a private teacher and another tutored them in music, voice, and dance, an essential social skill (George himself loved to dance). However, Jacky, the family scamp, exasperated his stepfather in ways that did not seem to affect his indulgent mother. George constantly fretted about the boy's laziness and proven ability to squander educational opportunities George coveted but did not have at a similar age. At thirteen Jacky was sent to study under Reverend Jonathan Boucher in Fredericksburg, Virginia. It did not go well. In December 1770 Boucher reported that "I never did in my Life know a Youth so exceedingly indolent, or so surprisingly voluptuous: one would suppose Nature had intended Him for some Asiatic Prince."

By the early 1770s, Patsy's health was in decline and George took to noting the girl's frequent seizures in his calendar. On June 19, 1773, she passed away at seventeen "without uttering a Word, a groan, or scarce a Sigh" said George in a letter to his brother-in-law. He told him of "the distress of this family. . . this Sudden, and unexpected blow, I scarce need add has almost reduced my poor Wife to the lowest ebb of Misery." Jack, who had recently announced his engagement to Eleanor "Nelly" Calvert, dropped out of King's College (later Columbia University) and married her in February 1774. George did not put up a fight, finally resigned that his stepson was no scholar and that his presence near Mount Vernon would be a comfort to Martha. His ever-present disappointment and concern flared up though when Jack, hoping to become an instant squire in northern Virginia, naively purchased property in Fairfax County under outrageous and impossible terms. George was aghast when he learned the details, and the disastrous deal hung over the family for years at considerable cost.

When the Continental Congress chose George Washington to lead its new army in June 1775, his first thought was what this would do to the family. "My great concern upon this occasion," he told Jack, "is the thoughts of leaving your Mother under the uneasiness which I know this affair will throw her into." He need not have worried. Martha managed Mount Vernon in his absence, and during eight years of war, they spent more than half that time together during the long winter months when military campaigning ceased. The first winter, in Cambridge, Massachusetts, she hauled with her everything necessary to make herself and the general comfortable, from a large wardrobe to piles of quilts, and she took along Jack and Nelly for company. They moved into army headquarters—the vacated home of a Loyalist—sharing it with her husband's staff and young soldiers sprawled throughout the mansion. She promptly organized new household procedures, and everyone around the general saw how much her vivacious presence meant to him. Some of Martha's closest friendships developed during the war with the wives of other officers.

Later winter accommodations fared poorly in comparison. At Valley Forge, the Washingtons and the staff crammed into a small stone house during a freezing, disease-ridden, desperate time. The general ordered that a log cabin be built to serve as a dining room, and Martha led other officers' wives in knitting a mountain of warm socks for the soldiers. Despite the hardship of long, bumpy travel by horse-drawn coach and stressful conditions at her destination, Martha never considered not going to winter quarters.

Meanwhile, neither of Jack's parents wanted to see him as a soldier, nor did Jack himself. Elected a delegate from Fairfax to the Virginia General Assembly, he was amiable, often absent, and made no noticeable contributions. But in the late summer of 1781 he offered to assist his stepfather as a civilian aide and joined him at Yorktown. After the American victory, in what was to be the final major battle of the war, Jack, twenty-six, fell ill with typhus and died soon after.

After the war, the Washingtons prepared for a new phase in their lives, and George undertook a major renovation of Mount Vernon's grounds. In other

Edward Savage, *The Washington Family*, 1796. Oil on canvas.

The first family posed for this large portrait in New York City, the artist reworked it in Philadelphia, but the imagined setting—with a view of the Potomac River—is seemingly Mount Vernon. Although the figures appear awkward, the painting was a success and popular with the public. George is shown in several capacities: as a husband and father figure during his presidency while wearing his Revolutionary War uniform. He places his left hand atop the plans for the capital city named in his honor as Martha uses her fan to indicate on a map the boulevard that would become Pennsylvania Avenue and the site George had selected for the Executive Mansion, later known as the White House. They are shown with her grandchildren that she and George raised: George Washington Parke Custis, at left, and Eleanor Parke Custis, center. An enslaved house servant, partly hidden at the far right, is thought to be Christopher Sheels, a valet who attended the former president on his deathbed.

respects, though, the 1780s played out like the 1760s. Jack left behind four children and his widow soon remarried. The Washingtons went back to parenting, raising the two youngest, Eleanor Parke Custis, like her mother known as Nelly, and George Washington Parke Custis, called "Washy," "Wash," and sometimes "Tub." The similarities between the two eras did not end there—George adored young Nelly but Wash, like his father, was lazy and a near-constant headache to his step-grandfather. By age nine Wash was on "the high road to ruin" declared George's secretary, Tobias Lear, but the general was unwilling to upset Martha by taking strict measures with the youngster. The College of New Jersey (later Princeton) did, however, when it expelled Wash in 1797 for "various acts of meanness & irregularity."

Guests had always been a near-permanent feature at Mount Vernon, and following the war, they were more frequent, numerous, and sometimes long-term. Visitors included extended family, George's military comrades and political colleagues, friends, friends of friends or their relatives and their friends; foreign admirers, businessmen, sightseers, and nearly anyone passing through northern Virginia. George likened Mount Vernon to a "well resorted tavern" since "scarcely any strangers who are going from north to south, or from south to north do not spend a day or two at it." Some relatives transitioned from guests to full-time residents, living at the estate for years at a time. Lund Washington, a distant cousin, worked as the estate manager for twenty-one years, succeeded by George's favorite nephew, George Augustine Washington, in 1785. Martha's favorite and closest niece, Fanny Bassett, arrived after the war and eventually became a second lady-of-the-house.

As the vortex of Custis and Washington family life, Mount Vernon drew other young relatives who found in George and Martha vital sources of familial ties, seasoned advice, lodging and sustenance, and future loans. George served as co-executor of the estate for his late and deeply indebted younger brother Samuel, and he funded the expensive educations of his two orphaned nephews, George Steptoe and Lawrence, and expenses for their teenage sister, Harriot. (George remarked that Harriot was "very well provided with every thing proper for a girl in her situation: this much I know, that she costs me enough to place her in it.") Martha and George's already close-knit families were further bound together with the marriage of Fanny and George Augustine and the marriage of Martha's granddaughter Nelly to Lawrence Lewis, George's nephew.

After George was elected president in 1789, the Washingtons spent a year in the temporary capital of New York City and another seven in Philadelphia, taking Nelly and Wash with them. Their living arrangements involved multiple moves in both cities as Martha set up and oversaw the presidential household. At the end of summer in 1790, they finally settled for the long term in Morris House, which had been renovated for presidential habitation, office work, and entertaining. The family frequented Philadelphia's theaters, museums, and gardens, and the children attended school rather than being tutored at home.

The Washingtons returned to Mount Vernon for good in 1797, enjoying little over two years together there, in the throes of incessant company. After George and Martha died, his nephew Bushrod Washington inherited the estate in 1802. Nelly and Lawrence lived at Woodlawn plantation, then part of the Mount Vernon property and a wedding gift from her grandparents. Wash became a playwright, and both he and Nelly were significant sources for Washington family lore and history. The decay that had crept in about the mansion and the plantation in the Washingtons' absence during the presidency accelerated under subsequent owners. In 1858 the Mount Vernon Ladies' Association purchased the house and two hundred acres to preserve the estate and promote Washington's life and legacy. ☀

At Home with the House of Hanover

Thoughtful, amiable, conscientious, and—taking a thoroughly unconventional route—faithful to his wife, George III was an outlier among men in the House of Hanover. Whereas his great-grandfather, George I, and grandfather, George II, took mistresses, despised their eldest sons, and banished or imprisoned relatives they found annoying, George III set out to end these dynastic customs. He would be an altogether different father and monarch from his immediate predecessors, and with his queen, Charlotte, and their eventual fifteen children, would seek to embody virtue and domestic bliss for the rest of the country to emulate. As the king wrote to his son Prince Frederick, then seventeen, in 1781, "My ardent Prayer to Heaven is that the conduct of my Children may be the Channel by which I may receive the Commendation of the World."

The family resided at Kew Palace, and, as their numbers increased, at Windsor Castle, and when in London at the Queen's House (also known as Buckingham House and, later, as Buckingham Palace). The king kept a regular schedule, rising between six and seven and retiring in the evening at eleven: he attended chapel, walked in the garden, or rode his horse before breakfasting with the queen, their "children always playing about them the whole time," according to one observer. He often hunted later in the morning before tending to his correspondence. A playful and affectionate young father, he enjoyed spirited visits to the royal nursery. In the afternoon he received government officials and closely read state paperwork. Several times a week he attended afternoon levees (formal receptions) at St. James's Palace, where he met with prominent political, religious, social, and cultural figures as well as foreign visitors. Frequently he worked after dinner before joining the queen for the evening.

When in London, the king and queen spent several evenings each week visiting his mother, Princess Augusta, at her home; other weeknights were regularly given over to card parties or concerts. On occasion, the family visited museums, military units, and businesses, and they were regulars at the theater, where the king preferred light-hearted comedies. They religiously attended Sunday chapel service, and George, who read his Bible daily, was intent on instilling in his youngsters a strong moral foundation and reliance on their Christian faith, "which is the only real means of obtaining the Peace of mind that alone can fit a man for arduous undertakings," he told thirteen-year-old Prince William, a theme that regularly appeared in letters to his children. Music played a significant role in family life, and the king and queen greatly admired the work of George Frederick Handel. Most of the children were good musicians, occasionally joining the king (fiddle, flute, pianoforte) and queen (guitar, harpsichord) for at-home recitals or chamber music performances by the Queen's Band.

The king diligently supervised the boys' intensive eight-hour-a day schooling under various instructors, devising a comprehensive and demanding curriculum that included French, German, Latin, and Greek; mathematics; history, religion, law, and government; natural philosophy (physics and other sciences); "polite literature;" and hands-on practice in agriculture. In verbose letters to his sons (on the subject of the Almighty's commandments and eternal salvation, the king wrote Prince Adolphus, "I could write volumes"), he offered encouraging words, praise when warranted, and well-intentioned but usually unwelcome advice and admonishment. "You have not made that progress in your studies which . . . I might have had every reason to expect," he wrote his eldest son, George, the Prince of Wales, since "your love of dissipation has for some months been with enough ill-nature trumpeted in the public papers, and there are those ready to wound me in the severest place by ripping up every error they may be able to find in you." (The press did not need to look far in confirming the extravagant young man's scandalous behavior.) To seventeen-year-old Prince William, in the Royal Navy, the king noted that "your judgement does not ripen so fast as I could wish."

After their education at home, each teenage son went abroad for additional schooling or military training, most not returning home for years at a time. (The king kept the troublesome Prince of Wales in Britain, however, that he might not adversely influence his younger brothers while they studied outside the country.) George's methodical purpose was to train the boys from a young age for professional service to Britain. "My sons are the instruments I look to for assistance in putting this country into any degree of prosperity," the king wrote to Prince William in 1785, two years after the American Revolution, "but then they must by their behavior convince me they are deserving of such trust." In general, they did not.

Meanwhile, Queen Charlotte managed the girls' extensive education, hiring teachers and bringing in subject experts, and she even sat in on lessons for her own benefit. (Educated women, the queen explained, were just as competent as learned men.) The king followed their schooling with interest, and much of the older princesses' early training was in the expectation that, for diplomatic purposes, they would marry into foreign royal families. They studied English, French (the language used in European courts), German, history, geography, art, penmanship, music, dancing, and needlework. Eventually, both parents lost their fervor and intense personal involvement in the education of their younger children. These youngsters, born during the American Revolution, saw much less of their parents than their older siblings, received less discipline, and communicated with the king and queen primarily by correspondence. George and Charlotte were regularly on the go, commuting between their London and country residences ("We are often in three places in a week," said the queen, who made a point of being at Kew "on Friday and Saturday to see my children.")

Like the king during his own isolated upbringing, the royal offspring interacted with few others their age, and the adults they encountered daily were usually in their parents' employ: nurses, stewards, governesses and governors, teachers, equerries, and doctors, as well as courtiers. The girls, especially, confided in their governesses and teachers; the boys, however, with the king's consent, endured harsh discipline, including beatings and floggings, a long-time practice in British schools. There was some free time for play and roughhousing as youngsters, but at court, which was rigidly formal though low-key compared with the lavish and elaborate proceedings in pre-Revolutionary Paris, the royal teenagers were expected to attend receptions, concerts, and endure life on display. Of the thirteen surviving children, relying on each other as playmates and confidantes, most would remain in contact throughout their lives, but after the second eldest, Prince Frederick, left for Hanover in 1780, the entire immediate family was never all together again. They maintained a voluminous and devoted correspondence, however, and visited each other, even when living on different continents, with some pairs and groups of siblings becoming close despite significant age differences and far-flung residences. As a family they were inveterate gift givers, regularly treating each other to tokens of affection.

Away from court and formal occasions, the king and queen lived modestly by royal standards and were usually in plain attire. They preferred simple meals, the king favoring tea and eating moderately, the queen drinking coffee and dining heartily. Neither drank much alcohol. In the summer, the family spent long holidays at the seaside, particularly at Weymouth, a humble early resort town that held little interest for restless, inquisitive princesses denied the same measure of freedom their brothers enjoyed by their late teens. ("This place is more dull and stupid than I can find words to express," huffed Princess Mary.) The king often interacted with locals, especially those engaged in farming, and some members of the royal household were horrified to see the queen out and about as if she were an ordinary person.

Ultimately, the plan to promote virtue and familial harmony did not go as the king had hoped. With the exception of his two youngest boys, Octavius and Alfred, who died as young children, George, having set high moral standards for the others and selected their professions, came to regard most of his seven surviving sons as utter disappointments, especially where their private lives were concerned. The king found himself personally involved in marriage counseling, blackmail resolution, and child support payments for his sons. Other than Prince Adolphus, they were uninterested, unwilling or unable to follow their father's upright example as they cycled through mistresses, gambled, sank deeply into debt, drank excessively, publicly allied themselves with the king's opponents, repeatedly asked for military promotions and greater incomes, and complained to each other about his treatment of them. In the nineteenth century, the Victorians cast them as deadbeats and villains. The Duke of Wellington would refer to them as "the damndest millstone about the necks of any government than can be imagined." Their sisters, for the most part, cherished them.

In time, two sons, the shopaholic aesthete Prince

Parallel Lives

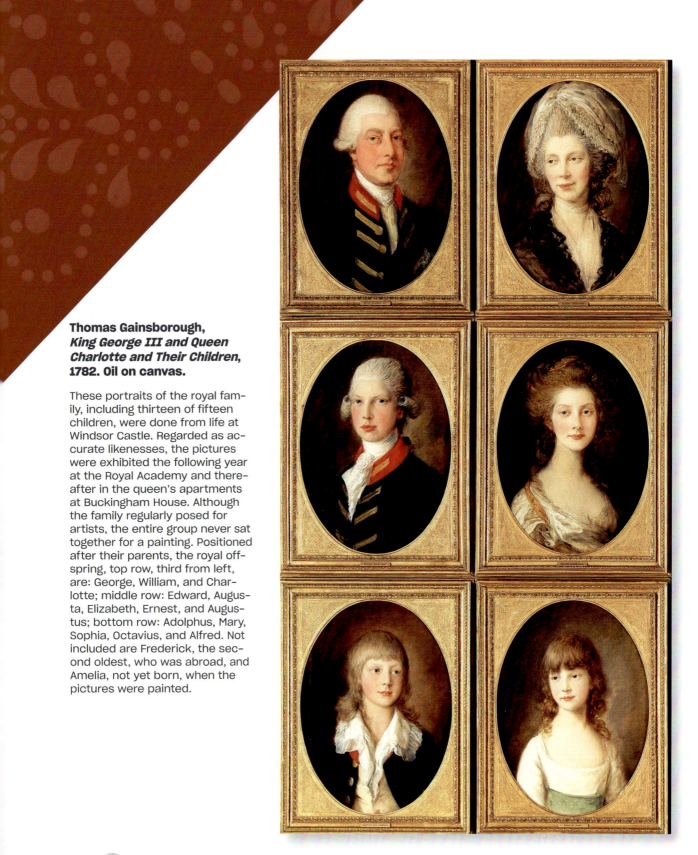

Thomas Gainsborough, *King George III and Queen Charlotte and Their Children*, 1782. Oil on canvas.

These portraits of the royal family, including thirteen of fifteen children, were done from life at Windsor Castle. Regarded as accurate likenesses, the pictures were exhibited the following year at the Royal Academy and thereafter in the queen's apartments at Buckingham House. Although the family regularly posed for artists, the entire group never sat together for a painting. Positioned after their parents, the royal offspring, top row, third from left, are: George, William, and Charlotte; middle row: Edward, Augusta, Elizabeth, Ernest, and Augustus; bottom row: Adolphus, Mary, Sophia, Octavius, and Alfred. Not included are Frederick, the second oldest, who was abroad, and Amelia, not yet born, when the pictures were painted.

Parallel Lives

of Wales and the successful, good-natured naval veteran William, Duke of Clarence, would accede to the throne as George IV and William IV, respectively. Frederick, Duke of York, became the well-regarded and reform-minded commander-in-chief of the army; the deeply unpopular Ernest, Duke of Cumberland, who some believed murdered his valet although he was officially cleared in the case, eventually became king of Hanover. Edward, Duke of Kent, served in Canada as commander-in-chief of North America, the first royal family member to reside there and to visit the United States, while the sickly Augustus, Duke of Sussex, became grand master of the masonic United Grand Lodge of England and the favorite uncle of Queen Victoria. Adolphus, Duke of Cambridge, served in the army, saw combat, and was made a field general before becoming viceroy to Hanover for his brothers George IV and William IV. Only Adolphus, who signed letters to his father as his "Most Dutiful and Affectionate Son and Subject," lived the wholesome life their father had expected and desperately wanted for all his sons.

Whatever heartache his sons caused him, George found great comfort in the company of his six well-read, witty, and talented daughters, so much so that he was later determined to keep them at home forever. Indeed, in 1797, the king cried—though not out of happiness—at the wedding of his eldest daughter, Charlotte, the Princess Royal, who later became queen of Württemberg, a small German kingdom. Although father and daughter corresponded frequently afterward, they never saw each other again, which figured into his thinking about losing the others. So, too, did the fact that his own sisters suffered greatly through politically arranged marriages that were utter debacles. Over time, the princesses assumed various roles within the family, as Sophia became their father's confidante and aide-de-camp, Elizabeth catered to their mother, and Augusta, a self-described good cricket player in her youth, served as the family news disseminator and documentarian. The youngest child, the amiable but headstrong Princess Amelia, was understood to be the king's favorite.

The princesses performed charitable works, engaged in endless art and craft projects, struggled with clandestine romances, and referred to their living quarters as "the nunnery." The queen was aware of their unhappiness as sheltered grown women, but the king seems not to have appreciated just how stifled they felt. Although they adored their father, the princesses were not only relentlessly bored by their social isolation but were traumatized by his bouts of mental illness and accompanying violent rages, which they witnessed far more than their scattered brothers. In 1805, with her elder daughters then in their thirties, the queen carefully broached the subject of marriage to the king, "which I have made it a rule to avoid" since "I know their opinions differ with Your Majesty's." Nonetheless, she wrote, "every one of them at different times assured me, that happy as they are, they should like to settle if they could, and I feel I cannot blame them."

During much of their own marriage, George and Charlotte enjoyed a close and happy relationship. The queen was deferential to her husband, quick to his defense, and when possible, she shielded him from news she knew would upset him. In private they enjoyed a warm and flirtatious rapport. Unlike most aristocratic couples, they shared a bedroom. That permanently changed, at Charlotte's insistence, with the king's penultimate bout of mental illness in 1804, after which the pair attended events together but lived apart, to George's bitter disappointment. The death of Princess Amelia in late 1810—brought on by tuberculosis and, according to her sisters, a doomed romance—contributed to the king's final loss of sanity. By 1811, George was no longer able to serve as monarch, and the Prince of Wales became the Prince Regent.

After discussions raised by his determined sisters, a sympathetic Prince Regent saw to it that their allowances were significantly increased and they could at last establish their own households and live as they pleased, or at least to the extent that propriety and familial obligations permitted. It was a wonder, Princess Sophia wrote him, that he did "not vote for putting us in a sack and drowning us in the Thames," and they were eternally grateful to him for ensuring their independence and liberty. With the king unable to object, Princesses Elizabeth and Mary, in middle age, welcomed husbands. Like her sister Princess Charlotte, Elizabeth married a German prince she barely knew and lived abroad for the rest of her life. The queen spent more time at Kew and at Frogmore Cottage at Windsor, and the king, blind and beyond recovery, disappeared for good into his apartments at Windsor Castle. The queen saw the king in June 1812, but after that brief visit, George and Charlotte never met with one another again.

"The Most Interesting Event": Managing Marriage

George III took a significant but unsuccessful step in trying to manage his family with the far-reaching and consequential Royal Marriages Act of 1772, which he proposed and Parliament reluctantly passed when his eldest child was just nine years old. The king did so after discovering to his horror that his youngest brother had recently married in secret knowing that George would not approve of the marriage. (Five months after the Act's passage, the king learned that *another* brother had been secretly married for six years.) The Act required descendants of George II younger than twenty-five years old to obtain permission from the sovereign to marry; the king wanted to ensure that his family members wed Protestant, high-ranking, strategically placed, and otherwise acceptable partners. However, the law wreaked havoc in his children's lives and would bring the Hanoverian dynasty in Britain to an end. Two sons—and possibly one daughter—later married secretly and illegally, and most of George's children, to his embarrassment, resorted to having relationships with commoners and those with no social standing whatsoever.

By 1817, George and Charlotte had numerous grandchildren, but with just one exception, all those offspring resulted from illicit liaisons or unsanctioned matrimony and thus they could never accede to the throne. When the only "legitimate" grandchild, Princess Charlotte of Wales, died that year at twenty-one, it set off a flurry of royal weddings in 1818. Sons William, Edward, and Adolphus—then in their forties and fifties—were rushed to the altar to provide the family with children eligible for the crown. It would be Edward's daughter, Victoria, born in 1819, who would emerge from her complicated generation as queen of the United Kingdom and the last British monarch from the House of Hanover. The Royal Marriages Act was not repealed until 2011, and the Succession to the Crown Act (2013) eliminated most nuptial impediments affecting the royal family.

The Washingtons did not have nearly as small or restricted a playing field as the royal family had for marital prospects, but it was not wide open either. George and Martha both came from the minor gentry and although Virginia society expected people to generally marry within their own class, there was some wiggle room. (Martha, in first marrying Daniel Custis, and George's brother Lawrence, in marrying Anne Fairfax, had both wed above their station.) "It has ever been a maxim with me, through life, neither to promote, nor to prevent a matrimonial connection, unless there should be something, indispensably requiring interference in the latter," George Washington, a veteran husband, wrote in 1785. "I have always considered Marriage as the most interesting event of ones life." Neither George nor Martha believed that romance should govern one's choice of partner; indeed, love might not even figure into the decision at all. Rather, critical factors to consider included compatibility, temperament, financial stability, and reputation.

When Martha's son, Jack Custis, nineteen, announced in 1773 his plans to leave college and marry Eleanor Calvert, sixteen, both Washingtons encouraged the young couple to wait a few years, until he had finished his education. Instead, Jack quit school and the giddy pair married the following year. Twenty years later, in a letter to his step-granddaughter Elizabeth "Eliza" Parke Custis, another teenager pining to marry, George Washington continued to advocate for practicality, advising that "Love is a mighty pretty thing; but like all other delicious things . . . love is too dainty a food to live upon alone." The most important thing, he explained, was that her intended "possess good sense—good dispositions—and the means of supporting you in the way you have been brought up . . . for be assured, and experience will convince you, that there is no truth more certain, than that all our enjoyments fall short of our expectations; and to none does it apply with more force, than to the gratification of the passions."

Filling Their Shelves

George III was a museum-quality collector: manuscripts, maps, clocks, scientific instruments, art, medals, gems, coins, prints, pamphlets, and books—*especially* books. As Prince of Wales, he had a personal library and a librarian to go with it, and for the rest of his life he maintained private libraries at Kew and Windsor Castle. He was in good company, as eighteenth-century Britain was well-stocked with serious book collectors and eccentric bibliophiles, and the rapidly growing print and publishing industry made even severe cases of bibliomania more affordable for the less well-to-do. Still, there was no national library, unlike in France and Spain, and only a handful of "public" but restricted libraries available. Royal libraries were even more inaccessible, but George III set out to change that.

George's book collecting went into overdrive soon after he became king. His first major purchase for the new royal library, at a whopping £10,000, was the 15,000-volume library of Joseph Smith, British consul at Venice (the king also purchased, for another £10,000, Smith's art collection). He acquired books from closed or impoverished monasteries, book dealers, estate sales, and some of his bibliophile ancestors. His Majesty also accepted donations, including those from authors savvy enough to present their works to the king's library, which quickly became one of the finest in the world.

At Buckingham House, his London residence, and under his close supervision, a grand new library emerged, conveniently located next to his bedroom. Construction began in 1762 and the last room was completed a decade later, as the king's vast book collection demanded ever more space. The library eventually comprised four huge rooms and floor-to-ceiling shelves (except in the spectacular central two-story Octagon Room). In assembling a deep and wide-ranging book and manuscript collection, the king initiated a unique purpose. He not only welcomed but urged scholars to make use of it. The library reflected the love of books Lord Bute had unleashed in George, and its very existence cataloged and archived scientific progress and artistic genius. Through this major center for scholarship, the king was disseminating knowledge and culture.

In 1774, his new royal librarian, Frederick Augusta Barnard (1742–1830), who would remain on the job for the next fifty-six years, brought a strategic approach to book acquisition as he filled subject area gaps and strengthened the collections. George sent him abroad on shopping trips, and agents in London purchased anywhere from individual volumes to entire libraries for the king. Early in his reign, he spent about a fifth of his personal annual income on books; toward the end of it, he maintained a small library staff, cataloging and bindery operations, and some 65,000 volumes on his shelves. Notable works included a Gutenberg Bible (1455); Chaucer's *Canterbury Tales* (1476), produced by William Caxton, the first book printed in England; and the first US presidential biography, John Marshall's landmark *Life of George Washington* (1804–1807), in five volumes and 3,311 pages. The holdings were especially strong in classical, British, and European literature and history; the king's favorite subjects came under the letter "A": agriculture, architecture, and astronomy.

One of the library's frequent users was Dr. Samuel Johnson. In 1762, the king granted him a £300 annual pension for his accomplishments as a lexicographer and a man of letters but had never met him. (Occasionally, Johnson advised Barnard on specific titles to acquire, recommending that he get "at least the most curious edition, the most splendid, and the most useful.") Five years later, the king encountered Johnson in the library sitting fireside, deep in a book, and engaged him in conversation. The surprised doctor was utterly impressed with the sovereign's book knowledge and informed line of questioning, later remarking that "they may talk of the king as they will; but he is the finest gentleman I have ever seen." Johnson's on-the-spot biographer, James Boswell, commented that "The accession of George the Third to the throne of these kingdoms, opened a new and brighter prospect to men of literary merit, who had been honoured with no mark of royal favour in the preceding reign."

Scholars of any political persuasion were welcome, and so was a visitor once deemed a traitor and enemy. In November 1783, John Adams, soon to be the first American ambassador to Britain, toured Buckingham House and was given access to the king's library. "Accordingly, in the absence of the royal family at Windsor, we had an opportunity at leisure, to see all the apartments," he reported in his diary. "The king's library struck me with admiration; I wished for

James Stephanoff, *Buckingham House: The Octagon Library*, 1818. Watercolor and bodycolor over pencil.

Early in his reign, George III needed more space for his rapidly growing book collection. On purchasing Buckingham House in 1762, he had it renovated and remodeled to include four library rooms, one of which was the spectacular two-story, 42-foot-wide Octagon Library that was adjacent to his bedroom. His former architecture tutor, Sir William Chambers, carried out the grandiose work. The king himself was thoroughly involved in the project, from drawing his own sample designs to overseeing the installation of shelves and the décor. On the matching octagonal desk in the center sits the first of the king's two astronomical clocks. One of the first to tour the new library, Caroline Lybbe Powys reported that "The books are said to be the best collection anywhere to be met with."

a week's time, but had but a few hours. The books were in perfect order, elegant in their editions, paper, binding, &c. but gaudy and extravagant in nothing. They were chosen with perfect taste and judgment; every book that a king ought to have always at hand."

Meanwhile, at Mount Vernon, George Washington was not much of a collector outside of wines, liquors, and tracts of land. He did, however, collect books, more for practical purposes than pleasure, keeping them in cabinets in his study and dining room. He had read plenty of books from Fairfax family libraries to understand the advantages of a useful collection immediately at hand. His patchwork education meant self-instruction was often a necessity, and Washington relied on books for each occupation he entered, as a surveyor, soldier, farmer, legislator, and president.

Washington's library, begun in childhood, gradually increased in the 1750s during his time in the Virginia regiment, as he acquired a thirty-year-old copy of Humphrey Bland's *Treatise of Military Discipline* (1727) and other military manuals. The collection grew noticeably once he established himself at Mount Vernon in the early 1760s and began reading everything that seemed beneficial on agriculture. Additional book titles ranged from politics, law, and economics to religion, fiction, poetry, encyclopedias and reference works, and travelogues. On two occasions he inventoried his library: he had only a few books specifically dedicated to physical sciences, but considerably more titles in natural history. In addition to gifts and purchases, tomes belonging to other family members also found their way onto Washington's shelves, including hundreds that once belonged to Martha's first husband, Daniel Parke Custis.

In the ongoing quest to properly educate his stepson, Jack, Washington purchased a generous starter library of fifty books for the fourteen-year-old student. A few years later, in 1771, he shared his educational philosophy with the Reverend Jonathan Boucher, Jack's tutor, commenting that "I conceive a knowledge of books is the basis upon which other knowledge is to be built." That same year, he ordered more personalized bookplates than he had books, perhaps in anticipation of a bibliographic growth spurt. Aside from its pragmatic purposes, a good library was a status symbol among gentlemen, and Washington craved that recognition, but his library also countered a view some shared that, in John Adams' words, Washington was "too illiterate, unlearned, unread for his station and reputation."

Once he became a famous general and a fixture in national life, authors and well-wishers sent him books as well, and he continued to consult book dealer catalogs, ordering publications that he would actually read.

In 1797 he tried enticing his nephew Lawrence Lewis to come to Mount Vernon, "to make this place your home," in exchange for unpaid help in organizing his presidential papers. As a perk, he offered Lewis the use of his library "as I have a great many instructive Books, on many subjects, as well as amusing ones"; perhaps Martha Washington's copy of *The Jilts: Or, Female Fortune-Hunters* (ca. 1756) being counted among the latter. At the end of his life, Washinton's library held more than nine hundred books and several hundred other publications, including journals and pamphlets.

During the golden age of pamphleteering, political issues in Revolutionary America prominently held the field. Commentators used the handy format to reach readers in greater depth than newspapers could, and they were much less expensive than books. George III collected some thirty thousand pamphlets; Washington had his neatly bound in thirty-six volumes for easy reference. Washington himself was the author of a pamphlet when his *Journal of Major George Washington* was published in Williamsburg and London in 1754 reporting on his mission to the commandant of French forces on the Ohio River. The publication introduced Washington's name to readers in America and Britain, and a copy of it appeared in the royal George's library as well.

Like King George, Washington envisioned a central repository for his library and his papers, which he modestly recognized would be of great import to historians, future presidents, and the nation. In retirement he began organizing his archive with plans to build a facility at Mount Vernon for their preservation. At his death, his library and papers went to his nephew, Bushrod Washington, and his books were eventually dispersed among family members. In 1847, book dealer Henry Stevens, who had acquired about a third of Washington's books, announced his intention to sell them to the British Museum. Alarmed that the largest remaining portion of Washington's library might end up outside America, the Boston Athenaeum raised $3,250 and purchased the collection. The rest of the original library is scattered, and Washington's books can be found at the Library of Congress, Mount Vernon, universities, and in private hands. Meanwhile, George III's enormous library was bequeathed to his son, George IV, who in turn donated it to the British Museum. In 1973 it became a cornerstone of the new national British Library, eventually moving into its specially built six-story glass tower at the library's St. Pancras location in London, where it continues to be used by the public.

Gardens and Landscapes: The Genius of the Place

Rome was the art capital of the Western world in the eighteenth century, and artists from all over Europe traveled there to study painting, sculpture, and architecture. As the Georgian era progressed, however, many also traveled within and to Britain to see its finest contribution to the era's visual arts: the English garden. The style would revolutionize gardening and landscape design in Europe and North America by recognizing and emphasizing what renowned satirist and garden consultant Alexander Pope described as "the genius of the place." Given that both Georges were wealthy landowners, avid hunters and farmers, knowledgeable admirers of nature, and appreciative of art, they readily participated in the flourishing English landscape movement. Although neither man was prone to puttering, in a garden or anywhere else, each ensured that his respective Edens were enticing places of leisure and impressive symbols of status, political civility, culture, aesthetic taste . . . and of course science.

Large-scale art on a vast natural canvas, the English garden was characterized by sweeping vistas, lakes, streams, and waterfalls; meadows, glades, and groves of trees; broad lawns and gentle grassy hills that gave way to grand views; and winding paths that led to classical-looking temples and statuary, sham ancient and medieval ruins ("follies"), tea houses, pavilions, and scenic bridges. The style drew inspiration from stage design and landscape painting, as natural settings were shaped and contoured to present pleasant "scenes." Two especially notable sources for these pastoral scenes were seventeenth-century French painters Claude Lorrain and Nicholas Poussin, whose arcadian subjects, traceable to classical texts, Greek mythology, and ancient Rome, greatly influenced British landscape design. As Pope succinctly put it, "All gardening is landscape painting." Both Georges understood this, and the king owned some of Lorrain's original works while Washington displayed engraved landscape prints after Lorrain at Mount Vernon.

In 1759, as he and his new family settled in at Mount Vernon, Washington ordered a copy of Batty Langley's three-decade-old book, *New Principles of Gardening* (1728). Langley and others urged practitioners to dispense with the rigidity and geometric style of Renaissance and Baroque gardens and let nature be natural. Langley's picturesque garden designs were in sync with the arcadian ideal, but, he assured readers, "*entirely New*, as well as the most grand and rural" and "after *Nature's own Manner*." Filled with detailed illustrations and step-by-step procedures, it was the primary reference book for Washington and thousands of affluent amateurs intent on "improving" and transforming ordinary grounds into naturalistic gardens and asymmetrical landscapes. Langley hoped that with his book "I might do no inconsiderable Service to my Country." This was purpose-driven gardening as a national upper-class endeavor.

Langley's book was not out of date by the time Washington got his hands on it, or even later, after the Revolutionary War, when he revisited it and other gardening publications, because the "new principles" continued to be applied all over England. (Washington also relied on Langley's *Builder's and Workman's Treasury of Design* in selecting interior architectural designs for his mansion.) Returning home after the war as the most beloved and admired man in America, Washington braced himself for an onslaught of guests, invited or not, as well as eager tourists, and he was determined that Mount Vernon not disappoint. From 1784 to 1787, he reimagined and refashioned the grounds, ripping out the rectangular geometric garden layouts he had installed a decade earlier, moving and razing old outbuildings, and tearing down unsightly walls. He designed a bowling green bordered by a serpentine gravel walk, shrubs, and forest trees, which in turn were flanked by shield-shaped ornamental and vegetable gardens. Next to the ornamental garden, he built a well-lit, large two-story greenhouse—then an unusual sight in America—to raise tropical plants. He added a "fruit garden," and his small botanical garden functioned as a horticultural laboratory, where Washington experimented with non-indigenous plants, whose seeds he obtained from friends throughout America and his international connections.

In the English manner, Washington created picturesque landscape views guided by the "genius" of Mount Vernon's natural setting. On the western side of the mansion, beyond the bowling green, he crafted a dramatic, curving, near mile-long approach to the house that greeted visitors with a series of undulating, tree-lined greenswards that perfectly framed his white walled, red roofed home. To enhance the already magnificent eastern view across the Potomac River, he had a broad lawn put in from the mansion portico that sloped down toward the riverbank, further improving the scene by removing the outhouse facility. He replaced fencing with sunken "ha-ha" barriers that kept out animals and allowed for uninterrupted pastoral views. As part of the riparian landscape, Washington also installed an eighteen-acre deer park, importing English deer that joined an American variety, making it clear that it was not for hunting but for "tranquility and rural amusements." (He was almost as fond of the deer as he was his favored sheep.) Although Washington had never been to Britain, Julian Ursyn Niemcewicz wrote in 1798 that "after seeing his house and his gardens one would say that [Washington] had seen the most beautiful examples in England."

Some of those "most beautiful examples" belonged to George III. As a young man studying drawing, he was partial to sketching imaginary classical landscapes with architectural features. As king, he funded and followed with great interest major, multi-decade gardening projects, although developing the pleasure grounds of Kew and Richmond had been carried out by his mother, Princess Augusta, and his grandmother, Queen Caroline, respectively. At Windsor Great Park, he sponsored the transformation of a pond into Virginia Water, a two-mile-long lake that fed the Cascade, whose waterfall tumbled over a stone grotto. Begun before George's reign, the work lasted nearly forty years. In 1792, following the death his former tutor, Lord Bute, who held the position of ranger at Richmond Park, the king appointed himself to the office, and saw to various improvements while granting greater access to the public. His greatest landscaping legacy was the official union of Richmond and Kew gardens (which later became the Royal Botanic Gardens at Kew), a plan held up for some thirty-seven years over ancient rights-of-way. The king eventually resolved the conflict by building a new highway.

His Majesty also surrounded himself with some of the best horticultural and gardening talent available. After receiving a box of "new discovered specimens" from Philadelphia botanist John Bertram, the king hired him in 1765 to explore Florida, newly acquired from Spain, and prepare a report. Other botanical samples Bertram collected in his travels along the Atlantic Seaboard were also sent to Kew and cataloged. Meanwhile, the king appointed the soon to be legendary Lancelot "Capability" Brown as a royal master gardener at Hampton Court Palace and commissioned him to design a new landscape at Richmond. (Brown's nickname was derived not from his own skill but telling clients that their properties were "capable" of improvement.)

At Kew, Brown designed the Hollow Walk, which survives as the Rhododendron Dell, and transformed the flat landscape with varied elevations. The king also brought on his wealthy friend and science advisor, the naturalist Sir Joseph Banks, to serve at Kew Gardens. Under Banks, the gardens and its 5,600 plant species thrived. The king and Banks saw to it that nearly every British expedition included a Kew scientist to obtain seeds and other horticultural specimens. (Two Kew botanists on board the HMS *Bounty* perished in the South Pacific following the famed mutiny in 1789.) For all its scientific importance, Kew was a place of respite for the king; having grown up playing in the gardens it was there that he could take walks unaccompanied and where, recovering from serious illness in 1789, he found further restoration in strolling through the genius of the place.

Samuel Vaughan, *Plan of Mount Vernon*, 1787. Ink and watercolor.

After meeting George Washington through the Philadelphia Society for Promoting Agriculture, Samuel Vaughan, a merchant and plantation owner, proceeded to shower the general with gifts, including this large hand-drawn plan of Mount Vernon. Washington had just completed a two-and-a-half year landscaping project of his own composition and was back in Philadelphia presiding over the Constitutional Convention when Vaughan arrived at Mount Vernon in August 1787.

Staying for nearly a week, Vaughan made himself useful by sketching a detailed plan of the new landscape in his journal, which he used to create this large presentation watercolor. With the Potomac River at the top, the plan depicts the mansion and its outbuildings, the circular carriage drive, the bowling green flanked by the Upper Garden on the left, used as an ornamental showplace, the Lower Garden, on the right, for growing vegetables, and tree groves, as well as a ground level floorplan and a view of the mansion's west-facing elevation.

In a letter dated November 12, 1787, the former surveyor offered Vaughan his "sincere and hearty" thanks for the Mount Vernon plan before noting its general accuracy as well as some slight errors. The watercolor turned out to be more than a token of appreciation from Vaughan; it has been a gift as well to preservationists in restoring the grounds that Washington installed during his sojourn as an amateur landscape designer.

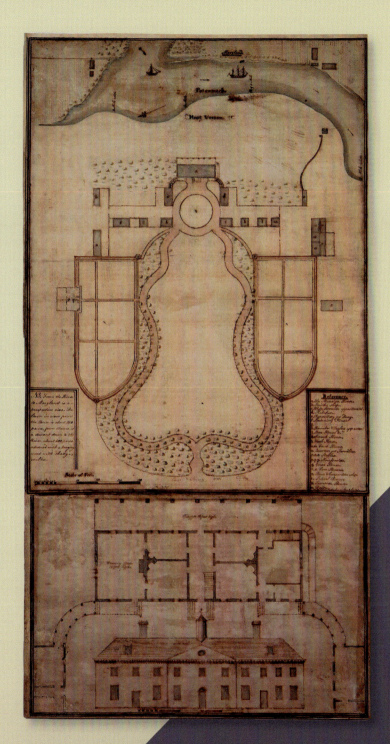

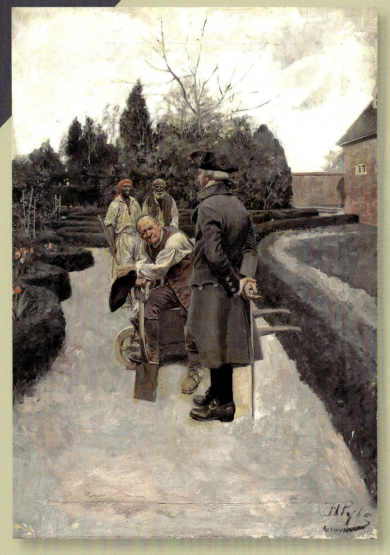

Howard Pyle, *Washington in the Garden at Mount Vernon*, 1896. Oil on illustration board. Published in *Harper's New Monthly Magazine*, September 1896.

Washington hired white men as head gardeners, and both indentured and enslaved men tended the lawns, ornamental and vegetable gardens, orchards, and greenhouse plants. Howard Pyle, a nineteenth-century illustrator, depicted Washington conversing with Philip Bateman, head gardener from 1773 to 1785 ("indulge him in getting Drunk now and then, and he will be Happy—he is the best Kitchen gardener to be met with" advised Lund Washington, George's cousin and farm manager), and two enslaved assistants.

In 1789 Washington hired his first professionally trained European gardener, John Christian Ehlers, who had apprenticed in Hanover, Germany, at the Montbrillant royal gardens, belonging to none other than George III. During his presidency, Washington sent his estate manager lengthy and detailed gardening instructions and regularly expressed concern about inefficiencies, writing Anthony Whitting in October 1792 that "the ever-greens must be removed when they can be taken up with a compact & solid body of frozen earth to the Roots, otherwise the labour will be lost, and another year will pass away without accomplishing my design; as abundant experience has incontestably proved."

William Elliott after William Woollett, *A View of the Palace from the North Side of the Lake, the Green House & the Temple of Arethusa, in the Royal Gardens at Kew***, ca. 1766. Hand-colored engraving.**

At Kew Palace, her summer residence, the widowed Princess Augusta enlarged and enhanced the existing gardens, creating a world-famous landscape that later became the national botanic garden. Her son George III knew the grounds and its architectural follies well; many were built by his architecture tutor, William Chambers, who designed the neoclassical Temple of Arethusa seen at left. Elsewhere Chambers' pleasure garden included his ten-story chinoiserie Great Pagoda, a mosque with Turkish-style minarets, and a Moorish-inspired salon, called the Alhambra.

At the center of the gardens, a lake was constructed, where, Chambers later wrote, "originally the ground was one continued dead flat: the soil was in general barren, and without either wood or water. With so many disadvantages it was not easy to produce anything even tolerable in gardening; but princely munificence, guided by a director, equally skilled in cultivating the earth, and in the politer arts, overcame all difficulties. What was once a Desert is now an Eden."

In June 1755, theater manager and producer John Rich, known for his spectacular productions at Covent Garden, made a majestic, eighteen-foot-tall swan boat as a gift to Prince George on his seventeenth birthday. Named *The Augusta*, the "pleasure barge" successfully imitated the bird's natural motions in water, its feet serving as oars, and it seated ten passengers. Set afloat at Kew, the swan boat was an instant success. *The Gentleman's Magazine* reported that "The novelty of the design, and the elegance of the execution, afford a particular pleasure to the royal family."

The Georges on the Go

Though George Washington and George III both played key roles in world politics in the second half of the eighteenth century, neither traveled as much as some of their contemporaries, such as American founders Benjamin Franklin and Thomas Jefferson, or the king's predecessor, George II, and successor, George IV. Washington traveled more extensively than His Majesty, visiting Barbados in his youth, leading surveying and military expeditions past the Appalachian Mountains, moving up and down the Eastern Seaboard during the Revolutionary War, and making several tours of the young United States during his presidency. The king, meanwhile, never left southern England. Instead, he preferred to be an armchair traveler via his extensive map collection. When he did travel beyond London and its vicinity, it often was for health reasons, such as his numerous visits to Weymouth to enjoy the soothing waters, or to review military installations.

Washington had never been more than two hundred miles from where he was born when he took his first major trip, a four-month excursion to Barbados with his brother Lawrence in 1751. Lawrence, suffering from tuberculosis, hoped the warm weather there would bring him relief. The brothers stayed outside the capital city of Bridgetown—the largest settlement Washington had ever seen—with a view of Carlisle Bay. George toured the many fortifications that dotted the coast, Charles Fort being the first of many he would come to inspect.

The Barbados excursion was also a pleasure trip for George, who dined with gentlemen, exposing him to new social circles. On November 14, he attended his first play, *The London Merchant; or, The History of George Barnwell*, by George Lillo, an old play still popular with the London theater scene. He also contracted smallpox, protecting him from future outbreaks, but possibly also rendering him sterile. The Barbados trip was George's only venture off the North American mainland, though he hoped to see London, writing in 1759, of his "longing desire…of visiting the great Matropolis."

Washington's early profession as a surveyor led him to future states such as North Carolina, West Virginia, and Ohio, in addition to work within his native Virginia. He visited the Great Dismal Swamp on the border between North Carolina and Virginia in 1763, cofounding the Dismal Swamp Company that hoped to drain it for settlement. He also served in the Virginia militia in western Pennsylvania before and during the French and Indian War, reaching the outskirts of modern Erie.

Travel in eighteenth-century America was not pleasant, and Washington, often traveling on horseback, complained of dust, heat, poor roads, exhausted horses, bad weather and dangerous water crossings, and uncomfortable accommodations. Trying to be as efficient as possible, each day he would leave early in the morning, briefly stopping for breakfast and dinner on the road. He noted in his diary he usually traveled about five miles per hour, slightly above average for the time.

For the duration of the Revolutionary War, Washington was on the road. After receiving his commission in June 1775, he spent the next eight years leading the Continental Army, not permanently returning to Mount Vernon until he resigned his commission in December 1783. During the conflict, he fought in battles in Massachusetts, New York, New Jersey, Pennsylvania, and Virginia. It is estimated he spent the night in 280 houses during the conflict, inevitably leading to the cliché that "Washington slept here."

Washington's most extensive travels were during his presidency. Within a few weeks of his inauguration in 1789, he wrote to members of his inner circle, including Vice President John Adams, with questions concerning etiquette and precedent. The eighth query asked,

> Whether during the recess of Congress, it would not be advantageous to the interests of the Union for the President to make the Tour of the United States, in order to become better acquainted with their principal Characters, & internal circumstances, as well as to be more accessible to numbers of well informed Persons, who might give him useful information & Advice on political Subjects?

Washington believed such trips would connect him with his new constituents, helping to unite the country under the new Constitution after the fractious Confederation period. Ten days before he departed on his first tour of New England, he wrote in his diary

 Chapter 3

that he hoped "to acquire knowledge of the face of the Country[,] the growth and Agriculture there of[,] and the temper and disposition of the Inhabitants towards the new government." Referring to his colleagues in the new government, Washington wrote that they thought his trip "a very desirable plan and advised it accordingly."

He left New York City on October 15, 1789, and returned November 3, venturing as far north as the future state of Maine, then part of Massachusetts. The following April, he spent four days traveling around Long Island, and in August 1790 he went to Rhode Island by boat, accompanied by Secretary of State Thomas Jefferson.

During his presidential trips, he hoped that when he arrived in a given town, it would be "without any parade, or extraordinary ceremony," as he wrote John Hancock prior to arriving in Boston in 1789. For the most part he did not get his wish. Instead, he got parades, military salutes, dinners, songs of praise, and cheering visitors who lined up to see the famous general and president. Local dignitaries wrote speeches ahead of time and sent them to Washington's aide who then drafted a reply for Washington to recite. However, one of Washington's requests did prevail on these trips: he insisted on paying for his stay in inns and taverns rather than be hosted in private homes.

The longest trip Washington took was the 1791 Southern tour. Starting in the new capital of Philadelphia, he and a group of eight men journeyed through seven states, as well as the future capital city of Washington, DC, traveling 1,900 miles to Georgia and back. The party included two enslaved men, Paris and Giles, though Giles only made it as far as Mount Vernon before becoming sick. Washington visited Annapolis, Maryland; Richmond, Virginia; Wilmington and Salem, North Carolina; Charleston, South Carolina; and Savannah, Georgia. According to writer Warren L. Bingham, it was perhaps the longest single trip taken by an American at that point in the nation's history. When entering a city, Washington often did so astride his white charger, Prescott, cutting an imposing figure. In between towns, his entourage rode in a carriage outfitted with a depiction of the four seasons as well as Washington's coat-of-arms, giving off a quasi-royal air. The monarchical splendor of the trip was not lost on critics. Indeed, his immediate successors John Adams, Thomas Jefferson, and James Madison declined to take long tours to avoid the appearance of royal grandeur.

George III, for his part, reestablished a waning precedent of monarchical travel. The traditional royal "progress" of visiting the countryside was central to the sixteenth-century reign of Elizabeth I, who was well-attuned to how she was viewed by the populace. Nevertheless, the Stuart monarchs and the first two Hanoverian monarchs in the eighteenth century did not travel extensively in Great Britain. George I and George II preferred to return to their native Hanover than tour the British countryside. For the first twenty years of his reign, George III generally stayed closer to London and his wife, who was usually pregnant. His first visit well outside the city was to Portsmouth in 1773, to attend a Royal Navy review, when he was thirty-five years old.

Although he would make frequent trips during the middle part of his reign, and he studied maps and charts that he collected, his sense of adventure did not move beyond the page. Secretary to the Treasury George Rose, with whom the king stayed at Cuffnells Park several times, said the king "had no taste for what was called the fine wild beauties of nature. He did not like mountains and other romantic scenes, of which he had sometimes heard much." After 1804 he traveled little, due to his illness and failing eyesight.

The city of Weymouth on the south coast of England is closely associated with George III, who visited fourteen times between 1789 and 1805. George had considered visiting Hanover after recovering from mental illness in 1789, but his doctor Francis Willis suggested the English coast instead. Weymouth itself was recommended by the king's brother William Henry, the Duke of Gloucester and Edinburgh, who had first stayed there in 1780 (and had previously experienced similar symptoms as George in 1771 and 1777). It was such common knowledge that George spent time there that Thomas Hardy included a vignette of him visiting Weymouth in the novel *The Trumpet Major* (1880). According to historical weather data, the 1780s saw fewer prevailing westerlies than in other decades, and thus the southwest coast of England would have been quite pleasant.

The king's other journeys included odd day trips to review a fleet or military parade. He also enjoyed spending time at country estates of the gentry. During a 1778 excursion to Winchester and Salisbury, George and Queen Charlotte made a stop at Stonehenge, which "their majesties examined very attentively" according to a newspaper report. Similar to other aspects of his personality, George was a good guest, not

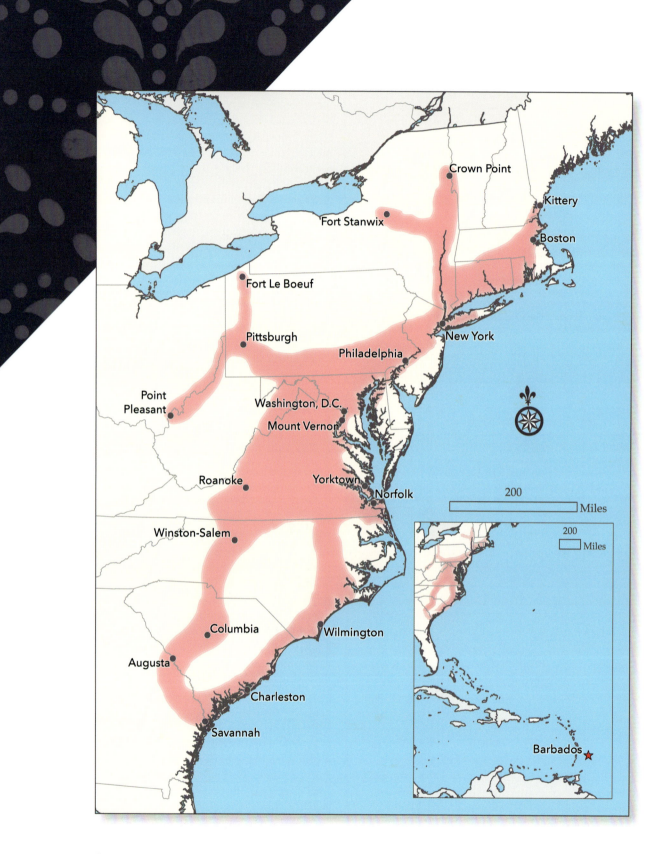

Tim St. Onge, Maps showing travel areas for George Washington (left) and George III (below), 2024.

The areas shaded in red are approximations of the Georges' travel throughout their lives. Despite ruling an empire that stretched from North America to South Africa to India, George III never left southern England. Washington traveled to Barbados as a youth and later in life as a general, private citizen, or president visited all thirteen original states, though he never traveled to Europe.

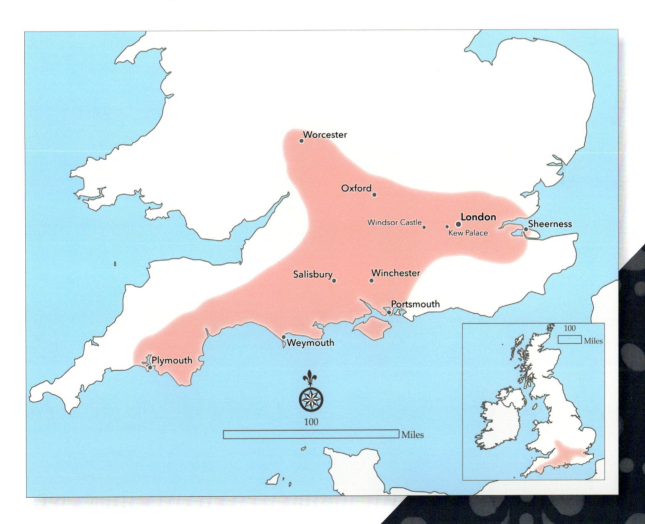

demanding too much of his hosts. He even remarked upon a visit to the Duke of Marlborough's magnificent Blenheim Palace that "we have nothing equal to this." While making these trips, he often donated to local schools, charities, or churches. When Salisbury Cathedral reopened in 1792 after three years of renovations, the king, queen, and six princesses attended as special guests.

Though he did not travel long distances, the king enjoyed planning his trips. Letters in his hand detail itineraries, specifications for housing, and other logistics. Instead of leaving this up to his bevy of servants, he took an active role to ensure his travels were to his satisfaction. During these rambles through the countryside, throngs gathered. "Every town and village within twenty miles seemed to have been deserted, to supply all the pathways with groups of anxious spectators," Fanny Burney, the queen's keeper of the robes, wrote in July 1788.

Due in part to his limited travel, George met only one other monarch, his brother-in-law (and also first cousin) Christian VII of Denmark, who visited London in 1768. His lack of travel also stood out among monarchs of the era. Although Georges I and II had not traveled throughout Britain, they had regularly returned to the Electorate of Hanover during their reigns for lengthy visits and had visited other European regions before acceding to the British throne. Ironically, in considering abdication in 1783, George III suggested he would retire to his family's dominions even though he had never set foot on the European continent. In the end, he never visited Hanover, just as Washington never saw London. ☀

John Thomas Serres, *View of Weymouth*, August 12, 1803. Hand-colored etching.

Dedicated to George III, this etching depicts the Dorset resort town of Weymouth in the era when the king made yearly pilgrimages there. John Thomas Serres served as a maritime painter to George's court, and he may have included George's son William in the small boat in the lower right of the painting.

Parallel Lives 113

Chapter 4

Benjamin West, *George III*, 1779.
Oil on canvas.

Rupture: America Revolts

Charles Willson Peale, *George Washington at Princeton*, 1779. Oil on canvas.

Over George Washington's long and storied career, few moments loom larger than the victorious general's resignation of his military command at the Maryland State House on December 23, 1783. Nine months earlier, in the army's encampment at Newburgh, New York, Washington had defused a plot by Continental officers, many of whom had not been paid in months, to force Congress to compensate them for their service. Now, as he headed for Annapolis, he was determined to show that power in a republic belonged to the people and their representatives, not the military. At the stroke of noon, Congress' secretary summoned him into the State House chamber. After bowing to the assembled delegates, Washington read a brief statement in which he thanked the army for its service, then announced his retirement from "the employments of public life." The father of his country, as Americans were already calling the former commander, had no interest in being a Caesar.[1] By Christmas Eve, Washington was back at Mount Vernon, a "private citizen," as he wrote Baron von Steuben, tending his farm on the banks of the Potomac.[2]

Among the many people who noted this performance was another farmer, Washington's former sovereign, George III, King of Great Britain and Ireland. After Britain's humiliating defeat at Yorktown, the king asked the American-born painter Benjamin West if he knew what General Washington planned to do once the war was over. As captain general of the British Army, King George knew a thing or two about military politics. In 1779, West's most ambitious and successful royal portrait showed the king commanding troops on England's south coast during a threatened invasion by America's leading European allies, France and Spain. But even George seemed surprised by what the artist had to say. From everything he had heard, said West, Washington intended to return to private life. If he does, exclaimed the king, he will "be the greatest man in the world."[3] Despite the many points on which the two Georges differed, the importance of constitutional government was one on which they saw eye to eye.

For anyone who had followed the events of the previous two decades, this convergence was

Daniel Paterson, *Cantonment of His Majesty's Forces in N. America*, ca. 1767. Pen-and-ink and watercolor.

Daniel Paterson served as a cartographer to the quartermaster-general of the forces in the British Army. He created this map of British troop locations in North America from data compiled in March 1766, just a few years after the conclusion of the French and Indian War. Areas with a strong military presence include New England and Southern Canada, New York City, and the Gulf Coast. Parallel to the Appalachian Mountains is the Proclamation Line of 1763, indicating the western boundary of the colonies, while the remaining area to the east of the Mississippi River is marked "Lands Reserved for the Indians."

Though George III never visited the American colonies, he nonetheless maintained a profound interest in his overseas possessions. As commander-in-chief of the British military, he reviewed maps like this throughout his reign to understand army and naval operations, and he took an active role in overseeing the deployment of troops.

The Repeal, or the Funeral of Miss Ame= Stamp, March 18, 1766. Etching.

This British satirical cartoon uses the metaphor of a funeral to mock Parliament's repeal of the Stamp Act. Prime Minister George Grenville had introduced the bill to levy taxes on paper and documents in 1765 to help pay for the recently concluded French and Indian War. The Act was met with immediate outrage in the colonies, leading to protests and boycotts of British-made goods. George Washington viewed it "as a direful attack" upon colonists' rights. In October, members from nine colonies met in New York City and concluded that London had no right to tax the colonies since the colonies did not have representation in Parliament. This Stamp Act Congress was a pivotal moment in the fraying relationship between Britain and its colonies.

The protests in America led to discussions in Parliament to repeal it. George III had enthusiastically supported the original passage, and even as late as January 30, 1766, he made it known privately to his former governor, Lord Harcourt, that "he was strenuously for supporting and asserting the right of Great Britain to impose the tax," according to the diary of Elizabeth Grenville, wife of the prime minister. However, just a few weeks later he changed course, giving cover to MPs who supported repeal, saying that if it could not be modified then "Repealing [was] infinitely more eligible than Enforcing, which could only tend to widen the breach between this Country & America." The House of Commons voted for repeal in late February, and the Lords in March; George gave his royal assent on March 18, and the Stamp Act was repealed. Ironically, given the colonists' opprobrium a decade later, the king was hailed as a hero for agreeing to the repeal, and his popularity increased. His birthday celebrations in June 1766 were more lavish than usual in Boston, Philadelphia, and New York.

This anonymous cartoon–published the day of the royal assent–depicts Grenville carrying a small coffin for "Miss Ame[rica] Stamp" while Lord Bute, George III's former mentor and another proponent of the bill, walks behind him in mourning. In the bottom right corner, metaphorical cases of stamps have been returned from America, unused, while a statue of William Pitt the Elder is loaded onto a boat headed back, a nod to Pitt's popularity in the colonies for opposing the tax. (Four months after this cartoon was printed, Pitt became prime minister.) The print sold two thousand copies within four days.

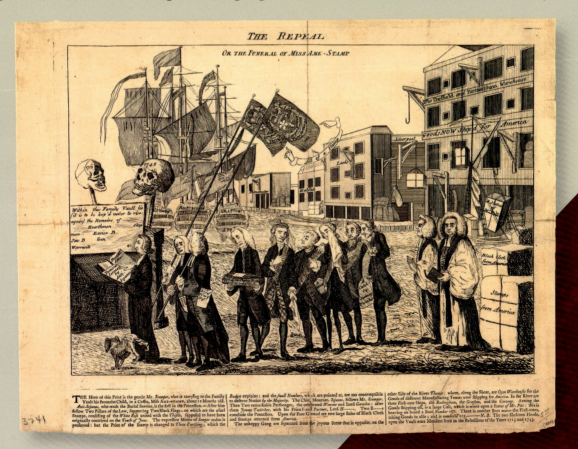

Rupture: America Revolts

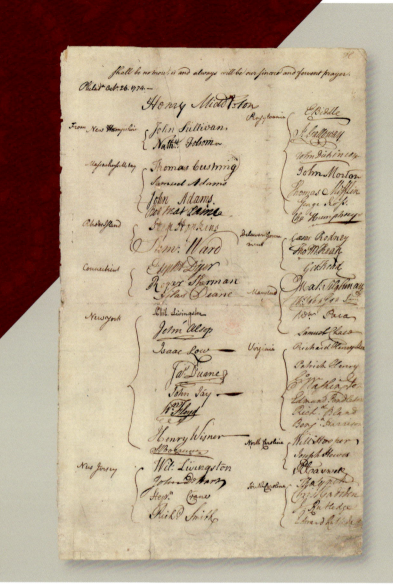

Petition of the Continental Congress to King George III, October 26, 1774. Manuscript document in the hand of Timothy Matlack.

In October 1774, Congress submitted a list of grievances to George III from "we, your Majesty's faithful subjects." The document served as a response to the Intolerable Acts, which were passed in the wake of the Boston Tea Party to punish Massachusetts. The petition arrived in London in December 1774, and colonial agents Benjamin Franklin, Arthur Lee, and William Bollan brought it to the attention of Lord Dartmouth, the secretary of state for the colonies. The petition was formally presented to Parliament by Lord North on January 19, 1775.

Though the colonists concluded by stating "we therefore most earnestly beseech your Majesty, that your royal authority and interposition may be used for our relief: and that a gracious answer may be given to this petition," the king never responded, and it received little attention in Parliament.

George Washington's signature can be seen third from the top in the list of Virginia signers.

in some ways remarkable. Like many Americans, Washington initially viewed Parliament's attempts at colonial taxation, first with the Sugar and Stamp Acts of 1764 and 1765, then with the Townshend Duties of 1767, as misguided and unconstitutional but hoped cooler heads would eventually prevail. But as the standoff deepened, Washington became convinced that "our lordly Masters in Great Britain," as he wrote George Mason in 1769, were bent on destroying American freedom.[4] When Congress declared independence, Washington joined patriots in denouncing the British king as a tyrant. For his part, George III thought colonial opponents of parliamentary taxation were "deluded," and he came to believe that armed force was the only way to avert "open and avowed rebellion."[5] Such attitudes inevitably colored British views of the rebellion's military leader. Washington, wrote one of the officers tasked with carrying out the king's orders in America, was a "little paltry colonel of militia," and the soldiers under his command contemptible "banditti."[6] There was nothing legal about his actions.

Yet even as they impugned each other's motives, the American general and the British king remained true to what each saw as his constitutional duty. For Washington, this at first meant duty to the *British* constitution. Although the Declaration of Independence severed all ties to the crown, the revolution started as a quarrel with Parliament, not George III, leading some Americans to hope that the king would intervene on their behalf. During the war's first year, Washington referred to the British forces opposing him as the "ministerial" or parliamentary army, insisting that he was the king's most loyal subject. Following the opening engagement in Massachusetts, he told his English friend George William Fairfax that most patriots could not "yet prevail upon ourselves to call them the King's Troops."⁷ As it did for many Americans, Washington's moment of truth arrived in early January when news of George III's October 26, 1775, speech to Parliament declaring the colonies to be in rebellion reached North America. According to Washington, the speech was "full of rancour and resentment." As he told John Hancock, the king "ought to promote the blessings of his people . . . not their oppression."⁸ Washington's sense of betrayal was palpable.

Had George III been willing to follow Washington's wishes and overrule Parliament, the American Revolution might have ended differently—perhaps with the colonies subject to the crown, while being independent of the British government and legislature in the same way that Canada, New Zealand, and a number of other members of the Commonwealth are independent today. George, however, was a constitutional monarch. His first and most important duty was to support Parliament. When British kings defied the legislature and attempted to rule on their own, they either lost their head, as happened to Charles I in 1649, or their throne, which had been James II's fate in 1688. After France joined the war as an ally of the United States in 1778, the king's ministers reluctantly offered Congress the sort of commonwealth status that Washington had once hoped for, but the offer did not come from George alone, who personally opposed making any concession, but had the backing of both the

Thomas Colley, *The Belligerent Plenipo's*, December 8, 1782. Hand-colored etching. Published by W. Richardson.

As peace negotiations drag on among European powers and the United States, George III, left, sports only half a crown after losing America. He tells the three maimed center figures, plenipotentiaries representing France, Holland, and Spain, that "I gave them independence," prompting each to ask for a portion of the British Empire as part of their own peace agreements with Britain. At George's feet are the plenipotentiaries' missing body parts, signs of their military sacrifices. Ireland, floating above, calls for its own constitutional freedom with a joke about potatoes as America, right, wearing an Indian headdress, blithely announces that "I have got all I wanted–Empire!"

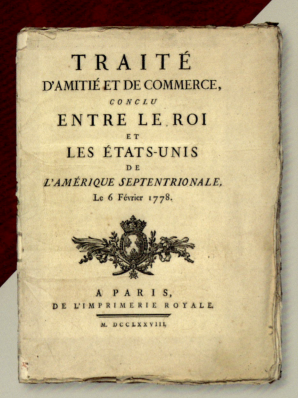

Traité D'Amitié et de Commerce Conclu Entre le Roi et les États-Unis de l'Amerique Septentrionale [Treaty of Friendship and Commerce Concluded Between the King and the United States of North America], February 6, 1778, Paris.

France, encouraged by the American victory over Britain at Saratoga in October 1777, signed two treaties with the United States: this Treaty of Amity and Commerce and the Treaty of Alliance. These two treaties, signed in Paris by American diplomats Benjamin Franklin, Silas Deane, and Arthur Lee, established the alliance between the United States and its first foreign ally.

The alliance with France was crucial to the outcome of the Revolutionary War. Even before the war officially began, it was clear that allying the country with a European power would greatly help the cause. In March 1774, Lee, living in London, wrote to his brother Richard Henry Lee in Virginia that "America may yet owe her salvation" to the "interposition" of European powers.

After submitting the treaty to Congress on February 16, 1778, the diplomats wrote, "This is an Event that will give our States such an Appearance of Stability as must strengthen our Credit, encourage other Powers in Europe to ally themselves with us, weaken the Hopes of our internal as well as external Enemies, fortify our Friends, and be in many other Respects so advantageous to us that we congratulate you upon it most heartily." That sentiment was echoed in George Washington's response to the treaty's ratification: "I believe no event was ever received with a more heart felt joy." He led his troops in chants of "Long live the king of France" on learning the news.

On the other side of the Atlantic, Britain viewed the new alliance with great concern. With increasing certainty of a war with France, the British sent a peace offering to America on March 16, 1778, hoping to prevent a two-front war. But the offer did not include independence and it was rejected in April. The king had disapproved of Lord North's decision to try to negotiate a peace with the colonies, instructing him to "Bring America back to a sense of attachement to the Mother Country" through force, not reconciliation.

As a result of the treaties, France recognized the United States as an independent nation, agreed to terms of trade, made significant loans to the American war effort, and contributed some 12,000 soldiers and 32,000 sailors to the cause.

---

king and Parliament. (In America, the gesture came too late to change most minds, though Benedict Arnold mentioned it as a pretext for switching sides.[9]) As long as Parliament claimed the authority to govern the British Empire as it saw fit, that was King George's position too.

Ironically, George III's loyalty to the British constitution ensured that he ultimately had to accept the independence of Washington and the former colonies. Although no one tried harder than the king to keep America from leaving the empire, Parliament's support for the war evaporated after Yorktown, leaving him no choice but to sue for peace. During the king's historic speech to Parliament on December 5, 1782—before a chamber hung with tapestry celebrating the defeat of the Spanish Armada and a gallery packed with American spectators, among them Benjamin West and his fellow painter, John Singleton Copley—those present noted that when he came to the words, "offer to declare," he stopped. Whether he was "embarrassed in reading his speech," the explanation given by New England merchant Elkannah Watson, who sat next to General Howe's brother, Admiral Lord Howe, during the oration, or unable to see the text because of the "darkness of the room," or because he was "affected by a very *natural emotion*," was impossible to say. Whatever the reason, the troubled monarch paused, collected himself, then resumed. He had offered, King George said in a strained voice, to declare the colonies "*free and independent states.*"[10] The rupture of Britain and America was complete.

Independence, of course, did not mean total separation. During the same interview where he asked Benjamin West about Washington's postwar plans, George III wanted to know how Americans were likely to "act towards this country" once they were independent. West's response, that most revolutionary leaders remained well disposed to Britain, so moved Queen Charlotte that she began to cry.[11] In neither Britain nor America were feelings quite as friendly as West suggested, but the royal family's curiosity is a reminder of the many ties—commercial, linguistic, religious, familial, and cultural—that continued to bind the two English-speaking peoples together, even as their formal political connection was severed. Among the most important of these was a shared commitment to constitutional government. Although they may have agreed on little else, the two Georges had that in common. ☀

— Eliga H. Gould

John Mitchell, *A Map of the British Colonies in North America*, ca. 1755, manuscript annotations ca. 1782 by George III. Hand-colored engraving.

John Mitchell first created this map at the outset of the French and Indian War, compiling it from information provided by British governors of the colonies. It remained the definitive map of British sovereignty toward the end of the Revolutionary War. During the 1782-83 negotiations that led to the Treaty of Paris, this map was used to establish boundaries of the United States. At the negotiations, secretary to the British delegation Robert Oswald marked the boundary of the new nation in red, and on presenting a copy to George III, the king wrote (just east of North Carolina) "Boundary as described by Mr. Oswald." The map then was known as "The Red Line Map."

In the final treaty, the new borders of the United States did not actually extend to the farthest line. George IV donated his father's copy to the British Library, but access to the map remained guarded, lest Americans claim Canadian lands as their own. It was not until 1896 that the British government eased the restrictions on viewing the map.

"My Inclinations Are Strongly Bent to Arms": The Georges at War

Both George III and George Washington played leading roles in their countries' militaries. The king served as commander-in-chief of all British forces, taking an active role in planning and disseminating orders across the British Empire, even though he never left southern England. Washington served in the colonial militia as an officer, extending the empire's aims in North America. During the American Revolutionary War, he took up arms against Britain as commander-in-chief of the Continental Army. Later, he also served as commander-in-chief while president of the United States, though unlike the king, he accompanied troops toward a possible battle—in what might have been the biggest military blunder of his career.

Although he enjoyed playing with toy soldiers as a child, George III never trained in the British armed forces. This was in contrast to his male predecessors. The tradition of English kings leading their armies on the field dated back centuries, and each one from Charles I in the 1640s to George II had done so. But George's lack of service was not by choice. In 1759, he wrote his grandfather, "Now that every part of the Nation is arming for its defence, I cannot bear the thoughts of continuing in this inactive state. … Permit me . . . To request of your Majesty to give me an opportunity of convincing the World that I am neither unworthy of My high Situation, nor of the blood that fills my veins." But George II declined the Prince of Wales' offer to serve.

Nevertheless, as monarch himself, George III held a keen interest in the efforts of the British Army and Royal Navy. He recruited Hessian mercenaries from his ancestral home of Hanover to fight in North America and elsewhere. The king was also interested in the minutiae of the American Revolutionary War, even inquiring about how many blankets were required for troops, or the size of war pensions, and he received a cask of sauerkraut like those sent to soldiers overseas to sample himself. He personally appointed generals William Howe, Henry Clinton, and John Burgoyne, reviewed draft instructions to generals, read rebel newspapers, and signed off on official documents that pertained to the war. Though the cabinet occasionally overruled his proposed strategies, he nonetheless vigorously prosecuted the war, stating "If others will not be active, I must drive." (Prime Minister Lord North even complained that the king meddled too much in the conflict.) George aggressively pushed to subdue the American rebellion, believing a British loss would be catastrophic to the country, saying: "We must stretch every nerve to defend ourselves, and must run some risks, for if we are to play only a cautious game ruin will inevitably ensue." He viewed the American Revolution as "the most serious crisis this nation ever knew."

During most of his reign, the king regularly reviewed troops and fleets, inspected military installations, watched training exercises, and he hoped to serve as inspiration to servicemen and the nation. In popular culture, his presence at the head of the British armed forces appears in the lyrics to a ballad printed in 1778 that ended each patriotic verse with "George our King," such as:

> Now let's nobly advance,
> And crush the pride of France,
> Honour 'twill bring,
> Those who back the rebel's cause,
> Can never gain applause,
> Enemies to all laws,
> And George our king.

Across the Atlantic, George Washington prepared for military service as very young man. He was fourteen when his half-brother Lawrence believed that Washington needed "adventure" and should join the Royal Navy as a midshipman. Lawrence had served in the War of Jenkins' Ear, fighting the Spanish in the Caribbean. However, Mary Washington prevented her oldest son's enlistment, especially after her brother Joseph Ball Jr. informed her of the brutal treatment lower-ranking sailors received.

Still, inspired by tales of warfare from Lawrence, and in reading about the exploits of famous military commanders such as Alexander the Great and Julius Caesar—one of the first books he ever purchased, at age fifteen, was a biography of a seventeenth-century German soldier—Washington maintained his dream of fighting. After Lawrence died in 1752, George pushed to get his brother's title in the Virginia militia, although he was not initially successful. He nonetheless joined the militia where his skill as a surveyor likely was viewed as a benefit for scouting terrain, writing in 1754 that "my inclinations are strongly bent to arms." At twenty-one, he had become a major, with an annual salary of 100 pounds, despite no prior formal military training. He then was appointed to lead a diplomatic mission to the Ohio River Valley carrying an order signed by King George II, demanding the French vacate lands the British claimed themselves.

In 1754, along with Seneca chief Tanacharison, he returned to western Pennsylvania to push out the French. Washington led the attack, and he and his troops killed ten French soldiers including the commander, Joseph Coulon de Jumonville, who was allegedly leading a similar mission to secure land from the British. One month later, the French retaliated, attacking the British at Fort Necessity. Washington, commanding about four hundred men, surrendered the fort, which, perhaps due to his lack of tactical training, was easily exposed to enemy fire. These two engagements precipitated the French and Indian War, the North American theater of the Seven Years' War, considered the first global war.

The next year, Washington, now a colonel, participated in the expedition led by General Edward Braddock to take Fort Duquesne (modern Pittsburgh) from the French. Serving as an aide-de-camp, Washington witnessed firsthand the massive British failure, in which a smaller French army overwhelmed the British. Upon being mortally wounded, Braddock gave Washington his ceremonial sash, which Washington kept (and is held at Mount Vernon). Writing to his mother of the battle, he shared that "I luckily escapd witht a wound, tho' I had four Bullets through my Coat, and two Horses shot under me."

Washington's bravery leading the remnants of Braddock's force back to safety earned him plaudits. Various Virginia luminaries wrote to him praising his conduct, with Lt. Governor Robert Dinwiddie calling him the "hero of Monongahela" for his "gallant Behavior." Washington tried to parlay this newfound admiration into a commission in the British Army

George Washington's commission as commander-in-chief signed by John Hancock and Charles Thomson, June 19, 1775. Holograph on vellum.

In June 1775, two months after the battles at Lexington and Concord, the Continental Congress commissioned George Washington as commander-in-chief of the Continental Army. Washington was selected over other candidates, including John Hancock, based on his previous military experience and the hope that a leader from wealthy, populous, and centrally located Virginia could unite the colonies. Informing his wife Abigail of Washington's unanimous selection on June 15, John Adams described the new general as "modest and virtuous, the amiable, generous and brave George Washington Esqr." However, on the 18th, Washington wrote to his wife Martha that the appointment "fills me with inexpressible concern... I assure you in the most solemn manner, that, so far from seeking this appointment, I have used every endeavor in my power to avoid it." Nevertheless, Washington left for Massachusetts within days of receiving his commission and assumed command of the Continental Army in Cambridge on July 3, 1775.

Rupture: America Revolts

commanding regular troops. When that effort failed, he then formed his own militia unit, the Virginia Regiment, which saw action in the continuing conflict with France for another three years.

Washington resigned his commission in the Virginia militia in December 1758, marrying Martha Custis a month later, but his experiences fighting the French, however disastrous they were, served as real-life military education that he otherwise lacked. He also held fond memories of his military service during the next decade and a half. In the earliest surviving portrait of Washington, a Charles Willson Peale painting from 1772, he proudly wears his former uniform. Similarly, in 1774 when he served in the First Continental Congress, he wore his uniform often in Philadelphia, reminding his fellow delegates of his service.

When the Continental Army was created in response to the violence at Lexington and Concord, Washington's military experience was fresh on the delegates' minds. On June 16, 1775, Congress unanimously elected Washington commander-in-chief. He declined a salary, only requesting that his expenses be reimbursed at the end of the war. Upon receiving his commission, Washington wrote to his stepson, Jack Custis, that "it is an honor I neither sought after, or, was by any means fond of accepting." However, he knew his duty was to the American cause, "as the partiality of the Congress has placed me in this distinguished point of view, I can make them no other return but what will flow from close attention and upright intention—for the rest I can say nothing."

Despite such hesitancy, Washington remained the leader of the Continental Army for the next eight years. Throughout the war, he lost more battles than he won, but by keeping his army intact, he outlasted the British. With an inferior number of troops, he adopted a strategy of avoiding as many direct confrontations with the enemy as possible. This was a necessary approach after half of the army's initial recruits, irregularly paid and inadequately provisioned, left the service by the middle of 1776. Washington made clear how important this issue was in a lengthy letter to John Hancock that September, stating "it is in vain to expect that any (or more than a trifling) part of this Army will again engage in the Service on [just] the encouragement offered by Congress" unless they receive adequate pay. Even the men who did get paid often scattered when the shooting started, as at the Battle of Kips Bay—which led to Washington yelling at his retreating troops, "Are these the men with whom I am to defend America?"

But Washington knew that by remaining in the field, the Continental Army could keep the revolution alive. Wags in Britain derided this strategy, calling Washington "Fabius," a reference to Roman general Quintus Fabius Maximus who was so cautious during the Second Punic War that he was known as the "Delayer." But these insults did nothing to dissuade Washington from his strategy, nor from taking decisive action when needed, as at the Battles of Trenton, Princeton, or Yorktown. Washington also developed and relied on an extensive espionage network throughout the war, believing "much will depend on early Intelligence, and meeting the Enemy before they can Intrench." He authorized funding for spy operations and oversaw the Culper Ring of spies in New York City run by Major Benjmain Tallmadge (Washington's code name was Agent 711).

After the Treaty of Paris was signed in September 1783 ending the Revolutionary War, Washington headed back to Mount Vernon. On the way home, he stopped in Annapolis, Maryland, and on December 23, in a carefully orchestrated event, he resigned his commission and acceded authority to civilian control, an unprecedented act in Western military history.

Perhaps the best summation of Washington's military success during the Revolutionary War came from Benjamin Franklin. Writing to a British contact in August 1784, he boasted that "An American Planter who had never seen Europe, was chosen by us to Command our Troops and continu'd during the whole War. This Man sent home to you, one after another, five of your best Generals, baffled, their Heads bare of Laurels, disgraced even in the Opinion of their Employers."

In 1789, Washington was elected president, and under the new constitution, he served as the commander-in-chief, just as George III exercised that right in Britain. During Washington's presidency, there were some small-scale wars with Native Americans, such as the Northwest Indian War (1785–1795). But his biggest military challenge in office was the Whiskey Rebellion. In 1794, Washington called up thirteen thousand troops to suppress a series of protests over federal excise duties on whiskey in western Pennsylvania. The taxes, at a rate comparable to the taxes Britain had decreed in the 1760s, were part of Treasury Secretary Alexander Hamilton's plan to pay off debt from the Revolutionary War. When peaceful protests went unheeded by the Washington administration and tax collectors, violence erupted, including the old tactics of tarring and feathering the local revenue officials.

Washington, incensed at the uproar, overruled Pennsylvania governor Thomas Mifflin's plan for the courts to legally try the protestors. He called the Pennsylvania militia into federal service and even paid a tailor to create a uniform for him based on his old one from the Revolutionary War. Although he did go to western Pennsylvania and reviewed the troops, on the day of a potential clash with the rebellious distillers, he decided at the last minute not to appear—and neither did most of the protestors. Though there was no battle, he became the only president to lead troops in a campaign aimed at his own citizens, as his forces arrested about 150 men. Only two protestors were convicted of treason, but Washington pardoned them, perhaps out of embarrassment for overreaching.

Fortunately for Washington, that low point was not his last contribution to the American military. In July 1798, John Adams, now president, appointed him "Lieutenant-General and Commander in Chief of all the armies raised or to be raised for the service of the United States." Washington was touched, writing his former vice president "I can not express how greatly affected I am at this new proof of public confidence." But he accepted only on the condition that "I shall not be called into the field until the Army is in a situation to require my presence or it becomes indispensable by the urgency of circumstances." Indeed, Washington never saw action as lieutenant general—he mostly worked on building up the officer corps in case of war with France, selecting Alexander Hamilton as his second in command. Yet it was the highest military rank he achieved in his lifetime.

However, it was not the highest rank he ever attained.

After Washington died in 1799, other American generals received higher rank, such as John Pershing in the immediate aftermath of World War I. As a result, Congress passed legislation, effective July 4, 1976, promoting Washington to general of the armies, the highest possible rank in the United States Army; the legislation stated that his promotion would "have rank and precedence over all other grades of the Army, past or present." Thus, Washington, a man strongly inclined to arms, will never be outranked by another American general.

George Washington's Oath of Allegiance, May 12, 1778. Printed document with manuscript sheet.

On February 3, 1778, the Continental Congress passed a resolution that all officers in the Continental Army sign a loyalty oath. Even George Washington, commander-in-chief of the American forces, was required to do so, signing his form while stationed at Valley Forge. Occasionally Washington served as a witness to such oath signings for other officers. The oath required the officers to declare "no allegiance or obedience to George the Third." Although Washington had already been at war against the king for nearly three years, this oath was official proof that the two Georges had become sworn enemies.

Loudest Yelps: The Slavery Metaphor

At the beginning of the American Revolutionary War in 1775, approximately 20 percent of British North America's 2.5 million residents were enslaved. Slavery was not a cause of the Revolutionary War, as it was of the American Civil War, but it was always simmering just beneath the surface. Ironically, enslavers themselves used slavery as a metaphor to describe their own condition under what they termed corrupt British rule.

In 1746, an anonymous treatise caused a stir in London. Titled *An Essay Concerning Slavery*, it maintained that further importation of Africans to Jamaica—where there already was a ten-to-one ratio between the enslaved and white populations—would lead to revolts. The author, who historians have since documented was the sitting Jamaica governor Edward Trelawny, was personally conflicted over slavery, writing that "I cou'd wish with all my Heart, that Slavery was abolish'd entirely, and I hope in time it may be so." Yet he believed immediate abolition would be "a great Evil, and a Ruin to Thousands whose Wealth" was based on slavery. Still, he condemned the enslavers "who know the Value of Liberty, who prize it above Life" for believing the captive people they imported would not be motivated to find such liberty themselves.

Indeed, many enslavers and other Americans, in writing about the growing conflict with Britain in the prewar period, so strenuously believed in their own liberty, that they referred to themselves as slaves to the British political system. The *Boston Gazette and Country Journal*, in the midst of the Stamp Act Crisis, warned its readers on October 7, 1765, to "AWAKE!" to "defeat the Designs of those who enslave us and our Posterity." Two years later, in the second of his *Letters from a Farmer in Pennsylvania*, John Dickinson wrote that if Britain "can order us to pay what taxes she pleases … we are as abject slaves as France and Poland can shew in wooden shoes, and with uncombed hair." Benjamin Rush said two months prior to the Boston Tea Party that "The baneful chests contain in them a slow poison in a political as well as a physical sense. They contain something worse than death—the seeds of Slavery." Samuel Adams, who unlike Dickinson and Rush did not enslave people, asked in 1772, "is it not High Time for the People of this Country explicitly to declare, whether they will be Freeman or slave?" Even as the conflict headed to its conclusion, Thomas Jefferson used the comparison to slavery to justify the war retroactively, writing a Kaskaskia chief in June 1781 that the British had "made us carry all our wealth to their country, to enrich them; and, not satisfied with this, they at length began to say we were their slaves, and should do whatever they ordered us."

The slave metaphor even made its way to England, in the mouths of those who supported the colonists. In a speech in the House of Lords, Charles Pratt, Earl of Camden, invoked slavery to attack the Declaratory Bill. This bill aimed to save face in the aftermath of the Stamp Act Crisis, emphasizing Parliament's right to tax the colonies despite the lack of representation. Camden concluded, "The forefathers of the Americans did not leave their native country, and subject themselves to every danger and distress, to be reduced to a state of slavery: they did not give up their rights; they looked for protection, and not for chains, from their mother country; by her they expected to be defended in the possession of their property, and not to be deprived of it: for, should the present power continue, there is nothing which they can call their own." Later, Thomas Howard, Earl of Effingham, stated, upon resigning his commission in the British Army instead of fighting the Patriots, that Americans "have made the most respectful remonstrances, you answer them with bills of pains and penalties; they know they ought to be free, you tell them they shall be slaves."

George Washington was no stranger to this rhetoric. During the summer of 1774, when Washington and other colonists in Virginia debated, drafted, and signed the Fairfax Resolves stating Britain could not impose laws without the Americans' consent, he routinely used the slavery metaphor in a series of letters to his childhood friends, the brothers Bryan and George William Fairfax. In June, he wrote George William that Parliament was "endeavouring by every piece of art and despotism to fix the Shackles of Slavery upon us." In July, two days after the Fairfax Resolves' passage, he wrote Bryan that the colonies must push back on Britain's encroachment lest they be reduced "to the most abject state of Slavery that ever was designd for Mankind." And a couple of months later, he made the metaphor even more explicit in another letter to Bryan, writing that "the Crisis is arrivd when we must assert our Rights, or [Britain] will make us as tame, & abject Slaves, as the Blacks we Rule over with such arbitrary Sway."

Six weeks after the battles of Lexington and Concord, Washington justified the Patriot attack on "Ministerial Troops" in another letter to George William by stating "Unhappy it is though to reflect, that a Brother's Sword has been sheathed in a Brother's breast, and that, the once happy and peaceful plains of America are either to be drenched with Blood, or Inhabited by Slaves. Sad alternative! But can a virtuous Man hesitate in his choice?" And upon giving his troops orders on July 2, 1776, the general in charge of the Continental Army stated, "The time is now near at hand which must probably determine, whether Americans are to be, Freemen, or Slaves; whether they are to have any property they can call their own."

The biggest example of contradictory language regarding the slave metaphor was in the Declaration of Independence. Drafted by Jefferson, who enslaved more than six hundred people throughout his life, it boldly states "All men are created equal," a phrase that in practice only applied to white men. In a letter discussing the Declaration, English abolitionist Thomas Day pointed out this inconsistency, writing "If there be an object truly ridiculous in nature, it is an American patriot, signing resolutions of independency with the one hand, and with the other brandishing a whip over his affrighted slaves."

Many who opposed slavery as well as the American cause agreed with Day, rushing to point out the hypocrisy. Enslaved American poet Phillis Wheatley—who sent Washington a copy of her book of poems—wrote of "the strange Absurdity of [American enslavers'] Conduct whose Words and Actions are so diametrically, opposite. How well the Cry for Liberty, and the reverse Disposition for the exercise of oppressive Power over others agree, I humbly think it does not require the Penetration of a Philosopher to determine." Over in England, political writer Josiah Tucker, who believed the Americans should be independent but also came to despise them, wrote that Washington and President of Congress Henry Laurens were "the greatest American champions for the unalienable Rights of Mankind" but "have shewn by their own Examples, that they have no Objections against Slavery, provided they shall be free themselves, and have the Power of Enslaving Others." The fact that Washington enslaved people while leading an army dedicated to "liberty" led diarist Nicholas Cresswell to deride Washington as "a Negro-driver … with a ragged Banditti of undisciplined people."

Lexicographer and writer Samuel Johnson had the most famous retort. In his 1775 pamphlet *Taxation, No Tyranny*, he called colonists "these demigods of independence" while defending the Coercive Acts and admonishing Americans that they could move to Great Britain and purchase an estate if they cared about voting for representatives in Parliament. His quip "How is it that we hear the loudest yelps for liberty among the drivers of negroes" perfectly summed up this inherent contradiction in the Americans' revolutionary rhetoric.

Lord Dunmore's Proclamation

In November 1775, the royal governor of Virginia, John Murray, Earl of Dunmore, issued the proclamation declaring martial law in the colony. Dunmore had incensed local colonists by seizing Williamsburg's armory seven months earlier. With this proclamation, he further incited Virginians by decreeing that any indentured or enslaved person "appertaining to Rebels" who joined "his Majesty's Troops" would be granted freedom. (People enslaved by Dunmore himself or other Loyalists were exempt.)

Colonists feared this would lead to an insurrection. The Virginia Convention declared on December 17, 1775, "all negro or other slaves, conspiring to rebel or make insurrection, shall suffer death." Thomas Jefferson, in Philadelphia when the proclamation was issued, made plans for his family to flee should his enslaved workers at Monticello rebel. According to Edward Rutledge, a South Carolina delegate to the Continental Congress, Dunmore's proclamation did more "to work an eternal separation between Great Britain and the Colonies, than any other expedient."

Meanwhile, that December, George Washington wrote that "If the Virginians are wise, that Arch Traitor to the Rights of Humanity, Lord Dunmore, should be instantly crushd, if it takes the force of the whole Colony to do it." He feared that the proclamation would have a cascading effect "like a snow Ball in rolling," recruiting thousands of enslaved people to fight for the British.

All told, between eight hundred and one thousand enslaved persons in Virginia fled to the British in response to the proclamation (at the time, the colony had approximately 210,000 enslaved people). The proclamation followed a pattern of rumors that percolated throughout the enslaved community in the eighteenth century that the king—whomever it was at the time—secretly was their protector and sought their freedom. For example, the preachers who led an aborted slave uprising in South Carolina earlier in 1775 claimed that King George II had gone to hell for ignoring the commands of a mysterious book that ordered him to set enslaved people free. However, the young King George III was a believer in this book, and, according to the leaders of the revolt, "was about to alter the World and set the Negroes Free."

Though George III did not abolish slavery, nonetheless the British Army used the promise of freedom in Dunmore's proclamation to recruit soldiers, exacerbating tensions with the colonies. And in turn, tens of thousands of enslaved people throughout the colonies fled to the British, with approximately twenty thousand men serving in the British armed forces.

Lord Dunmore's Proclamation, Williamsburg, VA, November 7, 1775.

Rupture: America Revolts

Melted Majesty

On July 6, 1776, John Hancock sent a copy of the Declaration of Independence to George Washington, stationed in New York, requesting that he "have it proclaimed at the Head of the Army in the Way you shall think most proper." Three days later, with British ships visible offshore, Washington had the Declaration read aloud to the assembled troops. Later that night, a crowd inspired by revolutionary sentiments pulled down a golden equestrian statue of George III in Bowling Green.

The statue by William Wilton had been dedicated in April 1770 in honor of George III for "the deep Sense this Colony has of the eminent and singular Blessings received from him during his most auspicious Reign." At the time of its unveiling, it was the only equestrian statue in the future United States. However, it soon became a target of vandalism, in part because the shine from the gold leaf temporarily blinded passersby. In 1771 a fence was erected to prevent it from becoming "a receptacle of all the filth & dirt of the Neighbourhood." Two years later an anti-vandalism ordinance was passed to further protect it. The fenceposts even resembled crowns, which were torn down along with the statue.

After the statue was toppled, a factory in Litchfield, Connecticut, created 42,088 bullets out of it for the war effort. The *Freeman's Journal* of New Hampshire suggested that the bullets would "assimilate with the brains" of the redcoats. The postmaster of New York, Ebenezer Hazard, wrote General Horatio Gates that British "troops will probably have melted Majesty fired at them." (Not all these bullets hit their targets, as some are still occasionally found in Revolutionary War battlefields.).

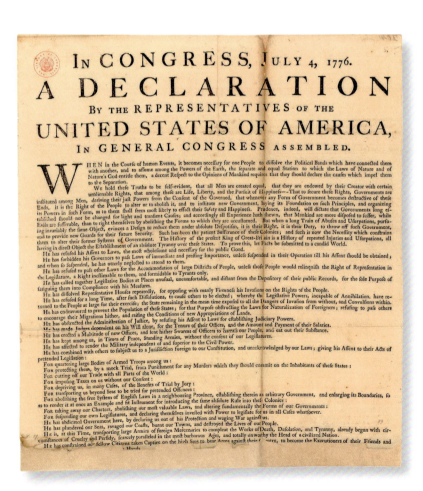

Declaration of Independence, printed by John Dunlap, July 4-5, 1776. Philadelphia.

As soon as the Continental Congress approved the Declaration of Independence, John Hancock, president of Congress, ordered it printed by John Dunlap. This copy was enclosed in a July 6 letter from Hancock to George Washington requesting he read the Declaration to the Continental Army.

Andre Basset, *La destruction de la statue royale a Nouvelle Yorck*, based on Franz Xavier Habermann's *Die zerstorung der koniglichen bild saule zu Neu Yorck*, ca. 1776-1779. Hand-colored etching.

This drawing, originally created in Augsburg then printed in Paris, is a fanciful depiction of the night the New York statue of George III was torn down. The architecture is much more European than colonial, and the statue depicted is not equestrian. Although it shows enslaved people lowering the statue, their participation is not documented. Nonetheless, this image circulated widely in Europe.

A Worthless, Diabolical Tyrant: King George in the Eyes of the Founders

As the crisis between Britain and its American colonies led to war, the revolutionaries' anger shifted from Parliament to George III. The king became more entrenched in his commitment to restrain the Americans, and invective against their former sovereign grew. Their fury manifested itself in propaganda, designed to sway the public to the Patriots' cause, and the harshness of their words underscored the fractured relationship between George and his rebellious subjects.

For the first dozen years of George's reign, the colonists viewed him relatively favorably. When Parliament passed the Stamp Act in 1765, taxing anything that was printed, such as newspapers or playing cards, colonists aimed their anger at Parliament and thanked the king for intervening once it was repealed. Similarly, in the aftermath of the 1767 Townshend Acts, the Virginia House of Burgesses directly appealed to the king for "royal interposition" to support the rights of the Americans. Even in the 1770s, when the exacerbated tensions evolved into warfare, approximately 20 percent of the colonists remained Loyalists, still revering George and believing he was faithfully executing his duties as the sovereign.

After the Boston Tea Party in December 1773, the relationship between the colonists and the king further deteriorated. As Parliament passed harsher measures to pay for its military expenditures in North America and to punish Massachusetts for the interruption to commerce, Americans turned to the king. But several petitions begging him to intercede were rejected or ignored. Little did they know that the king had written his prime minister, Lord North, on September 11, 1774, "The dye is now cast, the colonies must either submit or triumph. I do not wish to come to severer measures, but we must not retreat... once vigorous measures appear to be the only means left of bringing the Americans to a due submission to the mother country the colonies will submit." Two months later on November 18, he wrote "blows must decide whether" the colonies "are to be a subject to this country or independent." And on November 30 he told Parliament that "you may depend upon my firm and stedfast resolution to withstand every attempt to weaken or impair the supreme authority of this Legislature over all the dominions of my Crown."

Though the king was just exercising his constitutional duty, the Americans did not consider it respectful. Echoing George's own language, Abigail Adams declared "the die is cast." The November 1774 speech "would strain with everlasting infamy the reign of" George III, she wrote, and "the reply of the house of commons and the house of Lords shew us the most wicked and hostile measures will be persued against us." A year later, six months after the Battle of Lexington started the Revolution, the king was even more cantankerous at the opening of Parliament on October 26, stating he would "be ready to receive the Misled with Tenderness and Mercy" should the "unhappy and deluded Multitude ... become sensible of their Error." Though the British public praised the speech as restrained and forbearing, the Americans viewed it as incendiary and foreboding. George Washington called it "full of rancor and resentment." In January 1776, Samuel Adams vehemently wrote, "I have heard that [George] is his own Minister —that he follows the Dictates of his own Heart. If so, why should we cast the odium of distressing Mankind upon his Minions & Flatterers only. Guilt must lie at his Door. Divine Vengeance will fall on his head; for all-gracious Heaven cannot be an indifferent Spectator of the virtuous Struggles of this people." With the sovereign clearly aligned against the Americans, George III was now the face of British oppression and his stature in the colonies dwindled.

Of all the founders, perhaps the two Thomases, Paine and Jefferson, despised George III the most. Paine, who was born in Norfolk, England, and emigrated to America in 1774, described the king as "a sottish, stupid, stubborn, worthless, brutish man" in his pamphlet, *The Crisis*. He had supported George until the Battle of Lexington, but in his pamphlet *Common Sense* (1776), he wrote that "No man was a warmer wisher for a reconciliation than myself, before the fatal nineteenth of April, 1775, but the moment the event of that day was made known, I rejected the hardened, sullen-tempered Pharaoh of England for ever; and disdain the wretch, that with the pretended title of FATHER OF HIS PEOPLE, can unfeelingly hear of their slaughter, and composedly sleep with their blood upon his soul." (The invective against the king did not go unheeded in Britain; some even agreed. Diarist Sylas Neville reported that he "particularly" enjoyed the part where Paine "treats Geo. III as the dog deserves.")

Thomas Jefferson particularly reviled George III. He mocked the king by calling him "George Hanover," "Brunswick," (an allusion to his duchy in Germany) and "Guelph" (the family name of the House of Hanover), and prominently listed his perceived offenses and failures in the Declaration of Independence. Jefferson's rough draft of the Declaration included the phrase "future ages will scarce believe that the hardiness of one man adventured within the short compass of twelve years only, to build a blatant and undisguised tyranny over a people fostered & fixed in the principles of freedom." Although that part was removed by the Continental Congress when it revised Jefferson's draft, his less inflammatory statement, that "The history of the present King of Great Britain is a history of repeated injuries and usurpations" made the final version. The completed Declaration also listed twenty-seven grievances that justified American independence, two-thirds of which begin with "He," explicitly blaming George III. Jefferson concluded the list asserting that "A Prince whose character is thus marked by every act which may define a Tyrant, is unfit to be the ruler of a free people."

Jefferson's utter contempt extended to the monarchy as a concept, not just George III himself. In a 1787 letter, he referred to kings as a "class of human lions, tygers, and mammo[th]s." The next year, in a letter from Paris to George Washington, the sage of Monticello observed that "there is not a crowned head in Europe, whose talents or merits would entitle him to be elected vestryman by the people of any parish in America."

Even after the king died in January 1820, Jefferson could not help but get another dig in. The following December he wrote a contact in Liverpool that "the obstacle" to better relations between the young American republic and Britain had been "in the obstinate and unforgiving temper of your late king, and a continuance of his prejudices kept up from habit after he was withdrawn from power. I hope I now see symptoms of sounder views in your government."

(Jefferson's sentiment that George had been a mad king bent on exacting pain from his colonists remained in the public firmament well after the founding generation had died. Even Abraham Lincoln wrote in 1855 "we were the political slaves of King George, and wanted to be free.")

Not all founders detested the king, especially after the war. John Adams, who as America's first minister

The Horse America, Throwing His Master, 1779. Etching. Published by Wm. White.

This anonymous cartoon mocks the flailing British effort to suppress the rebellious colonies, as George III is thrown from his horse; his whip made of swords, bayonets, and cutting tools not accomplishing the task of mastering the animal symbolizing America. A jaunty Frenchman with a fleur-de-lis flag marches in the background, a reminder of the Franco-American alliance enacted the previous year.

Rupture: America Revolts

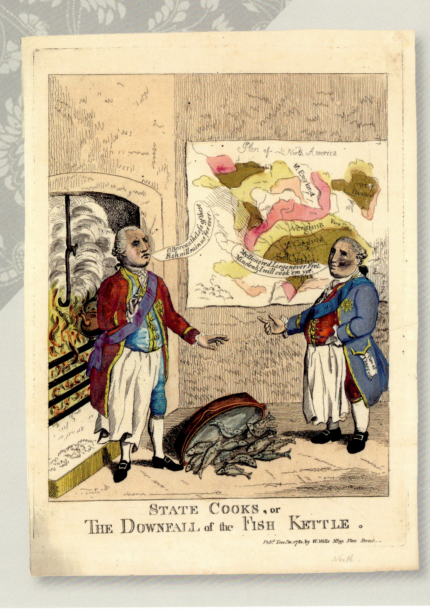

State Cooks, or the Downfall of the Fish Kettle, December 10, 1781. Hand-colored etching. Published by Wiliam Wells.

This print was published shortly after word reached London that General Cornwallis had surrendered at Yorktown in Virginia. On the left, the king (looking very much like George Washington), tells Lord North that "the loss of these fish will ruin us for ever." The fish in question are the American colonies, spilling out of a kettle, a reference to the phrase "a kettle of fish," meaning a mess. Playing up an imaginary worst-case scenario, Quebec, Florida, and Nova Scotia are also shown with the colonies that actually broke away. This is the first print to depict Yorktown on a map after the decisive battle. The reference to "Minden" by Lord North is a quip about George Germain who was accused of cowardice at the 1759 Battle of Minden in the Seven Years' War, a charge that dogged him throughout his term as colonial secretary during the Revolutionary War.

to Britain had to treat the king respectfully, later regretted the personal nature of the Declaration, writing that he "never believed George to be a tyrant." The criticisms of George were "expressions which I would not have inserted, if I had drawn it up, particularly that which called the King tyrant." (Adams had served on the committee that prepared the Declaration, though Jefferson had written the initial draft.) He also castigated Benjamin Franklin who "often and indeed always appeared to me to have personal Animosity and very severe Resentment against the King. In all his conversations and in all his Writings, when he could naturally and sometimes when he could not, he mentioned the King with great Asperity." (Franklin had attended the king's coronation in 1761, but in April 1782 wrote that "this King will, therefore, stand foremost in the list of diabolical, bloody, and execrable tyrants.") George Washington maintained a diplomatic tone with George III after Adams's time in London. In 1796, in a letter to the king introducing Rufus King as minister plenipotentiary, Washington described George as "our great and good friend" and stated that "I pray God to have your Majesty in his safe and holy keeping."

"The Flower of American Chivalry": How the British Viewed Washington

As leader of the Continental Army staging a rebellion against the British Empire, George Washington was often a target for insults from the British public. Yet he also developed something of a heroic reputation.

During the Revolution, even Loyalists who previously had warm relations with Washington became his enemy. Jonathan Boucher perfectly exemplified this change of heart. Boucher, a rector of Anglican churches in Virginia and Maryland, had run a school that counted Washington's stepson Jack Custis as a pupil. A staunch Tory, Boucher wrote a caustic letter to Washington in August 1775, denouncing him as a traitor. "We have now each of us taken and avowed our side. … those who with you are promoting the present apparently popular measures are the true enemies of their country. … You are no longer worthy of my friendship: a man of honour can no longer without dishonour be connected with you. With your cause I renounce you."

Emigrating to Britain—where he would remain for the rest of his life—Boucher wrote newly appointed secretary for America, George Germain, a lengthy letter on November 27, 1775, ending with a brief description of Washington. Though he viewed the Virginian as "honest," he nonetheless believed that "in the military line it is not possible his Merit can be considerable." Boucher thought that because Washington had "little personal experience" with warfare "and still less Reading, a thousand Difficulties must daily occur to Him." Although Boucher admitted that Washington's "extraordinary Coolness and Caution" might "acquit himself well," the rector predicted that Washington would be "defenceless" against "Manoeuvres of Art" and "perplexed and confounded by stratagems."

As the fighting commenced, some British generals and members of the press agreed with Boucher's assessment. John Burgoyne was so confident he could defeat Washington's army that while in London on leave in December 1776, he bet Whig MP Charles James Fox a pony—equivalent to fifty guineas—that, per the Brooks's Club betting register, he would be "home victorious from America by Christmas, 1777," even though he had yet to be appointed commander of the forces in Canada. In another equine-related mockery, newspapers reported on a horse named Washington that lost a race, likening him to General Washington who was "famous for retreat."

British generals who met him in the field treated him with disdain, believing that as a leader of a rebellion he should not be treated as an equal. On July 14, 1776, the Howe brothers, General William and Admiral Richard, received a delegation of American officers under a flag of truce to meet on Governor's Island in New York. There they gave the officers a letter of potential reconciliation addressed to "George Washington, Esq.," deliberately not recognizing his American military rank of general. The officers, under strict instructions not to accept any overtures should they fail to convey proper respect, refused to accept the message, declaring "All the world knew who General Washington was since the Transactions of Last Summer." Outraged, Ambrose Serle, William Howe's civilian secretary, thought Washington full of "vanity and insolence" for insisting on a title he was not given by the British Army. In response to the incident, Congress issued a positive defense of Washington stating, "That General Washington, in refusing to receive" the letter "acted with Dignity becoming his Station, and therefore this Congress do highly approve the same." The exchange was also published in British newspapers, furthering the overseas reputation of Washington and his men as noble and decorous.

In fact, unlike the British commanders who scoffed at Washington, many British commentators could not help but admire the American general and offer begrudging respect. After word reached Britain in August 1775 of Washington's appointment, initial sketches of the general largely painted a positive picture of him. *Scots Magazine* in October 1775 stated "His is a man of sense and great integrity; his is polite, though rather reserved. … There is much dignity and modesty in his manner."

Some Whig politicians and supporters even openly toasted Washington. Charles James Fox, the leader of the opposition, was ejected from a dinner party for proposing a tribute to Washington. Thomas Coke, a Whig MP from Holkham, said toward the end of his life that "Every night during the American War did I drink to the health of General Washington as the greatest man on earth." Not every Whig was so audacious, and indeed retribution against such acts could be violent: in Nottingham, Robert Dennison was "crushed" to the

Rupture: America Revolts

floor for toasting the general, and in Leeds, a clothier was tarred and feathered for drinking to his health. Some Whigs who supported Washington did so out of a belief that the colonists were justified in fighting for their rights as Englishmen, while others, seeing the writing on the wall, decided that trade with an inevitably independent America would be stronger if the war was brought to a swift conclusion.

The American leader was often compared favorably with the British commanders, a trend that began early on with Washington's first opposing general, Thomas Gage, the commander-in-chief of the British Army. The *Saint James's Chronicle* quipped that when Gage was recalled from his post in the fall of 1775, he took "with him the Portraits of Mess. Hancock, Adams, Washington, and [General Isaac Putnam]. We hope he means to apologize in the politest Manner, to a certain Royal Connoisseur, for not having been able to procure him the Originals." Colonel Isaac Barré, in a speech on October 26, 1775, in the House of Commons, declared that a missive from Gage that was much too "flowery" compared with Washington's "clear and manly" reply.

In the aftermath of Burgoyne's loss at Saratoga—so much for that pony—Washington allowed the British general to return home, even writing a letter defending Burgoyne's conduct. "I am ever ready to do justice to the merit of the gentleman and the soldier; and to esteem, where esteem is due, however the idea of a public enemy may interpose" he wrote. Burgoyne made sure the letter was widely reprinted, as he found himself defending his actions to a Parliament set on making him a scapegoat. As a result, one commentator wrote: "Let every Englishman contrast the behavior of General Washington with that of [the North ministry] since General Burgoyne's arrival." A few months earlier, the *Edinburgh Advertiser*, which historian Troy Bickham describes as "perhaps the most vehemently anti-American newspaper in Britain" even went so far as to write, "Let us not … disdain to learn virtue even from a REBEL."

The British also gave Washington high marks in his treatment of enemy soldiers and his generosity with his own men. British newspapers printed a letter allegedly intercepted from the French that said "Gen Washington is continually recommending humanity, and when any prisoners are made, he is the first to desire that they may not be ill treated … his courage and disinterestedness are equal to his humanity." On December 7, 1776, *Jackson's Oxford Journal*, a pro-Tory newspaper, referred to Washington as "The Flower of American Chivalry" while reporting he had sent men home for the fall harvest so "that the Country might not suffer for Want of Agriculture."

With such positive reports, the British public could not help but be impressed. *The Public Advertiser* stated on August 22, 1778, that "The Americans are indebted, for the Stand they hitherto made, to the Courage of the emigrant natives of this Island, the Conduct of George Washington." Perhaps *Westminster Magazine* best summed up the British view of Washington in August 1780: "It is somewhat singular, that even in England, not one reflection was ever cast, or the least disrespectful word uttered against him." Although this statement perhaps belies some of the aspersions cast on Washington at the start of the conflict, it nonetheless spoke to the universal acclaim he achieved during the war.

When Washington died in 1799, the British praise became even more laudatory than it had been while he was an enemy combatant. Memorial services were held in London, the Royal Navy lowered their White Ensign to half mast, and the *London Morning Chronicle* was one of many newspapers to provide a glowing eulogy: "The world will hear the most sincere regret that this truly great and good man died" it began. "The whole range of history does not present to our view a character upon which we can dwell with such entire and unmixed admiration. … General WASHINGTON is not the idol of a day, but the hero of ages!"

Another convert to the cult of Washington was none other than Jonathan Boucher. In 1797, he dedicated a publication of his sermons to Washington, writing "I never was more than your political enemy; and every sentiment even of political animosity has, on my part, long ago subsided. Permit me then to hope, that this tender of renewed amity between us may be received and regarded as giving some promise of that perfect reconciliation between our two countries."

Receiving a copy of the book from Boucher, Washington thanked him for the "honor" of the dedication, asserting that "there is no man in either country, more zealously devoted to Peace and a good understanding between the two Nations than I am—Nor one who is more disposed to bury in oblivion all animosities which have subsisted between them, & the Individuals of each." ☀

The Curious Zebra. Alive from America! Walk in Gem'men and Ladies, Walk In, September 3, 1778. Hand-colored etching. Printed for G. Johnson.

In this British print, the colonies are represented as stripes of a zebra, with several political figures handling the animal. Despite having died eight years earlier, George Grenville is depicted loading a saddle on the animal labeled "Stamp Act," which America had resisted when he was prime minister more than a decade earlier. Lord North is tugging at the front stating "I hold the Reins and will never quit them until the Beast is Subdued." In the background three peace commissioners indicate America will only negotiate for peace if it is granted independence.

Notably, George Washington stands at the tail, referring to himself as "Fabius the Second," a legendary Roman general who was overly cautious in battle. Indeed this largely was Washington's strategy as commander-in-chief. He even told Congress, "we should on all occasions avoid a general action unless compelled by a necessity." Meanwhile, the British grew frustrated by his refusal to fight in open battle. British general Henry Clinton wrote to Whitehall in 1779: "To force Washington to an action upon terms tolerably equal has been the object of every campaign during this war." Despite this ridicule, Washington himself is not caricatured, appearing quite normal; later, British caricaturists would not show such restraint with Napoleon.

Rupture: America Revolts

The Deciding Battle

Surrender of the English Army commanded by my Lord Cornwallis to the combined armies of the United States of America and France under Generals Washington and Rochambeau at Yorktown and Gloucester in Virginia, October 19, 1781. Hand-colored map. Paris: Mondhare, ca. 1781.

General Washington arrived outside of Yorktown, on the coast of southern Virginia, in August 1781 to oversee preparations for a siege of the city, where British troops under Lord Cornwallis were garrisoned. On October 9, American and French forces began relentless artillery fire on British positions before storming Cornwallis' defenses. Overwhelmed, outnumbered, and surrounded, with a French fleet blocking their retreat by sea, the British conceded on October 19.

This French print celebrates the British surrender as ships of the French navy crowd the Yorktown shoreline and civilians gather between lines of allied soldiers and officers on horseback. Washington's response to Cornwallis' capitulation was measured, calling it "an important victory" and "a glorious event," but he was unsure of Britain's next move and worried that Americans would regard success at Yorktown as the end of their wartime commitment. When Britain's prime minister, Lord North, learned of the disaster five weeks later, he exclaimed, "Oh God. It is all over. It is all over." George III was disappointed but undaunted, because unlike North, he did not believe that the war had actually ended. The king was determined to continue the fight, and it was not until March 1782 that he had to accept the decision of a war-weary Parliament to seek peace with the United States.

The French had been an invaluable American ally, without whom the Patriot cause would almost certainly have failed. King Louis XVI had provided arms and provisions to outfit the Continental Army, and more than 2,000 French soldiers and sailors died assisting the Americans. It was appropriate, then, that the agreement that officially ended the war in 1783 was the Treaty of Paris.

Seizing the Prince

In September 1781, a month before the British surrender at Yorktown, sixteen-year-old Prince William, third child of George III, sailed to America with the Royal Navy. Stationed in New York City, then occupied by the British, the prince wrote his father: "When I came on shore I was received by an immense concourse of people, who appeared very loyal, continually crying out 'God Bless King George.'" The people who greeted the prince with enthusiasm were the Loyalists who remained in the city after the British captured it in 1776.

By the following spring, with British interest in continued warfare flagging and peace talks soon to begin, Prince William was quartered in a large house in Hanover Square—which had been named so after George I's accession to the British throne. Meanwhile, as George Washington kept his army intact and on alert should the British resolve to keep fighting, Colonel Matthias Ogden presented him with a scheme to snatch the young prince. Ogden and a crew of armed men would row across the Hudson from New Jersey in four whaleboats and "seize on" William, Admiral Robert Digby, and other naval personnel. Washington approved the plan, which he noted "merits applause," and instructed Ogden to "treat them with all possible respect, but you are to delay no time in conveying them to Congress." Perhaps Washington hoped to exchange them for American prisoners.

The Americans never captured their royal prey. A few days after authorizing the kidnapping, Washington, who had spies in the city, learned that the prince was well protected and advised Ogden that the plan could not succeed. Nearly five decades later, in 1830, Prince William became King William IV of the United Kingdom. On learning of the abandoned plot as king, William remarked to Louis McLane, the American ambassador, that "I am obliged to General Washington for his humanity, but I'm damned glad I did not give him an opportunity of exercising it towards me."

Benjamin West, *Portrait of Prince William as a Midshipman, standing on the deck of HMS Prince George,* **1779. Oil on canvas.**

"The Greatest Man in the World"

George Washington's greatest accomplishment as the nation's first general was not the British surrender at Yorktown nor any other military victory. His resignation of his military commission in Annapolis, Maryland, after the conclusion of the Revolutionary War, on December 23, 1783, distinguishes his leadership from the countless war heroes before him, who chose to embrace power rather than reject it. Washington's simple act guaranteed that civilian law, not military might, would govern the United States. It squelched any rumors that the new nation would follow the already trodden path of tyranny and dictatorship. In that sense, American democratic republicanism was born in Annapolis.

Washington arrived at the Senate chamber of the Maryland statehouse shortly before noon. The audience kept their hats on when he entered, not out of disrespect but as a gesture establishing the republican, not monarchical, practices of the new nation. As presiding officer of the Confederation Congress, Thomas Mifflin invited General Washington to speak. The protocol of the ceremony was scripted by Thomas Jefferson, who fully understood the historical import of the moment (see following page).

According to firsthand accounts, Washington's voice wavered at times. Others shed tears during his short speech. He closed his remarks by indicating his permanent resignation from government service: "Having now finished the work assigned me, I retire from the great theater of action; and bidding an affectionate farewell to this august body under whose orders I have so long acted, I here offer my commission and take my leave of all the employments of public life." After shaking the hands of each member of Congress present, Washington quickly left Annapolis on horseback, headed directly to Mount Vernon.

Washington's decision to retreat from military service was recognized globally as extraordinarily significant. American-born artist Benjamin West remarked that King George III was astonished to learn that Washington planned to retreat to private life if the American colonies gained independence. While sitting in the Queen's closet, distraught with the rebellion, he allegedly remarked to West: "If he (Washington) did that, he would be the greatest man in the world."

Washington returned to public life years later to serve as the first president of the United States, but did so reluctantly. He was persuaded by the argument that only someone with his stature and reputation could serve in this role. The Marquis de Lafayette wrote to Washington about the decision: "You alone can make this political machine operate successfully." The fact that Washington had resigned his military command at Annapolis only intensified public support for his candidacy. Because Washington had renounced unilateral authority and power once before, he was perfectly suited to serve as the world's first democratically elected independent executive. ☀

Charles Willson Peale. *His Excel: G: Washington Esq: L.L.D. Late commander in chief of the armies of the U.S. of America & president of the Convention of 1787.* Engraving.

Abel Buell, *A New and Correct Map of the United States of North America*, 1784. New Haven, Connecticut. On deposit to the Library of Congress from David M. Rubenstein.

The first map produced and published in the newly independent United States of America, Abel Buell's work depicts the nation and the territorial claims of its states. At this point, George III had recognized American sovereignty, but the mechanics of government remained a work in progress: the ratification of the Constitution (1788) and the inauguration of President George Washington (1789) were still a few years away. Virginia, North Carolina, South Carolina, and Georgia (as well as Spanish Florida) are shown with their western boundaries extending to the Mississippi River, as the new states maintained their colonial territorial objectives. Curiously, Connecticut, Buell's home state, in the northeast corner and outlined in green, optimistically leaps over New York, New Jersey, and Pennsylvania with an ambitious land claim that also reaches the Mississippi.

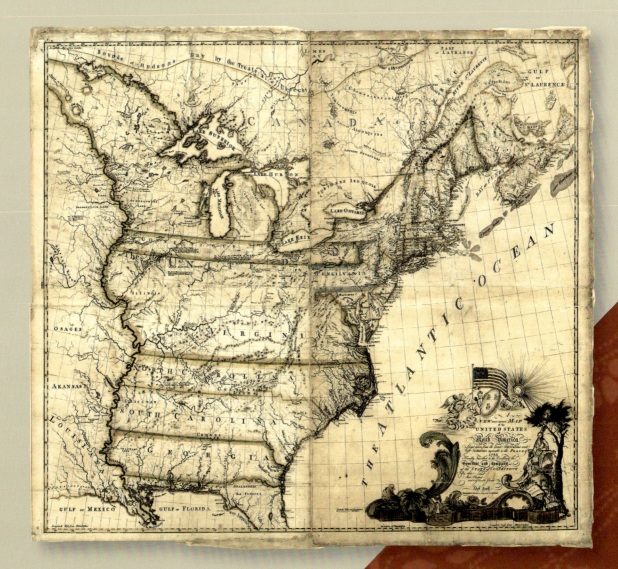

Rupture: America Revolts

John Trumbull, *General George Washington Resigning His Commission*, 1826. Oil on Canvas.

This massive twelve-by-eighteen-foot painting depicts the momentous occasion on December 23, 1783, in Annapolis, Maryland, when General Washington resigned as commander-in-chief of the Continental Army, thus establishing the precedent of civilian authority over the American military. It is on permanent display in the rotunda of the US Capitol.

Chapter 5

Thomas Lawrence, *George III*, 1818. Oil on canvas.

A King, a President, a Republic, and Executive Power

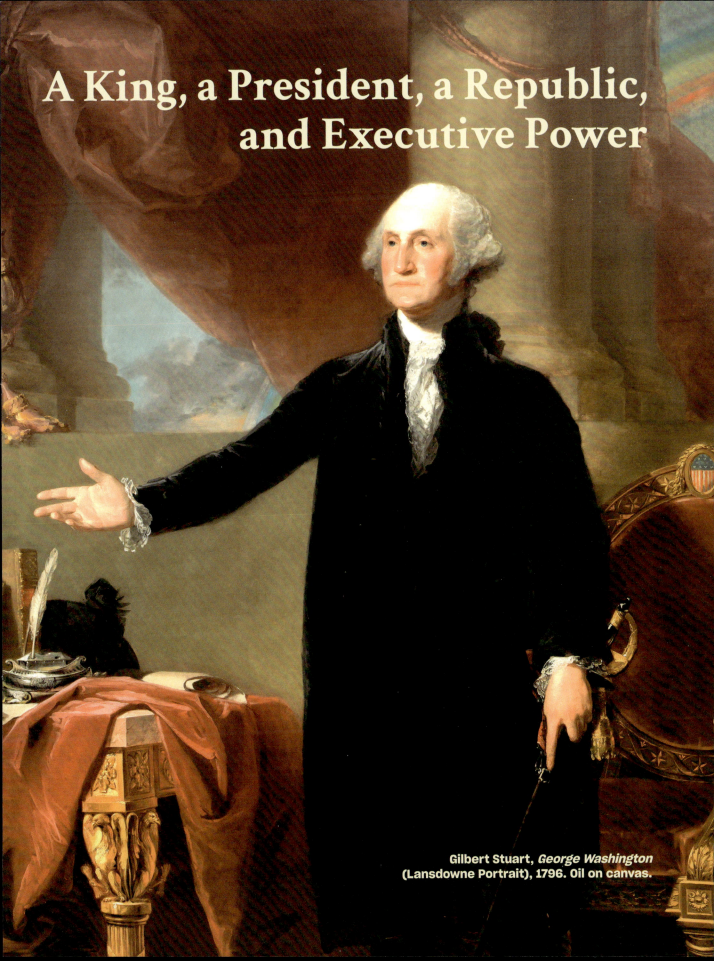

Gilbert Stuart, *George Washington* (Lansdowne Portrait), 1796. Oil on canvas.

From the outset of the American experiment in self-government, there has been a precarious equilibrium between the preservation of liberal ideals and the execution of effective governance.[1] The United States Constitution provided a novel solution to this dilemma with the creation of an independent, democratically elected chief executive. As the first president of the United States, George Washington accepted the unprecedented responsibility of protecting the individual liberties that a republic safeguards while at the same time exercising executive powers only previously discharged by hereditary monarchs.[2]

Before the existence of the United States, King George III encountered challenges to monarchical power, which had atrophied since the overthrow of King James II in 1688. While the American founding directly confronted the immense task of making the executive compatible with republican government, the story of George III and the transformation of the British monarchy is underappreciated.

Was George III a tyrant or a weakened figurehead?[3] The answer to that question is one of historical interpretation, but the intrinsic nature of executive power is both subordinate and insubordinate, weak and strong, reactive and instigating.[4] Such tension is evident in the leadership of both Georges. As king and president, they attempted to balance these competing demands by emphasizing the republican virtues of disinterestedness, civic duty, and patriotism.

With no written constitution in Britain, competing notions of monarchical legitimacy muddled interpretations of George III's executive leadership. The popular conception of George III is that he did little to defend the American colonists' rights before the Revolution and then subsequently, due to ineptitude, lost the war. Such a superficial treatment of this critical period in world history is unfortunate. From 1760 to 1784, George III protected executive power and consequently preserved components of monarchical influence. For example, at a time when the king's political power waned, George III exercised his authority to nominate the chief minister. He protected that right until the end of his active reign.[5] Perhaps of greatest interest is George III's conduct and leadership during the American Revolution. While his ministers wavered in prosecuting the war, the king did not. Consistent with a strong executive, George III led when Parliament squabbled. His rationale for continuing the war stemmed from his concern for the whole. The preservation of the empire was at stake, and thus Britain's ability to sustain its commercial and economic superiority.[6] As his chief minister, Lord North, equivocated, George III "roused him to action."[7] When Spain and France threatened Britain as the war's effect expanded beyond the colonies, "the king was undaunted." For the first time since Queen Anne, the monarch assembled the cabinet. During the meeting at his library in Buckingham House, he spoke for an hour, defending his position to continue fighting in America.[8]

The willingness of George III to enter the fray of politics and exert influence came at a cost. The public perception of George III as a "patriot king" who served the country above politics withered.[9] As his reign continued, George III's political opinions and preferences became well known amongst the London elite. The loss of America, allegations of favoritism and corruption, and many political tussles with Parliament threatened his independent executive authority.[10] The king who had promised to rise above faction became its casualty.

However, the 1784 election that elevated a youthful minister, Pitt the Younger, opened a new opportunity for George III to orchestrate a rebirth of his national popularity based largely on his role as head of state. He had been challenged by "republicanism abroad and faction at home," yet he did not cede the entirety of his executive authority.[11] The steadfastness of George III presented itself at a time in which Britain searched for reassurances of identity and shared culture. By stepping back from politics, George III found a new purpose and center of authority for the British monarchy. The change in the king's stature must have been palpable. His son Frederick wrote to his father, "The nation appears now to have at last opened its eyes, and to be convinced that it owes every thing to your Majesty's firmness."[12]

The idea that a vanquished George III dissolved into irrelevance is inaccurate. In fact, George III had strong ideas about governance and "particularly about the role of the king."[13] Post-revolution, George III's reign began the critical transition of the British monarchy from executive power rooted in inherent political influence to national symbolism. George III was the precursor of "that curious blend of assiduous domestic coziness interspersed with occasional bouts of public splendor which is the current royal trademark in Britain."[14] Even as the king's explicit political power diminished, George III fostered a reputation of respectability and patriotism. Britain had no simpler task than what the young American republic faced, namely determining how executive power, lodged for centuries in the hereditary monarchy, could support an evolving constitutional democracy.

Due to his laudable reputation, the reign of George III embodied many of the tenets of classical republicanism.[15] The personal qualities of stability, accessibility, perseverance, and patriotism strengthened his hand as he transformed into a national symbol. The king's actions shaped public opinion, providing reassurance about the monarch's role. For example, George III opened the Queen's library at Buckingham House in the summer months for the "inspection of the curious." He was happily married and without a mistress, unusual for European monarchs. The British people celebrated his recovery from illness in 1789 with galas reminiscent of his coronation. Since George III never left England, he was always at home for his birthday, which resulted in grand celebrations and many commemorative items.[16] As such, the king's image managed to blend regality with domesticity.[17] The transformation of the monarch into a powerful patriotic symbol is an important, yet underappreciated, component of British political development. His executive leadership buttressed and reinforced Britain's larger political transformation to a republic in the guise of a monarchy.

George Washington's contribution to establishing a balance between the independent strength of executive power and the liberty promised by republican government began before his election as president. After the war ended, Washington wrote to Thomas Mifflin, his former military aide, to inquire about how to offer his resignation as commander-in-chief of the Continental Army so he could "regulate" his "Conduct accordingly."[18] Washington astutely recognized that his resignation strengthened the hand of liberty within the fledgling republic. This unprecedented surrender of executive power may indeed be the most influential act in the history of the American republic. By subordinating executive power, Washington made its return possible. It is altogether appropriate that John Trumbull's painting of Washington's resignation at Annapolis adorns the United States Capitol, the seat of representative government. Washington's action at Annapolis literally and figuratively undergirds the American republic, and the country learned from him that the resignation of power is as crucial to a republic's vitality as is its exercise.

In 1787, Constitutional Convention attendees knew that the United States needed a national executive to administer the growing duties of government. Nonetheless, the specter of tyranny shrouded discussions of the independent executive. By nature, republics are wary of instilling power in one person. The only previous example of unitary executive power, after all, was hereditary monarchy. Before the American founding, the single executive had never been republicanized.[19] As with George III, the personal virtue of Washington affected the outcome. The expectation that Washington would serve as the first president mollified the fears of most framers and those charged with ratification of the Constitution.[20] Nonetheless, Washington was cognizant that the written Constitution did not resolve many questions of authority and that precedent would be determinative.

Rather than the Madisonian "separated powers" system, Washington was an enthusiastic sup-

William L. Breton, *Residence of Washington in High Street, Philada*. Engraving. Published in John F. Watson, *Annals of Philadelphia* (Philadelphia: E. L. Carey & A. Hart, 1830).

Eighteen months into George Washington's presidency, the federal government moved from New York City to Philadelphia for a temporary ten-year period (1790-1800), while the permanent federal capital was under construction in Washington, DC. The president's house shown here was located just a couple of blocks north of Congress Hall, where the legislative branch met, and the Pennsylvania State House. Robert Morris—who along with Roger Sherman was one of just two people to sign the Declaration of Independence, the Articles of Confederation, and the Constitution—leased the building to the Washington family. The president had the house enlarged to lodge more than two dozen residents, including family members, government staff, servants, and enslaved workers. He hosted weekly state dinners and receptions on the first floor, and the cabinet met in a remodeled former bathroom on the second floor.

porter of the British "mixed government" model, blending the components of democracy, aristocracy, and monarchy.[21] He yearned for a strong central government with fewer impediments to action. As president, Washington looked for ways in which he could strengthen relationships between the branches of government. This led to the establishment of an "energetic" executive who exercised the powers outlined in the Constitution, but also took advantage of the silences and ambiguities in the document. For example, Article II, Section 3, Clause 1 states that the president of the United States "shall from time to time give to the Congress Information of the State of the Union, and recommend to their Consideration such Measures as he shall judge necessary and expedient." Washington issued his report annually in person as part of a Joint Session of Congress, thus establishing the precedent that eventually became the State of the Union address.

Washington was careful, however, to remember the underlying lesson in the resignation of his military commission: he deferred to and consulted with Congress. In his First Annual Address, he introduced legislative recommendations but did not order Congress to act.[22] Such cooperation institutionalized the American presidency in a manner consistent with the Cincinnatus republican myth that the denial of executive power enables its strengthening.[23] More important, Washington's actions fortified the stability of the nascent republican government.

The president of the United States combined the "head of government" and "head of state" roles, which remain separated in constitutional monarchy. The celebrations of George III's birthday disappeared in America, but localities replaced them with similar fêtes commemorating the birthday of an elected leader, George Washington. The demise of monarchical authority did not mean the end of celebrating national purpose as exemplified through executive power. On the contrary, Washington utilized the "traditions and trappings" of the British monarchy to promote civic attachment to the young republic and emphasize a unity of national purpose. This was accomplished through "courtly rituals," the "creation of a title for him," and the celebration of "popular political festivals honoring Washington."[24]

However, much like George III, as Washington's political career progressed, his reputation as a "patriot king" diminished. Once again, Washington found strength in the abdication of power. After two terms in office, he chose to retire from public life, returning to Mount Vernon as a private citizen. Washington's presidency demonstrated that the novel experiment of combining the principles of republican government with the strength of an independent executive could succeed.

Such a merger, however, was not and is not self-executing. There is nothing perpetual about democratic republics or constitutional monarchies. What can be learned from George III and George Washington, who found themselves charged with wholly new orders and expectations of representative government? The eminence of the two Georges did not originate in written or unwritten constitutions, nor from the establishment of historical precedents. Instead, they earned veneration through their established reputations. The British and American people bestowed their executive leaders with public trust to fortify the positions they occupied. In turn, George III assured the continuation of the monarchy in Britain and George Washington established the American presidency. Both republics and monarchies depend upon executives motivated by disinterestedness and the greater collective good. As true as it was in the eighteenth century, principled leadership in the executive remains an effective antidote to the insidious threat of authoritarianism, the enemy of all popular governments and the individual rights they preserve. ☀

— **Colleen Shogan**

William Westall, *Buckingham House: The East Front*, 1819. Watercolor and bodycolor over pencil.

In early 1762, shortly after he married, George III bought Buckingham House (1705) in the heart of London for Queen Charlotte, and it became their primary city residence. The king added the structures alongside the main building to accommodate his library and his many children, all of whom except the eldest were born here. During George's reign it was generally known as the Queen's House, and he held court at nearby St. James's Palace (1536). His son, George IV, greatly enlarged the house, transforming it into Buckingham Palace.

God Save the King and Long Live Washington: Coronation and Inauguration Days

Coronation of George III: Tuesday, September 22, 1761, Westminster Abbey, London

Inauguration of George Washington: Thursday, April 30, 1789, Federal Hall, New York City

The coronation of King George and the inauguration of George Washington were momentous occasions of similar purpose, but of completely different scale. George III, king for nearly a year, looked forward to what literally was his crowning moment, when he would be formally invested with the royal regalia; Washington, officially elected president several months before his inauguration, dreaded but accepted his date with presidential destiny. For both Georges, these ceremonies marked the public assumption of significant commitments, which each took seriously.

In Britain, archbishops of Canterbury had been crowning monarchs in Westminster Abbey since 1066 and elsewhere before that. The ancient ceremony was rooted in the oaths of good governance and ideals of kingship; modified over time, it was also a glittering spectacle. Above all, though, it was a Christian ceremony, with prayers, reading from scripture, and communion service. It bound together sovereign and subjects through presentation and recognition of the king, solemn pledges, and consecration of the monarch with holy oil. George III, just twenty-three years old and with a long reign ahead of him, promised to defend the church and uphold the law, and he would later remind his government ministers of his coronation oaths when he felt pressed on positions he had taken.

In the United States, the inauguration—initially at least—was brief and modest. Robert Livingston, the chancellor of New York and the highest-ranking judicial figure in the state, presided over the secular event, the first of its kind. The US Constitution provided little guidance on how to proceed; all that was required was that the president-to-be "solemnly swear that I will faithfully execute the office of President of the United States, and will to the best of my ability, preserve, protect and defend the Constitution of the United States." Washington, reluctantly coming out of retirement at fifty-seven, would be careful to carry out the oath he took that day, and his conscientiousness extended to the precedents he set as the first president.

In anticipation of George III's coronation, savvy homeowners near Westminster Abbey rented out their houses and spectators purchased seats on scaffolding from which to view the king's procession. Abbey officials sold tickets, with the best seats in the church going for ten guineas, a sum well out of reach for the average citizen. Package deals were also available; one advertisement announced: "Seats are to let in WESTMINSTER ABBEY, from the West Door to the Choir. Rooms are built for withdrawing, and the best refreshments provided, and every convenience studied that can make it fit for the reception of Ladies and Gentlemen." Those attending received dress code instructions that called for coronation robes and "Under-Habits of very rich Gold or Silver Brocades, white silk Stockings, and white Shoes."

On Coronation Day, King George and Queen Charlotte left St. James's Palace at 9 am traveling in sedan chairs to Westminster Hall. (The dazzling new 21-foot long, four-ton Gold State Coach that George had ordered was not yet ready.) Cheering crowds and yeoman guards lined the streets to watch the lengthy procession, which took an hour and a half to parade from the hall to Westminster Abbey, a journey that was usually just a two-minute walk.

Led by the king's herb-woman and her six maids, strewing flora and spices as they went, those following included richly adorned musicians, sheriffs, the privy council, chief justices of the courts, the Westminster children's choir, the master of the jewel house, knights, officials in the royal household, clergy, peers and peeresses, Great Officers of State, government ministers, the archbishops of York and Canterbury, the queen "in her Royal Robes of Crimson Velvet, on her head a circlet of Gold, adorned with Jewels" and her entourage; Princess Augusta, the king's mother; nobles carrying the king's regalia; his brothers, the royal dukes; and finally the king himself in a bright vermillion suit.

In a sparkling but exhausting six-hour ceremony steeped in history, symbolism, and music—eight lengthy anthems were performed—Thomas Secker, the archbishop of Canterbury, placed St. Edward's crown on George's head and the principal nobles, led by the king's brother Prince Edward, the Duke of York, pledged their allegiance to him. Restless, hungry attendees opened picnic baskets or sent out for meals, the consumption of which and the accompanying sound of cutlery echoed throughout the abbey.

Coronation regalia (1661) used by George III, September 22, 1761. Gold, rubies, amethysts, sapphires, emeralds, diamonds, and other gemstones, pearls, velvet, and ermine.

Nearly a year after George III took the throne, the Archbishop of Canterbury crowned the king and Queen Charlotte, his wife of two weeks, in a marathon coronation ceremony at Westminster Abbey. Through rituals dating to the tenth century and the use of the seventeenth-century coronation regalia, the king formed a covenant with his people. The regalia includes St. Edward's crown, a solid gold and bejeweled symbol of kingship; the sovereign's orb, standing for the monarch's authority in a Christian world; gold spurs, representing knighthood; the sovereign's scepter, in three parts, signifying worldly power and good governance; the eagle-shaped ampulla, containing holy oil; and a set of gold armills (bracelets).

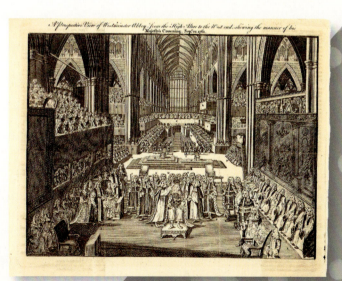

A Perspective View of Westminster Abbey from the High Altar . . . Showing the Manner of His Majesty's Crowning, ca. 1761. Engraving.

A King, a President, a Republic, and Executive Power 151

Despite the impressive pageantry, disorganization, missing items (the sword of state, canopies and chairs for the king and queen) and other mishaps plagued the coronation but shed light on George's character. Catherine Talbot, who lived in Secker's household, wrote that the heralds continually erred but the king "had much patience and good humour in bearing their numerous mistakes, and stupidities, as quickness and attention in setting them right." He had studied the proceedings and apparently knew the parts of others as well as his own, but the "confusion, irregularity, and disorder," as one attendee put it, led George to confront the organizer, the Earl of Effingham, who was acting in a hereditary post and might not have been the best person for the job. The earl allowed that there had been some failures, but he assured His Majesty that he would see to it that "the *next* coronation" went smoothly. (The next coronation was sixty years later, when the king, of course, was dead and the earl long gone.) Tickled by this disarming response, the king prompted Effingham to repeat the quip several more times that day.

The festivities concluded with a lavish banquet in Westminster Hall, lit with nearly three thousand candles. Tables were loaded with venison and a variety of game, and those seated in the galleries, who had paid to watch the dinner, lowered handkerchiefs tied together to those sitting below who filled them with provisions to be hauled back up. Later, the king's mounted champion, in white armor, entered the hall and threw down his gauntlet to challenge in combat anyone who denied that George III was the rightful king. After their majesties and guests had departed around 10 pm, crowds still waited outside, and as one account noted, "the hall doors were thrown open according to custom, when the people immediately cleared it of all moveables such as victuals, cloths, plates, dishes, etc. and, in short, everything that could stick to their fingers."

Twenty-eight years later and more than three thousand miles away, George Washington's inauguration as first president of the United States was an exercise in simplicity (and perhaps minimal planning on short notice), a decided effort not to mimic the grandeur of a coronation. The concept of an elected chief executive holding office only for a prescribed period, with powers defined and limited by a written constitution, was extraordinary in contrast to the world's prevailing model of hereditary leadership. Installation of a president called for a different approach, but one that captured the solemnity and significance of the moment. (Even so, despite Washington's efforts to appear respectable—rather than regal—some criticized him for veering into royal territory.) After decades of protest, warfare, and effort to forge a new system of government, the inauguration was also a celebratory affair and the president's swearing-in marked the second of three federal government branches at last churning into existence.

Washington left Mount Vernon on April 16, 1789, and "from Alexandria to George-Town he was attended by a voluntary company of private gentlemen—neighbors, friends and children of the man, who had saved their country and them," reported the *Gazette of the United States*. Staying at public inns and receiving rapturous welcomes along the way, Washington was tired of adulation when he arrived to great fanfare in New York City, the temporary federal capital, a week later. Meanwhile, Martha remained at Mount Vernon, taking her time organizing the household's relocation.

Inauguration Day opened to the sound of artillery fire and church bells. Washington rode from Franklin House, the newly rented presidential mansion on Cherry Street, to Federal Hall in a state coach accompanied by a procession of senators and representatives, a military escort, the French and Spanish ambassadors, and spectators who joined in.

Gathering in the Senate chamber, Washington and the inaugural party, including Vice President John Adams, dressed in their best suits, stepped out onto the second-floor balcony before a crowd that filled Broad and Wall Streets and assembled on neighboring rooftops. At 2 pm, Chancellor Livingston administered the efficient oath of office as Washington placed his hand upon a bible acquired in a last-minute panic from a nearby Masonic lodge. Livingston presented him to the crowd, declaring "Long live George Washington, president of the United States!" Washington acknowledged the cheers with a bow but did not speak, instead delivering his ten-minute inaugural address in a soft, shaking voice to Congress in the Senate chamber.

Chapter 5

Hartford Woolen Manufactory brown broadcloth coat, ca. 1780s, belonging to George Washington.

For his presidential inauguration on April 30, 1789, George Washington specially ordered a dark brown wool suit from Hartford, Connecticut, likely the one shown here, to wear on the occasion. He had two aims for the suit. First, he wanted to support local American "homespun" businesses, and the aggressive advertising campaign of the Hartford Woolen Manufactory had caught his eye. Marketing products with catchy names like "Congress Brown," the company promoted its goods as patriotic by virtue of their being made in America. In a letter to a company agent, Washington wrote "I shall always take a peculiar pleasure in giving every proper encouragement in my power to the manufactures of my Country." This propensity for domestic fabric extended to other leaders; John Adams and the entire Connecticut delegation also wore Hartford-made clothes to the inauguration.

Second, Washington did not want to appear as a king, and indeed the outfit was relatively simple. The suit was embellished only with buttons engraved with eagles on them. He also wore a dress sword, a symbol of his military career and future power as commander-in-chief. The bottom half of his suit was more stylish, with silk stockings and shoes with diamond buckles.

A King, a President, a Republic, and Executive Power

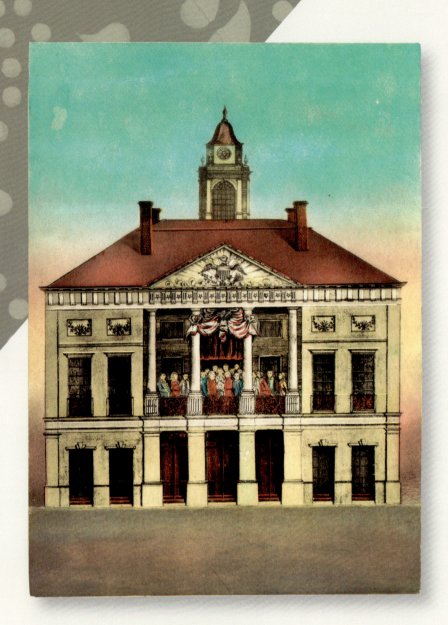

Amos Doolittle, *Federal Hall, N.Y. 1789 - First Capitol of the United States,* **1790. Engraving; hand colored after publication.**

George Washington taking the presidential oath of office.

Washington's speech addressed grand themes, such as national unity, as might be expected but it was also notably personal: he spoke of his "anxieties" in being chosen by the Electoral College to a position he had not sought, preferring to retire to Mount Vernon, "the asylum of my declining years;" his "conflict of emotions" in accepting the presidency; and being conscious of his "own deficiencies" in taking on the "weighty and untried cares before me." But he had returned to public life because he was "summoned by my Country, whose voice I can never hear but with veneration and love."

Afterward, Washington and the inaugural party attended a prayer service at St. Paul's Chapel. The new president then dined alone at Franklin House and closed out the day with Livingston and several others at Bowling Green watching a two-hour firework display that lit up Manhattan. The streets were so crammed with well-wishers and partygoers that the president of the United States of America could not return to Franklin House by coach and instead made his way home on foot.

The Patriot King: The Impossible Executive Ideal

King George III and George Washington ruled and governed under the auspices of a common ideal, attributed to Viscount Bolingbroke. A Tory, Bolingbroke grew concerned with corruption in British politics, especially during the ministry of Sir Robert Walpole. He wrote *The Idea of a Patriot King* in 1738, arguing that the remedy for such political problems was a virtuous monarch who could stand above factions, bribery, and private interest.

Eliminating partisan attachments was the keystone of the ideal. Bolingbroke stated, "To espouse no party, but to govern like the common father of his people, is so essential to the character of a Patriot King, that he who does otherwise forfeits the title." Before becoming the reigning monarch, George III studied the ideas contained in Bolingbroke's treatise and vowed to implement them. When he acceded to the throne in 1760, he averred, "I glory in the name of Britain."

Unfortunately, Bolingbroke's maxims were difficult to implement, particularly given that British constitutional government was continuing to evolve into a parliamentary democracy. For example, George III believed he should choose ministers based upon their moral virtue rather than whether they were able to maintain a stable legislative majority. This led to a particularly tumultuous time in British governance, punctuated by a revolving door of political leaders.

It is unclear whether George Washington ever read Bolingbroke. Nonetheless, he was clearly attuned to the principles of leadership contained in the treatise, particularly the emphasis on governing above faction or parties. As president, Washington attempted to emulate the ideals of the patriot king, but negotiating the growing political divide between the political factions represented by Thomas Jefferson and Alexander Hamilton proved impossible. Eventually, Washington moved toward Hamilton's Federalist faction in his second term of office, though he despised the perception that he had supported the nascent development of political parties in the United States.

Both George III and George Washington returned to the concept of the Patriot King near the end of their public lives. Washington famously warned against the "baneful effects of the spirit of party" in his 1796 Farewell Address. According to Washington, parties represented a "small but artful and enterprising minority of the community" and threatened to subvert public administration of the common good. The second half of George III's reign reflected a continued decline in the positive political power of the monarchy. But that decline coincided with a resuscitation of British patriotism, exemplified through the king and his family. Thus, the embodiment of virtue, a Bolingbroke ideal, bolstered the legacy of George III and helped to secure the longevity of the British monarchy.

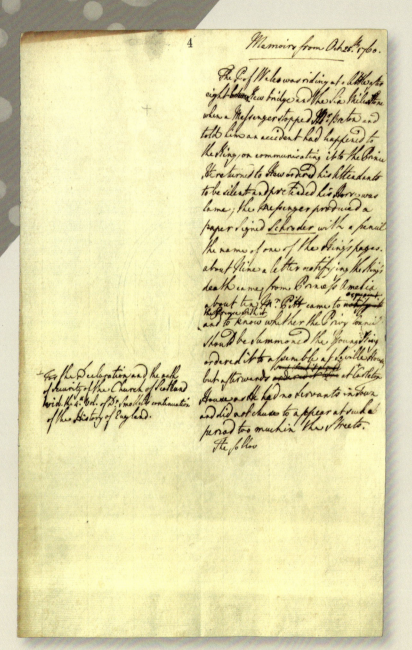

George III's memoir, in his own hand, on becoming king on October 25, 1760. Undated manuscript.

George, the Prince of Wales, was just twenty-two years old and out for an early morning horseback ride when his life irrevocably changed, as he knew it someday would. A messenger stopped the prince's companion, who passed word to George that "an accident had happened to the king." The prince returned to Kew when soon a message arrived from his Aunt Amelia, addressing him as "Your Majesty," and telling him her father, George II, was dead. Soon after, William Pitt the elder, cabinet leader, "came to acquaint the prince with it and to know whether the Privy Council should be summoned," wrote George III, referring to himself in third person. "The young King ordered it to assemble at Saville House but afterwards at Carleton House as he had no servants in town and did not choose to appear at such a period too much in the streets." Telling a friend of his sudden accession to the throne, he said simply, "A most extraordinary thing [has] just happened."

Creating the Presidency

After his inauguration in 1789, George Washington found himself as the popularly elected occupant of an office with no previously established precedents or established modes of order. The newly ratified Constitution painted broad strokes in Article II to create the American presidency while Washington was left to fill in the details concerning how the office would actually function.

Washington faced a difficult task. The decisions he made would establish practices that would be followed by future presidents, undoubtedly influencing the overall efficacy and success of the American experiment in republican government. To this end, Washington paid careful attention to the balance between democratic familiarity and monarchical splendor. The president was not a king, yet the office he occupied had been entrusted with embodying the national character of the newly formed United States.

To thread this needle, Washington proceeded deliberately, combining elements of British pomp and circumstance with new republican traditions. At the first inauguration, Washington wore a single-breasted suit woven in Connecticut rather than a military uniform. The open-air ceremony emphasized democratic citizenry rather than aristocratic nobility. As president, Washington received public guests twice a week; a levee for men on Tuesdays and tea parties for both sexes on Friday afternoons. In his first term, he visited every state, reminiscent of a kingly tour of the realm, but with the goal to become more accessible to citizens. Washington gave his annual address to Congress in person, not unlike the British monarch's tradition of speaking to Parliament. However, in the British tradition, parliamentarians stood when the monarch spoke. When Washington began to speak in the Senate chamber, members of Congress were seated, indicating their status as a co-equal branch of government.

As president, Washington exercised republican powers with monarchical origins. He vetoed a bill in 1792, discharged his role as commander-in-chief, and issued the first presidential pardon in 1795. In all of these actions, Washington was acutely aware of the strong criticism that had emerged during the Constitutional Convention about the single executive. Edmund Randolph of Virginia had described the presidency as the "fetus of monarchy." As he fulfilled his official duties, Washington carefully blended British precedent with democratic sensibilities, thus creating a wholly new republican executive.

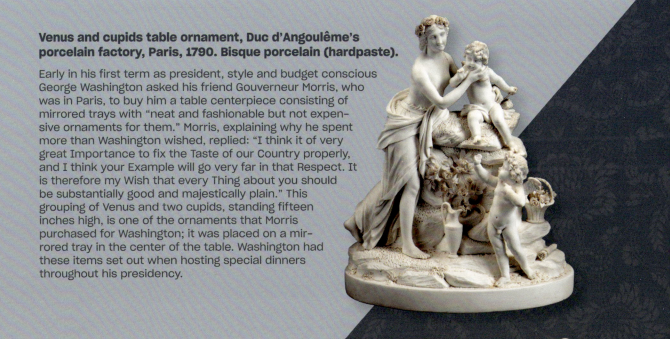

Venus and cupids table ornament, Duc d'Angoulême's porcelain factory, Paris, 1790. Bisque porcelain (hardpaste).

Early in his first term as president, style and budget conscious George Washington asked his friend Gouverneur Morris, who was in Paris, to buy him a table centerpiece consisting of mirrored trays with "neat and fashionable but not expensive ornaments for them." Morris, explaining why he spent more than Washington wished, replied: "I think it of very great Importance to fix the Taste of our Country properly, and I think your Example will go very far in that Respect. It is therefore my Wish that every Thing about you should be substantially good and majestically plain." This grouping of Venus and two cupids, standing fifteen inches high, is one of the ornaments that Morris purchased for Washington; it was placed on a mirrored tray in the center of the table. Washington had these items set out when hosting special dinners throughout his presidency.

A King, a President, a Republic, and Executive Power

King George Considers Early Retirement

"America is lost!" a devastated George III began an undated essay, mimicking one written by Arthur Young, following the British surrender at Yorktown and Parliament's decision to stop prosecuting the war. The humiliating and unfathomable loss of wealth and prestige prompted the king to consider abdicating. Then, in early 1783, the Fox-North coalition of opposing Whigs and Tories ousted Lord Shelburne's government for the purpose of assuming power, despite no chance of long-term cooperation with each other. This bizarre alliance, under the nominal heading of the Duke of Portland, appalled the king, who had long despised the pro-America Charles James Fox and was now estranged from Lord North, his once-cherished former prime minister. Unwilling to accept such a government and still grappling with a new world order, George again considered giving up the throne, leaving the dais of a reduced empire for the near obscurity of a place he had never been, his family's ancestral home in Hanover.

In his drafted but undelivered message to Parliament, the king blamed the Shelburne ministry's collapse on bad actors unwilling to put the good of the country first. He expressed the hope that his abdication, an astonishing act of martyrdom, would prompt Parliament to rally around a fresh new monarch, paving the way to a stable government.

His message read, in part:

> I cannot at the most serious, as well as most painful moment of My Life, go out of the Great Assembly, without communicating to You My Intentions, not asking Your Advice.
>
> The first time I appeared as Your Sovereign in this place now above twenty-two years, I had the pleasing hope that being born among You, I might have proved the happy instrument of conciliating all Parties and thus collecting to the Service of the State the most respectable and most able Persons this Kingdom produced. Of this object I have never lost sight, though sad experience now teaches me that selfish Views are so prevalent that they have smothered the first of Public Virtues, attachment to the Country . . .
>
> A long Experience and a serious attention to the Strange Events that have successively arisen, has gradually prepared my Mind to expect the time when I should be no longer of Utility to this Empire: that hour is now come; I am therefore resolved to resign My Crown and all the Dominions appertaining to it to the Prince of Wales my Eldest Son and Lawful Successor and to retire to the care of My Electoral Dominions the Original Patrimony of my Ancestors.

George III did not give up the crown, but the fact that he even pondered it illuminates the depth of his despair and frustration. He might have written this piece as a cathartic exercise or to force government officials to do his bidding to avoid an unfortunate abdication. In any event, within weeks of drafting this message, the king gritted his teeth, held his nose, and reluctantly accepted the Fox-North government. It failed before the year was out, and George remained on his throne—for another thirty-seven years. ☀

"America is Lost!" from essay by George III, undated.

Chapter 5

Excerpt from George III's draft of an abdication message to Parliament, March 1783.

that hour is now come; I am therefore resolved to resign My Crown and all the Dominions appertaining to it to the Prince of Wales my Eldest Son and Lawful Successor and to retire to the care of My Electoral Dominions the Original Patrimony of my Ancestors. For which purpose I shall Draw up and Sign an Instrument to which I shall affix my Private Seal. I trust

A King, a President, a Republic, and Executive Power

When John Adams Met George III

George Washington never met George III, but other founders did indeed meet the king. In 1785, the Confederation Congress appointed John Adams the first US minister to Great Britain. When he learned of his new position, Adams wrote to an acquaintance, "I know not whether I shall meet a candid or even a decent Reception in England. It is not to be expected that I should be cherished and beloved." Only nine years previously, Adams had been on the committee of the Continental Congress that had drafted the Declaration of Independence. Now, after lengthy fratricidal warfare, he had the uncomfortable task of coming face-to-face with his former king. How the king would respond to a leader of the recent rebellion was an open question.

After arriving in May and presenting his credentials to the minister of foreign affairs, the Marquis of Carmarthen, Adams received an invitation to meet George III on June 1. Inauspiciously, it was raining that day. Carmarthen explained that Adams must bow to the king upon entering the room, as he approached the king, and a third time once he stood in front of the king. He also told Adams that it was customary for ministers to give a brief but courteous speech.

Upon entering the chamber, Adams did the requisite bows, but due to nerves, mumbled his speech. He stated his assignment as minister plenipotentiary was "to cultivate the most friendly and liberal Intercourse … between People who, tho Seperated by an Ocean and under different Governments have the Same Language, a Similar Religion and kindred Blood."

What King George said in response is in minor dispute, because Adams wrote down three slightly different versions. Exact wording aside, the king expressed his pleasure that John Adams was chosen US minister and acknowledged that Adams's conduct during the war was out of duty to his country. His Majesty said that while he was the last person to agree to the separation of the colonies from Britain, he would be the first to greet the United States of America as a friend. The king ended by echoing Adams' observation that the two countries' shared culture would be the bedrock of a new relationship.

In a letter to Thomas Jefferson, Adams wrote that the meeting went better than he had expected. "The Mission was treated by his Majesty with all the Respect, and the Person of with all the Kindness, which would have been expected or reasonably desired."

The British press was less forgiving. The London *Morning Herald and Daily Advertiser* wrote "An Ambassador from America! Good heavens what a sound!" and continued to say that "tis hard to say which can excite indignation most, the insolence of those who appoint the [ambassador], or the meanness of those who receive it." The *Times* noted the irony that Adams "who was formerly proscribed as a *rebel* to this country, now appears invested with all the privileges and rank *annexed* to the representative of a free state; and the title of *Excellency* is now substituted by those very persons who formerly stiled him *traitor*."

This vitriol did not go by unnoticed by Abigail Adams, who remarked, "The Tory venom has begun to spit itself forth in the publick papers as I expected, bursting with envy that an American Minister should be received here with the same marks of attention, politeness, and civility which is shewn to the Ministers of any other power."

Though George III had every reason to show disdain for Adams, like the press did, that he instead treated him just as he would any other diplomat emphasized his ability to put his duty to his country over any personal feelings of resentment.

Gilbert Stuart,
John Adams, ca. 1800-1815.
Oil on canvas.

John Adams to Thomas Jefferson, June 3, 1785. In Adams' secretary's hand.

> to the Court of Great Britain. The Mission was treated by his Majesty with all the Respect, and the Person with all the Kindness, which could have been expected or reasonably desired, and with much more, I confess than was in fact expected by me.

Abigail Adams and the Two Georges

Gilbert Stuart, *Abigail Smith Adams (Mrs. John Adams)*, ca. 1800-1815. Oil on canvas.

Abigail Adams was one of only a few people to attend the court of King George III in London and the "republican court" of George Washington in New York, and to describe them both. In letters to her family, she revealed what it felt like, as the wife of the first US minister to Great Britain, to represent a new country to its old enemy. And then, as the wife of the first vice president of the United States, to help re-create a scene that both was and was not like the Court of St. James.

In June 1785, a few weeks after John Adams was presented to King George, Abigail Adams went to St. James's Palace in London to be presented herself. The king, she wrote her son, John Quincy Adams, on June 26, "look'd very jovial and good humourd when I was presented to him," but she felt sorry for Queen Charlotte, whom she thought seemed "embarrassed and confused," and their daughters. "To have to go round to every person and find something to say to all," she wrote of the princesses, "is paying dearly for their Rank. They do it however with great affability, and give general satisfaction, but I could not help reflecting with myself during the ceremony, what a fool do I look like to be thus accutored and stand here for 4 hours together, only for to be spoken too, by 'royalty.'"

What Abigail Adams perceived as confusion and embarrassment on the part of the queen was, as Charlotte's own letters express, real unhappiness. In January 1797, after enduring decades of court assemblies, the shy queen wrote her husband that she "found the Fatigue almost too much for me, & at times was so spent that the Princesses can witness how often I was inclined to beg leave of you to be excused the going out on Wednesday evening & Thursdays to court."

In 1789, John Adams was elected vice president of the United States and Abigail Adams became a central participant in the Friday evening levees hosted by Martha Washington. Once critical of the pomp she witnessed in London, Abigail Adams now agreed with her husband when he advised George Washington that an American president was justified in projecting "splendor and majisty." In a letter to her sister on January 5, 1790, she described the hierarchical seating arrangement at these events, and offered a glimpse of the president defending her place near Martha. She jabbed at those who, arguing that Americans should not uphold "distinction" between social classes, criticized the Washingtons' assemblies as too regal.

The room, she wrote, "was as much crowded as a Birth Night at St James, and with company as Briliantly drest, diamonds & great hoops excepted my station is always at the right hand of Mrs W. [T]hrough want of knowing what is right, I find it some times occupied, but on such an occasion the President never fails of Seeing that it is relinquishd for me, and having removed Ladies Several times, they have now learnt to rise & give it me, but this between our selves, as all *distinction* you know is unpopular." ☀

Joseph Brant: Mohawk Leader

Joseph Brant (Thayendanegea) was a Mohawk leader of the Haudenosaunee (the Six Nations of the Iroquois Confederacy) and a British military officer. Born in the Ohio region in 1743, Brant was a charismatic and complex figure fluent in multiple languages and cultures, who sought to unify his people against American encroachment on their land. He regarded the Americans as a greater threat than the British, who in the Proclamation of 1763 prohibited westward settlement beyond the Appalachian Mountains.

Brant travelled to England in 1775 hoping to get British assistance for Haudenosaunee losses in the French and Indian War and to secure their lands. He met briefly with George III, was the toast of London, and came to an understanding with Lord Germain, the colonial secretary, that Haudenosaunee grievances would be dealt with after the American rebellion was snuffed out.

Brant fought alongside his Loyalist allies, and after his Seneca warriors joined British units in attacking a settlement in Cherry Valley, New York, in 1778, General Washington announced an award for his capture. Washington referred to Brant as a leader of "Banditti" that continually harassed American frontiers, erroneously blaming him for atrocities committed by others, and ordered wholesale destruction of Indian villages in revenge. The Haudenosaunee bitterly called Washington *Hanödaga:yas, or* "Town Destroyer." In 1792, a decade after the war ended, Brant and other tribal leaders met in Philadelphia with their former enemy, who had become the president of the United States. Washington now described him as "the celebrated Captain Joseph Brant" and sought to express "the equitable intentions of this government toward *all* the nations of his colour." Brant was dubious.

At a subsequent meeting of Shawnees and Delawares at the rapids of the Miami River in Ohio, Brant warned them to be wary of Washington: "I desire you Brothers Shawnees and Nephews Delawares

John Raphael Smith, *Joseph Fayadaneega [Thayendanegea], Called the Brant, the Great Captain of the Six Nations,* **ca. 1776. Mezzotint.**

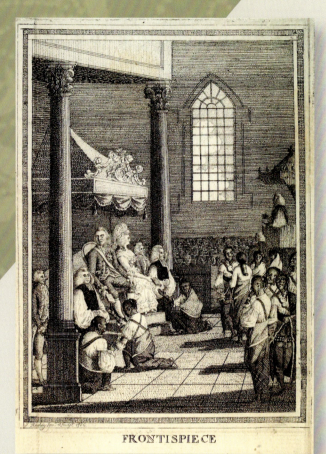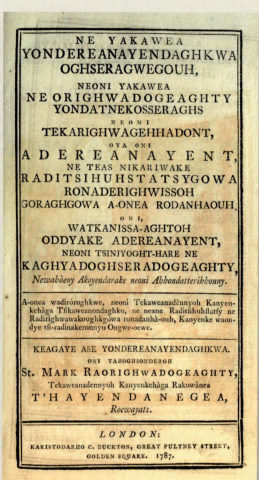

The Book of Common Prayer and the Gospel According to St Mark; translated into the Mohawk language. Frontispiece and title page. London: Printed by C. Buckton, 1787.

This edition of the Church of England's *Book of Common Prayer* appears in the Kanyen'kéha language, as it had before, but "To Which Is Added the Gospel According to St. Mark, Translated into the Mohawk Language, by Captain Joseph Brant, An Indian of the Mohawk Nation." Brant was a firm Anglican, and in the preface to the book, the Society for Propagation of the Gospel in Foreign Parts noted that His Majesty King George "was pleased to express much satisfaction" that the publication, paid for by his government, would be "for the use of the Mohawks." The book was also known as the "Mowhawk bible."

This edition was published two years after Brant's second meeting with George III, in 1785, and the frontispiece illustrates that event, as the Mohawk leader and his companions are presented to the king and queen. Brant also met with the home secretary, dined with the Prince of Wales, and posed for portraits, leaving England with some £15,000 for his people and a clear signal that British military assistance against rapacious American land grabbers would not be forthcoming.

to take care and be aware of what we are about—General Washington is very cunning, he will try to fool us if he can—he speaks very smooth, will tell you fair stories, and at the same time want to ruin us—Perhaps in a few days, he may send out a flag—that will be only to blindfold us.—It will not do for one man to turn about and listen to that flag—We must be all at it, as we are all united as one man."

Although Brant was able to secure some land for the Mohawks and spent the rest of his life working for their interests, neither King George nor President Washington fully satisfied his requests. Disheartened, he and his family ultimately left the United States for Canada, where he died in 1807.

William Birch, *New Lutheran Church in Fourth Street, Philadelphia*, 1804. Hand-colored etching and engraving.

This image, which first appeared in William Birch's landmark book, *The City of Philadelphia, in the State of Pennsylvania North America; As It Appeared in the Year 1800*, depicts a Native American delegation visiting the city, then the US capital. Such delegations were common as Indian tribes sought treaties to protect their interests and shriveling territory. George Washington attended services at the New Lutheran Church seen here (also known as the Zion Lutheran or German Lutheran church).

A King, a President, a Republic, and Executive Power

Escaping from George and Martha

When the federal government moved from New York City to Philadelphia in 1790, George Washington faced an obstacle as a slaveholder. Ten years earlier, Pennsylvania's legislature was the first to pass a slavery abolition act. The Gradual Abolition Act emancipated any enslaved person born in Pennsylvania after its passage when they reached the age of twenty-eight or any enslaved person brought into the state, of any age, after they lived there for six months. However, it exempted people already legally enslaved in Pennsylvania, as well as people held by members of Congress who were living in Philadelphia.

Thus, when the Washington family moved to Philadelphia, it was unclear if this exception applied to the people enslaved by the presidential family. On the advice of attorney general Edmund Randolph, the Washingtons set up a system whereby they rotated their enslaved workers between their house in Philadelphia and their Mount Vernon estate to skirt the six-month limit—even though this violated a 1788 amendment that sought to close such a loophole. The Washingtons were never prosecuted for this, and the issue of whether the law pertained to the president remained unsettled.

Despite Washington's precautions, the people he enslaved nonetheless found the allure of freedom while living in the north inviting, given the free Black community that was there. Washington, in turn, did not hesitate to recapture enslaved workers who escaped. Back in 1761 he had advertised in the *Maryland Gazette* for the capture of four enslaved men, Cupid, Jack, Neptune, and Peres, who had fled from Mount Vernon. Now as president, he had his household steward, Frederick Kitt, place this advertisement (opposite) for the return of an enslaved young woman named Ona "Oney" Judge who had escaped from the executive mansion.

Centuries later, these advertisements serve a purpose different from the one Washington intended: they preserve information that, even though it comes from an unfriendly source, is still a valuable record of the lives of five people, including details about their appearance, characters, and histories. The names of the four men, however, conceal more than they reveal. Owners often gave their African slaves classical first names, and they rarely recognized their slaves' last names adopted in America. In contrast, Washington's ad for Ona Judge, who was born in Virginia to an enslaved mother and a white father, includes her first and last names.

In the older advertisement, Washington wrote that the four men "went off without the least Suspicion, Provocation, or Difference with any Body." In 1796 he, or Kitt on his behalf, also expressed bafflement, even using the same language, writing that Judge's escape "happened without the least provocation." Even though Washington came to believe that slavery ought to be abolished, he never accepted that theft of liberty was more than enough provocation for people held in bondage.

Washington recovered the four men, but he never recaptured Ona Judge. After walking out of the president's house in Philadelphia, she traveled by boat to New Hampshire, where she spent the rest of her life as a free woman.

Advertisement for Ona Judge, *Claypoole's American Daily Advertiser*, May 24, 25, 27, 1796.

Ten Dollars Reward.

ABSCONDED from the household of the President of the United States, on Saturday afternoon, ONEY JUDGE, a light Mulatto girl, much freckled, with very black eyes, and bushy black hair—She is of middle stature, but slender and delicately made, about 20 years of age. She has many changes of very good clothes of all sorts, but they are not sufficiently recollected to describe.

As there was no suspicion of her going off, and it happened without the least provocation, it is not easy to conjecture whither she is gone—or fully, what her design is; but as she may attempt to escape by water, all masters of vessels and others are cautioned against receiving her on board, altho' she may, and probably will endeavour to pass for a free woman, and it is said has, wherewithal to pay her passage.

Ten dollars will be paid to any person, (white or black) who will bring her home, if taken in the city, or on board any vessel in the harbour; and a further reasonable sum if apprehended and brought home, from a greater distance, and in proportion to the distance.   FRED. KITT, Steward.

May 24   ¶3

Slave Trade Legislation: Slow, Sure, and Imperceptible

George Eyre and Andrew Strahan, "An Act for the Abolition of the Slave Trade," in *A Collection of the General Statutes Passed in the 47th year of the Reign of His Majesty King George III*, **March 25, 1807.**

Britain and the United States abolished the international slave trade (but not slavery) roughly in parallel. The US Constitution, drafted in 1787, over which George Washington presided, allowed the international slave trade to continue.

Washington's annotated copy of a draft of the federal Constitution, below, indicates that the delegates had agreed upon a clause prohibiting the ban on the importation of slaves until 1808 (see the first clause of section 9). This clause, delaying legislation on the slave trade for twenty years, aligned with Washington's view, expressed in 1786, that he wished slavery would be ended by "slow, sure, & imperceptable degrees."

In 1789, British abolitionist and member of Parliament William Wilberforce first proposed elimination of the British slave trade, but Parliament did not pass the Slave Trade Act until 1806. Submitting to political reality, George III signed it, even though he believed the British colonial system depended on slavery. The act went into effect in 1807 (the published version is at left).

Meanwhile, in December 1806, in his annual message to Congress, President Thomas Jefferson, recognizing that the twenty-year ban was expiring, called on Congress to fulfill the terms of the Constitution and end the international slave trade. In January 1807 Congress did so, passing An Act Prohibiting Importation of Slaves, to take effect in 1808.

Despite the end of the slave trade, enslavers, including Jefferson and Washington and Custis family members, continued to legally buy, sell, and own people in the United States and the British Caribbean. Britain finally passed a bill prohibiting slavery in its West Indian colonies in 1833, while in the United States legal slavery ended after the Civil War with ratification of the Thirteenth Amendment in 1865.

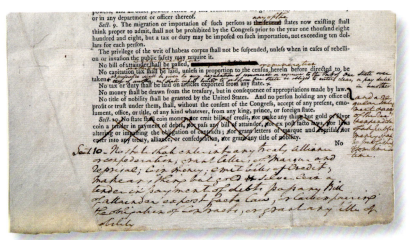

George Washington, *Draft United States Constitution, Report of the Committee of Style, Article 1, Section 9, page 2 on the abolition of the slave trade*, **ca. September 8 and 12, 1787.**

George and George, Church and State

The two Georges were both Anglicans but of very different sorts. Personally, the king was free and open in sharing his religious beliefs; Washington was circumspect. The king remained steadfast in his faith, but Washington's views were nuanced and evolving. Politically, George III was the executive head of the Church of England and "defender of the faith," having promised at his coronation to protect the state church. His subjects were overwhelmingly Anglican, with tiny minorities of Dissenters, Catholics (except in Ireland, where they prevailed) and Jews; and a mix of Presbyterians, Baptists, and small sects in Scotland. In the new United States, Protestant denominations were dominate and varied, but other faiths were practiced as well and there was no official state religion. As president, Washington was ecumenical in his relations with religious groups, promoting tolerance and supporting a strong wall between church and state.

In the sixteenth and seventeenth centuries, Parliament, fearful of papal influence and interference, passed penal laws that prohibited Catholics from practicing their religion, voting, owning land and other valuable property, or serving in public office. But in the later eighteenth century, with the Protestant Hanoverians securely on the throne and Pope Clement XIII's acknowledgment of George III as Britain's king, there was less concern about Catholic participation in public life. Yet the penal laws remained on the books, and Prime Minister William Pitt sought to repeal them. Despite having Catholic friends, George III believed that as defender of the faith, it was his sworn duty to oppose revocation of the laws, stating that "I had rather beg my bread from door to door throughout Europe than consent to any such measure."

Nevertheless, Parliament passed the Catholic Relief Act in 1791, granting Catholics freedom of worship, the right to operate their own schools, to hold minor public offices, and even to reside in London. The king objected to Catholics holding high public office and military positions, but he was tolerant of their private faith. Following the union of Ireland and Britain in 1801, Pitt's efforts to expand Catholic rights were an attempt to win over the Irish public, but he could not win over his king. George worried that if Catholics entered Parliament, they would join forces with his greatest opponents, the radical Whigs. Eventually, the king extracted a promise from Pitt, whom he respected immensely, not to raise the issue again. After George III's death, the Catholic Emancipation Act of 1829 nullified nearly all the remaining penal laws.

In the American colonies, religion was a constant and intense presence of tremendous variety, born out of a history of religious freedom. During the Revolutionary War, Washington attended army chaplain services and encouraged soldiers to do so as well. After the war, and for reasons he kept to himself, he stopped receiving communion, but he sensed that he had a certain calling in life having survived two wars and multiple serious illnesses. He returned home to a changing religious landscape, as the Anglican Church in America, which had once prayed for and pledged loyalty to George III, transformed into the Episcopal Church and ceased being the official church of Virginia.

Washington's military and political careers exposed him to a breadth of religious practices and viewpoints, and it reinforced his support for religious pluralism. As president he corresponded with numerous congregations, and in 1790 he famously assured the Jewish community in Newport, Rhode Island, that "happily the Government of the United States … gives to bigotry no sanction, to persecution no assistance." Respectful of both the faithful and the non-believer, Washington despised religious zealotry and took care to remind his fellow Americans in his 1796 presidential Farewell Address "that morality can be maintained without religion."

Farmer George, John Bull, and All the Rest: George III in Caricature

George III's reign coincided with what historians have dubbed the golden age of caricature. The British Museum has more than ten thousand unique prints from 1760 to 1830, and an additional two thousand not in their catalog appear in the British cartoon collection, which the Library of Congress purchased from the royal collection at Windsor Castle in 1921. Cartoons from this era usually had print runs of 500 to 1,500 copies; black-and-white prints generally sold for one shilling and those in color for two. They were sold in bookshops, print shops, and coffee houses, and their dimensions often conformed to the windowpanes of such establishments, where they attracted public attention.

Famous caricaturists of the day included James Gillray, Isaac Cruikshank and his sons George and Robert, and Thomas Rowlandson. These men (and they were overwhelmingly men, though women such as Gillray's publisher and landlord Hannah Humphrey did play roles) owed a debt of gratitude to William Hogarth, whose series *A Harlot's Progress* and *A Rake's Progress* in the 1730s had established a tradition of British satirical engravings. These artists used subtlety and symbols for references. For example, Charles James Fox, who came to power as a Whig in 1782 in opposition to the king's policies, often wore a coat of buff and blue to mimic George Washington's army uniform; cartoons regularly portrayed him as a literal fox dressed in such clothes. Other cartoons used crude humor to get their point across. Gillray's famous 1793 cartoon, *The French Invasion, or John Bull Bombarding the Bum-Boats*, depicts the king as the geographic outline of England defecating boats across the English Channel at the French coast. The title is a play on the word "bumboat," a small ship used to ferry supplies to larger vessels.

Despite these occasional lewd cartoons, caricaturists enjoyed relative freedom in mocking the royal family and government officials. Unlike other countries in Europe, Britain had a strong tradition of freedom of the press. The law allowing pre-publication censorship of prints had lapsed in 1695. Lawsuits for libel against caricaturists and printers were rare in the late eighteenth century, especially compared with book authors, in part because such a precedent had yet to be set. Though the threat of prosecution would grow in the 1790s as the royal family was increasingly on edge after the French Revolution, they gave tacit approval to these prints *because* of the revolution. As historian Kenneth Baker notes on British caricatures of the Georgian era: "when British people can laugh at their monarchs they do not cut off their heads."

Of all the public figures ridiculed during this period, none received as much direct attention from the satirists as King George did. Caricatures of him were so common that he became the first British monarch that the public could identify by sight. Cartoonists commented on both his personal and public life, whether it was false allegations that his mother was having an affair with Lord Bute, the revolving slate of government ministries in the 1760s, his perceived miserliness, his failure to keep the American colonies, or his piety. This lampooning of George as an authority figure tapped into a widespread, albeit not universal, dislike of George. (Even musicians were disdainful: London theaters only played "God Save the King" four times from 1760 to 1781). As well-traveled cleric John Wesley wrote in 1775 on the eve of the war with America: "The bulk of the people in every city, town and village … heartily despise his Majesty, and hate him with a perfect hatred."

Still, in the years succeeding the American Revolution, the satires became gentler, "God Save the King" was performed much more frequently, and George's popularity rose significantly. A combination of the steadiness of William Pitt as prime minister, the public's empathy through the king's illness of 1788–89, and the increasing threat posed by Revolutionary and Napoleonic France coalesced into George's transformation as a symbol of British resoluteness. He often was depicted as John Bull, the national everyman, or as Farmer George, a homespun friendly agrarian (see page 76). In 1809, Samuel Romilly, a Whig member of Parliament, stated "From the beginning of his reign to the close of the American War, he was one of the most unpopular princes that ever sat upon the throne. He is now one of the most popular."

By contrast, George Washington was more or less universally beloved by the public at large throughout his career as general and then president. Even the British respected him. One of the few British political

 Chapter 5

cartoons during the American Revolution to depict Washington portrayed him without exaggeration or caricaturizing his features (see page 137). Such respect for a foreign adversary did not extend to Napoleon during his later forays against the British.

The king mostly enjoyed the caricatures, amassing a large collection of prints—even the particularly nasty ones or those that depicted him as a commoner. His three eldest sons and two of his daughters also collected prints by the leading satirists. During the king's health crisis in 1788, the Prince of Wales used the art form to bolster the argument for a regency. He hired Thomas Rowlandson to create anonymous prints supporting his rule as regent, countering caricatures—some even by Rowlandson himself!—that had lampooned the prince's own faults.

Despite the king's enjoyment of cartoons, some of their subtle references perhaps went over his head. In March 1788, Fanny Burney recorded that the previous month she and some other members of the court were laughing at a cartoon by Henry Bunbury (who also was an equerry to George's son, the Duke of York), when "His Majesty entered the room; and, after looking at [the print] a little while, with much entertainment, he took it away to show it to the Queen and Princesses." The print contained oblique references to the illegal marriage of the Prince of Wales, something that would have not have amused the king if he had fully understood the cartoon.

Nevertheless, George admired the ability of the satirists to draw notable figures of the day. A popular anecdote recorded in an 1830 memoir showed that the king appreciated Gillray's work. Reviewing a traditional portrait of Charles James Fox by Joshua Reynolds, the king said, "Sir Joshua's picture is finely painted, a fine specimen of art;—but Gillray is the better limner. Nobody hits off Mr. Fox like him—Gillray is the man—for the *man of the people*. Hey! My Lord—hey! Like as my profile on a tower halfpenny—hey!" Charles Knight, the son of a bookseller whose shop George visited in Windsor, wrote in his memoirs that satires of the king "were more likely to provoke the laughter of his family, than to suggest any desire to stifle the poor jests by those terrors of the law which might have

James Gillray, *The King of Brobdingnag and Gulliver.-Vide. Swift's Gulliver: Voyage to Brobdingnag*, June 26, 1803. Hand-colored etching and aquatint. Published by Hannah Humphrey.

In one of his most famous cartoons, James Gillray contrasts George III and the diminutive Napoleon Bonaparte. The king tells the French general he is "one of the most pernicious, little odious reptiles, that nature ever suffer'd to crawl upon the surface of the Earth," a line inspired by the King of Brobdingnag in Jonathan Swift's 1726 novel *Gulliver's Travels*. Gillray included a version of this caricature in the background of his later cartoon, *Very Slippy-Weather* (see next page).

A King, a President, a Republic, and Executive Power

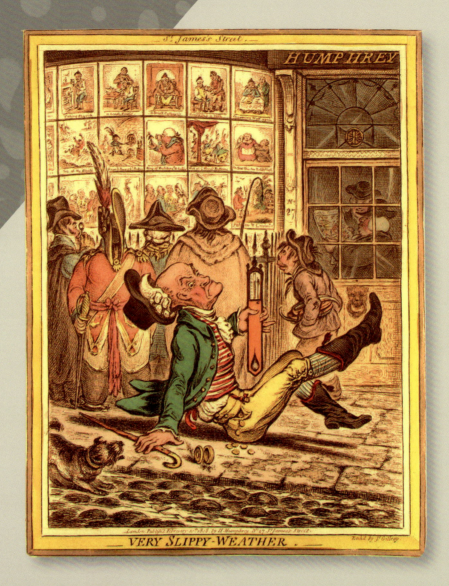

James Gillray, V*ery Slippy-Weather*, February 10, 1808. Hand-colored etching. Published by Hannah Humphrey.

In this very meta cartoon, James Gillray (1756-1815) depicts a scene outside 27 St. James's Street, the location of his publisher Hannah Humphrey's print shop. Despite a man falling down, his coins cascading to the ground and his hat and wig falling off his head, five people stare intently at Humphrey's window, where each pane is covered by a real Gillray print. Most prominent of these cartoons, in the middle of the second row, is *The King of Brobdingnag and Gulliver* depicting George III staring at a miniature Napoleon who stands on the palm of the king's hand. Establishments such as Humphrey's readily advertised their wares in this manner. Such displays proved to be a haven for pickpockets, whose victims were easily distracted by the cartoons, as evidenced by the oblivious crowd in this print.

Humphrey (ca. 1745-1818) was one of the most successful publishers of satirical prints during the reign of George III. She published around 650 by Gillray, approximately 70 percent of his output, and he worked exclusively with her starting in 1791. She also rented a room to him at 27 St. James's where he lived for the last twenty years of his life. Around the time George III was confined to Windsor due to his mental instability, Gillray also experienced bouts of insanity. In July 1811, he attempted suicide by jumping out of Humphrey's attic window. Although he survived, he spent the last four years of his life in her care.

been easily commanded. … The daubs of the caricaturist provoked no contempt for 'Farmer George and his Wife.'"

There were limits to his magnanimity, however. He particularly took exception when his mother was attacked, especially the rumors involving Lord Bute. In July 1756, he wrote Bute that "They have also treated my Mother in a cruel manner (which I shall never forget nor forgive to the day of my death). I do therefore here in the presence of Our Almighty Lord promise that I will remember the insults, and never will forgive anyone who shall venture to speak disrespectfully of her." In addition, the royal family, especially the Prince of Wales, occasionally bought all copies and the printing plate of particularly sensitive prints to prevent their dissemination. One such suppressed print from 1811 depicted the Prince Regent being punched in the face by Lord Yarmouth as Lady Yarmouth emerges from behind a screen (festooned with caricatures, in fact). He also sometimes bribed printmakers to halt production of scurrilous prints.

These efforts increased upon the regent's accession as George IV in 1820. However, while the caricaturists continued in the succeeding decade, it was a swansong for the genre. By 1830, when William IV became king, the popularity of political prints had waned; artists were instead focusing on book, magazine, and newspaper illustration. But it had been a remarkable seventy-year run of political satire. Reflecting on the golden age and its key figure George III, satirist Peter Pindar punned, "The King has been a good subject to me, but I have been a bad subject to his Majesty." ☀

The Georges' Cabinets

As king and president respectively, George III and George Washington were each advised by a cabinet, a group of counselors who provided guidance, research, and headed various departments and staffs of their own. Though the British and American versions differed in particulars—the British cabinet called its members "ministers," the American cabinet called its members "secretaries"—they shared common traits that aided the executives in their quest for principled leadership. Each leader played key roles in shaping their cabinets. During George III's reign, the power of the cabinet consolidated, with the role of the prime minster becoming enshrined. As the first president, Washington organized the original American cabinet, thus establishing a precedent followed to this day.

The British cabinet had its origins in the privy council, members of Parliament who advised the monarch. The name cabinet originated from the small room, or cabinet, where they met, and the first usage of "cabinet" to refer to the body of advisers dates to 1644. In the aftermath of the Glorious Revolution (1688), the cabinet grew in importance. Although it was met with distrust in certain political corners, which viewed it as a cabal operating in the shadows, it nonetheless became enshrined in custom, if not law, by the middle of the eighteenth century.

Around that time, the role of the prime minister emerged. This minister, who usually was the first lord of the treasury, led the cabinet in the execution of its powers and liaised with the king. Robert Walpole, who served as first lord of the treasury from 1721 to 1742, is considered the first prime minister, though he personally rejected the title; indeed, it was his opponents who used it to attack him for having too much power. Several of George III's early chief ministers eschewed the title as well.

George III initially found that the responsibility of choosing ministers was a burden. In his first decade as king, he went through six prime ministers, as he tried to balance supporting ministers friendly to him with those that were better suited to govern. His first appointment, a comfortable but boyish choice, was his former tutor, John Stuart, Lord Bute. Bute served for about a year from May 1762 to April 1763, but stepped down in the aftermath of an unpopular cider tax that threatened to mark George III's reign as authoritarian. Others, such as George Grenville (1763–1765), were more adept at working with Parliament, but irritated George by providing him unsolicited advice and meddling with other cabinet appointments.

It was not until the ministry of Frederick, Lord North (1770–1782) that George found a minister that provided stability. Lord North was only thirty-eight when he became prime minister, but he had served in Parliament for sixteen years. While he was perhaps not the perfect choice for a wartime ministry—he once stated "upon military manners I speak ignorantly, and therefore without effect"—he nonetheless was popular enough to win easy majorities in Parliament in the general elections of 1774 and 1780, despite his flailing effort to suppress the rebellion in America.

Indeed, the American Revolution galvanized the cabinet system. George became more involved in the cabinet's affairs as he aggressively pursued the war. In an extraordinary moment, he called the entire cabinet, not just the prime minister, to his residence in 1779, something that had not been done in more than sixty years. He broke with protocol by having all the members sit down. Although they thought he might dismiss them, he instead urged them to stay strong during the war, to pursue it to the end. In short, he "expected firmness and support from his ministers." Later that day he wrote North, emphasizing that the cabinet "can alone hope for my Support by shewing zeal, assiduity, and activity." However, as the war dragged on, his cabinet showed less and less enthusiasm for the costly conflict, with the king rejecting multiple offers from North to resign, until, in 1782, it was clear the minister had lost the confidence of Parliament.

During North's ministry, twenty-four men served in twelve distinct cabinet roles. Most of these ministers were peers in the House of Lords, though some served in the Commons. John Montagu, fourth Earl of Sandwich, who served as first lord of the admiralty, and Lord George Germain, secretary of state for the colonies, played key roles in the American War. Sandwich oversaw British naval operations, while Germain similarly coordinated the land war. Both received heavy criticism for losing the colonies; Sandwich for conservatively keeping most of the fleet in Europe to defend a potential French invasion and Germain for issuing confusing orders that betrayed a lack of knowledge of American geography.

Following on the heels of the American Revolu-

Chapter 6

tion, the threat posed by the French Revolution as well as George III's episodes of mental illness encouraged further consolidation of executive powers in the cabinet and the rise of an active, robust prime minister. William Pitt the Younger (1783–1801, 1804–1806) readily embraced the role (and the title), shaping the position into something approaching its modern form of head of government. In 1803, while out of power, he remarked that the "first minister" should maintain "the principal place in the confidence of the King" and "the chief weight in the [cabinet] council."

As George came to respect and even rely on Pitt, he showed his favoritism by providing royal patronage, particularly in granting him the lucrative sinecure of warden of the Cinque Ports. Indeed, George often played favorites with members of the cabinet, writing in 1792, "I never love throwing favours on enemies and love rewarding steady friends."

When George Washington became president, it was clear that he could not just reward his friends with appointments to government positions. The British system had drawn contempt from colonists before and

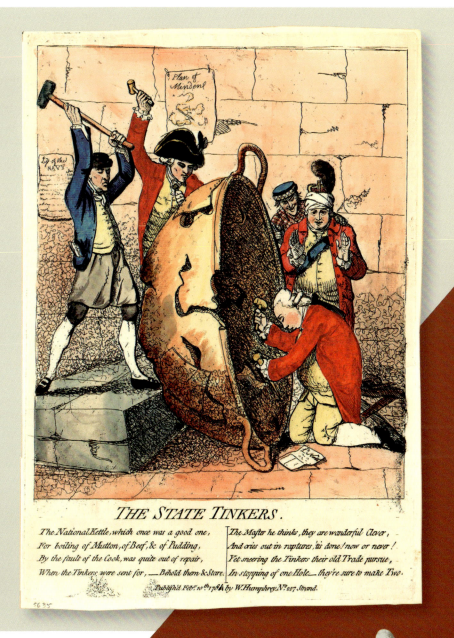

James Gillray, *The State Tinkers*, February 10, 1780. Color engraving. Published by W. Humphrey.

After going through six prime ministers in his first decade as king, George III finally found a steady hand in Lord Frederick North, who served as the leader of the cabinet from 1770 to 1782. In this cartoon, North is seen bending on the ground hammering at "the national kettle," per the poem James Gillray includes below the scene, while George raises his hands in gleeful surprise. Also depicted from left to right are: the Earl of Sandwich, who as first lord of the admiralty is identified by a "list of the Navy" on the wall; Lord George Germain, secretary of state for the colonies, chiseling the kettle in front of the "Plan of Minden," a reference to a battle where he had shown cowardice; and lastly Lord Bute, a former prime minister, who wears a tartan pattern identifying him as Scottish.

A King, a President, a Republic, and Executive Power

James Gillray, *A Block for the Wigs - or, the New State Whirligig*, May 5, 1783. Etching. Published by Hannah Humphrey.

Master of the satirical cartoon, James Gillray comments on what would be a tumultuous, short-lived Fox-North coalition government that many, including George III, considered shameless, having ousted Lord Shelburne as prime minister during peace negotiations with the United States. Outside the "Crown and Royal Bob" pub, representing the United Kingdom, John Bull, the personification of the country, obliviously sits outside with his tankard warbling "Tis Liberty! Tis Liberty. Dear Liberty alone" as thieves help themselves to goods from the pub's upper window. Meanwhile, the kilted Lord Mansfield, Scottish president of the Privy Council, grins as leading members of the king's cabinet hold tight to a speeding merry-go-round precariously propped up with pegs representing the Treasury, Navy, and Army. Among the many illustrated puns, the cartoon's title refers to George III's powdered wig and wig block (for holding and shaping a wig, in the profile of the king, hence a "blockhead") as the center beam of the carousel. Charles James Fox, the pro-American leader of the Whigs, at far right, is a fox hoisting a bag of money; on his left, Lord North, a Tory and prime minister during the American Revolution, literally takes a back seat to Fox and loses his own wig.

during the Revolution. "The late violent measures, and some others equally vindictive, which are now carrying on, were all concerted in a cabinet-council," wrote one South Carolina newspaper in 1770. Two months before Lexington and Concord, John Adams wrote to a correspondent in London that Americans expected "the knavery in the cabinet" to worsen the situation with the Mother Country. While trying to recruit soldiers from the Passamaquoddy Tribe in December 1776, Washington wrote, "Now Brothers never lett the Kings Wicked Councellors turn your Hearts Against Me and your Bretheren of this Country." Another South Carolina newspaper stated in 1779 that in the British cabinet "the voice of the people is only heard with contempt."

But what to do instead was unclear. The Constitution did not prescribe the details of a cabinet. Article II, Section 2, Clause 1 states, in part, that the president "may require the Opinion, in writing, of the principal Officer in each of the executive Departments, upon any Subject relating to the Duties of their respective Offices" but it does not say anything about meetings of the department heads. Indeed, when Washington eventually did decide to meet with secretaries of the various departments starting in 1791, he often sent them questions in writing ahead of time, and he would require written responses when his advisers disagreed with each other. His experience requesting similar advice when a general in the Continental Army influenced his presidential behavior.

Not wanting to operate like a monarch, Washington appointed government officials based on merit, or what he called "fitness." In choosing his cabinet secretaries, he initially sought political and geographic balance; his first four secretaries came from Virginia, New York, and Massachusetts, and later replacements also hailed from Connecticut, Pennsylvania, and Maryland. He wanted a wide range of viewpoints, and he did not appoint people based solely on social prestige or personal connections, unlike George III who preferred rewarding his friends. This also applied to any government position the president had control over. When his nephew Bushrod Washington asked to be appointed a US attorney, Washington declined, writing "My political conduct in nominations, even if I was uninfluenced by principle, must be exceedingly circumspect and proof against just criticism."

Washington first assembled the cabinet in person on November 26, 1791, more than thirty months after he took the oath of office. According to historian Lindsay Chervinsky, "the delayed emergence of the cabinet is the strongest evidence showing that Washington sought to avoid comparisons to the British cabinet." "The cabinet" in Washington's first two years was so disparate that even three months before its first meeting, Alexander Hamilton, the secretary of the treasury, wrote a British minster, "we have no Cabinet, and the heads of Departments meet on very particular occasions only." Besides Hamilton, the November 1791 meeting included Attorney General Edmund Randolph, Secretary of State Thomas Jefferson, and Secretary of War Henry Knox; they joined Washington in his private study on the second floor of the President's House in Philadelphia. These secretaries continued to meet a few more times in 1791 and 1792 before meeting weekly in 1793.

As the meetings became more regular, so did the word "cabinet" to refer to Washington's chief advisers. On February 25, 1793, Jefferson wrote a memo titled "Cabinet Opinions on Indian Affairs" while Hamilton also noted a "Cabinet Meeting" that discussed paying France for debt amassed during the Revolution. Later that June, James Madison, a congressman at the time, asked Jefferson, "Did no such view of [the Neutrality Proclamation] present itself in the discussion of the Cabinet?" By the end of the year, the term was widespread in the press as well.

But there was one exception: Washington himself. Still wary of the implications of being advised by a similar group to the king, as president he never once used the term "cabinet meeting" to refer to such gatherings. Instead, he would simply indicate he was meeting with his secretaries, whom he called "the gentlemen of my family." He also wrote, in a letter to the Marquis de Lafayette, "I feel myself supported by able Co-adjustors who harmonise extremely well together."

Unlike the members of the British cabinet, who were drawn from Parliament, the members of Washington's cabinet had been appointed by him without any direct election by the public—though the Senate confirmed their appointment. Thus, in the American system, the first cabinet worked to enhance and expand Washington's presidential authority, rather than restrain it, in the way British ministers served as a check on the monarch.

Perhaps surprising given their disdain of the British cabinet, the American public for the most part failed to criticize Washington's cabinet as a concept.

A King, a President, a Republic, and Executive Power

Washington and His Cabinet. **Lithograph. Published by Currier & Ives, ca. 1876.**

President George Washington, left, with cabinet members Secretary of War Henry Knox, Secretary of the Treasury Alexander Hamilton, Secretary of State Thomas Jefferson, and Attorney General Edmund Randolph. The vice president did not partake in cabinet meetings until the twentieth century thus John Adams is not represented here.

They understood that a brand-new executive needed guidance from others. Rather, critics of Washington's administration, especially in his first term, focused on individuals within the cabinet and on policy decisions that came out of its deliberations. Hamilton came to bear the brunt of the criticism, especially his ambitious plan to absorb the states' debt from the Revolutionary War as well as his pro-British stance. Some critics feared Hamilton was amassing power a la a prime minister, with some even comparing him and his policies to that of Robert Walpole, the first British prime minister.

Jefferson especially grated at Hamilton's outsize role, resigning from the cabinet in 1793. Hamilton himself would follow in 1795. Washington addressed conflict in the cabinet in his second term; he appointed only Federalists, writing in 1795 "I shall not … bring a man into any Office of consequence knowingly, whose political tenets are adverse to the measures, which the general government are pursuing. For this, in my opinion, would be a sort of political Suicide."

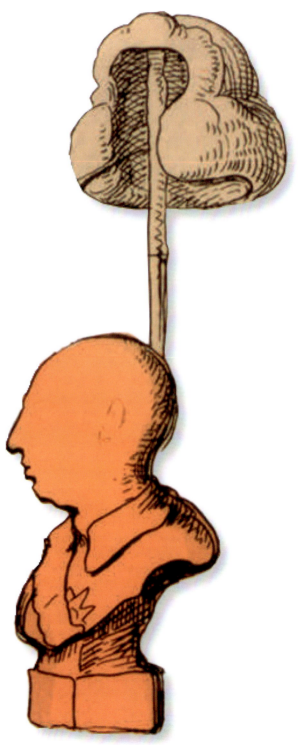

Not Exactly Déjà Vu: Reckoning with the French Revolution

On Tuesday, July 14, 1789, George Washington was in New York City, just ten weeks into his presidency and recuperating from painful (and secretive) surgery to remove an infected growth in his leg. King George was seaside in Weymouth, enjoying his summer holiday, having recovered earlier that spring from a serious bout of mental illness. Late in the afternoon, an angry crowd in Paris, in search of weapons and gunpowder, stormed the Bastille, a medieval fortress and state prison slated for demolition. Mutinous soldiers of the French Guard, some of whom had fought in the American War for Independence, soon joined in with cannon. And the indecisive, reserved King Louis XVI, detached from society, went to bed that night in his palace at Versailles having described the day in his diary in one word: *rien* ["nothing"]. The next morning he learned that there *had* been something: the Bastille had fallen. Louis allegedly enquired, "Is it a revolt?" "No, sire," replied the Duke de La Rochefoucauld. "It is a revolution."

The Bastille was a long-hated symbol of absolute monarchy and autocratic tyranny, a place where the king's political opponents historically found themselves jailed without trial. Its surrender ignited an already simmering cauldron of grievances. Of the French Revolution's many causes, including the immediate issues of food shortages and soaring prices, two were rooted in the young United States: the successful American Revolution inspired those seeking to destroy the *ancien régime*—the old order—and the heavy debt France incurred as America's ally brought about oppressive taxation and social unrest.

Americans in general and British radicals in particular joyfully welcomed word of the revolution, viewing it as a continuation of the "Spirit of '76" and proof that political enlightenment had asserted itself in France. But ever since the wartime French and American alliance in 1778, Washington had anticipated that one day France might erupt in fury, given the "ruinous" financial and military investment young Louis XVI made in America to fight Britain. Four years after the war ended, Washington's friend the Marquis de Lafayette had told him that the French were "tired to pay what they Have not Voted. The ideas of liberty Have Been, since the American Revolution, spreading very fast." Indeed, fear surged among the aristocracy and crowned heads of Europe that anarchy and mob violence in the name of *liberté, égalité, fraternité* might come for them as well.

In October 1789, after learning more of the events in Paris, Washington wrote to his friend Gouverneur Morris, who was in the French capital, with a positive but prescient reaction. "The revolution which has been effected in France is of so wonderful a nature that the mind can hardly realise the fact—If it ends as our last accounts to the first of August predict that nation will be the most powerful and happy in Europe; but I fear though it has gone triumphantly through the first paroxysm, it is not the last it has to encounter before matters are finally settled." The same week as the president's letter, Queen Charlotte wrote her asthmatic son Prince Augustus, who was in the south of France for his health, with a different take: "France furnishes greater, but melancholy news. I often think that this cannot be the 18th century in which we live at present, for ancient history can hardly produce anything more barbarous and cruel than our neighbours in France."

George III expressed concern for the safety of Louis XVI and his family, who were soon under house arrest and later in June 1791 caught attempting to escape. He did not, however, join international efforts to rescue a fellow sovereign whose country was regularly at war with his own. Lafayette and Washington were both hopeful that the constitutional monarchy King Louis was forced to accept in September that year would be a lasting, peaceful accommodation that guaranteed liberty and "the natural rights of man" to French citizens. Instead, rioting, violence, and extremism escalated, and many who had initially supported the revolutionaries' cause were appalled by the chaos and bloodshed that characterized the movement.

King George and his prime minister, William Pitt, tread firmly but carefully in combatting "the French disease" from within and without, as galvanized radicals, demanding parliamentary reform, grew more prolific in public and in print. In part two of his bestselling bombshell pamphlet, *Rights of Man*, published in February 1792, the English-born

American Thomas Paine accused George III of despotism, called for universal suffrage and abolishing the monarchy, and declared that British governance had been "eclipsed by the enlarged orb of reason, and the luminous revolutions of America and France." In May that eclipsed government issued a royal proclamation in the king's name denouncing the "wicked and seditious Writings … endeavouring to vilify and bring into Contempt the wise and wholesome" British constitution. It ordered local magistrates to report libelous or seditionist publications and gatherings, but in notable cases at subsequent trials for sedition and treason, the defendants were either acquitted or received moderate prison sentences. No pamphleteer or publisher went to the gallows.

Concurrent with the pamphlet war in Britain,

James Gillray, *The hopes of the party, prior to July 14th "from such wicked crown & anchor-dreams, good Lord deliver us"*, July 19, 1791. Hand-colored print. Published by S.W. Fores.

British radicals, who supported the French Revolution, are shown after a celebratory dinner at the Crown & Anchor tavern commemorating the second anniversary of the attack on the Bastille in Paris. Whig leader Charles James Fox, center, masked and raising an executioner's axe, is seen about to decapitate George III, who is held by John Horne Tooke, a fervent parliamentary reformer, on the left, and MP Richard Sheridan on the right. The king cries out "What! What! What!" (a well-known verbal tic of his), "What's the matter now?" In the upper right corner, Queen Charlotte and Prime Minister William Pitt have been strung up on streetlights, and those below wave their hats in approval. As the violence increased and France spiraled toward the Reign of Terror, fear that such a scene could come to Britain eventually disillusioned James Gillray, who had long lampooned the king. The cartoonist's later drawings found him an ardent supporter of the crown, and his depictions of the revolution cast its figures as horrid, ghastly, and unwashed, bent on destroying civilization.

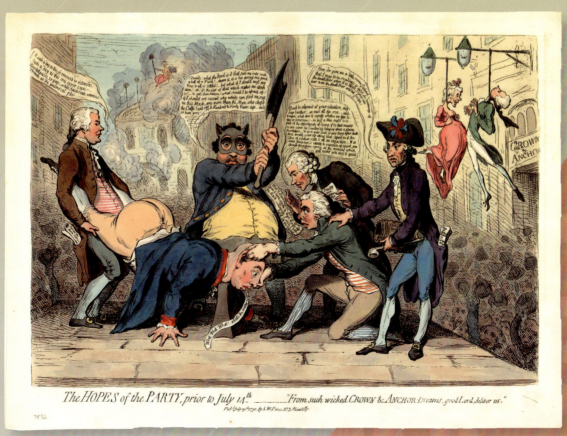

A King, a President, a Republic, and Executive Power

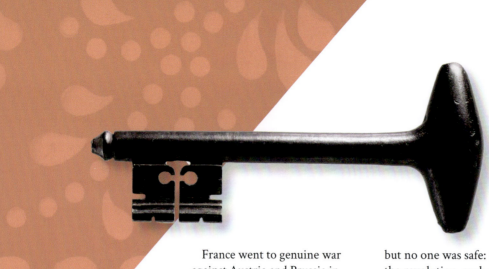

France went to genuine war against Austria and Prussia in the spring of 1792, and King George agreed with his government that British neutrality was the best option. In August the revolutionary French government imprisoned King Louis and the next month declared France a republic. At the same time, it awarded George Washington, Alexander Hamilton, James Madison, and Thomas Paine honorary French citizenship for their service in "the cause of liberty." Meanwhile, King George, who referred to the revolutionaries as "cruel wretches" and "savages," complained that the movement was "destroying all religion, law, and subordination . . . without the smallest inclination after this destruction to build up anything." As the year ended, French troops occupied all of the continental Channel ports, putting Britain in grave danger.

The execution of Louis XVI at the guillotine in January 1793 marked a significant turning point. George III expelled the French ambassador, France declared war on Britain in February, and the British public, thankful for his adherence to the constitution and the stability he provided, was more supportive than ever of their Patriot King. For the rest of his active reign, until the regency of his son in 1811, the king was closely involved in the defense of the nation as the revolution in France gave way to the military dictatorship of Napoleon Bonaparte and his wars across Europe.

The French king's incarceration and death unleashed frenzied butchery, and the governing Committee of Public Safety's consolidation of power produced the Reign of Terror. Tens of thousands of "counter-revolutionaries" accused of treason were arrested, executed, or otherwise perished in an extraordinary national descent into hysteria and paranoia. Most victims were peasants and working-class people, but no one was safe: even high-profile supporters of the revolution, such as Lafayette, who had favored a limited monarchy, and Paine, who wanted to abolish it, were imprisoned in Moravia and France, respectively, and the self-destructive Committee executed some of its own leaders as well. In the United States, the changed tenor of the revolution divided government and public opinion.

Notably, Jefferson and Madison continued to back the cause and tolerated its excesses and atrocities. As Jefferson put it early on, one could not expect to move "from despotism to liberty, in a feather-bed." But Washington and Hamilton, the secretary of the treasury, grew horrified and despondent over the situation. "If there be anything solid in virtue—the time must come when it will have been a disgrace to have advocated the Revolution of France in its late stages," Hamilton would later write in 1794. "This is a language to which the ears of the people of this country have not been accustomed."

With France and Britain at war, and France going to war with ever more of Europe, Washington and his cabinet wrestled over whether to remain loyal to America's benefactor or stay out of the conflict. The president had publicly supported the French—"Very Great and Good Allies" in his carefully chosen words—despite his private distress. Other concerns weighed on his mind as well. American trade with Britain was far more important and much more convenient than it was with France. Americans preferred to buy British, and he was convinced that keeping the peace with them was essential. He was also determined that as a new nation still gaining its footing, the United States must avoid further European "entanglements" and concentrate on its own development.

In April 1793, President Washington issued a neutrality proclamation stating that the United States

Chapter 6

would "pursue a conduct friendly and impartial toward the belligerent Powers." Regarded by many as ingratitude toward an old friend, the proclamation would become the cornerstone of American foreign policy for the next hundred years. However, its provisions barring American citizens from aiding and abetting belligerents did not stop the recently arrived and popular new French minister, Edmond-Charles Genêt, from setting off a major diplomatic crisis. Known by revolutionary nomenclature as Citizen Genêt, he urged Americans to violate the proclamation.

Wheeling and dealing his way north from Charleston, Genêt commissioned Americans as privateers, recruited others to fight for France, and armed former British ships captured by French privateers in American ports. He then threatened to publicly embarrass the president by demanding withdrawal of the proclamation. Frostily, Washington received him in Philadelphia and turned loose Hamilton, the king of pamphleteering, and others to respond in print condemning Genêt's actions and threatening to disclose devastating revelations. Having failed to draw Americans into its war, the French government recalled its infuriating minister home to face trial for not being revolutionary enough, which Washington knew was a certain death sentence. Despite clashing with the French diplomat, he nonetheless permitted Citizen Genêt to live quietly in New York, as Washington's own days as a political revolutionary drew to a close.

Key to the Bastille and display case.

In the summer of 1790, George Washington received a striking gift from the Marquis de Lafayette, who commanded the national guard in Paris overseeing the demolition of the Bastille. The package contained a drawing of the crumbling building and a 1.3 pound, 7.3-inch-long wrought iron key, its teeth cut to reveal the shape of the royal fleur-de-lis. It was the main key to the Bastille. Washington displayed it in a glass and gilded wood case in the dining room of the executive mansion in Philadelphia during his presidency, then installed it and the framed drawing in the central hallway of his mansion at Mount Vernon. Lafayette would set eyes on the key once more, in 1824, on a tour of the United States, when he visited Mount Vernon with his son, George Washington Lafayette.

A King, a President, a Republic, and Executive Power

The Illness of King George

George III experienced several bouts of intense mania, the last of these persisting for the final decade of his life, leading to the regency of his son, the future George IV. The potential causes of these outbursts have long been debated, including arsenic poisoning from wig powder, as well as George's diet. The accepted theory for much of the twentieth century was that George's illness was caused by the genetic disease porphyria. Symptoms of this disease include abdominal pain, mental illness, nausea, and dark colored urine, all things George experienced periodically throughout his life. However, that theory has since been debunked. The abdominal pains he experienced were fleeting and not debilitating, and his urine might have been dark because of all the medicines and tinctures his doctors prescribed. Instead, he most likely suffered from bipolar disorder. Regardless of the exact cause, these episodes of serious illness greatly affected him, his family, and even the governance of Britain.

George's first serious bout of illness was in 1765. After falling from a horse, he developed such symptoms as feverish cold, chest pain, high pulse rate, and peculiar behavior, what might be considered manic episodes. Queen Charlotte and the king's doctors actively hid the king's symptoms from the public. He described it as "my late Indisposition, tho; not attended with danger," yet a regency plan was privately drawn up just in case.

The next major episode was preceded with physical symptoms in June 1788 that lasted until the following spring. After a bilious attack, his doctors suggested he take the waters, and so he spent a month at the spa town of Cheltenham. But in August when he returned to London, he had more stomach pains, cramps, and a rash. By October, he was taking laudanum and laxatives. On October 24 at a levee, his speech was slurred and his behavior irrational. In early November, signs of mental illness set in as he attacked the Prince of Wales and began giving orders to people who were long dead or non-existent. From November 18 to 19, he talked for nineteen hours straight. He was physically violent, once trying to throw himself out of a window.

With the king's doctors flummoxed, Francis Willis, who ran a successful asylum in Lincolnshire, joined the medical care team in December. Although the king's physicians scoffed at Willis, since he initially had been trained as a clergyman, Willis and his son John were given full control over the king's recovery. While many of the Willises' treatments were horrific—including placing His Majesty in a straitjacket, what George called his "coronation chair," for hours at a time—some of them were cutting-edge techniques in treating mental illness. Willis believed that psychosis could be cured by imposing order on the patient, and he took full control of the king's actions, instituting a reward-punishment system based on the king's ability to rein in his symptoms. Willis taught George to recognize when he said things that were inappropriate, and as the monarch behaved better, he was given privileges such as shaving himself, reading Shakespeare, and receiving visits from his family. Though George would come to detest Willis for the painful and intense treatment he received at his hands, the symptoms did start to recede in the winter of 1789.

While Willis treated the king, George's condition led to a political crisis. Doctors feared the king faced imminent permanent insanity, yet hoping to temper panic, they refused to commit to such a prognosis in public statements. This uncertainty was further exacerbated by speculation on what the Prince of Wales would do if he were to become regent. Many thought the prince, who was allied with the king's political opposition, was likely to dismiss the Tory government under William Pitt. Thus, Pitt tried to limit a potential regent's powers, even preparing himself for the prospect of having to return to his law practice. Eventually, the king's recovery resolved the crisis, and a regency bill passed on February 12, 1789, was put aside.

Despite George's recovery, his weakened body and gaunt features showed signs of the struggle. Even Queen Charlotte changed, as her hair turned from brown to white. The king was not oblivious to such suffering by his wife, writing her on March 6, 1789, "I cannot but be deeply impressed at how much you must have been affected by the long continuum of my illness."

Surprisingly, this bout of illness increased George's standing with the country. Large crowds gathered to witness him attend St. George's Day at St. Paul's Cathedral in April, and the nation celebrated his recovery with fireworks, parties, and loud renditions of "God Save the King." Medals celebrating his return to health and honoring his doctors were created, and the Willises were feted for their "cure" of His Majesty. Francis Willis received a gold watch personally from the king, as well as a £1,000 annual pension from Parliament for twenty-one years.

Just a week after the service of thanksgiving for King George, George Washington was inaugurated as president in New York City on April 30, 1789. The previous December, Jefferson had reported to Washington: "The lunacy of the King of England is a decided fact." Washington, meanwhile, believed that whatever "Be the cause of the British king's insanity what it may, his situation … merits commiseration." Gouverneur Morris passed on a rumor to Washington that, in a fit of mania, the king believed he was "no less a personage than George Washington at the head of the American Army. This shows that you have done something or other which sticks most terribly in his stomach." Although there is no direct historical record of George III confusing himself with the other George, his illness nonetheless did manifest itself in out-of-body experiences.

His illness returned in 1801 and lasted on and off throughout the year, though it was not quite as severe as the 1788–1789 episode. At one point a treatment called for the king to be tied to a chair and placed in front of a fire, a practice he described as being "roasted alive for six hours." The king's doctors encouraged Charlotte to remove herself from his presence, some-

Thomas Rowlandson, *Filial Piety*, **November 25, 1788. Hand-colored etching.**

Published at the height of the king's second bout of serious mental illness, this satirical print is the first one to show him indisposed. Prince George, the heir apparent, barges in on a priest providing communion to the king, and two lackeys (George Hanger, a future equerry of the prince, and dramatist and MP Richard Brinsley Sheridan) drunkenly burst in as well. The Prince of Wales says with glee "Damme, come along, I'll see if the Old Fellow's –– or not," suggesting the prince hoped his father would be too ill to reign, leading to a regency for himself.

A King, a President, a Republic, and Executive Power

thing she described in a letter to him, dated April 22, 1801, as a "painful necessity" that would "deprive myself of so satisfactory a pleasure."

The next major episode, in 1804, was caused in part by stress related to the cabinet. The king began to show an uncharacteristic aversion to the queen, with whom he'd always had a loving relationship. He threatened to take a mistress and became more erratic around women. The queen stopped travelling with him and barricaded her door. His various episodes of illness along with his advanced age contributed to failing eyesight, and by 1805, he was virtually blind. His speech to Parliament in that year was the last he gave in person to start a session.

The final occurrence began late in 1810, following the death of his youngest child, Princess Amelia, from tuberculosis. George's last public appearance had been a jubilee celebration on October 25, 1810, marking fifty years on the throne. Though there was hope he would recover in the spring of 1811, it was clear he had become too disabled. The regency bill was finally enacted, and the Prince of Wales became the Prince Regent.

While living in Windsor Castle and separated from his family for the next decade, George occupied his time by playing the flute, harpsichord, and violin. He imagined conversations with his two youngest sons, Prince Alfred and Prince Octavius, who had died in the early 1780s. In 1818, when Queen Charlotte died, the courtyard outside his rooms was strewn with straw to prevent the noise of his wife's funeral carriage from disturbing him.

George died on January 29, 1820, in the sixtieth year of his reign. At the time, he was the longest reigning British monarch, surpassed since by his granddaughter Victoria and subsequently by his great-great-great-great-granddaughter Elizabeth II.

The drama of the "mad" king lingered in the imagination of poets and playwrights long after the king's demise. Written in the penultimate year of the king's reign (though published posthumously in 1832), Percy Bysshe Shelley's sonnet, "England in 1819," opens with references to George III and his sons:

> An old, mad, blind, despised and dying king,
> Princes, the dregs of their dull race, who flow
> Through public scorn- mud from a muddy spring,
> Rulers who neither see, nor feel, nor know,
> But leech-like to their fainting country cling.

In 1845, *Punch* ran four satirical poems by William Makepeace Thackeray, imaging potential inscriptions to be engraved on statues of the four Georgian monarchs. For George III's statue, the poem ends with these couplets:

> My guns roar'd triumph, but I never heard;
> All England thrilled with joy, I never stirred.
> What care had I of pomp, or fame, or power,-
> A crazy old blind man in Windsor Tower?

Thackeray later extended his satire of the Hanoverian monarchs into a series of lectures he later published in 1861 under the title, *The Four Georges: Sketches of Manners, Morals, Court, and Town Life*.

Two hundred years after George's most serious episode, the best-known modern artistic interpretation of his illness premiered. *The Madness of George III* (1991), an award-winning play by Alan Bennett and a later a feature film (1994) focused on the king's illness in 1788–1789. It depicted George's experience in all its gory detail, showing the tortuous treatments used on the king. Coinciding with decades of historical revisionism over his reign, it facilitated something of a redemption in the British public's mind.

George III's recurring experiences of mental illness overshadowed his legacy, drew public attention away from other important aspects of his reign, and reduced him in popular culture to simply that of a "mad" monarch. The king was aware of the negative affect his bouts of illness had on his reputation; while shut away in Windsor, he once remarked, "I must have a new suit of clothes and I will have them black in memory of George III." ☼

Sèvres porcelain factory, Tasse à thé (part of a tea and coffee set), 1789. Soft paste porcelain and gilded decoration.

After becoming seriously ill in November 1788, the king started to show signs of return to health by April, when it appeared he was over the worst of it. On June 9, 1789, the Spanish ambassador to the United Kingdom organized a gala to celebrate the king's recovery. For the occasion, he commissioned a Sèvres porcelain tea and coffee set as well as dessert service. Each piece bore a different sentiment, such as this one with the inscription "Huzza The King is well." Sèvres porcelain was a highly sought-after luxury item, being the official royal porcelain of France.

As the king recovered, thanksgiving services were held around the country, and other celebratory items were produced. George's doctor Francis Willis even had medals created with his own likeness and the phrase "Britons Rejoice, Your King's Restored."

Chapter 6

Hiram Powers, bust of George Washington, 1838-44, carved after 1844. Marble.

The Apotheosis Perplex

Peter Turnerelli, jubilee bust of George III, 1812 version. Marble.

George Washington excelled, all his life, at retreat. As a military man, his genius lay not least in knowing when to advance to the rear, saving his troops for another try on a better day when others would have battled on to the last man. As a victorious commander-in-chief, he gained international acclaim in late 1783, when he beat his sword into a ploughshare and retired "from the great theater of action" to his country seat at Mount Vernon, a modern Cincinnatus.[1] He stepped aside from the United States presidency after two terms, when many would have had him linger, a demi-king. His Farewell Address, in 1796, had far more enduring impact than both of his inaugurals combined.

So it is no surprise that George Washington, master of departure, excelled, too, at the *ars morendi*. Death did not catch him especially young; he was sixty-seven, just shy of his biblically allotted three-score-and-ten, when he succumbed to a "putrid sore throat" in December 1799. But it seized him with a narratively satisfying suddenness. If Washington was prepared—and it is hard to imagine him, ever, unprepared—the fractious people of the young United States were not. The way the country's first and best actor left the stage, this last time, allowed for an orgy of grief and a sterling remembrance, unalloyed by difficult realities.

George III had no such virtue and no such luck. He was known, in the United States, as the sovereign who held on too tightly for too long, clinging to prerogatives he might have yielded, to ministers he should have sacked, to colonies he could have loosed within the silken bands of empire before their people cut the cord completely. He waged war against them, relentlessly and fruitlessly, long after it should have been clear he was licked. He held the throne even into madness and extreme old age becoming, in the mind's eye of the early United States, a parable of monarchy as death-in-life.

George III was eighty-one when he succumbed. Finally as decrepit as he had long seemed to Americans, he had not been seen in public for a decade. Few would ever have guessed that he had been the younger of the two Georges headlining the Anglo-American saga, born six years after the sainted Washington. No longer the archfiend who engrossed all the good verbs in the Declaration of Independence, the king who lost America had softened into something pitiable, like the mad Lear, with George's preening profligate son and regent subbing in for the Shakespearian king's cruel daughters.[2] At best, the long serving king dissolved into John Bull, symbol of the roast beef vitality of the nation's constitutional monarchy. At worst, he was remembered as "George the Third-rate," as one twentieth-century British historian quipped.[3]

* * *

Death became George Washington's pinnacle, his greatest achievement, his *apotheosis*, as many works that mourned his passing styled it. By the end of 1800, print buyers could choose from myriad images that commemorated the late lamented father of his suffering country, from memorial engravings of his bust portraits available at a variety of price points, to landscapes of Mount Vernon, to gothic depictions of his tomb, to funerary scenes that became the subjects of schoolgirl embroidery. Shorn of his wig, with a stone tablet in his right hand and the British lion trembling at his feet, a stern-faced Washington played Moses, "giving the laws to America."[4] You could sleep surrounded by bed-hangings depicting Washington, Franklin, and Liberty in heaven; and pour water from a pitcher emblazoned with a berobed Washington borne aloft by angels and eagles and bearing the legend, *Apotheosis*.[5]

By mid-century, he had stepped into the New Testament. The German painter Heinrich Weishaupt, who had once drawn a lovely neo-renaissance lithograph of Christ on the cross, rendered Washington as a coyly draped nude, his well-muscled arms outstretched in a cruciform pose, with stains on the cloth covering his legs suggesting stigmata.[6] In 1865, when Abraham Lincoln was murdered, the Son became the Father. A popular *carte de visite* printed that year showed the first president—dressed as if he had stepped out from Gilbert Stuart's *Lansdowne* por-

Washington Giving the Laws to America, ca. 1800. Engraving and etching.

Heinrich Weishaupt, *Apotheosis of George Washington,* ca. 1830-50. Hand-colored lithograph.

The Apotheosis Perplex

S. J. Ferris, *Washington & Lincoln (Apotheosis)*, ca. 1865-1867. Carte-de-visite.

trait—awaiting the slain Emancipator in heaven.[7] We the People, the implied viewers, become the third leg of the Trinity, the holy spirit of America.

Pictures were hardly the only agents of Washington's apotheosis. Histories and schoolbooks, fables and plays all did their parts transforming a man of his season into a mind out of times. The man who would not be king became the boy who could not tell a lie, and then no man at all, but an emblem, an allegory, our foremost Founding Father, with skin of marble and heart of gold.

* * *

Surely George Washington did not want this republican brand of divinity. He had hated to be painted. He called the portraitists' frenzied work to capture him a tax on the American people and likened himself in the painter's chair to a dray horse trudging round the thill.[8] But he had no power to stop his apotheosis. And so, will-he, nill-he, he rose, mythic and marmoreal, far above the workaday stuff of history. The distortions, the elisions, the fantasies, and the outright lies of posterity couldn't hurt him. But they hurt us, The People, as we prostrated ourselves at his alabaster feet, no pose for participants in a robust republic.

In the twentieth century, historians trained as scientists rather than artists began to expose

 Chapter 6

the man behind the myth. Grant Wood's *Parson Weems' Fable* uses a hard-edged realism to puncture the soft surface of fable. The painting, completed in 1939—the year MGM's *The Wizard of Oz* mesmerized Americans still reeling from Depression—is a droll exposé: there's no wizard, nor even a full-grown man behind the curtain. Wood's Washington appears literally cut down to size, a boy wearing the hoary head of the hackneyed portrait on every dollar bill.

Like Wood's painting, many recent histories thrum with the negative energy of iconoclasm, glorying in the smashed idol, the emptied pedestal. Historians, whose tribe spent a century and a half extracting Washington from his place in time, have gradually reintroduced the complex realities of eighteenth-century Anglo-America to his biography. Since the 1990s, scholars have paid far more attention than their predecessors did to Washington's full-throated participation in the violence of the colonial enterprise, including his speculation in Western lands, his murderous military actions against Native peoples during two global wars, and especially his role as the captor of more than three hundred men, women, and children held in bondage.[9] As a slaveholder, Washington was exceptional neither in his cruelty nor in his magnanimity. He gave people as wedding presents. He moved workers around his vast landholdings, separating families in the process. When people he owned ran away—whether from Mount Vernon or from the President's House in the vexingly free city of Philadelphia—he had them posted and hunted.[10] Mount Vernon looks very different when a massive slave labor encampment is restored to the core of a pastoral fantasy. We cannot unlearn what the historian Henry Wiencek unearthed in his 2003 biography, *An Imperfect God*: when Washington smiled, as he surely did in life if not in the painter's chair, he smiled through dentures that included teeth extracted from his slaves.[11]

Where Gilbert Stuart gave us the ethereal Washington of the late eighteenth century, and Emanuel Leutze created the fervid, Delaware-crossing Washington of the mid-nine-

Grant Wood, *Parson Weems' Fable*, 1939. Oil on canvas.

The Apotheosis Perplex

Titus Kaphar, *Shadows of Liberty*, 2016. Oil and rusted nails on canvas.

teenth, it is the African-American painter Titus Kaphar who has created the Washington of the twenty-first century. In Kaphar's *Shadows of Liberty*, the familiar figure of the general on horseback dissolves into loose ribbons of canvas bearing the texts of runaway advertisements. Kaphar's Washington looks as if he can't hold out much longer. Soon to be swallowed by once-hidden truths made manifest, his fall seems complete.

Reintegrating a more complex—which is to say, truer—George Washington into the American national story has proved contentious.

However factually untenable, Washington's apotheosis still tacitly organizes our politics. "Look, if we brought George Washington here and we said, we have George Washington, the Democrats would vote against him. ... Didn't he have a couple of things in his past?" President Donald Trump quipped during a press conference in September 2018.[12] On the Right, it remains hard to admit that Washington, still in his heaven, had any past at all. Yet it seems nearly as difficult, on the Left, to admit that he had any virtues. In the index of a 2018 anthology on indigenous history in the age of Revolutions, the entry for George Washington reads, "*See* Connotacarious," Washington's Iroquois (Haudenosaunee) name, which translates, roughly, as Town Destroyer.¹³

* * *

George III neither rose as high nor fell as hard. During the War of 1812, American cartoonists tried in vain to resuscitate him as a villain. *A Boxing Match, Or Another Bloody Nose for John Bull* (1813) shows the red-coated sovereign, one eye blackened and crown askew, duking it out with a bantam James Madison. Both men wear the wigs of the 1770s, like zombies of the Revolution reanimated for a new age. The frail Madison's punches land better than the wan joke. The new American president looks as superannuated as the ancient English king, whose great role in the American story had ended decades earlier. The hapless Hanoverian's next big appearance in American prints came not with his death, in 1820, but with the United States centennial. In 1876, images of American patriots toppling the king's statue on New York's Bowling Green were once again in vogue. Long after his death, George III fell, and fell again.¹⁴

In Lin-Manuel Miranda's musical blockbuster *Hamilton* (2015), though, the posthumous George III has the last laugh. Miranda's George Washington is bloodless, as if already crushed under the weight of history which, he croons vaguely, "has its eyes" on him.

But oh, that king. It is 1776, and he is young and sneering and sassy, taunting the Americans on the stage and in the audience with his campy break-up number, an anthem of rising and falling. "You'll Be Back," he sings, and we wish we were. Three times, at long last, he steals the show.¹⁵ ☼

— **Jane Kamensky**

William Charles, *A Boxing Match, Or Another Bloody Nose for John Bull*, 1813. Etching with watercolor.

An Edinburgh-born cartoonist, William Charles, who lived in New York and Philadelphia from 1806 until his death in 1820, created this print at the height of the War of 1812, which saw Americans fighting Britain again. Alluding to the defeat of the British ship *Boxer* by the American *Enterprise* in September 1813, President James Madison punches a beleaguered George III, saying "You thought yourself a Boxer, did you? I'll let you know we are an enterprising Nation and ready to meet you with equal force any day." Meanwhile, George—who by this point had become permanently disabled and replaced by his son as regent—says "Stop...Brother Jonathan, or I shall fall with the loss of blood." Brother Jonathan was the personification of the United States prior to Uncle Sam.

The Apotheosis Perplex

Farewells and Funerals

Washington in His Last Illness, 1800. Hand-colored etching with watercolor on paper.

Following George Washington's death, the Washingtoniana industry accelerated with the production of memorial items that ranged from expensive marble busts to modestly priced prints such as this one. Various deathbed depictions soon appeared on the market, and this popular print shows Doctors Craik and Brown tending to the stricken Washington, who died from a throat infection, as Martha Washington sits nearby. Beneath the image is a stanza typical in sentiment and folk style to the innumerable tributes made in Washington's memory: "Americans behold and shed a grateful tear/For a man who has gained your freedom most dear/And now is departing unto the realms above/Where he may ever rest in lasting peace and love."

Samuel William Reynolds, *George III*, early version ca. 1820 and published version February 24, 1820. Mezzotint.

Samuel William Reynolds created these two mezzotint portraits of the king in the last few months of his life, based on a sketch by the sculptor Matthew Wyatt who worked at Windsor. The one on the left is a more realistic rendering of the king with long hair and beard. The Prince Regent requested alterations to provide a more elegant image of George III in preserving his legacy as the longest serving monarch in the nation's history up until that point. The revised portrait was first published a month after the king's death.

 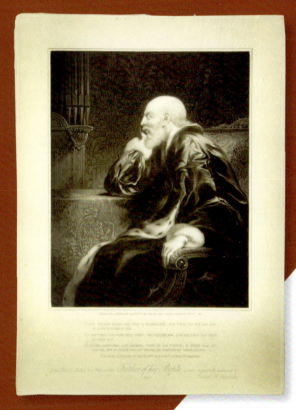

William Birch, *High Street from Country Market Place with the Procession in Commemoration of the Death of General George Washington*, 1800. Hand-colored engraving.

The day of George Washington's funeral and burial at Mount Vernon, Congress, meeting in Philadelphia, learned of his death. It sent letters of condolence to Martha Washington and to President John Adams, Washington's successor, acknowledging that "on this occasion, it is manly to weep." Congress implemented the country's first rites of presidential mourning, with a proclamation calling for thirty days of observance, and it immediately organized a national memorial service held on December 26, 1799, at the New Lutheran Church in Philadelphia, which Washington had attended during his presidency.

The memorial procession began at Congress Hall, and a lone trumpeter on horseback led to the church local and federal dignitaries, the cabinet, members of Congress, clergy in white scarves, bands with drums muffled, cavalry units, and foot soldiers representing various military organizations as thousands of citizens lined the route. As depicted here, a riderless horse, representing a fallen soldier, leads a draped but empty bier on which rests a tricorn hat and crossed swords. An account in the *Connecticut Currant* called it "one of the most . . . impressive scenes ever witnessed." The church, the largest in the area and seating 2,500, was jammed with some 4,000 in attendance. Congress tapped Henry "Lighthorse" Lee to deliver the eulogy, and the former Continental Army calvary officer declared Washington "First in war, first in peace, and first in the hearts of his countrymen." It was a sentiment that would resonate in a burgeoning American culture and serve as a primary text in mythologizing Washington.

George Cruikshank, *Funeral Procession of George III*, February 16, 1820, Windsor Castle. Ink on paper.

King George died of pneumonia on January 29, 1820, at the age of 81, after being out of the public eye for nearly a decade. The funeral was held eighteen days later, to allow for the elaborate preparations and all the participants to assemble. As carriages clogged the roads to Windsor, the king lay in state on February 15 and 16 in the castle's audience chamber, and some 30,000 ticketed mourners passed through. The day of the funeral, guns fired every five minutes from 8 am until the funeral procession departed for St. George's Chapel at 9 pm. Black-robed dukes and other members of the peerage carried a purple velvet canopy and accompanied the bier holding the king's draped coffin, atop which was affixed a velvet cushion holding the imperial crown. Second son Prince Frederick, the Duke of York, served as chief mourner since the new king, George IV, formerly the Prince Regent, was too ill to attend. After the hour-long service, the king's coffin was lowered into the royal vault. "And thus ended the most ... magnificent ceremony which any British subject now living ever witnessed in this country," reported *The European Magazine, and London Review*, "a ceremony . . . rendered sublime by the voluntary and heartfelt homage of countless thousands of affectionate subjects, who had thronged to the last obsequies of their King . . . to shed a last tear over the grave of a father and friend."

Allies and Apotheosis

His Royal Highness the Prince of Wales at the Tomb of Washington, October 1860. Wood engraving. Published in *Harper's Weekly*.

On the eve of the American Civil War, President James Buchanan invited George III's great-grandson, Albert Edward, Prince of Wales (later King Edward VII), to visit Washington, DC, during his upcoming three-month tour of North America. The prince was acquainted with Buchanan, who had become friendly with his mother, Queen Victoria, while he was US minister to Britain in the 1850s. As the president had predicted, the prince was met by cheering crowds everywhere he went–he was even greeted with a rendition of "God Save the Queen" by a brass band on arrival in Baltimore. During his stay at the White House, the prince could see the early construction of the Washington Monument, then only a stub of stone.

Accompanied by President Buchanan and his niece, Harriet Lane, who served as first lady, the prince toured Mount Vernon on October 5, 1860, writing his mother that it "is a much revered spot by the Americans, as the House in which General Washington lived and also died stands there. The visit therefore was a very interesting one; the house itself is unfortunately in very bad repair and is rapidly falling into decay; we saw all the different rooms and the one in which Washington died. We also visited his grave which is a short distance from the house, and by the wish of the President I planted a Chestnut [tree] near it." As a memento of his visit, the prince received a wooden fragment from Washington's original coffin, and the piece remains in the royal collections. The prince's tour was a great success, and afterward the queen wrote Buchanan that "I fully reciprocate towards your nation the feelings thus made apparent and look upon them as forming an important link to cement two nations of kindred origin and character."

Constantino Brumidi, *Study for The Apotheosis of George Washington*, US Capitol, Washington, DC, ca. 1859-1862. Oil on canvas.

Americans were not done deifying George Washington more than a half-century after his death. In an eleven-month decorating spree in 1865, muralist Constantino Brumidi painted a massive fresco, covering 4,664 square feet, in the eye of the Capitol rotunda, 180 feet above the floor. The timing was fortuitous, as the American Civil War had drawn to a close, and the country Washington and his generation had founded was preserved at a terrible and bloody cost. Brumidi enthroned Washington, revered by both the North and the South, as a symbol of national unity. Set atop a central celestial cloud, wearing his general's uniform and draped with a purple robe in the style of victorious Roman generals, Washington presides in heavenly glory, flanked by Liberty and Victory, and surrounded by classical gods, goddesses, and American figures.

The Apotheosis Perplex

Pop History

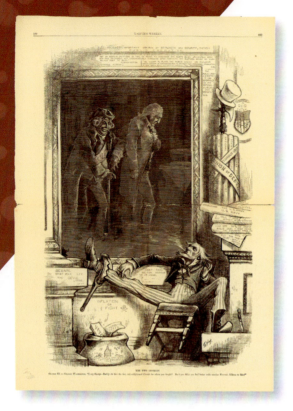

Thomas Nast, *The Two Georges*, March 23, 1878. Wood engraving. Published in *Harper's Weekly*.

Even one hundred years after the Revolutionary War, George III and George Washington could be used as symbols of the—now friendly—rivalry of their two nations. In this print, legendary political cartoonist Thomas Nast depicts a ghost of the king mocking the specter of his former enemy Washington, by pointing out that Uncle Sam is falling down on the job: "I say, George - Daddy - is that the free and enlightened Cherub for whom you fought? Don't you think you had better write another Farewell Address to him?" The cartoon is rife with allusions to American political issues of the 1870s, including the currency debate over the silver and gold standards; labor versus capital; reduction of the military; and the public debt.

"Mad Salutes the Bicentennial Year," *Mad* magazine, no. 181, March 1976. E. C. Publications.

A gap-toothed *Mad* mascot Alfred E. Neuman assumes the persona of George Washington on the cover of an issue featuring "Historical Reenactments We'd Like to See" during America's bicentennial celebrations. The country's bestselling humor magazine at the time, *Mad* parodied American culture and roasted public figures. Satirizing Gilbert Stuart's famous but incomplete portrait of Washington (1796), the cover includes a handwritten note from the president: "Dear Mr. Stuart, I really do not believe this to be a good likeness of me! It would best remain unfinished! George Washington." Stuart never completed what became known as the Athenaeum portrait since he used it only as a reference copy in making additional Washington portraits for clients. Stuart's rendering later served as the model for Washington's appearance on US postage stamps; *Mad's* version epitomized Washington's image as traditional shorthand for referencing the Revolution in American popular culture.

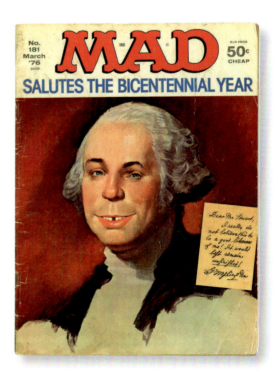

Jonathan Groff as King George III in *Hamilton*, ca. 2016. Photograph.

Lin-Manuel Miranda's mega hit musical *Hamilton: An American Musical* (2015) depicts the struggle in founding the United States through a series of hip-hop songs and Broadway show tunes. The main conflict centers on American founding fathers and rivals Alexander Hamilton and Aaron Burr, while George III appears as a campy secondary antagonist and George Washington is played straight, as a father figure to Hamilton. Though he is only onstage for about nine minutes total, His Majesty steals the show, prancing around the stage in regal garb and predicting "You'll Be Back," a number Miranda wrote as a taunting breakup letter from the king to the former colonies.

Hamilton won eleven Tony Awards, the Grammy Award for Best Musical Theater Album, and the Pulitzer Prize for Drama. It revitalized interest in the Revolutionary period, especially its title character and King George, and its inclusive casting and rapping attracted younger, diverse crowds who made the show a cultural phenomenon.

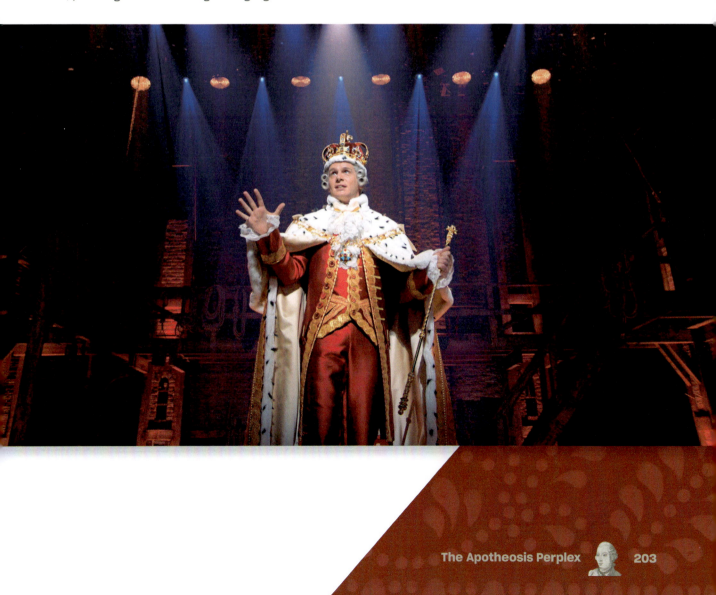

Portrait Gallery:
Lives and Legacies in Oil and Marble

Allan Ramsay, *George III*, ca. 1761-62. Oil on canvas.

Newly crowned George III, young and robust, dressed in a bright vermillion suit and ermine coronation robe, is shown in a life-size official state portrait. The heavy bejeweled crown of Saint Edward, a symbol of the king's authority, sits nearby on the table. The portrait was in such demand that Allan Ramsay, principal painter to the king, and his assistants spent two decades making copies, including smaller cropped versions. This painting belonged to George himself and was displayed in his mother's home at Carlton House and later at Buckingham Palace. Replicas hung in other royal residences, institutions, businesses, and on the walls of British colonial offices and corporations worldwide.

Charles Willson Peale, *George Washington as First Colonel in the Virginia Regiment,* **1772. Oil on canvas.**

Martha Washington commissioned this three-quarter-length portrait from Charles Willson Peale long after the period depicted here, when her husband served as the commander of the Virginia Regiment (1755-1758) during the French and Indian War. Washington wears the provincial colonial uniform of a colonel, including a sash and a silver gorget around his neck bearing Britain's coat of arms, both items signifying his status as an officer. Denied a commission in the regular British Army, he resigned his post in 1759. The painting hung next to a portrait of Martha in the Washingtons' front parlor at Mount Vernon until her death thirty years later.

Lives and Legacies in Oil and Marble

John Wollaston, *Martha Dandridge Custis*, 1757. Oil on canvas.

Traveling painter to the rich and famous, John Wollaston produced this pricey portrait of Martha, the earliest known image of her, when she was about twenty-six years old and shortly before her first husband, Daniel Custis, died suddenly. She was soon Mrs. Washington, and she paired this painting with one she commissioned of her new husband in their Mount Vernon mansion. Young and stylishly dressed, Wollaston's Martha bears little resemblance to the pleasant grandmother she appears to be in popular images that circulated during George's presidency and ever since. More than forty years after it was made, Polish statesman Julian Urysn Niemcewicz saw it as a guest at Mount Vernon and was underwhelmed; he described the painted Martha as having "a blue gown with her hair dressed a half an inch high and her ears uncovered. In her right hand she carries a flower. This portrait, which was never good, is in addition badly damaged."

Portrait Gallery

Thomas Gainsborough, *Queen Charlotte*, **1781. Oil on canvas.**

Through the enthusiastic patronage of George III, the Royal Academy in London for the Purpose of Cultivating and Improving the Arts of Painting, Sculpture, and Architecture was established in 1768 and took on a mission as expansive as its name. Leading portraitist Thomas Gainsborough was among the Royal Academy's founders, later becoming a favorite artist with the royal family. In his full-length painting of the queen, who was thirty-seven when she posed, Charlotte appears in a large, contoured powdered wig that was very much of the moment, unlike her hoop dress, then declining in fashion. For the rest of her life, the queen required that women at court continue to wear her preferred, outdated style, though not everyone managed to maneuver around in it as effortlessly as Her Majesty. The king had the painting installed in Buckingham House's dining room, where it primarily remained on display into the reign of their granddaughter Victoria.

Lives and Legacies in Oil and Marble

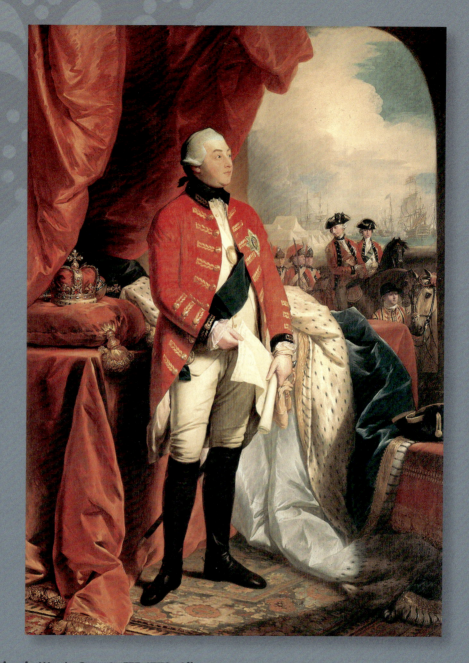

Benjamin West, *George III*, 1779. Oil on canvas.

Benjamin West created this portrait, one of the king's favorites, the same year Spain declared war on Britain, leading to the possibility of a naval invasion by Spain and France. West portrays the king as a man of action, having set aside his crown and robes, appearing in a bright red military coat as commander-in-chief, and gripping a document recording troop positions. In the background, a groom leads the king's horse followed by military advisors the Marquess of Lothian and Lord Amherst. West, who was born in the Pennsylvania colony but spent most of his life in England, shared the same life dates (1738-1820) as George III, and the king appointed him historical painter to the court, commissioning some eighty paintings from the artist. Four years after this portrait was done, West painted his friend and monarch wearing a suit of armor, perhaps to improve his military image following the loss of America.

Charles Willson Peale, *George Washington at Princeton*, 1779. Oil on canvas.

Charles Willson Peale depicts a confident-looking General Washington after the Battle of Princeton, which occurred in January 1777. The Supreme Executive Council of Pennsylvania commissioned the artist, himself a Revolutionary War soldier, to commemorate the victory that drove the British out of New Jersey; the painting was for the council's room in Independence Hall. Washington wears his uniform as commander-in-chief; in the distance Princeton college can be seen, along with British prisoners-of-war. Peale made eight copies of the painting, and replicas were in high demand.

Lives and Legacies in Oil and Marble

Thomas Lawrence, *George III*, 1818. Oil on canvas.

George III is seen here in his elaborate velvet robe and accoutrements as head of one of the world's oldest surviving chivalric orders, the Most Noble Order of the Garter. Edward III established it in 1348, inspired by the legend of King Arthur and the Knights of the Round Table, and some four hundred years later, as a young prince, George was installed in the elite association. His solid gold chain collar comprises heraldic knots and medallions, below which hangs a figure of St. George astride a white charger, spear raised, slaying a dragon. An enormous tassel fastens the king's robe, and below his left knee he wears the order's namesake apparel. The king regarded knighthood in the order as a rare but "public testimonial of my approbation," offered to those of high rank and merit. In 1786, George expanded membership, originally limited to the monarch, the Prince of Wales, and twenty-four knights, to include his many sons.

Gilbert Stuart, *George Washington* **(Lansdowne Portrait), 1796. Oil on canvas.**

Former British prime minister Lord Shelburne (later known as the Marquess of Lansdowne), who oversaw the treaty ending the American Revolutionary War and was eager to establish strong postwar trade relations, was the first to own this iconic painting. The president appears in plain but formal civilian dress, a black velvet suit distinguished by a high-collared white ruffled shirt. Gilbert Stuart based this and his many other portraits of Washington on an unfinished painting he had quickly made from life. Symbols of the new republic include books on recent American history, carved eagles, a stars-and-stripes medallion under laurel, as well as the rainbow in the upper right indicating a peaceful calm after the storm of war. Lord Lansdowne was delighted with the life-size work when it reached him in London, writing a friend that "A very fine portrait of the greatest man living in a magnificent frame found its way into my hall" where on seeing it his guests "turn away from every thing else, to pay their homage to General Washington."

Lives and Legacies in Oil and Marble 213

Peter Turnerelli, jubilee bust of George III, 1812 version. Marble.

As part of the golden jubilee celebrations marking the king's fifty years on the throne, Peter Turnerelli modelled the official bust, depicting George at the age of seventy-two with his Star of the Order of the Garter pinned on his coat. The sculptor was an art tutor to the king's daughters, later becoming sculptor-in-ordinary to the royal family. Turnerelli sometimes portrayed his prominent subjects in neoclassical cloaks and drapery, which was then the style (as with the bust of George Washington), but he also introduced the practice of rendering them in their regular attire, as seen here. The bust was exhibited at the Royal Academy during the jubilee, and another eighty marble copies were produced and sold to institutional and private purchasers. The version shown here dates to 1812, a few years after the original was presented to His Majesty on October 25, 1809, at Windsor Castle.

Hiram Powers, bust of George Washington, 1838-44, carved after 1844. Marble.

Prominent American sculptor Hiram Powers based his life-size bust of George Washington on the work of French artist Jean Houdon, who had made a plaster life mask of the fifty-three-year-old general in 1785 for reference in producing a full-size statue. By placing Washington in classical drapery, Powers connected his subject to the democratic virtues of classical Greece and the republican ideals of ancient Rome. So popular was the piece that the sculptor carved some three dozen replicas with the help of Italian stonecutters, and this representation of the founding father became the quintessential version reproduced by later artists and manufacturers.

Lives and Legacies in Oil and Marble

Acknowledgments

The editors gratefully acknowledge the assistance of their Library of Congress colleagues, especially Julie Miller (Manuscript Division), the curator of the *Two Georges* exhibition; the exhibition team of John Powell, Carroll Johnson, Naomi Coquillon, and Cheryl Regan (ret.); Tim St. Onge (Geography and Map Division), who created new maps of the Georges' travel; Kevin Butterfield (Kluge Center), Julie Stoner (Geography & Map Division), and Nicki Saylor, Judith Gray, and Michael Pahn (American Folklife Center) for reviewing all or parts of the text.

In addition, Barbara Bair and Timothy Stutz (Manuscript Division); Amanda Zimmerman (Rare Book and Special Collections Division); Lena Denis (Geography & Map Division); and Sara Duke (Prints and Photographs Division) provided expert guidance and assistance with their divisions' collections.

Many thanks go to our Publishing Office colleagues Becky Clark, Pete Devereaux, Hannah Freece, Aimee Hess, and to interns Jane Brinley, Grace Conroy, Polina Lopez, and Jude Souazoube; Tijuana Goldring and Michelle Williams (Office of the Librarian), who provided invaluable programmatic support; and David Mandel (Center for Exhibitions & Interpretation), Mike Munshaw, and Marlena Rivera (Design Office).

Thanks also to Kate Heard, senior curator of prints and drawings, Daniel Partridge, and Karen Lawson (Royal Collection Trust); Andrew Jackson O'Shaughnessy (University of Virginia) for reviewing the chapter opening essays; Paige Emerick (University of Leicester) for sharing her thesis and original maps of the royal travels of George III; Dawn Bonner (Mount Vernon) for generously providing us with images; and Benjamin Justice (Rutgers University) for sharing information and images of the Seal of Quebec.

Contributors

Arthur Burns (1963–2023) was a Professor of Modern British History at Kings College London. A widely published specialist in the cultural and institutional history of religion focused on the Church of England, Professor Burns was also a pioneer in the field of Digital Humanities via his co-leadership of The Clergy of the Church of England Database, 1540–1835. He was the academic director of the Georgian Papers Programme, a project which, via digitization, similarly opened up new archival materials to researchers both within the academy and beyond.

Flora Fraser, historical biographer, has published, among other books, *Beloved Emma: The Life of Lady Hamilton*; *Princesses: The Daughters of George III*; *The Washingtons: George & Martha*, which won the 2016 George Washington Book Prize; and in 2023, a life of Jacobite heroine, Flora Macdonald. A Mount Vernon Georgian Papers Fellow in 2017 and a trustee of the London National Portrait Gallery for ten years, she was awarded an honorary doctorate from King's College, London in 2019. Flora Fraser is also co-founder and Chair of the Elizabeth Longford Prize for Historical Biography.

Eliga Gould is professor of history at the University of New Hampshire. His books include *Among the Powers of the Earth: The American Revolution and the Making of a New World Empire* (2012). Named a Library Journal Best Book of the Year, it received the SHEAR Book Prize from the Society for Historians of the Early American Republic and was a finalist for the George Washington Book Prize. Gould has held fellowships from the John Simon Guggenheim Memorial Foundation, the Robert H. Smith International Center for Jefferson Studies at Monticello, the National Endowment for the Humanities, and the Charles Warren Center at Harvard. Gould is the 2025-2026 Harmsworth Visiting Professor American History at Oxford University.

Jane Kamensky is a historian of British America and the United States. She is the author of numerous books, including *A Revolution in Color: The World of John Singleton Copley* (2016), which won four major prizes and was a finalist for several others, and *Candida Royalle and the Sexual Revolution*, published by W. W. Norton in March 2024. A former Commissioner of the Smithsonian National Portrait Gallery, Kamensky serves as a Trustee of the Museum of the American Revolution, and as one of the principal investigators on the NEH/Department of Education-funded initiative, Educating for American Democracy, among many other public history roles. For thirty years, she worked as a history professor and higher education leader, most recently as Jonathan Trumbull Professor of American History at Harvard University and Pforzheimer Foundation Director of the Schlesinger Library on the History of Women in America at Harvard Radcliffe Institute. In January 2024, she became the president of Monticello/the Thomas Jefferson Foundation.

Julie Miller oversees early American manuscripts in the Manuscript Division at the Library of Congress, and she is the curator of *The Two Georges* exhibition. She is the author of *Abandoned: Foundlings in Nineteenth-Century New York City* (NYU Press, 2008) and *Cry of Murder on Broadway: A Woman's Ruin and Revenge in Old New York* (Three Hills, Cornell University Press, October 2020), articles in academic and popular publications, including the *New York Times* and *Washington Post*, and many posts on Library of Congress blogs. She has been the recipient of awards and fellowships from the New York State Historical Association, the New-York Historical Society, and the Kluge Center at the Library of Congress. Before coming to the Library of Congress she taught in the history department of Hunter College, City University of New York.

Colleen Shogan is the 11th Archivist of the United States. Previously, she served as the Senior Vice President of the White House Historical Association, the Vice Chair of the Women's Suffrage Centennial Commission, and a senior executive at the Library of Congress. She has taught the presidency and the history of American political development at George Mason University and Georgetown University. Dr. Shogan holds a BA in Political Science from Boston College and a PhD in American Politics from Yale University. She is a member of Phi Beta Kappa, the Order of the Cross and Crown, and the Washington, DC Literary Society.

Karin Wulf is the Beatrice and Julio Mario Santo Domingo Librarian and Director of the John Carter Brown Library and Professor of History at Brown University. A historian of gender, family, and political culture in 18th century British America, she was the academic co-director of the Georgian Papers Programme from its inception to 2021. Her works include *Lineage: Genealogy and the Power of Connection in Early America* (2025).

For the Library of Congress Publishing Office:

Zach Klitzman is a writer-editor in the Publishing Office at the Library of Congress. He is the coauthor of *American Feast: Cookbooks and Cocktails from the Library of Congress* (2023), and he edits the Library of Congress Crime Classics series. A former *Jeopardy!* Champion, he previously worked at President Lincoln's Cottage, a national monument and national historic landmark where Abraham Lincoln wrote the Emancipation Proclamation. He holds an MA in history from American University and a BA in history from the University of Pennsylvania.

Susan Reyburn is a writer-editor in the Publishing Office at the Library of Congress. She is the author of *Rosa Parks: In Her Own Words* (2020), *Football Nation: Four Hundred Years of America's Game* (2014), *Women Who Dare: Amelia Earhart* (2006), and a coauthor of A*merican Feast: Cookbooks and Cocktails from the Library of Congress* (2023), *Baseball Americana: Treasures from the Library of Congress* (2009), *The Library of Congress World War II Companio*n (2007), and *The Library of Congress Civil War Desk Reference* (2002). She holds an MLS from the Catholic University of America and a BA in history from UCLA.

The Two Georges Partnership

The *Two Georges: Parallel Lives in an Age of Revolution*, both this publication and the accompanying exhibition, grew out of the Library of Congress's participation in the Georgian Papers Programme (https://georgianpapers.com). An ambitious initiative begun in 2015, the GPP digitized, conserved, catalogued, interpreted, and disseminated 425,000 manuscript pages held in the Royal Archives and Royal Library at Windsor Castle in London. This partnership included the following institutions:

The Library of Congress

Founded in 1800, the Library of Congress in Washington, DC, is the oldest federal cultural institution in the United States. The largest library in the world, it provides Congress with non-partisan research, administers the national copyright system, and collects books, manuscripts, original works of fine art, photographs, films, sound recordings, sheet music, maps, and more in documenting all fields of human inquiry and creativity. Visit https://www.loc.gov.

The George Washington Papers held in the Manuscript Division of the Library of Congress constitute the largest collection of original Washington papers in the world. They consist of approximately 77,000 items accumulated by Washington between 1745 and 1799, including correspondence, diaries, and financial and military records. Also documented is his management of Mount Vernon, his plantation home in Virginia, and the lives of his family and servants, and the enslaved people on whose labor his wealth depended. Because of the wide range of Washington's interests, activities, and correspondents, which include ordinary citizens as well as celebrated figures, his papers are a rich source of information about almost every aspect of life in early America.

The Royal Collection Trust

The Royal Collection Trust, established in 1993, is a department in the British Royal Household responsible for overseeing art collections, manuscripts, and public access to royal residences. It preserves, presents, and interprets items and properties in its custody to encourage public appreciation and understanding. Visit https://www.rct.uk.

The Royal Collection Trust holds thousands of items related to George III as a subject, creator, collector, and commissioner, including manuscripts, paintings, prints, illustrations, clocks and scientific instruments, furniture, housewares, and jewelry.

Omohundro Institute of Early American History & Culture

An independent research organization in Williamsburg, Virginia, the Omohundro Institute was created in 1943 to support the study of North America, its indigenous and immigrant peoples, cultures, and geography, as well as transatlantic slavery, trade, and colonization from the mid-fifteenth century to the early nineteenth century. Visit https://oieahc.wm.edu/.

George Washington's Mount Vernon

The mission of the Mount Vernon Ladies' Association is to preserve, restore, and manage the estate of George Washington and to educate visitors and people throughout the world about the life and legacies of George Washington. Resources include primary and secondary source collections, educational videos, and interactive online tools. The George Washington Presidential Library provides access to the Papers of George Washington and offers research fellowships. Visit https://www.mountvernon.org/.

King's College London

King's College London, founded in 1829, provided the academic lead for the Georgian Papers Programme. Research and teaching for the period covered by the GPP is supported by the significant library and archive holdings at King's College, including the library of the Foreign and Commonwealth Office, the historic medical libraries of St Thomas's, Guy's and King's College Hospitals, and gifts of libraries by nineteenth century antiquarian collectors and bibliophiles. Visit http://www.kcl.ac.uk/.

Contributors

Selected Sources and Notes

Note to Readers

The enormous amount of primary and secondary source material on the Two Georges that exists and continues to be generated centuries after their deaths is extraordinary but not surprising. In producing *The Two Georges*, authors consulted a range of resources, from original manuscripts to a wealth of digitized media that allowed for advanced research and access to previously unavailable documents. Authoritative works by leading historians shed further light on the personalities, the milieus, and the events featured here and are essential for a deeper understanding of the Georges and their world. Many good biographies on the pair exist, but two essential and definitive works include *George Washington: A Life* (2010) by Ron Chernow and *The Last King of America: The Misunderstood Reign of George III* (2021) by Andrew Roberts. Other biographies consulted include *You Never Forget Your First: A Biography of George Washington* (2020) by Alexis Coe, *George III: America's Last King* (2006) by Jeremy Black, and *George III: A Personal History* (1998) by Christopher Hibbert. For in-depth looks at the men's families, see Flora Fraser's *The Washingtons: George and Martha, Partners in Friendship and Love* (2015) and *Princesses: The Six Daughters of George III* (2006); Janice Hadlow's *A Royal Experiment: Love and Duty, Madness and Betrayal: The Private Lives of Kinge George III and Queen Charlotte* (2015) and *Martha Washington: A Life* (2005) by Patricia Brady.

For coverage of the Georges at war, readers will find Andrew O'Shaughnessy's *The Men Who Lost America: British Leadership, the American Revolution and the Fate of the Empire* (2013) and *General George Washington: A Military Life* (2005) by Edward G. Lengel particularly worthwhile. Other works consulted include *The American Revolution: A World War* (2018) edited by David K. Allison and Larrie D. Ferreiro; *Making Headlines: The American Revolution as Seen through the British Press* (2009) by Troy Bickham; and *Iron Tears: America's Battle for Freedom, Britain's Quagmire: 1775–1783* (2005) by Stanley Weintraub.

Lindsay Chervinsky's comprehensive book, *The Cabinet: George Washington and the Creation of an American Institution* (2020), provides valuable insight into the first presidential administration, while both Linda Colley's *Britons: Forging the Nation, 1707–1837* (1992, rev. 2009) and Peter Jupp's *The Governing of Britain, 1688–1848: The Executive, Parliament and the People* (2006) are informative examinations of British national politics. For expert analysis of the era's cartoons, see *George III: A Life in Caricature* (2007) and *George Washington's War in Caricature and Print* (2009) both by Kenneth Baker; Tim Clayton's *James Gillray: A Revolution in Satire* (2022); *The Age of Caricature: Satirical Prints in the Reign of George III* (1996) by Diana Donald; and *George III and the Satirists from Hogarth to Byron* (1992) by Vincent Carretta.

Notable works on Washington and slavery include *Washington at the Plow: The Founding Father and the Question of Slavery* (2021) by Bruce Ragsdale; *The Only Unavoidable Subject of Regret: Washington, Slavery, and the Enslaved Community at Mount Vernon* (2019) by Mary V. Thompson; and *Lives Bound Together: Slavery at George Washington's Mount Vernon* (2016) edited by Susan P. Schoelwer. *The Indian World of George Washington: The First President, the First Americans, and the Birth of the Nation* (2018) by Colin Calloway explores in detail Washington's consequential experiences and relations with Indian nations. For data and analysis of the population traveling between Britain and America, see Julie Flavell's *When London Was Capital of America* (2010).

Online, readers can search and delve into the transcribed papers of George Washington and other founders through the National Archives' Founders Online website at https://founders.archives.gov/. The Library of Congress holds more than three dozen of Washington's diaries as well his examples of his school copy books, maps, letter books, general correspondence, financial papers, and military papers at https://www.loc.gov/collections/george-washington-papers. Mount Vernon provides extensive and valuable coverage of Washington and his family, his Virginia estate, and slavery at https://www.mountvernon.org/. A variety of George III's papers and those of Queen Charlotte and other family members are available through the Georgian Papers Programme at https://georgianpapers.com/. See the Royal Collection Trust at https://www.rct.uk/ for artwork, furniture, household goods, and other items commissioned by, owned by, or related to George III and his family.

Manuscript Collections

John Adams Papers. Library of Congress, Manuscript Division.
Benjamin Franklin Papers. Library of Congress, Manuscript Division.
Royal Archives, Georgian Papers Programme. Royal Collection Trust (RA GEO).
Thomas Jefferson Papers. Library of Congress, Manuscript Division.
George Washington Papers. Library of Congress, Manuscript Division.
Papers of George Washington, Mount Vernon Ladies' Association and the University of Virginia (PGWDE).

Published Primary Sources

Adams, John. *The Adams Papers Digital Edition*, ed. Sara Martin. Charlottesville: University of Virginia Press, Rotunda, 2008–2020.
Aspinall, A., ed. *Later Correspondence of George III*. 5 vols. Cambridge: Cambridge University Press, 1962–1970.
Barrett, Charlotte, ed. *Diary and Letters of Madame D'Arblay*. 4 vols. London: S. Sonnenschein, 1893.
Fortescue, John, ed. *The Correspondence of King George the Third*. 6 vols. London: Macmillan, 1927–28.
Murdoch, David H., ed. *Rebellion in America: A Contemporary British Viewpoint*, 1769–1783. Santa Barbara, CA: Clio Books, 1979.
Simmons, R. C. and P. D. G. Thomas, eds. *Proceedings and Debates of the British parliaments Respecting North America* 1754–1783. 6 volumes. Millwood, NY: Kraus International, 1982–1986.
Smith, Paul H., ed. *Letters of Delegates to Congress*, 1774–1789. Washington DC: Library of Congress, 1976.
Walpole, Horace. *The Letters of Horace Walpole, Earl of Orford*, edited by Peter Cunningham. London: Bickers and Son, 1877.
Washington, George. "Letters of George Washington to Lord Dunmore." *The William and Mary College Quarterly Historical Magazine* 20, no. 2 (1940): 162–66. https://doi.org/10.2307/1922674.

Secondary Sources

Allison, David K. and Larrie D. Ferreiro, eds. *The American Revolution: A World War*. Washington, DC: Smithsonian Books, 2018.
Baker, Kenneth. *George III: A Life in Caricature*. New York: Thames & Hudson, 2007.
———. *George Washington's War in Caricature and Print*. London: Grub Street, 2009.
Bellion, Wendy. *Iconoclasm in New York: Revolution to Reenactment*. University Park: Pennsylvania State University Press, 2019.
Bickham, Troy O. "Sympathizing with Sedition? George Washington, the British Press, and British Attitudes during the American War of Independence." *The William and Mary Quarterly* 59, no. 1 (January 2002): 101–122. https://doi.org/10.2307/3491639.
———. *Making Headlines: The American Revolution as Seen through the British Press*. DeKalb: Northern Illinois University Press, 2009.
Bingham, Warren L. *George Washington's 1791 Southern Tour*. Charleston, SC: History Press, 2016.
Black, Jeremy. *George III: America's Last King*. New Haven, CT: Yale University Press, 2006.
Bradley, Patricia. "The Boston Gazette and Slavery as Revolutionary Propaganda." *Journalism & Mass Communication Quarterly* 72, no. 3 (Autumn 1995): 581–596.
Brady, Patricia. *Martha Washington: An American Life*. New York: Penguin Books, 2006.
Bullion, John L. "The Prince's Mentor: A New Perspective on the Friendship between George III and Lord Bute during the 1750s." *Albion* 21, no. 1 (1989): 34–55. https://doi.org/10.2307/4049865.
Burnard, Trevor. "Slavery and the Causes of the American Revolution in Plantation British America." In Shankman, *The World of the Revolutionary American Republic*, 54–76.
Calloway, Colin G. *The Indian World of George Washington: The First President, the First Americans, and the Birth of the Nation*. New York: Oxford University Press, 2018.
Cannon, John. "George III and America." *The Historian* 85 (Spring 2005): 20–26.
Carlson, Peter. "John Adams' Bow to King George III." *American History* 47, no. 5 (Dec 2012): 28.
Carretta, Vincent. *George III and the Satirists from Hogarth to Byron*. Athens: University of Georgia Press, 1992.
Chernow, Ron. *Washington: A Life*. New York: Penguin Press, 2010.
Chervinsky, Lindsay M. The *Cabinet: George Washington and the Creation of an American Institution*. Cambridge, MA: Belknap Press, 2020.
Clayton, Tim. *James Gillray: A Revolution in Satire*. New Haven, CT: Paul Mellon Centre for Studies in British Art, 2022.

Colley, Linda. *Britons: Forging the Nation*, 1707–1837. Rev. ed. New Haven, CT: Yale University Press, 2009.
Coe, Alexis. *You Never Forget Your First: A Biography of George Washington*. New York: Penguin Books, 2020.
Cresswell, Donald H., comp. *The American Revolution in Drawings and Prints: A Checklist Of 1765–1790 Graphics in the Library Of Congress*. Washington, DC: Library of Congress, 1975.
Cunliffe, Marcus. "The Two Georges: The President and the King." *American Studies International* 24, no. 2 (1986): 53–73. http://www.jstor.org/stable/41278850.
Donald, Diana. *The Age of Caricature: Satirical Prints in the Reign of George III*. New Haven, CT: Paul Mellon Centre for Studies in British Art, 1996.
Dorsey, Peter A. *Common Bondage: Slavery as Metaphor in Revolutionary America*. Knoxville: University Press of Tennessee, 2009.
DuVal, Kathleen. *Independence Lost: Lives on the Edge of the American Revolution*. New York: Random House, 2015.
Edelson, S. Max. *The New Map of Empire: How Britain Imagined America Before Independence*. Cambridge, MA: Harvard University Press, 2017.
Edwards, Sam. "A Great Englishman? British Views of George Washington, from Revolution to Rapprochement." *Journal of the American Revolution*, March 17, 2022. https://allthingsliberty.com/2022/03/a-great-englishman-british-views-of-george-washington-from-revolution-to-rapprochement/.
Ellis, Richard J. *Presidential Travel: The Journey from George Washington to George W. Bush*. Lawrence: University Press of Kansas, 2008.
Emerick, Paige Nicole. "Monarchy on the Move: The Royal Visits of George III and George IV, 1760–1830." PhD thesis, University of Leicester (UK), 2023.
Erby, Adam T., J. Dean Norton, and Esther C. White. *The General in the Garden: George Washington's Landscape at Mount Vernon*. Mount Vernon, VA: Mount Vernon Ladies' Association, 2015.
Ferling, John. "John Adams, Diplomat." *The William and Mary Quarterly* 51, no. 2 (1994): 227–52. https://doi.org/10.2307/2946861.
Flavell, Julie. *When London Was the Capital of America*. New Haven, CT: Yale University Press, 2010.
Fraser, Flora. *Princesses: The Daughters of George III*. New York: Knopf, 2005.
———. *The Unruly Queen: The Life of Queen Caroline*. New York: Knopf, 1996.
———. *The Washingtons: George and Martha*. New York: Alfred A. Knopf, 2015.
Freeman, Douglas Southall. *George Washington: A Biography*, 7 volumes. New York: Charles Scribner's Sons, 1948–1957.
Furstenberg, Francois. *In the Name of the Father: Washington's Legacy, Slavery, and the Making of a Nation*. New York: Penguin Books, 2006.
George M. Dorothy. *Catalogue of political and personal satires preserved in the Dept. of Prints and Drawings in the British Museum*. Vol. 5. London: British Museum, 1935.
Gould, Eliga. *Among the Powers of the Earth: The American Revolution and the Making of a New World Empire*. Cambridge, MA: Harvard University Press, 2012.
Gould, Eliga and Peter S. Onuf, eds. *Empire and Nation: The American Revolution in the Atlantic World*. Baltimore: Johns Hopkins University Press, 2005.
Hadlow, Janice. *A Royal Experiment: Love and Duty, Madness and Betrayal: The Private Lives of King George III and Queen Charlotte*. New York: Picador, 2015.
Hart, Katherine W. *James Gillray: Prints by the Eighteenth-Century Master of Caricature*. With the assistance of Laura Hacker. Hanover, NH: Hood Museum of Art, Dartmouth College, 1994.
Hibbert, Christopher. *George III: A Personal History*. New York: Basic Books, 1998.
———. *George IV: Prince of Wales*, 1762–1811. New York: Harper & Row, 1972.
———. *George IV: Regent and King*. New York: Harper & Row, 1975.
Isaac, Amanda C. and Michele Lee. *Take Note! George Washington the Reader*. Mount Vernon, VA: Mount Vernon Ladies' Association, 2013.
Jefcoate, Graham. "'Most Curious, Splendid and Useful': The King's Library of George III," in *Enlightenment: Discovering the World in the Eighteenth Century*. Kim Sloan, ed., the British Museum. Washington, DC: Smithsonian Books, 2003.
Justice, Benjamin. "The Art of Coining Christians: Indians and Authority in the Iconography of British Atlantic Colonial Seals, 1606–1767." *Journal of British Studies* 61, no. 1 (2022): 105–37. https://doi.org/10.1017/jbr.2021.118.
Jupp, Peter. *The Governing of Britain, 1688–1848: The Executive, Parliament and the People*. London: Routledge, 2006.
Kay, Emma. *Dining with the Georgians: A Delicious History*. Stroud, Gloucestershire, UK: Amberley Publishing, 2014.
Knox, Tim. "The King's Library and Its Architectural Genesis" in *Enlightenment: Discovering the World in the Eighteenth Century*. Kim Sloan, ed., the British Museum. Washington, DC: Smithsonian Books, 2003.
Lambert, Andrew. "The British Grand Strategy." In Allison and Ferreiro, *The American Revolution*, 34–51.
Lancelott, Francis. *The Queens of England and Their Times: From Matilda, Queen of William the Conqueror, to Adelaide, Queen of William the Fourth*, 2 volumes. D. Appleton, 1859.

Lee, Jean B. *Experiencing Mount Vernon: Eyewitness Accounts*, 1754-1865. Charlottesville: University of Virginia Press, 2006.

Lengel, Edward G. *General George Washington: A Military Life*. New York: Random House, 2005.

MacLeod, Jessie. "Kitchen Confidential." *Mount Vernon*, Winter 2021.

Marschner, Joanna, David Bindham and Lisa L. Ford, eds. *Enlightened Princesses: Caroline, Augusta, Charlotte, and The Shaping of the Modern World*. New Haven, CT: Yale Center for British Art, 2017.

McLeod, Stephen A, ed. *Dining with the Washingtons: Historic Recipes, Entertaining, and Hospitality from Mount Vernon*. Mount Vernon, VA: Mount Vernon, Ladies Association, 2011.

Meacham, Jon. *Thomas Jefferson: The Art of Power*. New York: Random House, 2012.

Morgan, Philip D. "'To Get Quit of Negroes': George Washington and Slavery." *Journal of American Studies* 39, no. 3 (2005): 403–29. https://doi.org/10.1017/S0021875805000599.

"Office-Holders in Modern Britain," in *Office-Holders in Modern Britain: Volume 11 (Revised), Court Officers, 1660–1837*. London, 2006. *British History Online*. https://www.british-history.ac.uk/office-holders/vol11.

Onuf, Peter S. "The Empire of Liberty: Land of the Free and Home of the Slave." In Shankman, *The World of the Revolutionary American Republic*, 195–217.

O'Shaughnessy, Andrew Jackson. "'If Others Will Not Be Active, I Must Drive': George III and the American Revolution." *Early American Studies: An Interdisciplinary Journal* 2, no. 1 (2004): iii, 1-46. https://doi.org/10.1353/eam.2007.0037.

———. *The Men Who Lost America: British Leadership, the American Revolution, and the Fate of the Empire*. New Haven, CT: Yale University Press, 2013.

Palmer, Dave R. *George Washington's Military Genius*. Washington, DC: Regnery Publishing, 2012.

Paxton, James W. *Joseph Brant and His World: Eighteenth-Century Mohawk Warrior and Statesman*. Toronto: James Lorimer, 2008.

Philbrick, Nathaniel. *Travels with George: In Search of Washington and His Legacy*. New York: Viking, 2021.

Preston, David. "When Young George Washington Started a War." *Smithsonian Magazine*, October 2019. https://www.smithsonianmag.com/history/when-young-george-washington-started-war-180973076/.

Prochaska, Frank. *Royal Bounty: The Making of a Welfare Monarchy*. New Haven, CT: Yale University Press, 1995.

Quarles, Benjamin. "Lord Dunmore as Liberator." *The William and Mary Quarterly* 15, no. 4 (1958): 494–507. https://doi.org/10.2307/2936904.

Ragsdale, Bruce A. *Washington at the Plow: The First Farmer and the Question of Slavery*. Cambridge, MA: Harvard University Press, 2021.

Roberts, Andrew. *The Last King of America: The Misunderstood Reign of George III*. New York: Viking, 2021.

Rosenberg, Chaim M. *The Loyalist Conscience: Principled Opposition to the American Revolution*. Jefferson, NC: McFarland, 2018.

Sainsbury, John. *Disaffected Patriots: London Supporters of Revolutionary America, 1769–1782*. Kingston, Ontario: McGill-Queen's University Press, 1987.

Schama, Simon. *Rough Crossings: Britain, the Slaves and the American Revolution*. New York: HarperCollins, 2006.

Selig, Robert A. "Hessian Savages, Frog-Eating Frenchmen, and Virtuous Americans." In Allison and Ferreiro, *The American Revolution*, 170–186.

Shankman, Andrew, ed. *The World of the Revolutionary American Republic: Land, Labor, and the Conflict for a Continent*. New York: Routledge, 2014.

Schoelwer, Susan P., ed. *Lives Bound Together: Slavery at George Washington's Mount Vernon*. Mount Vernon, VA: Mount Vernon Ladies' Association, 2016.

Sloan, Kim, ed., the British Museum. *Enlightenment: Discovering the World in the Eighteenth Century*. Washington, DC: Smithsonian Books, 2003.

Thomas, P.D.G. "George III and the American Revolution." *History* 70, no. 228 (1985): 16–31. http://www.jstor.org/stable/24414920.

Thompson, Mary V. *"The Only Unavoidable Subject of Regret": George Washington, Slavery, and the Enslaved Community at Mount Vernon*. Charlottesville: University Press of Virginia, 2019.

Van Cleve, George William. "Founding a Slaveholders' Union, 1770–1797." In *Contesting Slavery: The Politics of Bondage and Freedom in the New American Nation*, edited by John Craig Hammond and Matthew Mason, 117–137. Charlottesville: University of Virginia Press, 2011.

Weintraub, Stanley. *Iron Tears: America's Battle for Freedom, Britain's Quagmire: 1775–1783*. New York: Free Press, 2005.

Wiencek, Henry. *An Imperfect God: George Washington, His Slaves, and the Creation of America*. New York: Farrar, Strauss and Giroux, 2003.

Wills, Gary. *Cincinnatus: George Washington and the Enlightenment*. Garden City, NY: Doubleday, 1984.

Websites

American History Collection, Rotunda. University of Virginia. https://rotunda.upress.virginia.edu/founders/.
Founders Online. National Archives. https://founders.archives.gov/.
Georgian Papers Programme. https://georgianpapers.com/.
James Gillray: Caricaturist. Created by Jim Sherry. https://www.james-gillray.org/.
Journal of the American Revolution. https://allthingsliberty.com.
Library of Congress. https://www.loc.gov/.
Mount Vernon. https://www.mountvernon.org/.
Royal Collection Trust. https://www.rct.uk.
Science Museum (London). https://www.sciencemuseum.org.uk/

Sources for Chapter 1

Anderson, Fred. *The Crucible of War: The Seven Years War and the Fate of Empire in British North America, 1754–1766*. New York: Alfred A. Knopf, 2000.
Black, Jeremy. *George III: America's Last King*. New Haven, CT: Yale University Press, 2009.
Chernow, Ron. *Washington: A Life*. New York: Penguin, 2010.
Colley, Linda. *Britons: Forging the Nation, 1707–1837*. New Haven, CT: Yale University Press, 1992.
Ditchfield, G. M. *George III: An Essay in Monarchy*. Houndmills, Basingstoke, Hampshire, UK: Palgrave Macmillan, 2002.
Fraser, Flora. T*he Washingtons, George and Martha: Partners in Friendship and Love*. New York: Anchor Books, 2016.
Gikandi. Simon. *Slavery and the Culture of Taste*. Princeton, NJ: Princeton University Press, 2011.
Gould, Eliga. *The Persistence of Empire: British Political Culture in the Age of the American Revolution*. Williamsburg, VA: Omohundro Institute of Early American History & Culture, 2000.
Hilton, Boyd. *A Mad, Bad and Dangerous People? England 1783–1846*. New York: Oxford University Press, 2006.
Kamensky, Jane. *A Revolution in Color: The World of John Singleton Copley*. New York: W. W. Norton, 2016.
Langford, Paul. *A Polite and Commercial People: England 1727–1783*, revised edition. Oxford: Oxford University Press, 1998.
O'Shaughnessy, Andrew Jackson. *The Men who Lost America: British Leadership, the American Revolution, and the Fate of Empire*. New Haven, CT: Yale University Press, 2013.
Thornton, John K. *Africa and Africans in the Making of an Atlantic World, 1400–1800*, second edition
Cambridge: Cambridge University Press, 1998.
Trans-Atlantic Slave Trade Database. https://www.slavevoyages.org/.

Notes for Chapter 2

1   Bartholomew Dandridge (1691–ca.1754), *Frederick, Prince of Wales*, NPG 1164; John Kerslake, *Early Georgian Portraits* (London: Her Majesty's Stationery Office, 1977), I: 79–80, and II, plate 216; Emma Lauze, "Bartholomew Dandridge," *Oxford Dictionary of National Biography* (Oxford: Oxford University Press, 2019), https://doi.org/10.1093/ref:odnb/7105. For the connection between the London and Virginia Dandridge brothers, see: Kevin J. Hayes, "William Dandridge (1689–1744)," *Encyclopedia Virginia* (Virginia Foundation for the Humanities, 2013), http://www.EncyclopediaVirginia.org/Dandridge_William_1689-1744. My thanks to Flora Fraser for drawing my attention to this portrait.

2   Douglas Southall Freeman, *George Washington: A Biography* (New York: Scribner's, 1948), 1:15.

3   Martha Saxton, *The Widow Washington: The Life of Mary Washington* (New York: Farrar, Straus and Giroux, 2018). Joseph Ball's letters to his half-sister and her family are in: Joseph Ball Letterbook, 1743–1759, MMC-1790, Manuscript Division, Library of Congress.

4   T. Pape, "Appleby Grammar School and its Washington Pupils," *William and Mary Quarterly* 20 (October 1940): 498–501.

5   For the overseas studies and marriages of George III's family members, see Flora Fraser, *Princesses: The Six Daughters of George III* (New York: Knopf, 2005) and Janice Hadlow, *A Royal Experiment: The Private Life of King George III* (New York: Henry Holt, 2014).

6   *George Washington's Barbados Diary, 1751–1752*, ed. Alicia K. Anderson and Lynn A. Price (Charlottesville: University of Virginia Press, 2018).

7   Joseph Ball to George Washington, September 5, 1755, Joseph Ball Letterbook, 1743–1759, MMC-1790, Manuscript Division, Library of Congress.

8   "Bulletts whistle": George Washington to John Augustine Washington, May 31, 1754, in *London Magazine*, August, 1754, 371. George II's comment is in Horace Walpole, *Memoirs of the Reign of King George II*, 2nd ed. (London, 1847), 1:400.

 Selected Sources and Notes

9   On the social status of surveyors in colonial Virginia, see: Philander D. Chase. "A Stake in the West: George Washington as Backcountry Surveyor and Landholder," in *George Washington and the Virginia Backcountry*, ed. Warren Hofstra (Madison, WI: Madison House, 1998), 161.

10   Stuart E. Brown, *Virginia Baron: The Story of Thomas, Sixth Lord Fairfax* (Berryville, VA: Chesapeake Book, 1965).

11   George Washington to John Augustine Washington, May 28, 1755. Citations from George Washington's letters and diaries are, unless otherwise noted, from *The Papers of George Washington* ed. W. W. Abbot (Charlottesville: University of Virginia Press, 1985–2018), on Founders Online, http://founders.archives.gov, and in George Washington Papers, Manuscript Division, Library of Congress, https://www.loc.gov/collections/george-washington-papers/about-this-collection/.

12   Washington's sales of his tobacco and purchases of imported goods are documented in his copybooks of letters and invoices, volume 3, 1754–1766, and volume 4, 1767–1775, Series 5, George Washington Papers, Manuscript Division, Library of Congress. Not published, viewable on https://www.loc.gov/collections/george-washington-papers/about-this-collection/. Garnet necklace (March, 1759, 3:249); toy coach (March, 1759, 3:252); "treatise of agriculture," (May 1, 1759, 3:19); surveying instruments from Martha Ayscough (September 28, 1760, 3:60, 3:286); carriage (June 6, 1768, 4:25); *Covent Garden Magazine*, almonds, anchovies, capers, (July 10, 1773, 4:100). George III bought a telescope from James Ayscough, Alan Q. Morton and Jane A. Wess, *Public and Private Science: The King George III Collection* (London: Oxford University Press in association with the Science Museum, 1993), 500. Martha Ayscough, his widow, continued the business after his death. See her advertisement in *Public Advertiser* (London), November 16, 1759.

13   George Washington to Richard Washington, September 20, 1758.

14   James Thomas Flexner repeatedly described Mary Ball Washington as a "termagant," T*he Indispensable Man* (New York: New American Library, 1974), 5, 13, 39. Samuel Eliot Morison called her "grasping, querulous, and vulgar," *The Young Man Washington, an Address Delivered at Sanders Theatre, Cambridge, February 22, 1932* (Cambridge, MA: Harvard University Press, 1932), 10. Douglas Southall Freeman wrote of her: "Mistress of much or of little, mistress she was resolved to be, and in nothing more certainly than in deciding what should be done by her first-born, her pride and her weakness," *George Washington*, I:193. For Princess Augusta's reputation see John Brooke, *King George III* (London: Constable, 1972), 29. She was viciously caricatured by the cartoonists of the era, see Cynthia E. Roman, "Disrespect: Undermining the Royal Image," in Joanna Marschner, ed., *Enlightened Princesses: Caroline, Augusta, Charlotte, and the Shaping of the Modern World* (New Haven, CT: Yale University Press, 2017).

15   For the Washingtons' marriage see Flora Fraser, *The Washingtons: George and Martha,"Join'd by Friendship, Crown'd by Love"* (New York: Alfred A. Knopf, 2015). For the marriage of King George and Queen Charlotte, see Hadlow, *Royal Experiment*, 154–181. George III was certainly not a feminist. He explained to his son, the Prince of Wales (later George IV): "Believe me, submission in a woman always secures esteem . . ." in Brooke, *King George III*, 350.

16   Prince George to King George II, July 26, 1759, *Letters from George III to Lord Bute, 1756–1766*, ed. Romney Sedgwick (Westport, CT: Greenwood Press, 1981; reprint, London: Macmillan, 1939), 25.

17   Address to George Washington from his officers on his retirement from the Virginia Regiment, December 31, 1758, George Washington Papers, Manuscript Division, Library of Congress.

18   George Washington to Francis Dandridge, September 20, 1765.

19   George III, Memorandum, [February 11, 1766], T*he Correspondence of King George the Third*, ed. John Fortescue, (London: Frank Cass, 1967), 1:269. Jeremy Black, *George III: America's Last King* (New Haven, CT: Yale University Press, 2006), 81–86.

20   John L. Bullion, "The 'Ancien Regime' and the Modernizing State: George III and the American Revolution." *Anglican and Episcopal History* 68 (March 1999): 67–84; A. J. O'Shaughnessy, "If Others Will Not Be Active, I Must Drive," *Early American Studies* 2 (Spring 2004): 1–46; P. D. G. Thomas, "George III and the American Revolution," *History* 70 (February 1985): 16–31.

21   George III to Lord North, September 11, 1774, Fortescue, *Correspondence*, 3:131.

22   George Washington belonged to the Virginia House of Burgesses, which in 1769 and 1774 passed resolutions protesting British impositions. See *Revolutionary Virginia: The Road to Independence*, comp. William J. Van Schreeven, ed. Robert L. Scribner (Charlottesville: University Press of Virginia,1973), 1:73–77, 97–98. Washington also signed the Fairfax County Resolves in 1774:

https://www.loc.gov/collections/george-washington-papers/articles-and-essays/fairfax-resolves. And in October, 1774, as a Virginia delegate to the First Continental Congress, he signed a petition to the king, which outlined the colonies' complaints. See Benjamin Franklin Papers, Series 1, Volume 10, Manuscript Division, Library of Congress. All of these documents of protest included statements of loyalty to the king.

23   George Washington to George William Fairfax, May 31, 1775.

24   Brooke, *King George III*, 390n7.

25   My thanks to Andrew Jackson O'Shaughnessy, Martha Saxton, Colleen Shogan, Stephanie Stillo, and Daniele Turello for their comments on drafts of this essay.

Notes for Chapter 3

1. Norman Hampson, *The Enlightenment: An Evaluation of its Assumptions, Attitudes and Values* (London: Penguin, 1968; 2014), 35–39; Kim Sloan, ed., *Enlightenment: Discovering the World in the Eighteenth Century* (London: British Museum Press, 2003), 12–13; Dorinda Outram, *The Enlightenment* (Cambridge: Cambridge University Press, 2019), 123–138.
2. Mary V. Thompson, *"In the Hands of a Good Providence": Religion in the Life of George Washington* (Charlottesville: University Press of Virginia, 2008), xiii; PGWDE, To the Hebrew Congregations of Philadelphia, New York, Charleston, and Richmond, 13 December 1790.
3. G. M. Ditchfield, *George III: An Essay in Monarchy* (Houndsmill, Basingstoke, Hampshire, UK: Palgrave, 2002), 77–108.
4. Christopher Hibbert, *George III: A Personal History* (London: Viking, 1998), 191–96; James Fisher, "George III: Notes on Agriculture," Royal Collection Trust (January 2017), 1–4; Bruce Ragsdale and G. Page West, "George Washington: Innovative Farmer," in *Lessons in Leadership*, eds., D. Bradburn & S. Thomas, George Washington Leadership Institute, Fred W. Smith National Library for the Study of George Washington, Mount Vernon, 2017, 1–25.
5. RA GEO/ADD/32/1-2485, George III Essays.
6. Francis Russell, "Lord Bute and George III," in *The Wisdom of George the Third,* ed. Jonathan Marsden (London: Royal Collection Enterprises, 2006), 28–42.
7. RA GEO/MAIN/54129, Frederick, Prince of Wales to Prince George [1745–1751]; RA GEO/ADD/32/1-2485, George III Essays.
8. David Watkin, *The Architect King: George III and the Culture of the Enlightenment* (London: The Royal Collection, 2004), 55–75.
9. PGWDE, School Exercises [Ferry Farm, 1744–1748], and n. 9.
10. PGWDE, George Washington's Professional Surveys [22 July 1749–25 October 1752].
11. See https://www.loc.gov/collections/george-washington-papers/articles-and-essays/george-washington-survey-and-mapmaker/washington-as-public-land-surveyor/surveyor; Don Higginbotham, ed., "Washington and Colonial Military Tradition," in *George Washington Reconsidered,* ed. Don Higginbotham (Charlottesville: University Press of Virginia, 2001), 43–51; https://www.mountvernon.org/george-washington/house-of-burgesses.
12. PGWDE, Settlement of the Daniel Parke Custis Estate. I. Queries to John Mercer, Williamsburg, April 20, 1759 and Editorial Note.
13. Mary V. Thompson, *"Only Unavoidable Subject of Regret": George Washington, Slavery, and the Enslaved Community at Mount Vernon* (Charlottesville: University Press of Virginia, 2019), 117–18.
14. PGWDE, Settlement of the Daniel Parke Custis Estate, Appendix D, Inventory of the Books in the Estate [ca. 1759]; PGWDE, List of Books at Mount Vernon [ca. 1764].
15. Flora Fraser, *The Washingtons: George and Martha* (New York: Alfred A. Knopf, 2015), 77–80, 89.
16. PGWDE, George Washington to Burwell Bassett, 20 June 1773.
17. Olwen Hedley, *Queen Charlotte* (London: J. Murray, 1975), 114.
18. Michael Kassler, *The Diary of Queen Charlotte, 1789 and 1794,* vol. 4 in *Memoirs of the court of George III* (London: Pickering & Chatto, 2015) passim; Flora Fraser, *Princesses: The Daughters of George III* (New York: Anchor Books, 2006), 68.
19. Charlotte Campbell Orr, "Queen Charlotte and Her Circle," in *The Wisdom of George the Third,* ed. Jonathan Marsden (London: Royal Collection Enterprises, 2006), 162–78.
20. James Boswell, *Life of Johnson* (London: Robert Riviere, 1906), 337–42; John Martin Robinson, *Buckingham Palace: A Short History* (London: Michael Joseph 1995), 11–43.
21. Bruce Redford, ed., *Letters of Samuel Johnson,* vol. 5, 1776–1779 (Princeton, NJ: Princeton University Press, 1992), 347 and n10.
22. Flora Fraser, *The Unruly Queen: The Life of Queen Caroline,* (London: Knopf, 1996), 32–36, 38–39; Christopher Hibbert, *George IV: Prince of Wales, 1762–1811* (London: Longman, 1972), 90.
23. Higginbotham, W*ashington and Colonial Military Tradition,* 43–51; Bruce A. Ragsdale, "George Washington, the British Tobacco Trade, and Economic Opportunity in Pre-Revolutionary Virginia" in *George Washington Reconsidered,* ed. Don Higginbotham , 67–93; https://www.mountvernon.org/george-washington/house-of-burgesses.
24. PGWDE, Commission from the Continental Congress [Philadelphia, 19 June 1775].
25. PGWDE, George Washington to Lund Washington, "Camp at Cambridge," August 19, 1775; John Ferling, *Almost a Miracle: The American Victory in the War of Independence* (Oxford: Oxford University Press, 2007), 523–39.
26. William M. S. Rasmussen and Robert S. Tilton, *George Washington: The Man Behind the Myths* (Charlottesville: University Press of Virginia, 1999), 205–10.
27. Fraser, *The Washingtons,* 253–54, 301–2, 314–15.

Selected Sources and Notes

28 Joseph E. Fields, ed., *"Worthy Partner": The Papers of Martha Washington* (Westport, CT: Greenwood Press, 1994), 351–52, 345–47, 354–56, 384–85.

29 PGWDE, George Washington's Last Will and Testament [Mount Vernon, 9 July 1799]; Thompson, *"Only Unavoidable Subject of Regret"*, 293–314.

30 David Cannadine, *Victorious Century: The United Kingdom, 1800–1906* (London: Allen Lane, 2017) 79–80.

31 Passage of Slave Trade Abolition Bill in House of Lords, prior to Royal Assent on 25 March 1807 https://www.parliament.uk/about/living-heritage/transformingsociety/tradeindustry/slavetrade/overview/parliament-abolishes-the-slave-trade/.

32 Christopher Hibbert, *George IV: Regent and King, 1811–1830* (London: Harper & Row, 1975), 289–91.

33 RA MED/16/14/185-219, Letters from the King's Physicians to the Prince Regent for January 1820; Richard Thomson, *A Faithful Account of … the Coronation …of King George III and Queen Charlotte* (London: J. Major, 1820), 55.

Notes for Chapter 4

1 Robert Middlekauff, *The Glorious Cause: The American Revolution, 1763–1789* (New York: Oxford University Press, 1982), 582–84.

2 George Washington to Friedrich Wilhelm Ludolf Gerhard Augustin, Baron [von] Steuben, 23 December 1783, *Founders Online*, National Archives, last modified June 13, 2018, http://founders.archives.gov/documents/Washington/99-01-02-12226; accessed January 18, 2019.

3 Joseph Farington, *The Farington Diary*, ed. James Greig, 8 vols. (London: Hutchinson, 1922–1928), 1:278.

4 George Washington to George Mason, 5 April 1769, *Founders Online*, National Archives, http://founders.archives.gov/documents/Washington/02-08-02-0132.

5 Andrew Jackson O'Shaughnessy, *The Men Who Lost America: British Leadership, the American Revolution, and the Fate of the Empire* (New Haven, CT: Yale University Press, 2013), 24–25.

6 Eliga H. Gould, *Among the Powers of the Earth: The American Revolution and the Making of a New World Empire* (Cambridge, MA: Harvard University Press, 2012), 115.

7 William D. Liddle, "'A Patriot King, or None': Lord Bolingbroke and the American Renunciation of George III," *Journal of American History* 65, no. 4 (1979): 965.

8 Washington to Hancock, Cambridge, Jan. 4, 1776, and Washington to Nicholas Cooke, Cambridge, Jan. 6, 1776, *Founders Online*, https://founders.archives.gov/documents/Washington/03-03-02-0013, and https://founders.archives.gov/documents/Washington/03-03-02-0025, accessed May 20, 2024.

9 Isaac N. Arnold, *The Life of Benedict Arnold: His Patriotism and His Treason* (Chicago: Jansen, McClurg, 1880), 331.

10 Winslow C. Watson, ed., *Men and Times of the Revolution; or, Memoirs of Elkanah Watson* (New York: Dana, 1856), 178–79.

11 Farington, *Diary*, 1:278.

Notes for Chapter 5

Dr. Shogan wrote her essay while serving as a senior executive at the Library of Congress, prior to her appointment as Archivist.

1 For example, see Steven Levitsky and Daniel Ziblatt, *How Democracies Die* (New York: Crown, 2018) and Aziz Huq and Tom Ginsberg, "How to Lose a Constitutional Democracy," *UCLA Law Review* 65 (2018): 80–169.

2 Harvey C. Mansfield, Jr., *Taming the Prince: The Ambivalence of Modern Executive Power*. (New York: The Free Press, 1989), xvi.

3 G. M. Ditchfield, *George III: An Essay in Monarchy* (Houndsmill, Basingstoke, Hampshire, UK: Palgrave Macmillan, 2002), 5.

4 Mansfield, *Taming the Prince*, xvi.

5 Ditchfield, *George III*, 75.

6 Andrew Jackson O'Shaughnessy, "'If Others Will Not Be Active, I Must Drive': George III and the American Revolution," *Early American Studies: An Interdisciplinary Journal* 2, no. 1 (Spring 2004): 21.

7 O'Shaughnessy, 31.

8 O'Shaughnessy, 33–34.

9 Lord Bolingbroke, a British politician and political philosopher, coined the term "patriot king" in opposition to George I and George II, who he believed had more loyalty and allegiance to Hanover rather than Britain. Henry St. John Bolingbroke, *Letters, on the Spirit of Patriotism: on the Idea of a Patriot King: and on the State of Parties at the Accession of King George the First.* (London: Printed for A. Millar, 1749).

10 Ditchfield, *George III*, 138.

11 Ditchfield, 140.

12 Ditchfield, 140.
13 Herbert Butterfield, "George III and the Constitution," *History* 43, no. 147 (1958): 21.
14 Linda Colley, "The Apotheosis of George III: Loyalty, Royalty, and the British Nation 1760–1820," *Past & Present* 102 (February 1984): 108.
15 Ditchfield, *George III*, 159.
16 Ditchfield, 145.
17 Ditchfield, 143.
18 "From George Washington to Thomas Mifflin, 20 December 1783," *Founders Online*, National Archives, http://founders.archives.gov/documents/Washington/99-01-02-12212.
19 Mansfield, *Taming the Prince*, 247–78.
20 Thomas E. Cronin, "The President's Executive Power" in *Inventing the American Presidency*, Thomas E. Cronin, ed. (Lawrence: University Press of Kansas, 1989), 193–94.
21 Glenn A. Phelps, "George Washington: Precedent Setter" in Cronin, *Inventing the American Presidency*, 264.
22 David P. Currie, *The Constitution in Congress: The Federalist Period 1789–1801* (Chicago: University of Chicago Press, 1997), 29.
23 Garry Wills, *Cincinnatus: George Washington and the Enlightenment.* (New York: Doubleday, 1984), 3–25.
24 Simon P. Newman, "Principles or Men? George Washington and the Political Culture of National Leadership," *Journal of the Early Republic* 12, no. 4 (Winter 1992): 480.

Notes for Chapter 6

1 Washington's address resigning his army commission, December 23, 1783, appears in *The Papers of Thomas Jefferson*, vol. 6, *21 May 1781–1 March 1784*, ed. Julian P. Boyd (Princeton, NJ: Princeton University Press, 1952), 412.
2 Andrew Jackson O'Shaughnessy, *The Men Who Lost America: British Leadership, the American Revolution, and the Fate of the Empire* (New Haven, CT: Yale University Press, 2013), 17–46, esp. 44–46.
3 Alexander Gordon quoted in Jeremy Black, *George III: America's Last King* (New Haven, CT: Yale University Press, 2006), 418.
4 See for examples, "The Tomb of Washington," engraved by W. Woodruff Cunr. for the *Ladies Repository* (1800), Library of Congress; and "[George Washington] Lived Respected and Fear'd/ Died Lamented and Rever'd" (Philadelphia: Pember & [Luzarder], 1800); Library of Congress.
5 Creamware pitcher ca. 1800-1802 at the National Portrait Gallery: https://npg.si.edu/object/npg_NPG.2007.250.
6 Heinrich Weishaupt, "Apotheosis of George Washington," ca. 1830-50, The Metropolitan Museum of Art, https://www.metmuseum.org/art/collection/search/365736. For Weishaupt's 1839 *Chritus am Kreu*, see http://www.artnet.com/artists/heinrich-weishaupt/christus-am-kreu-E_1G6C3wWQe4xNUHXBP7Lw2.
7 "George Washington and Abraham Lincoln Apotheosis" (Philadelphia: Phil. Pho. Co, 1865), https://rememberinglincoln.fords.org/node/242.
8 Washington to Francis Hopkinson, 16 May 1785, George Washington Papers, Library of Congress. See also Hugh Howard, *The Painter's Chair: George Washington and the Making of American Art* (New York: Bloomsbury Press, 2009).
9 On Washington as speculator and Indian fighter, see (among other works), Colin G. Calloway, *The Indian World of George Washington: The First President, the First Americans, and the Birth of the Nation* (New York: Oxford University Press, 2018).
10 Erica Armstrong Dunbar, *Never Caught: The Washingtons' Relentless Pursuit of Their Runaway Slave, Ona Judge* (New York: Simon and Schuster, 2017); see also François Furstenberg, *In the Name of the Father: Washington's Legacy, Slavery, and the Making of a Nation* (New York: Penguin Press, 2006).
11 Henry Wiencek, *An Imperfect God: George Washington, His Slaves, and the Creation of America* (New York: Farrar, Straus and Giroux, 2003), 112–13.
12 Aaron Blake, "President Trump's U.N. Press Conference, Annotated," *Washington Post*, September 26, 2018, https://www.washingtonpost.com/politics/2018/09/26/president-trumps-un-press-conference-annotated/?utm_term=.eb1e04310c86.
13 Kate Fullagar and Michael A. McDonnell, *Facing Empire: Indigenous Experiences in a Revolutionary Age* (Baltimore: Johns Hopkins University Press, 2018), 355.
14 Wendy Bellion, *Iconoclasm in New York: Revolution to Reenactment* (State College, PA: Penn State University Press, 2019).
15 Lin-Manuel Miranda, *Hamilton: The Revolution: Being the Complete Libretto of the Broadway Musical, with a True Account of Its Creation, and Concise Remarks on Hip-Hop, the Power of Stories, and the New America* (New York: Grand Central, 2016), 52–67.

Selected Notes and Sources

Image Credits

Images from the Library of Congress are noted below using the following custodial division abbreviations:

G&M: Geography and Maps Division
LAW: Law Library of Congress
MSS: Manuscript Division
P&P: Prints and Photographs Division
RBSC: Rare Book and Special Collections Division
SER: Serial and Government Periodicals Division

The items from the Library's Prints and Photographs Division can be viewed and downloaded at loc.gov/pictures by entering the digital ID that is listed below. Many items from other divisions can be viewed or downloaded from the Library's online catalog at catalog.loc.gov. For assistance, contact the appropriate custodial division or Duplication Services (loc.gov/duplicationservices).

Cover (left): Royal Collection Trust / © His Majesty King Charles III 2024

Cover (right): Courtesy of the Pennsylvania Academy of the Fine Arts, Philadelphia. Gift of Maria McKean Allen and Phebe Warren Downes through the bequest of their mother, Elizabeth Wharton McKean. 1943.16.2.

ii-iii: P&P, LC-DIG-ppmsca-13282

iv-v: Royal Collection Trust / © His Majesty King Charles III 2024

vi: Courtesy National Gallery of Art, Washington, Andrew W. Mellon Collection

vii: Royal Collection Trust / © His Majesty King Charles III 2024

xiv-xv: G&M, Title Collection

Chapter 1

xvi-xvii: P&P, LC-DIG-pga-14082

3: P&P, British Cartoon Prints Collection, LC-USZC4-6204

5: P&P, LC-USZ62-127377

6: P&P, British Cartoon Prints Collection, LC-DIG-ds-00040

8 (top): P&P, LC-DIG-ds-06918

8 (bottom): P&P, LC-DIG-ppmsca-13415

10: Private Collection, The Stapleton Collection/Bridgeman Images

11: P&P, LC-DIG-pga-04612

12: P&P, LC-DIG-ppmsca-19164

13: P&P, LC-DIG-pga-01698

15: G&M, G3801.A9 1770 .P6

16 (top): © The Trustees of the British Museum. All rights reserved.

16 (bottom): P&P, British Cartoon Prints Collection, LC-DIG-ppmsca-31020

21: G&M, G3300 1755 .M51

22: G&M, G3300 1755 .B61

24: G&M, G3301.E1 1800 .G3

27: Benjamin Justice and the Royal Mint

29: P&P, American Cartoon Prints Collection, LC-USZC4-5321

Chapter 2

32: Royal Collection Trust / © His Majesty King Charles III 2024

33: Courtesy of Washington and Lee University, University Collections of Art and History

35: National Portrait Gallery, London

36: Royal Collection Trust / © His Majesty King Charles III 2024

37: © Science Museum / Science & Society Picture Library — All rights reserved.

38 (top): Courtesy of Mount Vernon Ladies' Association

38 (bottom): MSS, George Washington Papers

40 (left): P&P, LC-DIG-ppmsca-46832

40 (right): Royal Collection Trust / © His Majesty King Charles III 2024

41: © The Trustees of the British Museum. All rights reserved.

43: P&P, LC-DIG-pga-02152

44: Royal Collection Trust / © His Majesty King Charles III 2024

44 (top): Royal Collection Trust / © His Majesty King Charles III 2024

45 (bottom): MSS, George Washington Papers

47: Alexandria-Washington Lodge No. 22, A.F. & A.M., Alexandria, Virginia

48: National Portrait Gallery, London

50: Courtesy of Mount Vernon Ladies' Association

51: RBSC, AP4 .G3

52: G&M, G3884.A3G46 1749 .W3

53: G&M, G3882.M7 1766 .W3

Chapter 3

54: Courtesy of Washington and Lee University, University Collections of Art and History

55: Royal Collection Trust / © His Majesty King Charles III 2024

60: Royal Collection Trust / © His Majesty King Charles III 2024

61: Courtesy of Mount Vernon Ladies' Association

66 (top): P&P, British Cartoon Prints Collection, LC-DIG-ds-17204

66 (bottom): P&P, British Cartoon Prints Collection, LC-DIG-ds-17203

67: P&P, British Cartoon Prints Collection, LC-DIG-ds-17205

69: P&P, British Cartoon Prints Collection, LC-DIG-ds-17252

72: Courtesy of Mount Vernon Ladies' Association

74: MSS, George Washington Papers

76: Royal Collection Trust / © His Majesty King Charles III 2024

77: P&P, British Cartoon Prints Collection, LC-DIG-ds-17206

78 (left): Royal Archives / © His Majesty King Charles III 2024

78 (right): MSS, George Washington Papers

79 (top): G&M, G3882.M7 1793 .W34 1801 TIL

79 (bottom): MSS, George Washington Papers

82: © Science Museum / Science & Society Picture Library — All rights reserved.

83 (top and bottom): Courtesy of Mount Vernon Ladies' Association

84: Royal Collection Trust / © His Majesty King Charles III 2024

85: Royal Archives / © His Majesty King Charles III 2024

86: Royal Collection Trust / © His Majesty King Charles III 2024

89: Courtesy National Gallery of Art, Washington, Andrew W. Mellon Collection

94-95: Royal Collection Trust / © His Majesty King Charles III 2024

100: Royal Collection Trust / © His Majesty King Charles III 2024

102: Yale Center for British Art, Paul Mellon Collection

105: Courtesy of Mount Vernon Ladies' Association

106: Boston Public Library, Arts Department

107: Yale Center for British Art, Paul Mellon Collection

110 and 111: Tim St. Onge, G&M

113: Royal Collection Trust / © His Majesty King Charles III 2024

Chapter 4

114: Royal Collection Trust / © His Majesty King Charles III 2024

115: Courtesy of the Pennsylvania Academy of the Fine Arts, Philadelphia. Gift of Maria McKean Allen and Phebe Warren Downes through the bequest of their mother, Elizabeth Wharton McKean. 1943.16.2.

116: G&M, G3301.R2 1767 .P3

117: P&P, British Cartoon Prints Collection, LC-DIG-ppmsca-15709

118: MSS, Benjamin Franklin Papers

119: P&P, British Cartoon Prints Collection, LC-DIG-ppmsca-37323

120: RBSC, E249 .F81 1778b

121: British Library, London, UK. From the British Library archive/Bridgeman Images

123: MSS, George Washington Papers

125: National Archives and Records Administration, Washington, DC.

129: RBSC, Broadside portfolio 178 no. 18

130: RBSC, Broadside portfolio 39b

131: P&P, LC-DIG-ppmsca-17521

133: P&P, British Cartoon Prints Collection, LC-DIG-ppmsca-33532

134: P&P, British Cartoon Prints Collection, LC-DIG-ppmsca-13639

137: P&P, British Cartoon Prints Collection, LC-DIG-ppmsca-10751

138: G&M, G3884.Y6S3 1781 .M6

139: French & Company, New York

140: P&P, LC-DIG-ppmsca-17515

141: Courtesy of David Rubenstein

142-143: Architect of the Capitol

Chapter 5

144: Royal Collection Trust / © His Majesty King Charles III 2024

145: National Portrait Gallery, Smithsonian Institution; acquired as a gift to the nation through the generosity of the Donald W. Reynolds Foundation

148: RBSC, F158.3 .W2

149: Royal Collection Trust / © His Majesty King Charles III 2024

151 (top): Royal Collection Trust / © His Majesty King Charles III 2024

151 (bottom): © The Trustees of the British Museum. All rights reserved.

153: Courtesy of Mount Vernon Ladies' Association

154: P&P, Leonard Hassam Bogart Collection, LC-DIG-ds-05728

156: Royal Archives / © His Majesty King Charles III 2024

157: Courtesy of Mount Vernon Ladies' Association

158 and 159: Royal Archives / © His Majesty King Charles III 2024

 Image Credits

161 (top): Courtesy National Gallery of Art, Washington, Gift of Mrs. Robert Homans

161 (bottom): MSS, Thomas Jefferson Papers

162: Courtesy National Gallery of Art, Washington, Gift of Mrs. Robert Homans

163: P&P, LC-DIG-ppmsca-15712

164: University of Pittsburgh Library System

165: Philadelphia Museum of Art: Purchased with Museum and Subscription Funds from the Charles F. Williams Collection, 1923, 1923-23-227h.

167: SER

168 (top): Law Library, KD124 .G74

168 (bottom): MSS, George Washington Papers

170: The Metropolitan Museum of Art, New York, Harris Brisbane Dick Fund, 1917

172: P&P, British Cartoon Prints Collection, LC-USZC4-5779

175: P&P, British Cartoon Prints Collection, LC-DIG-ppmsca-10750

176: P&P, British Cartoon Prints Collection, LC-USZC4-6861

178: P&P, LC-DIG-pga-10098

181: P&P, British Cartoon Prints Collection, LC-DIG-ds-17202

182 and **183**: Courtesy of Mount Vernon Ladies' Association

185 and **187**: Royal Collection Trust / © His Majesty King Charles III 2024

Chapter 6

188: The Metropolitan Museum of Art, New York, Gift of Erving and Joyce Wolf, in memory of Diane R. Wolf, 1982

189: Royal Collection Trust / © His Majesty King Charles III 2024

191 (top): P&P, LC-DIG-ds-05302

191 (bottom): The Metropolitan Museum of Art, New York, Gift of Emily C. Chadbourne, 1952

192: Abraham Lincoln Library and Museum of Lincoln Memorial University.

193: Amon Carter Museum of American Art, Fort Worth, Texas, 1970.43

194: Titus Kaphar, Shadows of Liberty, 2016, Oil and rusted nails on canvas, 108 x 84 inches (274.32 x 213.36 cm), © Titus Kaphar, Courtesy Gagosian

195: P&P, American Cartoons Prints Collection, LC-DIG-ppmsca-10754

196: National Portrait Gallery, Smithsonian Institution

197 (right and left): Royal Collection Trust / © His Majesty King Charles III 2024

198: RBSC, F158.44 .B61a

199: © Museum of London

200: LC-USZ62-132327

201: Smithsonian American Art Museum, Museum purchase made possible by the American Art Forum, 2012.15

202 (top): P&P, Goldstein Foundation Collection, LC-DIG-ds-17201

202 (bottom): SER. Cover artwork from MAD magazine #181 (March 1976). © and TM E.C. Publications, Inc. Art by Norman Mingo. Used with permission.

203: WALT DISNEY PICTURES / Album / Alamy Stock Photo

Portrait Gallery

206: Royal Collection Trust / © His Majesty King Charles III 2024

207: Courtesy of Washington and Lee University, University Collections of Art and History

208: Courtesy of Washington and Lee University, University Collections of Art and History

209: Royal Collection Trust / © His Majesty King Charles III 2024

210: Royal Collection Trust / © His Majesty King Charles III 2024

211: Courtesy of the Pennsylvania Academy of the Fine Arts, Philadelphia. Gift of Maria McKean Allen and Phebe Warren Downes through the bequest of their mother, Elizabeth Wharton McKean. 1943.16.2.

212: Royal Collection Trust / © His Majesty King Charles III 2024

213: National Portrait Gallery, Smithsonian Institution; acquired as a gift to the nation through the generosity of the Donald W. Reynolds Foundation

214: The Metropolitan Museum of Art, New York, Gift of Erving and Joyce Wolf, in memory of Diane R. Wolf, 1982

215: Royal Collection Trust / © His Majesty King Charles III 2024

Index

Adams, Abigail, 26, 59, 123, 132, 160, 162, (162)
Adams, John, 26, 59, 99, 101, 108, 109, 126, 124, 132, 133-134, 136, 152, 153, 160, (161), 162, 177, 178, 198
Adams, Samuel, 127, 132
Adolphus, Prince, Duke of Cambridge (son of George III), 92, 93, 94, (94), 96, 98
Africa, xv, 1, 4, 5, 28, 65, 71
Agriculture, xii, 2, 35, 73-79, 92, 101, 105, 109, 136
Albert Edward, Prince of Wales, Edward VII (great-grandson of George III), 200, (200)
Alexandria, Virginia, 26, 47, 52, (52), 88, 152
Alfred, Prince (son of George III), 80, 93, 94, (95), 186
Algonquin (tribe), 24
Amelia, Princess (daughter of George II), 156
Amelia, Princess (daughter of George III), 16, (16), 94, 96, 186
American Civil War, 30, 127, 168, 200, 201
American colonies, 19–20, 25, 31, 33, 34, 44, 48, 50, 71, 112–113, 119, 121, 123–124, 132, 147, 152

American Indians/Native Americans (*see also* by tribe and nation), 4
    Haudenosaunee (Iroquois Confederacy, Six Nations) 7, 20, 24, 150, 163, 179
    Land, 23-25, 27–29, 162-165
American Revolution, 9, 10, 14, 15, 17, 34, 119, 122, 127-128, 132-134, 137, 180-181
American Revolutionary War, xiii, 21, 25, 26, 115-121, 122-124, 129, 130-131, 134, 136, 138, 139
    Lexington and Concord, battles of, 11, 39, 123, 124, 128
    Valley Forge, 13, 88, 125
    Yorktown and battle of, 14, 138, (138)
Anglicans and Anglican Church (*see also* Church of England), x, xi, xii, xiii, 7, 28, 58, 62, 88, 135, 164, 169
Anne, Queen, 23, 146
Arnold, Benedict, 120
Augusta, Princess of Wales (mother of George III), 34, 35, 36, 40-41, (41), 46, 47, 49, 65, 85, 92, 104, 107, 151, 170
Augusta, Princess (daughter of George III), 16, (16), 60, 94, (94), 96
Augustus, Prince, Duke of Sussex (son of George III), 94, (95), 96, 180
Ayscough, James, 37, 225n12

Ball, Joseph Jr., 34, 51, 122
Banks, Joseph, 104
Bassett, Fanny, 59, 90
Bastille, the, 60, 180, 181, 183
Bennett, Alan, 17, 186
Berryman, William, 8
Bonaparte, Napoleon, 137, 171, (171), 172, 182
Boston, 6, 9, 11, (11), 58, 80, 84, 109, 117
    Massacre, 11; Tea Party, 118, 130, 132
Boucher, Jonathan, 88, 135, 136
Bowen, Emanuel, 20, 22
Braddock, Edward, 123
Brant, Joseph (Thayendanegea), 163, (163), 164, (164)
British Empire, xii-xiii, 1, 4-6, 9, 10, 14, 18, 23, 28, 36, 56-57, 62, 64, 119, 120, 122, 135
Buckingham House (Queen's House, later Buckingham Palace), 57, 62, 68, 69, 84, 92, 94, 99-101, (100), 146, 147, 149, (149), 197, 206, 209
Buell, Abel, 141
Burgoyne, John, 123, 133, 136
Burney, Fanny, 62, 67, 68, 112
Bute, Lord (John Stuart), 40, 41, (41), 44, 45, 46-49, (48), 56, 99, 117, (117), 170, 172, 174, 175, (175)

Canada, 6, 14, 20, 26, 96, 116, 119, 135, 165
Caribbean ("West Indies") xv, 1, 3, 4, 5, 8, 9, 16, 22, 28, 29, 50, 65, 71, 122, 168
    Barbados, xii, xv, 4, 34, 60, 108, 111; Barbuda, 4; Cuba, xv; Dominica, 4; Grenada, 3; Hispaniola, xv; Jamaica, xv, 4, 6, 8, 127; St. Kitts and Nevis, 4
Caroline, Queen (grandmother of George III), 103
Charles III, King of Spain, 6, (6), 73, 75
Charlotte, Princess Royal (daughter of George III), 16, (16), 69, 94, (95), 96
Charlotte of Wales, Princess (granddaughter of George III), 98
Charlotte, Queen (wife of George III), 16, (16), 34, 49, (55), 56, 60, 62-63, 66, (66), (67), 68-69, 76, (76), 77, (77), 81, 85, 86, (86), 92-94, (94), 96, 98, 109, 121, 149, 150-151, 162, 164, (164), 180, 181, (181), 184-186, 209, (209)
Cherokee Nation, 23-25
Church of England (*see also* Anglican Church), xii, xiii, 2, 150, 164, 169
Clement XIII, 7, 169
Clinton, Henry, 12, 122, 137
Confederation Congress (1781-1789), 116, 139, 140, 160

Congress, US, 76, 108, 125, 148, 152, 157, 166, 168, 198
Constitutional Convention, 30, 59, 75, 105, 147, 157
Continental Congress (first, 1774; second, 1775-1781), 12, 13, 27, 37, 39, 88, 118, 119, 120, 123, 124, 125, 130, 133, 135, 137, 139, 160
Cornwallis, Lord Charles, 134, 138
Cruikshank, Isaac, 3, 16, 170
Custis, Daniel Parke, 58, 87, 98, 208
Custis, Eleanor Calvert (Nelly; stepdaughter-in-law of GW), 88, 90, 98
Custis, Elizabeth Parke (Eliza; step-granddaughter of GW), 98
Custis, George Washington Parke (step-grandson of GW), 64, 89, (89), 90
Custis, John Parke (Jacky, Jack; stepson of GW) 42, 56, 87-89, 98, 124, 135
Custis, Martha (Patsy; stepdaughter of GW), 56, 58, 87-88

Dandridge, Bartholomew, 34, 35
Declaration of Independence, 5, 13, 19, 25, 39, 119, 128, 130, (130), 133, 134, 148, 160, 190
Delaware Nation, 24, 163-164
Dinwiddie, Robert, 23, 51, 123
Dunmore, Lord (John Murray), 58, 129

Edward, Prince, Duke of Kent (son of George III), 28, 40, (40), 94, (94), 96, 98
Edward, Prince, Duke of York and Albany (brother of George III), 44, 151
Effingham, Earl of, *see* Howard, Thomas
Elizabeth, Princess (daughter of George III), 16, (16), 63, 93, (94), 96
Elizabeth I, Queen, 30, 109
Elizabeth II, Queen, 186
England, 2, 6, 7, 20, 36, 38, 64-65, 99, 103, 104, 109, (111), 116, 127, 128, 136, 160, 163, 164, 170, 186
Ernest, Prince, Duke of Cumberland (son of George III), 94, (95), 96

Fairfax, George William, 75, 119, 127, 128
Fairfax, Sally Cary, 46, 47
Fairfax, Lord Thomas, 34, 46-47, (47), 50
Fairfax, William, 46, 56
Fox, Charles James, 135, 158, 170, 171, 176, (176), 181, (181)
France, xv, 4, 20, 21, 23, 36, 65, 99, 116, 119, (119), 120, 124, 127, 146, 170, 177, 180-183
Franco–American alliance, 14, 199, 120, (120), 133, 180

232   Index

Franklin, Benjamin, 4, 29, 66, 108, 118, 124, 134, 190, (191)
Frederick, Prince of Wales (father of George III), 34-35, (35), 36, 40, 42, 49, 56, 83
Fredrick, Prince, Duke of York and Albany (son of George III), 92, 93, 94, 96, 146-147, 199
French and Indian War, 15, 20, 21, 23, 34, 36, 46, 49, 51
French Revolution, 14, 63, 170, 175, 180-183

Gage, Thomas, 136
Gainsborough, Thomas, 94, 208
Gates, Horatio, 130
George I (great-grandfather of George III), 34, 92, 109, 146n9
George II (grandfather of George III), 7, 20, 22, 23, 34, 36, (36), 40, 42, 45, 47, 50, 51, 56, 83, 92, 98, 108, 109, 122, 123, 129, 146n9, 156
George III
  Early life:
    Youth and education, xi, 35, 36, (40), 42, 44, (44), 45, 47, 49, 56; becomes king, 49, 56, 68, 156
  As King George:
    Abdication consideration, xiii, 112, 158-159
    Agricultural interests, xii, 56, 73, 75, 76, 78, 93, 99; as "Farmer George," 73, 76, (76), 77, (77), 170, 173
    As collector: artwork, 57, 99, 103, 206, 209, 210; books, 4, 57, 99-101; maps, 26-27, 57, 121; personal papers, 18, 68; scientific instruments, 35, 57, 80, 83, 84
    As a constitutional monarch, xii, 118-119, 146-147, 149, 155, 158, 174-175, 182
    Coronation, 7, 134, 147, 150-152, (151), 169
    Dining, 64-67, (66, 67), 92, 93
    Garden and park activities, 41, (41), 86, (86), 92, 103-104, 106, 107
    Library of, 57, 99-101, (100), 146, 149
    Marriage and family, 16, (16), 36, 40-41, (41), 42, 60, (60), 62-63, 80, 86, (86), 92-96, (94-95), 98, 107, 109, 173, 184, 186
    Mental illness, xii, 9, 57, 63, 96, 104, 109, 170, 174-175, 184-187
    Military interests and activities, 26, 45, (45), 108, 109, 116, 122, 182
    Music, xi, 92
    Regency crisis, 57, 63, 171, 184
    Religious faith and views, 56, 57, 80, 92, 99, 169
    Scientific interests, 80-86, (86), 104
    Slavery and views on, xii, 28-30, 168
    Statue of in New York City, 130-131, (131)
    Travel, xii, 4, 108-109, 111-113
      Viewed by others, 76, 96, 99, 132-134, 162, 170-173
    Death and funeral, xi, 186, 198, (198)

  Legacy and in memory, xii-xiii, 155, 186, 187, 190, 195, 202

George, Prince of Wales, Prince Regent, George IV (son of George III), 18, 19, 57, 63, 92-96, (95), 101, 108, 121, 149, 158, 164, 171, 173, 184-186, (185), 197, 199, 212
Genêt, Edmond–Charles (Citizen Genêt), 183
Germain, Lord George, 34, 135, 163, 174, 175, (175)
Gillray, James, 16, 66, 170-172, 174, 176, 181
Grenville, George, 117, (117), 137, (137), 174
Grenville, Lord William, 69, (69)

Hamilton: An American Musical (2015), 17, 195, 203
Hamilton, Alexander, 1, 29, 125, 166, 177, 178, (178), 182, 183
Hancock, John, 26, 109, 119, 123, 124
Handel, George Frederick, 92
Hanover, Electorate of, 1, 6, 34, 36, 49, 96, 106, 109, 111, 122, 139
Hanover, House of, 1, 92-96, 98, 133, 168
Harcourt, Lady Elizabeth, 62-63
Herschel, Caroline, 81
Herschel, William, 81
Hogarth, William, 170
Howard, Thomas, second Earl of Effingham, 152
Howard, Thomas, third Earl of Effingham, 127
Howe, William, 13, 80, 122, 135
Howe, Richard, 121, 135
Humphrey, Hannah, 69, 170, 171

Ireland, 4, 6, 9, 70, 118, (118)

Jefferson, Thomas, 108, 109, 127, 128, 129, 132-134, 140, 155, 160, 161, 168, 177, 178, (178), 182, 184
Johnson, Samuel, 57, 99, 128
Judge, Ona "Oney," 166, 167
Jumonville Glen and battle of, 20, 23, 123

Kaphar, Titus, 194
Kew, 42, 62, 65, 73, 75, 92, 93, 96, 99, 156
  Palace, 56, 68, 70; gardens: 40, (41), 85, 104, 107, (107)
Kimber, John, 3, (3)
Knox, Henry, 177, 178, (178)

Lafayette, Marquis de, 29-30, 42, 140, 177, 180, 182, 183
Latrobe, Benjamin Henry, 60, (61)
Lee, William, 29, 30, 68
Lewis, Eleanor "Nelly" Parke Custis (step-granddaughter of GW), 60, (61), 64, 65, 89, (89), 90

Lewis, Lawrence (nephew of GW), 30, 90, 101
Lincoln, Abraham, 133, 192 (192)
Livingston, Robert, 150, 152, 154
London, 10, (10), 23, 28, 34, 38, 56, 59, 62, 65, 68, 92, 108, 109, 112, 117, 127, 134, 137, 148, 150, 162, 163, 169
Louis XVI, King of France, 80, 86, 138, 180, 182

Madison, James, 108, 109, 177, 182, 195, (195)
Madness of George III/King George (1991), 22, 171
Mary, Princess (daughter of George III), 16, (16), 63, 93, 94, (94), 96
Mifflin, Thomas, 125, 140, 147
Miranda, Lin-Manuel, 17, 195, 203
Mitchell, John, 20, 21, 121
Mohawk (tribe), 24, 164
Mohican (tribe), 25
Montesquieu, Charles Louis de Secondat, 28, 30
Morris, Gouverneur, 157, 180, 185
Morris, Robert, 30, 148
Morris House, Philadelphia, 90, 148, (148)
Mount Vernon, (ii-iii), 6, 18, 26, 28, 42, 46, 50, 52, 53, 56, 57, 58, 59, 60, (61), 64, 65, 68, 70-75, 78-79, 80-81, 87-90, 101, 103-106, (105, 106), 116, 123, 152, 154, 166, 183, 190, 193, 198, 200, (200), 207, 208

Mount Vernon Ladies' Association, 90
Mozart, Wolfgang Amadeus, 62

Netherlands, (Holland) 20, 49, 119
New York City, 12, (12), 14, 90, 116, 124, (131), 139, 150, 152, 162, 180, 185, 195
Niemcewicz, Julian Ursyn, 58, 60, 70-71, 104, 208
North, Lord Frederick, 118, 120, 122, 132, 134, (134), 137, (137), 138, 146, 158, 174-176, (175, 176)

Occom, Samson, 23
Octavius, Prince (son of George III), 93, 186
Onondaga Nation, 24
Oneida Nation, 24, 25
Ostenaco, Otacity, 23

Paine, Thomas, 80, 132-133, 181-182
Paris, 14, 86, 93, 157, 180, 181, 183
Parliament, 4, 7, 16, 18, 30, 37, 39, 57, 63, 68, 98, 117, 118, 119-120, 127, 128, 132, 136, 138, 146, 157, 158, 168, 169, 174, 177, 185, 186
Peale, Charles Willson, 124, 140, 207, 211
Philadelphia, 5, 9, 12, 13, (13), 14, 30, 37, 57, 59, 68, 90, 104, 109, 117, 148, 163, 165, (165), 166
Pitt, William, (the Elder), 49, 117, 156

Index   233

Pitt, William (the Younger), 146, 169, 170, 180, (180)
Powers, Hiram, 215
Privy Council, 150, 156, 174, 176
Proclamation of 1763, 23-25, 116, 163

Randolph, Edmund, 157, 166, 177, 178, (178)
Regency (1811-1820), 56, 182, 186
Regency crisis, 57, 63, 171, 184, 185, (185)
Religion, 1, 2, 7, 56, 57, 62, 71, 92, 169, 182
Richmond, United Kingdom, and Richmond Palace, 62, 73, 78, 85, 104
Rowlandson, Thomas, 170-171, 185
Royal Academy, 194, 209, 214
Royal Marriages Act of 1772, 98

Seneca Nation, 23, 24, 123, 163
Servants, 10, 17, 28, 40, 68-70, 148, 156
Seven Years' War, 4, 7, 9, 36, 45, 49, 134
Shawnee (tribe), 163-164
Shelburne, Lord (Marquess of Lansdowne), 158, 176, 213
Slave trade, 1, 3, (3), 4, 8, 16, 57, 168
 Prohibition of, 30, 168; Royal African Company, 5
Slavery, 7, 28-30, 127-128
 Abolition efforts, 16, (16), 28-30, (29), 57, 59, 166; Slavery Abolition Act (1833), 30, 168; Thirteenth Amendment, 168
 Enslaved persons and labor, xii, 8, (8), 12, 16, 18, 23, 28-30, (29), 35, 38, 42, 56, 57, 59, 64, 68, 70-71, 72, (72), 74, 75, 87, 88, 106, (106), 109, 127-128, 129, 131, (131), 141, 166-167
Sophia, Princess (daughter of George III), 16, (16), 94, (95), 96,
Spain, xv, 4, 6, 20, 21, 22, 99, 104, 116, 119, 146, 210
Stamp Act and crisis (1765), 4, 36-37, 117, (117), 118, 127, 132, 137
 Stamp Act Congress, 12, 117
St. James's Palace, 36, 92, 149, 150, 162
Stockbridge-Munsee Nation, 25
Stuart, Gilbert, 178, 193, 202, 213
Succession to the Crown Act (2013), 98
Sugar, 4-5, 8, 10, 16, 28, 30, 35, 65
Sugar Act (1764), 118

Tanacharison ("Half King"), 23, 123
Townshend Acts (1767), 118, 132
Treaty of Paris (1763), 21, 49
Treaty of Paris (1783), 13, 14, 121, 124, 138
Turnerelli, Peter, 214
Tuscarora Nation, 23, 24, 25

United Kingdom, 1, 28, 73, 98, 176
United States, 1, 19, 20, 25, 76, 96, 108, (110), 119, 120, 121, 125, 138, 140, 141, (141), 146, 150, 154, 156, 168, 176, 182,183, 190, 195, 203
US Constitution, 14, 108, 124, 141, 146, 147, 148, 150, 157, 168, (168), 177

Vernon, Edward, 80
Victoria, Queen, 76, 96, 98, 186, 200, 209

Walpole, Horace, 42, 49
Walpole, Robert, 155, 174, 179
Washington, Anne Fairfax (sister-in-law of GW), 42, 50, 98
Washington, Augustine (father of GW), 40, 42, 43
Washington, Augustine (half-brother of GW), 34, 45, 52
Washington, Bushrod (nephew of GW), 90, 101, 177
Washington, DC, 79, 87, 89, 148, 201
Washington, George
 Early life:
 Youth, 34-35, 42-42, (43), 46, 47
 Education, xi, 45, 46, 56, 101, 124
 Surveyor, 1, 23, 26, 34-35, 37, 46, 48, 52, 53, 56, 80-81, 83, 101, 108, 122-123
 Journal of (1754), 51, 101
 Mission to Fort LeBoeuf, 7, 23, 46, 50, 101, 123
 Virginia Regiment, 7, 20, 46, 52, 101, 124, 207
 French and Indian War, 20, 23, 46, 108, 123, 207, 123
 Later life:
 Agricultural interests, 35, 45, 73-76, 78-79, 101, 105, 108-109, 136
 American Indian relations, 23-25, 163-165
 Commander-in-chief; Continental Army, xii, 13, 88, 122, 123-125, 137, 147, 190, 211, (211); United States, 124-125
 Resigns command, 108, 124, 140, 142, (142-143), 207
 Continental Congress, representative, 9, 20, 124
 Dining, 64-65, 87-88
 Gardens and gardening, 53, 90, 103-106, (105, 106)
 Land speculation and acquisition, 24-25, 34, 53, 79, 193
 Library and books, 101, 103, 122
 Maps drawn by, ix, 26, 79, (79), 52, (52), 53, (53)
 Marriage and family, 34, 38, 56-57, 58-59, 60, (61), 87-90, (89), 98, 148
 Political life and views, 30, 36, 39, 46, 76, 87, 118-119, 127-128, 146, 147-148, 157, 175, 177, 190, 192-193
 Religion and religious toleration, 56, 71, 80, 165, 169
 Scientific interests, 80, 101, 103
 Slavery, views and as enslaver, 28-30, 42, 68, 70-72, (72), 127-128, 166-167
 Travel, 34, 108-109, (110)
 Viewed by others, 101, 124, 128, 135-136, 140
 Presidency: 25, 26, 76, 90, 109, 146-149, 157
 Inauguration, 150, 152-154, (153, 154)
 Cabinet, 175, 177-179, (178)
 Neutrality Proclamation (1793), 182-183
 Whiskey Rebellion, 124-125
 Farewell Address, 155, 169, 190, 202
 End of life:
 Death and funeral, 18, 56, 190, 196, (196), 198, (198)
 Legacy and memory, xii-xiii, 90, 190-196, 200-202, (201)
Washington, George Augustine (nephew of GW), 90
Washington, George Steptoe (nephew of GW), 90
Washington, Harriot (niece of GW), 90
Washington, John Augustine (brother of GW), 46, 51
Washington, Lawrence (half-brother of GW), 34, 42, 46, 50, (50), 52, 98, 108, 122
Washington, Lawrence (nephew of GW), 90
Washington, Lund (cousin of GW), 90
Washington, Martha Dandridge Custis, 6, 18, 30, 34-35, 37, 38, (54), 56-57, 58-59, 60, (61), 64, 65, 70, 72, 80, 87-90, (89), 98, 101, 123, 152, 162, 166, 186, (186), 198, 207, 208, (208)
Washington, Mary Ball (mother of GW), 34, 35, 40-41, (40), 123
Washington, Samuel (brother of GW), 90
West, Benjamin, 114, 120, 140, 210
Wheatley, Phillis, 128
Whitting, Anthony, 71, 74, 106
Wilberforce, William, 3, 168
William, Prince, Duke of Gloucester (brother of George III), 109
William, Prince, Duke of Clarence, William IV (son of George III), 28, 30, 92, 93, 94, (95), 96, 98, 113, 139, (139), 173
Willis, Francis, 108, 109, 168–169, 184-185, 187
Windsor, 73, 75, 77
Windsor Castle, (iv-v), 49, 56, 57, 60, (60), 62, 68, 69-70, 77, 78, 86, (86), 92, 94, 96
Windsor Great Park, 73, 104
Wood, Grant, 192-193
Wyandot Nation, 24

Young, Arthur, 73, 75, 79, 158

234 Index

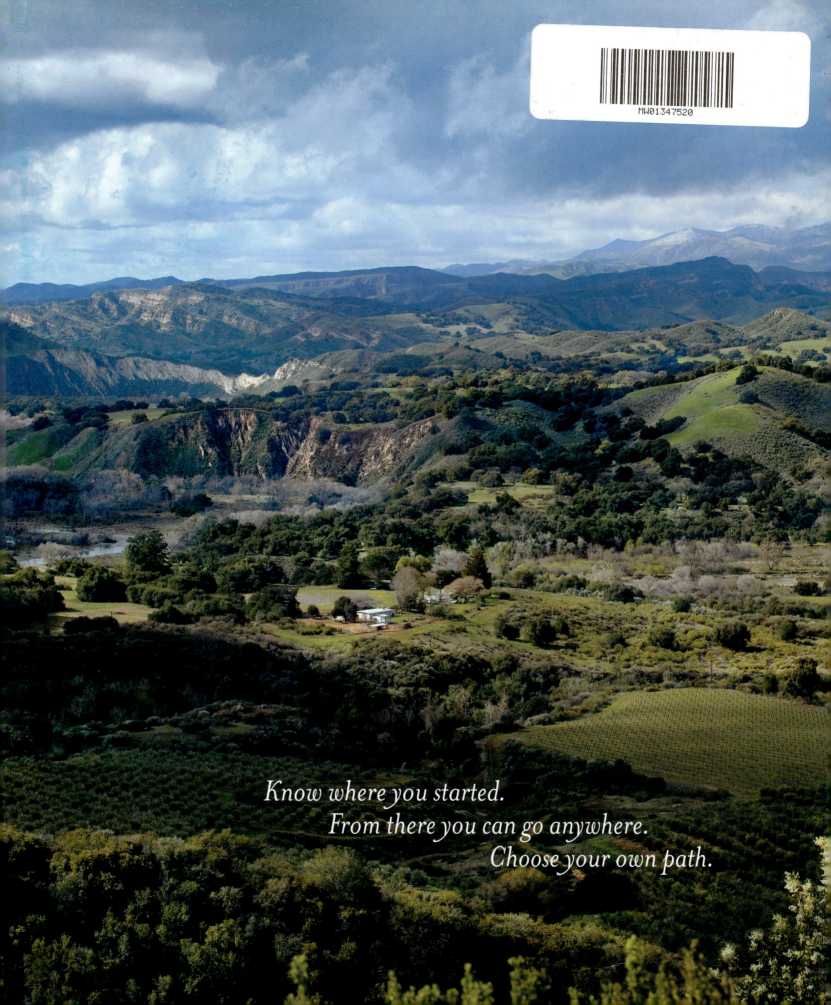
*Know where you started.
From there you can go anywhere.
Choose your own path.*

A Dash of Southern

A Dash of Southern

Classic Recipes for Family & Friends

Charlene,
From my Table to yours. Hope you enjoy my journey through food. Happy Entertaining!

Peg Ivy

Soup's On!
Peg Ivy
12/23/14

PUBLISHED BY

M27 Editions LLC
3030 State Street
Santa Barbara, California 93105
PHONE (805) 563-0099
FAX (805) 563-2070
EMAIL publish@m27editions.com
WEB www.m27editions.com

A Dash of Southern: Classic Recipes for Family & Friends
by Peg Ivy

WEB www.pegilicious.com
EMAIL info@pegilicious.com

Copyright 2014 by Peg Ivy and M27 Editions

All rights reserved. No part of this book may be reproduced or transmitted in any form or by any means electronic or mechanical, including photocopying, recording or by any information storage and retrieval system, without written permission from the author and publisher.

All trademarks, service marks, trade names, trade dress, product names and logos referenced or displayed in this book are the property of their respective owners. Any rights not expressly granted herein are reserved.

First Edition

ISBN 978-0-9659227-8-4
Library of Congress Catalog Number 2014946307

Design and Production by Media 27, Inc., Santa Barbara, California
Photography by Theresa Gingras, Mike Verbois, and Media 27

Printed and bound in China

Dedication

To my loving husband, Jarvis G. Ivy

My daughters, Deborah Dianne Hand
Teresa Darlene Hand-Bornhausen
Dana Denise McMahon

My sister, Mary Francis Simpson

Table of Contents

Starters and Light Fare	15
Appetizers and Dips	17
Salads and Dressings	39
Congealed Salads	54
Soups and Dumplings	63
Breakfast, Brunch, and Breads	73
Chef's Specialties	95
Side Dishes, Entrées, and Sauces	113
Vegetables, Pasta, and Rice	115
Entrées and Sauces	132
Desserts	143
Cookies	145
Pies, Puddings, and Other Pastries	155
Cakes	177
Ice Cream and Candy	197
Holiday & Party Punches and Specialty Drinks	205

Welcome to my world of cooking. Preparing and sharing food is basic to our lives. Enjoying food is universal. Please come and sit down at my table.

I'm Peg Ivy, and the recipes I am sharing here began as gifts from my mother, Grace Lee Martin. She was born in rural Georgia in 1901, a child of Cherokee and Dutch/Irish ancestry. With almost no schooling, she had more knowledge and greater wisdom than anyone I have ever known. People came to her to heal their aches and pains. They brought their sick and colicky babies. She would mix her herbs, a pinch of this, a drop of that. Colicky babies went home happy. Neighbors and friends were free of pain.

I am a living tribute to Mother's gift of healing. The youngest of nine children, I was born at home, arriving early and weighing in at three pounds. Nobody expected me to live, but here I am! The night I was born, Daddy was in a movie theater with another woman. He never came back, so I never met him.

Mother was our world. Even though there were lots of us to feed and money was scarce, we ate like royalty. The stuff of Mother's magic grew in her garden and in the natural woods around us. I grew up beside her in the kitchen, watching as she added a fistful of this and a pinch of that, stirring and tasting. Mother did not own a cookbook or even have a measuring cup. Over time I learned her secrets. Cooking became my world.

A teenage marriage was a mistake. I ran away to California where I met and married Jarvis Ivy—the best decision I have ever made. Our three daughters are now grown. When our oldest two were grown and on their own, our family moved to the Santa Ynez Valley where our youngest daughter grew up.

I began married life cooking Mother's food, and, little by little, I began exploring on my own. Soon I was adding my own creations. I loved it! And I never stopped, starting my own catering business in 1985.

I cooked in an ordinary kitchen on a stove with four burners and one oven, nothing fancy. I cook in that same kitchen today. Cooking in elegant kitchens for glamorous parties held in luxurious homes is fun, but fancy kitchens aren't necessary. These recipes can be fixed anywhere.

As you all know, when we're raising kids there are cookie sales, potluck dinners, and picnics. People began to ask me for recipes. There weren't any. Nothing was written down. As my girls grew up, they begged me to write down the recipes. So where to start? I would take a pinch of this and that, measuring teaspoons and cupfuls. Through trial and error, the recipes came together.

I started this book in 1997, and, after a lot of setbacks, I finally finished my work. As a chef, I know that you can only move your pot to the back burner so many times before it evaporates. Thankfully, I got to my pot in time.

Knowing how to fix Mother's food is my heritage. Preparing it is my joy. Adding my own creations is my way of honoring the gifts my mother gave me. Sharing it with you invites you to share her legacy.

My mother, Grace Lee Martin

After Dad left us, Mother moved us to Gadsden, Alabama, to be closer to her family. I was five months old. She dedicated her life to raising her children. She not only taught all us girls how to cook and sew, she taught the boys how to shoot a gun to hunt, how to fight to defend themselves, and how to treat a lady.

The women in our family worked in the Dwight Cotton Mill in Alabama City. Mother worked third shift from 11:00 pm to 7:00 am. When she arrived home, we were up and ready for school with breakfast on the table. We ate together and then Mother would send us off to school, clean up the kitchen, and sleep until we got home at 3:00 pm.

Mother's 85th birthday, Gadsden, Alabama: Sara Bellamy, Francis Simpson, Eloise Ware, Peggy Ivy, Grace Lee Martin

Each evening, she cooked dinner while we read the newspaper to her. The one luxury that Mother always managed to afford was the local newspaper. She believed it was important to keep up with what was going on. Also, it was the only thing in our house to read. When a recipe was in the paper, we gathered around, delighted to discuss it and excited about trying it out. It was from these written-down recipes that I learned to glean ideas that I would use as starting points for creating recipes of my own. I still have many of them, yellowed and worn.

Mom was a natural-born cook, and her meals were incredibly delicious. People were always coming to our house to eat. It was really the only entertainment we had, and our celebrations were always over food. Mama never owned a cookbook or measuring spoons or cups. Her cooking was based on flavor and appearance. Little did I realize at the time that she was developing our palates, which is the first step in becoming a great cook. She started teaching us to cook when we were very young.

She taught us to be resourceful and to be creative and make do with what we had. For a snack we took an apple from the tree or pulled carrots out of the garden. We never knew anything about packaged food. Our garden provided our staples, and we had chickens and fresh eggs. My brothers hunted, so we had game.

Although we were poor, with Mama, our lives were rich in so many ways.

I will never forget my first Thanksgiving in California, away from my family, alone, far from home, and feeling lost. Jarvis and I were dating, so I invited him to come for Thanksgiving dinner. He arrived with a dozen red roses and an electric knife for carving the turkey. What a guy! I had never had an electric knife and was very impressed. After dinner, Jarvis told me that my Thanksgiving dinner was the best he had ever had—even better than the ones his mother fixed. By the way he said it, I knew I had him hooked. My mother always told me that a way to a man's heart was through his stomach, and she was right. We were married before the next Thanksgiving came around.

I spent my early years cooking for family and friends but always wanted to do more. When I decided to venture into the catering world, I introduced myself by throwing a full-blown community party in the middle of the small town of Los Olivos. My best friend, Ruth Ann Sletten, was opening a new hair salon in town, and we decided to have an open house and invite the community.

This is where I met Ralph Story. Many in California will remember this wonderful TV personality that narrated the program, *LA Story*. A few years later, Ralph asked me to cater an open house for his art gallery, The Story Collection. He had an artist's palette made as my sign for the table that read, "Food Artistry by Peg Ivy." He truly believed that I was an artist when it came to food.

I designed our artist's smocks to wear using all his gallery logo colors, and we each wore a black Parisian floppy artist's beret. I designed the centerpieces by spray-painting carnations and pulling the heads through an artist palette for a splash of color. Then I stood the paint brushes up in the thumb hole. For this event, I prepared an array of hors d'oeuvres that were changed on the hour, every hour from 11:00 am to 7:00 pm. This gala for the opening of The Story Collection was not only a fun party but also a huge success! Ralph Story became one of my closest friends and staunchest supporters.

As with many events, this was a family affair. My daughters all helped out. Deb was born to cook and is very creative with food. She also designed the platters and came up with unique names for the dishes. Teresa, our fun-loving ambassador of cheer and good will, had a way of putting everyone at ease. She was the bartender on many occasions. She also traveled with me to the gourmet food shows, and with her there, we always sold out of everything we had. Dana, the youngest, was responsible for deciding the proper napkins, the style of fold, and place settings for the events. She truly had an eye for perfect and proper folding and display. This gal can fold a napkin into any shape you can possibly imagine!

Ruth Ann was my go-to person for sharing all my ideas. She was and still is my confidant, official taster, and the one who constantly encouraged me to go far beyond what I thought I could do. Talk about a test kitchen… her staff has tasted and endured many of my failures. They were brutally honest, marvelously supportive, and influenced me to become the chef I am today. Ruth Ann's daughter, Nicole, also worked in my catering business and has gone on to become a great chef and party planner!

By 1990, much to my boss's surprise and concern, I left a successful accounting career to follow my passion, catering full-time. Cooking is a creative endeavor that changes over time to keep up with the shifts in people's tastes. That is something I love about it. I prefer variety, and I'm notorious for trying something new when company is coming. That's the fun! Yes, there have been flops, but we had a laugh over them. The intrigue of thinking outside the box has always, and continues to be, a part of me. I love to experiment with new ideas. Those watching me work call me the mad scientist in the kitchen. In the kitchen is where I come alive, caught up in my passion to create a feast for family and friends.

For me, cooking is a labor of love. It's the way I connect with people. Meals have always been a celebration of good times with good people sharing good food. I like to entertain as a way of giving back. Birthday dinners, holiday get-togethers, thank-you luncheons, gala occasions that mark overcoming some obstacle—you name the occasion. I believe that celebrating by preparing and sharing food is a beautiful way to express the joy and love we have for others.

My mother was a magical cook. It was her creative gift, something she was born with. How blessed I am to have grown up beside her in the kitchen. She instilled in me the thrill of creating combinations of food and spices and herbs. She deftly arranged the dishes she prepared to resemble a piece of art. From her, I learned the love of cooking that is ingrained in the depths of who I am.

Ruth Ann

Soup's On!
Peg Avy

Zom not Mom

You will notice that a number of my recipes have the word Zom in the title, and in case you are wondering what that's all about, I can explain.

When Deb and Teresa were teenagers and Dana was a toddler, the big sisters were teaching the baby of the family how to say Mom. To make the lesson more fun and entertaining, they came up with the idea to use the letters of the alphabet, as though this were a game.

Going through the alphabet from A to Z, they substituted each letter for the M in Mom, so instead of the word Mom, Dana tried to copy her older sisters as they would say each word, beginning with Aom, followed by Bom, Com, Dom, and so forth. When they came to Z for Zom, they thought it was very funny. All three girls laughed and giggled in delight with the sound of their new word.

When Deb came home from school the following day, it was clear that she had shared the new word she had created, because she found out that not one other student had a Zom! They all had moms, so Deb asked if it would be all right if they called me Zom. Of course, they could, so Zom I became.

Zom is a term of endearment. Even the girls' school friends would call me Zom, and to this day, I still get cards addressed to Zom. I love it!

Oddly enough, after Dana grew up she started calling me Mom, but Deb and Teresa still call me Zom.

So there ya' go—Zom means Mom.

Starters and Light Fare

Appetizers and Dips

✦✦✦

Salads and Dressings

✦✦✦

Congealed Salads

✦✦✦

Soups and Dumplings

Peg's Cheese Pinecones

A client of mine had a goal, which was to meet a man and marry him. She also had a plan. That's where I came in. That plan was to have two parties a month for a year. Included on the guest lists would be a mix of new and returning guests, so there needed to be a new menu for each party—twenty-four different menus! I loved the challenge. Her plan worked. She was delighted. She married shortly after the New Year! Good food can make magic happen!

MAKES 4 CUPS OF SPREAD

- 16 ounces cream cheese, softened
- ⅓ cup beer
- 2 Tablespoons finely snipped fresh parsley
- 1 teaspoon paprika
- 3 cups shredded smoked sharp cheddar cheese, 12 ounces
- Sliced almonds
- Sliced apples
- Sliced pears
- Assorted crackers

◆ In a large bowl beat together the cream cheese, beer, parsley, and paprika until well blended. Stir in the cheddar cheese. Cover and chill the mixture for at least one hour.

◆ Divide the mixture in half. Using your hands, mold each portion into a pinecone shape and place both on a serving platter. Lay the almonds in rows over the molded cheese to resemble pinecones. Cover and chill several hours.

◆ Serve with apple slices, pear slices, and crackers.

PEG'S NOTES ~ When you put the almonds on the cheese, press the rounded edges in slightly, so the tips come up and overlap the rows a little; the result will look like a pinecone.

I slice my apples and pears just before serving and dip the fruit into a mixture of water and lemon juice to prevent it from darkening. You can sprinkle the slices with ascorbic acid color keeper, if you prefer.

I decorate my platter with a few artificial green pine twigs and real pinecones at the top of the cheese pinecones. This makes a colorful appetizer for Thanksgiving or a holiday party.

Gorgonzola Wafers

A friend of mine wanted something special to serve at the bar area of her home. Since I love Gorgonzola cheese, I decided it was going to be the base of my new recipe.

Serve these fantastic wafers alongside a basket of grapes; they are incredible with Chardonnay or other white wines. They make a lovely hostess gift, too: I stack some in a long cellophane sleeve and tie them to a bottle of wine. When I served these wafers at a party, my Italian friends could not believe that I had made them. They insisted that these were only made in Italy.

MAKES 2½ DOZEN WAFERS

- ¾ cup walnut pieces, toasted
- 1 cup all-purpose flour
- ½ teaspoon sea salt
- ½ teaspoon freshly ground pepper
- 3 Tablespoons cold butter, cut into pieces
- 4 ounces Gorgonzola cheese crumbles

◆ Process the walnuts in a food processor just until ground. Add the flour, salt, and pepper, and pulse until blended. Add the cold butter, and pulse 5 or 6 times or until crumbly. Add the cheese crumbles, and process until the dough forms and begins to leave the side of the bowl.

◆ Shape into two 5-inch logs. Wrap them in wax paper, and chill several hours or until firm. Cut the logs into ¼-inch slices, and place the slices on an ungreased cookie sheet.

◆ Bake at 350 degrees for 10 to 12 minutes, or until lightly browned. Cool 1 minute on the baking sheet, then remove to a wire rack to cool. Store in an airtight container up to 5 days.

PEG'S NOTES ~ *I always double this recipe, making 4 logs and 5 dozen wafers. I keep them in the refrigerator during the holidays and bake as needed. You will need to double the recipe for a party or to give out as gifts.*

Herb Brie En Croute

Brie is a favorite of mine, and I love to serve it at parties, but it was not something we had when I was growing up in Alabama. I was a young woman when I first tasted this mild, creamy cheese and thought it must be food for angels. That it came from Brie, France, only added to its mystique, and it was immediately added to my growing repertoire of recipes.

SERVES 12–14

- 1 17.6-ounce wheel ripe Brie cheese, chilled
- 1/3 cup minced shallots, about 2 large shallots
- 2 Tablespoons chopped fresh chives
- 2 teaspoons dry white vermouth
- 1/4 teaspoon white pepper
- 1 sheet frozen puff pastry, thawed
- 1 egg, beaten, for glaze

◆ Preheat the oven to 400 degrees.

◆ Cut the top off the Brie cheese and discard.

◆ Combine the shallots, chives, vermouth, and pepper in a small bowl, and mix until blended. Press the shallot mixture firmly over the top of the cheese.

◆ On a lightly floured surface, roll out the pastry to an 11-inch square. Lay the pastry over the cheese, and fold the dough under, enclosing the cheese completely. Turn the cheese over; press the pastry seams together, sealing them tightly. Turn the cheese right side up again, and place it on a baking sheet.

◆ Wrap the cheese in plastic, and refrigerate it for at least 30 minutes. This can be prepared one day ahead.

◆ Brush the top and sides of the pastry with the egg. Bake until the pastry is golden brown, about 25 minutes.

◆ Let stand 30 minutes before serving.

◆ Serve with fruit kabobs, crackers, and dry white wine.

PEG'S NOTES ~ *To chill the Brie, place it in the freezer for 30 minutes to an hour, and you'll be able to trim the top off easily.*

PEG'S NOTES ~ I freeze the Brie for 30 minutes, so I can remove the top rind more easily.

The longer this stands in the refrigerator, the more the pesto flavor gets into the cheese. I wrap it tightly, put the wheel of Brie back into the original wooden container, and refrigerate it for at least two days before I plan to serve it.

Don't worry about being exact with the measurements. Just throw in the basics and adjust them to your taste. You can add more cloves of garlic, if you like a lot of garlic. I include more of the tomatoes and pine nuts.

If you don't have a food processor, mash the garlic and chop the nuts, and blend them well with the other ingredients.

Sun-Dried Tomato Pesto Brie

Years ago, the employees where I worked had potlucks once a month, and they loved the dishes I brought. A group of women asked if I would teach a cooking class after hours. I loved the idea! All of us had fun! In this pesto recipe, I told them they could use as much garlic as they wished. One gal added twelve cloves! We could not get near her for a month—she smelled just like garlic!

I'm usually cautious with adding garlic so my guests won't take on an unexpected new aroma.

SERVES 16

- 1 2-pound wheel Brie cheese, chilled
- 5 Tablespoons minced parsley leaves
- 5 Tablespoons freshly grated Parmesan cheese
- 10 oil-packed sun-dried tomatoes, minced, plus additional, halved, for garnish
- 2½ Tablespoons oil from sun-dried tomatoes
- 5–6 cloves garlic
- 2 Tablespoons minced fresh basil, plus whole leaves for garnish
- 3 Tablespoons toasted pine nuts, plus additional for garnish

✦ Chill the Brie well before handling. Remove the rind from the top of the Brie, and place the cheese on a serving platter.

✦ Combine all the other ingredients except the pine nuts in a food processor. Pulse to blend well. Add the pine nuts, and pulse just a few more times to chop the nuts.

✦ Press the pesto into the top of the Brie, and decorate as desired with the sun-dried tomato halves, basil leaves, and pine nuts. Cover tightly with plastic wrap, and refrigerate overnight or longer.

✦ For optimum flavor, remove the Brie from the refrigerator, and allow it to stand 30 to 60 minutes before serving.

PEG'S NOTES ~ I use Breakstone's Jalapeño-Cheddar Gourmet Dip, and I always make this the day before, chilling it overnight to blend all the flavors.

Savory New Mexico Cheesecake

My husband hails from New Mexico, so of course our family loves Southwestern food, and our favorite chiles are Hatch green chiles grown in Hatch Valley, New Mexico, the place known as the Chile Capital of the World. When I first created this recipe, my husband called it **Pegilicious!**®

SERVES 16–20

Crust
- ⅔ cup finely crushed tortilla chips
- 2 Tablespoons butter

♦ Preheat the oven to 325 degrees.

♦ Combine the tortilla chip crumbs and the butter. Press the mixture onto the bottom of a 9-inch spring-form pan.

♦ Bake for 15 minutes.

Cheese layer
- 1 cup cottage cheese
- 24 ounces cream cheese, softened
- 4 eggs
- 1 10-ounce package sharp cheddar cheese, shredded
- ½ cup Hatch roasted green chiles, chopped, or 1 4-ounce can chopped green chiles

♦ Place the cottage cheese in a blender. Cover and process on high until smooth.

♦ In the large mixing bowl of an electric mixer, combine the cottage cheese and cream cheese, mixing at medium speed until well blended. Add the eggs, one at a time, mixing well after each addition.

♦ Blend in the cheddar cheese and chiles. Pour over the crust. Bake for 1 hour.

Topping
- 1 8-ounce container sour cream, plus additional for decoration
- 1 8-ounce container jalapeño-cheddar gourmet dip

♦ Combine the sour cream and dip; mix well. Spread the mixture over the cheesecake; return to oven and continue baking 10 minutes.

♦ Loosen the cake from the rim of the pan. Cool completely, then cover and refrigerate until chilled.

Garnish
- 1 cup chopped tomatoes
- ½ cup chopped green onions
- ½ cup pitted ripe olive slices
- Assorted crackers

♦ Top with the tomatoes, onions, ripe olives, and a dollop of sour cream in the center.

♦ Serve with assorted crackers.

Debbie's Jalapeño Poppers

My oldest daughter, Deborah, loves jalapeños. I was absolutely sure that they were too hot for me, and I wasn't about to eat one! That was before I knew about poppers, seeded jalapeño peppers filled with delicious concoctions. I tried them first in a restaurant, and it was love at first taste. Poppers joined my repertoire of recipes. Here we add two ingredients that are Deb's favorites, crab and goat cheese, to make this treat especially for her.

I have no doubt that these will be a big hit at your party!

MAKES 12 POPPERS

- 12 jalapeño peppers
- 1 cup lump crabmeat
- ½ cup fresh corn kernels
- 4 ounces cream cheese, softened
- 2 ounces goat cheese, softened
- ¼ cup shallots, chopped
- Juice of ½ lime
- Sea salt to taste
- ¼ cup crushed tortilla chips
- ¼ teaspoon chili powder

♦ Preheat the grill to medium low.

♦ Cut the jalapeños lengthwise, slicing off about one third of the flesh. Scrape out the white membrane (pith) and seeds.

♦ Blend the crab, corn, cream cheese, goat cheese, shallots, lime juice, and salt in a bowl. Stuff each jalapeño with a generous 3 tablespoons of the mixture.

♦ Combine the chips and chili powder, and sprinkle on the jalapeños.

♦ Grill the jalapeños, stuffing side up, for 10 minutes, or until charred but still firm.

PEG'S NOTES ~ *Wear gloves while handling the jalapeños to protect your hands from their volatile oils.*

You might want to position the jalapeños in the spaces between the grates of the grill to keep them from tipping over. Some cookware stores, such as Williams-Sonoma or Sur La Table, sell pans that hold poppers on the grill. I personally use a wire-mesh vegetable basket.

Sweet and Sour Meatballs

Most things in life change. Recipes have a way of doing the same thing. These meatballs have had ingredients tossed out and new ones added, until I barely recognize them. The changes have been for the better, however. While I liked them before, I love them now. Rarely are there any left when the party is over, and if there are, someone invariably asks to take them home.

Hungry guests will appreciate you for serving these.

MAKES 75–80 MEATBALLS

Meatballs

- 2½ pounds ground chuck or beef
- ½ pound pork sausage
- 1 medium onion, chopped
- ½ cup plain bread crumbs
- 2 eggs
- ½ teaspoon salt
- ½ teaspoon pepper

Sauce

- 1 8-ounce can crushed pineapple
- 1 16-ounce jar grape jelly
- 1 8-ounce jar currant jelly
- 2 12-ounce bottles Heinz Chili Sauce —catsup style

✦ Mix the meatball ingredients together, and shape into small balls. Cook in a lightly greased, heavy frying pan until brown. Remove to a paper-lined plate to drain.

✦ In a large Dutch oven, mix the sauce ingredients and simmer for 20 minutes. Then add the meatballs and simmer for an additional 20 minutes. Refrigerate overnight, and reheat just before serving in a chafing dish.

PEG'S NOTES ~
Make sure that the chili sauce is catsup style. It should be smooth and bright red, like catsup.

Peg's Heavenly Mushrooms

Recipes have found their ways to me from so many different places. This one came from a friend who thought it would be a wonderful addition to my repertoire. She was right. I'd had it for over a decade, when someone asked specifically for a mushroom appetizer. Aha! I just happened to have one. Of course, I always have to put my touch on everything—a touch that, in this case, made it heavenly! This rich savory dish should be served with a light entrée or when serving finger foods or appetizers.

Don't skip the caviar! It's essential! It adds saltiness and a dainty crunch to the smooth, mild richness of the cream cheese. The caviar is the magic ingredient!

MAKES 18–20 APPETIZERS

- 18 to 20 large mushrooms, each about 1½ inches in diameter
- 3 Tablespoons butter
- 2 Tablespoons black lumpfish caviar
- 8 ounces cream cheese, at room temperature
- 1 teaspoon dry dill weed
- 2 Tablespoons minced shallots
- ⅓ cup minced parsley

◆ Rinse the mushrooms well, and carefully remove the stems from mushroom caps. Reserve the stems for another use.

◆ Place the butter in an 8 by 12-inch baking dish. Put the dish in the oven, turn on the oven, and preheat to 350 degrees.

◆ When the butter is melted, remove the dish from oven. Swirl the mushrooms caps in the butter to coat evenly, then arrange the caps in the dish in a single layer, cut side up.

◆ Put the caviar in a fine strainer, and rinse under cold running water until the water runs clear. Set aside to drain well.

◆ Beat the cheese and blend in the dill weed and shallots. Stir in the caviar. Mound the cheese mixture equally in the mushroom caps.

◆ Bake, uncovered, in a 350-degree oven until the cheese mixture has a slight brown tinge, 15 to 20 minutes. Sprinkle with parsley and serve hot.

PEG'S NOTES ~ *These can be made ahead. Just cover the mushrooms, and chill overnight in the refrigerator. Allow 3 to 4 mushrooms per serving if this is your only appetizer. If you are serving other appetizers, you can get by with 2 per serving.*

Deb's Hot Crab Cocktail Dip

One of my catering-world highlights was to be asked to cater the reception after a Bob Hope Show. This was the Bob Hope Salutes the Troops show and was held at the Arlington Theater in Santa Barbara as a tribute to honor the veterans of the first Gulf War. This was a family event. My daughters, Deb and Teresa, were as excited as I was and loved adding their ideas to the event. The three of us decided that we'd set up several individual hors d'oeuvres tables in the courtyard so everyone could mingle, and we could manage the crowd.

This particular appetizer had Deb's touches all over it and was a fantastic hit! It was as good as the show!

SERVES 30

- 24 ounces cream cheese, softened to room temperature
- ½ cup mayonnaise
- ⅔ cup dry white wine
- ¼ teaspoon garlic salt
- 2 teaspoons Dijon mustard
- 2 teaspoons powdered sugar
- 1 teaspoon onion juice
- Dash of seasoned salt
- 1¼ pounds fresh crabmeat
- Assorted crackers and/or toasted rye cocktail bread

✦ Place the cream cheese, mayonnaise, and wine in a blender or food processor, and blend for about 45 seconds at medium speed. Add the garlic salt, mustard, sugar, onion juice, and seasoned salt, and blend for an additional 45 seconds.

✦ Place the blended ingredients in a double boiler, and heat over simmering water, stirring occasionally. Gently add the crabmeat to the ingredients in the double boiler. When the mixture is heated thoroughly, place it in a chafing dish to keep warm, and serve immediately.

✦ Serve with an array of assorted crackers or toasted rye cocktail bread.

PEG'S NOTES ~ *We found that a good dry California Chardonnay wine worked best.*

Famous Cheese Ball

I was promoted and transferred to another accounting office, where the staff had potlucks once a month. A co-worker, Frances Knudsen, brought this cheese ball to one of those potlucks and handed out the recipe. Everyone raved about it.

I prepared this cheese ball for the family Christmas-tree decorating party, where it became an instant tradition. The tree is set up, Nat King Cole Christmas songs are playing, and the cheese ball surrounded by crackers is on the coffee table. The entire family loves it, so I wouldn't dare fix something else for decorating the tree.

At one point, Kraft discontinued the Roca Blue Cheese Spread, but there was such a public outcry that they put it back on the market. During that time, I tried numerous substitutes, but nothing came close to the original version.

SERVES 8–10

- 1 5-ounce jar Kraft Roka Blue Cheese Spread
- 1 5-ounce jar Kraft Old English Cheese Spread
- 8 ounces cream cheese, softened
- 1 cup grated cheddar cheese
- Several dashes Worcestershire sauce
- Grated onion – about 2 teaspoons
- Sprinkle of garlic salt
- 2 cups chopped walnuts, or any other nuts

♦ Mix all ingredients except the nuts, and refrigerate overnight.

♦ Form into a ball and roll in chopped nuts just before serving.

PEG'S NOTES ~ I never measure the seasonings. I just dash the Worcestershire sauce to what I think tastes good, grate the onion over the bowl so that the juice of the onion goes into the cheese ball, then I sprinkle it with the garlic salt. Yummy!

I have always used chopped walnuts for this cheese ball, since I do not like the taste of pecans or pistachios with these flavors. But feel free to use whatever nuts your family prefers. This cheese ball goes well with stone ground wheat crackers.

The recipe is large enough to be divided into two balls for gift-giving.

APPETIZERS AND DIPS

Three-Cheese Fondue

Fondue was popular during the '60s and '70s, disappeared for a while, and is now making a comeback. And for good reason! It is tasty, warm and comforting. It's perfect for a wintry evening. This rich and fluffy fondue makes a hit whenever it is served. Everyone will love it!

MAKES 1 CUP

- ¼ cup dry white wine
- 2 Tablespoons shallots, minced
- ½ cup heavy cream
- ½ cup Boursin cheese, crumbled
- ⅓ cup blue cheese, crumbled
- 2 Tablespoons Parmesan cheese, grated
- 1 teaspoon fresh thyme, minced
- Freshly ground black pepper
- Juice of ½ lemon

✦ In a small saucepan, over medium heat, simmer the wine and shallots until the liquid is reduced by half, about 3 minutes.

✦ Add the cream, and reduce the heat to low. Gradually whisk in the cheeses until melted.

✦ Stir in the thyme, pepper, and lemon juice. Serve warm.

Hot Artichoke Dip

Artichokes are a perennial favorite, and this is no exception. And to make it even better, it is so easy to put together.

SERVES 8

- 1 cup Parmesan cheese
- 1 cup mayonnaise
- 1 6-ounce jar marinated artichoke hearts
- 1 4-ounce can chopped green chiles
- Stone ground wheat crackers

◆ Preheat the oven to 350 degrees.

◆ Drain and chop the artichoke hearts. Mix with the other ingredients. Pour into a small casserole dish.

◆ Bake for 20 minutes. Serve with crackers.

Deb's Artichoke Hearts Gratin

Feeling creative and using the hot artichoke dip recipe above as a starting point, Deb, who has become a chef in her own right, adds her magic touch, and with a few deft changes creates the following recipe, which has a totally different flavor from the original recipe.

SERVES 8

- 1 14-ounce can artichoke hearts
- ½ cup mayonnaise
- ½ cup grated Parmesan cheese
- 2 teaspoons mustard
- ½ teaspoon paprika

◆ Preheat the oven to 350 degrees.

◆ Butter a small, shallow baking dish, and set aside. Drain the artichokes and cut into small pieces.

◆ Combine the artichoke hearts with the other ingredients. Pour into the prepared dish.

◆ Bake for 15 to 20 minutes, or until browned and bubbly.

Peg's Crab Cakes

WITH A CHOICE OF SAUCES

Jarvis and I were chaperones for our youngest daughter Dana's eighth grade class U.S. history tour. I will never forget the delicious crab cakes that we enjoyed on the harbor in Maryland, and when I came home, I felt an impelling urge to recreate them. With a few trials and errors, there they were, delicious and worthy of a few special sauces.

The rave reviews abound at the parties I cater. Guests call them truly Pegilicious!®

MAKES 8 APPETIZERS OR 4 ENTRÉES

- 3 cups fine saltine cracker crumbs, divided
- 2 large eggs, lightly beaten
- ½ cup diced onion
- 3 Tablespoons mayonnaise
- 1 Tablespoon yellow mustard
- 2 teaspoons lemon juice
- ½ teaspoon grated lemon peel
- ¼ teaspoon Seafood Magic seasoning
- ½ teaspoon sea salt
- ¼ teaspoon black pepper
- ⅛ teaspoon ground red pepper
- ¼ teaspoon hot sauce
- 1 pound fresh lump crabmeat, drained*
- 2 Tablespoons butter
- 2 Tablespoons vegetable oil
- Mixed salad greens, for garnish
- Lemon slices, for garnish
- Fresh parsley sprigs, for garnish

♦ Stir together 2 cups of the cracker crumbs with the eggs, onion, mayonnaise, mustard, lemon juice, salt, peppers, and hot sauce. Gently fold in the crabmeat.

♦ Shape into 8 patties about 3 inches in diameter, and gently press them into the remaining cracker crumbs just to seal for frying.

♦ In a large skillet over medium-high heat, melt the butter in the oil. Add the crab cakes, and cook 4 minutes on each side or until golden.

♦ Remove the patties and place them on a serving platter. Garnish with mixed salad greens, lemon slices, and fresh parsley sprigs.

♦ Serve with Lemon-Dill Mayonnaise and Roasted Red Bell Pepper Sauce.

PEG'S NOTES ~ *In lieu of a dinner salad to start off a gourmet dinner, I serve these crab cakes as an appetizer on a bed of organic mixed greens on individual plates. I make both sauces and pass them around so guests can have a choice.*

*If using canned crab, you will need 3 6-ounce cans.

Lemon-Dill Mayonnaise

These two sauces are a "must" with the crab cakes.

MAKES 1¼ CUPS

- 1 cup mayonnaise
- 2 teaspoons grated lemon peel
- 1 Tablespoon lemon juice
- ¾ teaspoon dried dill weed
- ¼ teaspoon garlic powder
- ¼ teaspoon hot sauce

✦ Stir together all the ingredients.

✦ Cover and chill 1 hour.

Roasted Red Bell Pepper Sauce

MAKES 1¼ CUPS

- 1 large red bell pepper
- ½ cup mayonnaise, divided
- 2 teaspoons sherry
- ½ teaspoon garlic powder
- ½ teaspoon sea salt
- ¼ teaspoon pepper
- ¼ teaspoon hot sauce

✦ Cut the bell pepper in half, seed it, and place it cut side down on an aluminum foil–lined baking sheet. Broil on high until the pepper is blistered, turning it, if necessary.

✦ Place the pepper in a heavy-duty Ziploc® plastic bag, seal, and let it stand 10 minutes to loosen the skin.

✦ Peel the pepper and process it in a food processor with ¼ cup of the mayonnaise until smooth. Stir in the remaining mayonnaise, sherry, and seasonings.

✦ Cover and chill 1 hour.

PEG'S NOTES ~ You can bake the pepper at 450 degrees for 15 minutes, or leave the pepper whole, pierce it with a fork, and hold it over an open flame to blister the skin. Then place the pepper in the plastic bag for 10 minutes, peel it, and discard the seeds.

For this recipe, having roasted red bell peppers in the freezer comes in handy. Just thaw 1 pepper—or 2 halves—to room temperature before proceeding.

Peg's Fresh Fruit Salsa

The common association with the word "salsa" is a tomato-chili-based sauce to accompany Southwestern food, and there is no question that it is delicious. A fresh fruit salsa brings a meal alive. It makes a good dip and is also a perfect partner for many entrées. My husband, Jarvis, really loves fruit salsa and asked me to create one. After tasting several different kinds in restaurants, I developed these that he thinks are really delicious, especially the Peach-Avocado Salsa on page 100, that I often serve with pork. He also enjoys fruit salsa with fish.

Since I love to cook and he loves to eat, we make a good team.

MAKES 2¼ CUPS

- 1 cup papaya or mango, peeled and chopped
- 1 cup fresh pineapple, chopped
- ¼ cup red onion, finely chopped
- ¼ cup yellow, orange, or green bell pepper, finely chopped
- 3 Tablespoons snipped fresh cilantro
- 1 teaspoon finely shredded lime or lemon peel
- 2 Tablespoons lime or lemon juice
- 2 to 4 teaspoons finely chopped fresh jalapeño pepper
- 1 teaspoon grated fresh ginger

✦ In a medium-size bowl, combine all ingredients.

✦ Cover and chill in the refrigerator, so the flavors marinate for about 8 hours, or up to 24 hours.

PEG'S NOTES ~ Hot peppers contain volatile oils that can burn your skin. Wear rubber gloves when handling them. If your hands do touch the pepper, wash them well with soap and water before touching your face or eyes.

Peg's Mango Salsa

A best friend is one of life's greatest gifts to us, and I am blessed to have Ruth Ann for my very best friend. I love creating recipes for her. When we took a trip to Hawaii, I created special recipes for our trip, and since she loves mangoes, I thought a mango salsa would be an appropriate addition. She agreed.

MAKES 2 CUPS

- 1½ cups fresh mango, peeled and chopped
- 1 medium red bell pepper, seeded and chopped
- ¼ cup thinly sliced green onion
- 1 fresh jalapeño pepper, seeded and chopped
- 3 Tablespoons olive oil
- ½ teaspoon finely shredded lime peel
- 2 Tablespoons lime juice
- 1 Tablespoon white vinegar
- ¼ teaspoon sea salt
- ¼ teaspoon fresh ground black pepper

✦ In a medium-size bowl, combine all ingredients.

✦ Cover and chill in the refrigerator, so the flavors marinate for about 8 hours, or up to 24 hours.

PEG'S NOTES ~ A ripe mango has yellow skin blushed with red, and fragrant, juicy golden-orange flesh. If the fruit is not ripe, place it in a paper bag to ripen for 2 to 3 days at room temperature.

Hot peppers contain volatile oils that can burn your skin. Wear rubber gloves when handling them. If your hands do touch the pepper, wash them well with soap and water before touching your face or eyes.

APPETIZERS AND DIPS

PEG'S NOTES ~ I always use shallots in my dressings. I find them sweet and mild, and they do not overpower the recipe. I pick a small shallot, but if after chopping there is more than a tablespoon, I use all that I have chopped. For the grapefruit sections, I use Del Monte® Red Grapefruit, found in the produce section of the grocery store.

I **always** toss my salad greens with a sprinkle of dill weed when creating this salad.

It is very important that you toast your pecans: Preheat the oven to 350 degrees. Place the pecans on a cookie or baking sheet, and bake for 8 to 10 minutes. Ovens vary, so after 5 minutes I always check to see how the pecans are browning. Shake them around on the pan, and put them back into the oven for the additional 3 to 5 minutes. Do not bake longer than 10 minutes, as they will scorch or burn.

Fresh Southern Fruit Salad

with Honey-Pecan Dressing

This salad dressing is a family favorite. It is very refreshing and really cleans the palate before dinner. I have served it at many celebrations, holiday dinners, and quite a few birthday parties. It was the perfect salad for the 70th birthday dinner party for my special friend, Carol Garber, in Sarasota, Florida, on January 23, 2011. The rest of the menu that evening included individual beef Wellingtons with mushroom cream sauce, fresh asparagus, and fresh glazed carrots. The grand finale was my Southern Pecan Torte.

SERVES 4–6

Bibb or romaine lettuce

Dried dill weed

Fresh orange slices or mandarin sections

Grapefruit sections

Sliced avocado

Sliced strawberries

Other fresh berries, such as raspberries, blueberries, or blackberries

Any other fruit you like, such as grapes or melons

- Sprinkle the lettuce with dill weed. Place individual serving of lettuce on plates. Arrange the oranges, grapefruit, avocado, strawberries, and other berries or fruit over the lettuce leaves.
- Drizzle with Honey-Pecan Dressing.

Honey-Pecan Dressing

MAKES 2½ CUPS

- 3 Tablespoons sugar
- ½ cup honey
- 1 Tablespoon chopped shallots
- ¼ cup red wine vinegar
- ½ teaspoon dry mustard
- ¼ teaspoon sea salt
- 1 cup vegetable oil
- 1 cup chopped pecans, toasted

- Pulse the sugar, honey, shallots, vinegar, mustard, and salt in a blender or food processor 2 or 3 times until blended. With the blender running, pour the oil through the food chute in a slow, steady stream, and process until smooth.
- Stir in the pecans.
- If refrigerated, this dressing will keep for several weeks. Mine never lasts that long!

Ivy Manor Gourmet Salad
with Peg's Special Vinaigrette

I made this salad and served it for the first time to my family on Christmas Eve 1987. I had been extremely ill and after eight months was finally able to actually taste my food for the very first time. The dressing blended well with the other ingredients and tasted wonderful to me. The ingredients were a little expensive for a salad, but I was in a celebratory mood. It was the holidays, and everyone was coming home. You really don't need an excuse, however.

This was one of actor Efrem Zimbalist Jr.'s favorite salad dressings. He and TV personality Ralph Story tried to get me to produce it for commercial sales. I refused, though, because I believe the reason that it is so good is that it is made in small batches, and all the ingredients are fresh.

SERVES 8

- ½ pound bacon
- 2 bunches romaine lettuce, torn into bite-size pieces
- Dried dill weed
- 1 7.5-ounce can hearts of palm, drained and sliced
- 1 8.5-ounce can water-packed artichoke hearts, drained and quartered
- 4 ounces blue cheese crumbles

✦ Prepare Peg's Special Vinaigrette, and set aside. Keep at room temperature.

✦ Cook the bacon in a large heavy skillet over medium heat until crisp. Drain on paper towels. Cool completely. Crumble.

✦ Sprinkle the dill weed over the lettuce and toss. Keep the lettuce chilled in a Ziploc® bag in the refrigerator until ready to serve.

✦ On chilled salad plates, layer the lettuce, hearts of palm and artichokes, and sprinkle with the cheese and bacon crumbles.

✦ Drizzle the vinaigrette over the salad when you are ready to serve.

Peg's Special Vinaigrette

MAKES 1½ CUPS

- 1 small shallot, chopped
- 3 Tablespoons apple cider vinegar
- 2 teaspoons Dijon mustard
- ½ teaspoon sugar
- ½ teaspoon sea salt
- ¼ teaspoon freshly ground black pepper
- 1 cup vegetable oil

✦ Puree the shallot with the vinegar in a food processor. Blend in the mustard, sugar, salt, and pepper.

✦ Gradually add the oil in a thin, steady stream, and continue processing until thick. Pour into a salad jar, and keep at room temperature until ready to serve.

PEG'S NOTES ~ I make my salad dressing, cook the bacon, and prepare the lettuce early in the day. This gives the flavors in the dressing time to blend, and the lettuce can chill. Any leftover dressing will keep up to one month if refrigerated.

I drain and slice the hearts of palm and keep them covered in a small bowl. I drain the artichokes, cut them in half, and remove all of the artichoke fuzz from the hearts by taking a teaspoon and scooping it out. I then slice the halves to make quarters and keep them covered in a small bowl. At dinnertime, I just need to assemble the salads, which only takes a few minutes.

This salad is especially good when served with hot sourdough rolls.

Organic Salad Greens
with Sweet & Sour Dressing

This salad is truly "yummy." Of course, you can use the dressing on any salad, but it is really tasty here.

Salad

SERVES 4

- 1 bunch organic salad greens, washed and torn
- 1 cup frozen peas, thawed
- 1 cup shredded mozzarella cheese
- ½ cup toasted slivered almonds
- 6 bacon slices, cooked crisp and crumbled

◆ Combine all ingredients. Toss with Sweet & Sour Dressing just before serving.

Sweet & Sour Dressing

MAKES 1 CUP

- ⅓ cup honey
- 2½ Tablespoons red wine vinegar
- 1 Tablespoon diced shallots
- 1 teaspoon Dijon mustard
- ¼ teaspoon sea salt
- ¼ teaspoon garlic salt
- ⅛ teaspoon fresh ground black pepper
- ½ cup vegetable oil

◆ Pulse all ingredients except the oil in a blender 2 to 3 times until well blended. With the blender running, pour the oil through the food chute in a slow, steady stream, and process until smooth.

Ham and Spinach Salad

with Orange-Poppy Seed Dressing

There was a motive behind this salad. I wanted my family to eat more spinach, and the Orange–Poppy Seed Dressing did the trick. But just to be sure, I added ham, which they love. It worked! The addition of ham makes a nice entrée salad for lunch. It's very refreshing in the summertime!

SERVES 4

For the salad

- 7 cups fresh spinach
- 1 cup cubed or julienned fully cooked ham
- ½ medium red onion, thinly sliced and separated into rings
- ½ cup toasted pecan halves
- ½ small cantaloupe or ½ cup mandarin orange sections

✦ Arrange the fresh spinach on salad plates.

✦ Top with the ham, and add the onion rings, pecan halves, and fruit of choice. Drizzle with the Orange-Poppy Seed Dressing when ready to serve.

Orange-Poppy Seed Dressing

MAKES ¾ CUP

- 3 Tablespoons sugar
- 1½ teaspoons finely shredded orange peel
- 2 Tablespoons orange juice
- 2 Tablespoons vinegar
- 1 Tablespoon finely chopped shallot
- Dash of pepper
- ⅓ cup salad oil
- 1 teaspoon poppy seeds

✦ In a food processor or blender, combine and process the sugar, orange peel and juice, vinegar, shallot, and pepper. With the processor or blender running, slowly add the oil in a steady stream. Process until mixture is thickened.

✦ Stir in the poppy seeds. Cover and chill until needed. Shake before using. This keeps up to one week.

SALADS AND DRESSINGS

PEG'S NOTES ~ The buttermilk helps the cornmeal mixture stick to the tomatoes. Coat them heavily as some will be lost during frying. Use a flexible turner to gently turn the green tomato slices without dislodging the coating.

I like to make the dressing a day ahead, so that the flavors can blend. Stir before serving. For the perfect drizzle, place the dressing in an empty honey bottle, or a similar squeeze bottle. No bottle? No problem. Just pour about 1/2 cup of the dressing into a small plastic bag, snip one corner, and drizzle just a little over the salad. You don't want a lot of dressing on this salad, only a hint. Save the rest for another salad.

Ivy Manor Fried Green Tomato Salad

with Goat Cheese and Buttermilk Dressing

I love heirloom tomatoes, grow a lot of them, and eat them every day. Last year, I grew 17 different varieties and had to come up with new recipes so they wouldn't go to waste. It's a good thing my family likes them, too. Here is the salad I created for a family birthday party. It was a big hit. If you are a tomato lover, I think you will love it, too.

SERVES 4

For the green tomatoes

- 4 large green heirloom tomatoes
- Sea salt and pepper
- 2 cups cornmeal
- 1 cup panko bread crumbs
- 1 cup buttermilk
- Vegetable oil, for frying – do not use olive oil

For the salad

- 4 large ripe heirloom tomatoes, each cut into 2 slices, ¾ inch thick
- 1 15-ounce can black-eyed peas, drained and rinsed
- 4 ounces goat cheese crumbles
- Mixed salad greens
- Dried dill weed
- Buttermilk dressing

- ♦ Wash the green tomatoes, and cut each one into 2 slices, ¾ inch thick. The tomatoes need to be 4 to 5 inches in diameter, so large beefsteak tomatoes could be substituted.
- ♦ Sprinkle the green tomatoes with salt and pepper and set aside.
- ♦ Combine the cornmeal and panko, and place into a dipping pan. Pour the buttermilk into another dipping pan.
- ♦ Pour ¼ cup of the vegetable oil into a skillet, and heat on high until very hot.
- ♦ Dip the sliced green tomatoes first into the buttermilk, then into the cornmeal mixture. Immediately place them into the hot skillet, and fry until golden brown on one side. Gently turn the slices over, and continue cooking until the tomatoes are nice and golden. Remove and place on a paper towel-lined plate to absorb excessive oil. Keep warm.
- ♦ Sprinkle the mixed salad greens with the dill weed, divide the greens, and place a portion around the edge of four salad plates. In the center of each plate, place one slice of ripe tomato.
- ♦ On the top of the ripe tomato, place a fried green tomato slice. Repeat with a ripe tomato, then another fried tomato.
- ♦ Divide the black-eyed peas, and spoon them around the base of the tomatoes on each plate, adding a few peas on top of the fried green tomatoes.
- ♦ Sprinkle 2 tablespoons of goat cheese crumbles on each salad, and drizzle with a little Buttermilk Dressing. Serve immediately.

Buttermilk Dressing

MAKES 1½ CUPS

- ¾ cup buttermilk
- ½ cup mayonnaise
- ½ cup sour cream
- ½ teaspoon Dijon mustard
- 1 Tablespoon fresh lemon juice
- 1 Tablespoon minced shallot
- 1 garlic clove, minced
- ½ teaspoon salt
- ¼ teaspoon freshly ground pepper

- ♦ Whisk all the ingredients together. Cover and chill until ready to use.

Hawaiian Salmon Salad

I love Hawaii and thoroughly enjoy my visits. The abundance of tropical and other fresh fruits are an inspiration to me to create specials dishes in celebration of being there. The possible combinations seem endless. Talking about combinations, my best friend, Ruth Ann, and I make another great combination! We're a team in the kitchen, trying out new things and laughing a lot. This recipe honors her and all of our good times and great meals in Hawaii. Aloha!

SERVES 4

For the avocados

- 2 fresh avocados
- Flour, for dredging
- 1 beaten egg, for dredging
- Panko breadcrumbs, for dredging
- Vegetable oil, for frying

For the asparagus and salmon

- 16 stalks fresh asparagus
- Olive oil, for the asparagus and the salmon
- Sea salt and fresh pepper
- 4 6-ounce salmon fillets

For the salad

- Organic mixed salad greens
- Dried dill weed
- 2 Hawaiian papayas, peeled, halved, seeded, and cut into wedges
- 8 strawberries, halved
- Chopped macadamia nuts, optional

Mango-pineappple salsa

- 1 fresh mango, peeled and sliced
- 4 slices fresh pineapple, diced
- ¼ cup red onion, diced
- ¼ cup green pepper, diced
- ¼ cup red pepper, diced
- 1 jalapeño pepper, seeded and minced
- 2 Tablespoons lime juice
- 2 Tablespoons olive oil

Tropical salad dressing

- 1½ cups fresh pineapple chunks, plus additional, if needed
- ¼ cup diced shallots
- ¼ cup rice vinegar
- 1½ teaspoons Dijon mustard
- 2 teaspoons sugar
- ½ teaspoon sea salt
- ½ teaspoon white pepper
- 1 cup extra-virgin olive oil

- ✦ **Prepare the mango salsa.** In a bowl, combine all the salsa ingredients, and set aside.
- ✦ **Prepare the tropical salad dressing.** In a blender, blend all the dressing ingredients, adding the oil very slowly. Pour into a salad jar, and set aside until ready.
- ✦ **Prepare the avocados.** Cut each in half, remove the pit and peel, keeping the avocado half intact. Cut each half into 4 wedges. Dredge each wedge in flour. Dip first in the egg, then in the breadcrumbs. Fry in vegetable oil until golden.
- ✦ **Prepare the asparagus.** Brush the stalks with olive oil and sprinkle with salt and pepper. Grill for 2 to 3 minutes.
- ✦ **Prepare the salmon.** Brush the fillets with olive oil and season with salt and pepper. Then grill for 5 minutes on one side, flip, and grill for another 4 minutes, or until done.
- ✦ In a large bowl, sprinkle the salad greens with dill weed and toss with the Tropical Dressing. Divide the greens among four plates.
- ✦ Divide the asparagus, avocado, and papaya wedges among the plates, arranging them in clock formation. Place the strawberry halves next to the papaya. Place a salmon fillet on top in the middle of the salad, and top with the Mango Salsa. Sprinkle with the macadamia nuts, if using.

Curried Chicken Salad

with Mango and Cashews

One of the people I cooked for once a month was always requesting that I come up with new curry dishes. Whenever she invited guests to lunch, she was sure to request a curry dish. This dish is lovely served in baked puff pastry. She told me that her friends are still talking about that lunch.

You can adjust the seasonings to your taste in this recipe.

MAKES 3 CUPS

- ⅓ cup mayonnaise
- 2 Tablespoons apricot preserves
- ½ teaspoon curry powder
- Juice of ½ lime
- Sea salt and cayenne pepper to taste
- 2 cups cooked chicken, cubed
- 1 ripe mango, peeled and diced
- ½ cup celery, diced
- ¼ cup green onions, sliced
- 1 Tablespoon fresh cilantro, chopped
- ½ cup chopped cashews
- Pita bread or croissants

✦ Combine the mayonnaise, preserves, curry, lime juice, and seasonings in a large bowl.

✦ Add the chicken, mango, celery, green onions, and cilantro. Toss to coat.

✦ Stir in the cashews before serving with toasted pita bread or on a croissant.

PEG'S NOTES ~ Peel the mango with a vegetable peeler, then cut the flesh away from the large flat pit, and dice. You may reduce the amount of curry, if desired. This salad becomes a fancy dish when served between sheets of baked puff pastry. The dish will serve 4 to 6, depending on the size of the servings.

Shrimp and Avocado Salad

with Creamy Dill Dressing

SERVES 4

For the shrimp

- 1 cup water
- ½ cup dry white wine
- Juice and rind of ½ lemon
- 1 pound medium shrimp, peeled and deveined

For the salad

- 2 avocados, pitted and halved
- Lettuce leaves
- ½ cucumber, diced, optional

Creamy Dill Dressing

MAKES ½ CUP

- ¼ cup mayonnaise
- ¼ cup red onion, diced
- 2 Tablespoons fresh lemon juice
- 1 Tablespoon chopped fresh parsley
- 1 Tablespoon chopped fresh dill
- 2 teaspoons sugar
- Minced zest of 1 lemon
- Sea salt and pepper to taste
- Cayenne, optional

- ◆ In a saucepan over medium-high heat, simmer the water, wine, lemon juice, and rind.
- ◆ Add the shrimp and cook 3 minutes. Remove from the heat, and let stand until the shrimp are pink and firm, about 3 more minutes. Drain well.
- ◆ Prepare the dressing.
- ◆ Add the shrimp and cucumber, if using, to the dressing. Toss to coat, and chill until cold.
- ◆ To serve, place each avocado half on lettuce leaves, and spoon the salad into the center.

- ◆ Combine the mayonnaise, onion, lemon juice, herbs, sugar, lemon zest, and seasonings in a bowl.

SALADS AND DRESSINGS

Peg's Famous Crab Salad

In 1985, I wanted to start a catering business and was thinking about how I might do it. Then I had an idea. I would kick off my catering career by holding a street party in the middle of the small town of Los Olivos and invite the community to come. That way, they could find out for themselves that I made delicious stuff. These elegant bite-size servings disappeared as fast as we could refill the platters. Today, Crab Puffs are one of my most requested dishes.

Use the Cream Puff recipe on page 168 for making the puffs. It makes about 30 to 40 puffs.

SERVES 10–12

3 pounds fresh lump crabmeat

Sauce

1 cup mayonnaise
1 Tablespoon heavy cream
½ teaspoon curry powder
1 Tablespoon grated onion
1 Tablespoon minced parsley
¼ cup chili sauce
2 Tablespoons sherry
2 Tablespoons lemon juice
¼ teaspoon fresh ground black pepper

For serving and garnish

Lettuce cups
Tomato slices
Stuffed olives
Parsley sprigs

- Carefully remove the fibers from the crabmeat. Refrigerate the crabmeat, and keep it chilled while combining the ingredients for the sauce.
- Combine the mayonnaise, cream, curry, onion, parsley, chili sauce, sherry, juice, and pepper.
- Fold the crabmeat into the sauce carefully, so as not to break up the lumps. Chill thoroughly.
- Serve in lettuce cups garnished with tomato, olives, and parsley.

PEG'S NOTES ~ *You must use real crabmeat for this salad, the flavor improves after standing in the coldest part of the refrigerator. I make this salad the night before, and it really is flavorful the next day. This salad is excellent for picnics or served with hot biscuits or rolls for a delicious luncheon or dinner.*

This recipe will fill approximately 30 large or 40 small crab puffs. You should double the amount if you are serving 50 or more crab puffs.

SALADS AND DRESSINGS | 51

Turkey Salad

WITH CRANBERRY VINAIGRETTE

How on earth are we going to use up all this leftover Thanksgiving turkey? No more turkey sandwiches, please. Other leftovers helped me put this recipe together. My family was happy when I came up with this delicious turkey salad and cranberry vinaigrette.

SERVES 4

- 1 head romaine lettuce, torn
- Dried dill weed
- 4 bacon slices, cooked and crumbled
- 2 cups coarsely chopped cooked turkey
- 1 medium Fuji apple, thinly sliced
- ½ cup toasted chopped walnuts

- ✦ Toss the lettuce with the dill weed. Chill until ready to serve.
- ✦ Cook the bacon until crisp. Drain on a paper towel. Cool and crumble.
- ✦ Divide the lettuce among four salad plates. Top with the turkey and apples, equally divided among the plates. Sprinkle the walnuts and bacon on top equally.
- ✦ Drizzle the Cranberry Vinaigrette on the salad and serve the rest of the dressing alongside.

CRANBERRY VINAIGRETTE

MAKES 1 CUP

- ½ cup whole-berry cranberry sauce
- 2 Tablespoons balsamic vinegar
- ½ teaspoon grated orange rind
- 2 Tablespoons orange juice
- 1½ teaspoons Dijon mustard
- ½ teaspoon honey
- ⅛ teaspoon sea salt
- ¼ cup olive oil

- ✦ Stir together the cranberry sauce, vinegar, orange rind and juice, mustard, honey, and salt until blended. Stir in the oil, 1 tablespoon at a time, until well blended.

PEG'S NOTES ~ *I serve this with hot sourdough rolls or cranberry-walnut rolls. I use leftover fresh cranberry sauce in this recipe, and it is fantastic.*

Christmas Eve Salad

with Pomegranate-Lime Vinaigrette

Christmas Eve is a most festive time. Since red is one of the Christmas colors, I love using red in holiday meals. My pomegranate tree bears fruit from October through January, which makes it perfect for Christmas with its sweet, bright red seeds. The girls love this treat.

SERVES 4

- 1 bag mixed greens
- Dried dill weed
- 2 ruby red grapefruit, peeled and segmented
- 1 red apple, such as Pink Lady or Braeburn, diced
- 1 cup julienned jicama
- ½ cup pomegranate arils
- 1¼ cups sliced cooked beets

◆ In a large bowl sprinkle the salad greens with the dill and combine with the grapefruit, apple, jicama, and pomegranate arils.

◆ Drizzle the Pomegranate-Lime Vinaigrette over the salad, and toss to coat. Divide the salad among four plates, then layer the beets on the salad.

◆ Serve the salad immediately.

Pomegranate-Lime Vinaigrette

MAKES ½ CUP

- ¼ cup extra-virgin olive oil
- 3 Tablespoons pomegranate juice
- 2 Tablespoons fresh lime juice
- 2 teaspoons sugar
- ⅛ teaspoon cayenne pepper
- Sea salt and pepper to taste
- 1 Tablespoon chopped fresh cilantro leaves

◆ In a bowl whisk together the oil, juices, sugar, and cayenne pepper. Season with the salt and black pepper. Set aside.

◆ Add the cilantro to the vinaigrette just before serving the salad.

PEG'S NOTES ~ *I add the beets last, so their juice does not discolor the other ingredients of the salad. It is also much cheaper and less work to purchase a quart jar of Del Monte's® Red Grapefruit sections, rather than to peel and segment the fresh grapefruit. You can also purchase pomegranate arils. You can find both of these in the produce section of your local supermarket.*

Orange-Pineapple Salad

This combination of fruits and gelatin was created for Thanksgiving in the late sixties, back when gelatin salads were all the rage. I've been serving it ever since. I use a star mold, and the girls are always fighting over the points of the star. This is my daughter Dana's absolute favorite. She would try to hide any leftovers from her sisters.

On occasion, I've made this salad at the home of friends who don't have a star-shaped mold. It was delicious nevertheless. Sort of like me....my shape keeps changing, but my flavor stays the same.

SERVES 10–12

- 1 6-ounce box orange gelatin
- 2 cups hot water
- 1 20-ounce can crushed pineapple
- 2 11-ounce cans mandarin oranges, drained
- 2 cups miniature marshmallows
- 2 cups sour cream
- 4 Tablespoons mayonnaise
- 4 Tablespoons grated cheddar cheese
- Salad greens, if desired.

- ✦ Dissolve the gelatin in hot water. Add the pineapple, and chill until slightly thickened.
- ✦ Fold the mandarin oranges into the chilled pineapple-gelatin mixture. Pour into mold, and chill until firm. You can make the recipe to this point 1 to 2 days ahead. Keep it refrigerated.
- ✦ Mix the sour cream and mayonnaise and spread on the salad. Sprinkle with cheese.
- ✦ Serve on greens.

PEG'S NOTES ~ This recipe fills a 10 1/2 by 10 1/2 by 2 1/2-inch star mold that I bring out for the holidays. I unmold my star on a nice serving plate and spread the dressing on all sides. Then I sprinkle the cheese only on the top. It's as beautiful as a cake! If you dip your mold into hot water for a few seconds, the salad will slide right out of the mold. Then refrigerate the salad for a few minutes before icing it with the sour cream–mayonnaise dressing. I sometimes use pineapple rings and additional mandarin oranges for decoration instead of salad greens.

You can divide the recipe in half for a smaller portion to fill an 8 by 8 by 2-inch mold.

Peg's Fruit and Cranberry Mold

My sisters—remember, I was the youngest of nine, so they are quite elderly now—would never think of having a Sunday dinner or reunion without having what they call a "Congealed Salad." In honor of my Southern heritage, I am including their favorites. Of course, I had to create my own versions. I made this recipe on November 8, 1981.

SERVES 6–8

- 1 6-ounce package cherry gelatin
- 2 cups hot water
- 1 cup mayonnaise
- ¾ cup evaporated milk
- ½ pound fresh cranberries
- 1 seedless orange, peeled
- ¾ cup sugar
- ½ cup chopped pecans
- 1 cup crushed pineapple with juice
- 1 Tablespoon lemon juice

✦ Dissolve the gelatin in hot water, and set aside to cool. When it's cool, stir in the mayonnaise and milk. Chill until syrupy.

✦ In a food processor or blender, grind the cranberries and whole orange; keep the juices with the fruit. Add the sugar to the fruit.

✦ After the gelatin is syrupy, add the pecans, pineapple, and lemon juice, to the fruit, and fold the fruit mixture into the gelatin. Mix well.

✦ Pour into a 2-quart ring mold, and chill overnight.

Frannie's Salads

These salads were passed down to me from my sister Frannie. They were her real "pony show." I can see her now, proudly bringing her creations to the family table for everyone to devour. Whenever I serve either of these salads, I feel like she's right there in the room with me. I have no idea why she named one Watergate, but I serve this one with ham sandwiches during the Christmas holidays.

FRANNIE'S WATERGATE SALAD

- 1 20-ounce can crushed pineapple, undrained
- 1 3.4-ounce package pistachio instant pudding mix
- 1 12-ounce container Cool Whip
- 1 cup chopped pecans
- 1 cup miniature colored marshmallows

✦ Mix all the ingredients together. Put into a pretty glass serving bowl.

✦ Cover and chill until ready to serve.

FRANNIE'S CONGEALED SALAD

- 1 20-ounce can crushed pineapple in its own juice
- 1 6-ounce package peach gelatin
- 2 cups buttermilk
- 1 16-ounce container Cool Whip
- Chopped nuts, optional

✦ In a heavy saucepan, bring the crushed pineapple to boil over moderate heat. Add the peach gelatin, and continue to cook until the gelatin is dissolved. Remove from heat and cool.

✦ Stir in the buttermilk and blend in the Cool Whip. Add nuts, if using.

✦ Pour into a serving dish. Chill until set and ready to serve.

PEG'S NOTES ~ The colored marshmallows in the green pudding of Frannie's Watergate Salad makes a really pretty dish at holiday time, so this recipe is not only good to eat, it is also good looking.

Frannie's Congealed Salad was another creative idea from Frannie. She never named this salad, so the family just referred to it as "Frannie's." It's simple, unusual, and delicious.

V.I.P. Salad

VERY IMPORTANT PINEAPPLE

I created this salad for a 50th wedding anniversary held in December. My beautiful star mold seemed very appropriate for Christmas time, and also complemented the salad which is as delicious as it is beautiful. The secret is the port wine and cranberry/raspberry combination that pairs so perfectly with ham.

SERVES 10–12

- 1 20-ounce can crushed pineapple
- 1 envelope unflavored gelatin
- 1 6-ounce package raspberry gelatin
- 1 cup boiling water
- 1 16-ounce can whole cranberry sauce
- 1 cup port wine
- 1 cup chopped walnuts
- 8 ounces cream cheese, softened
- 1 cup sour cream
- 1 4-ounce can sliced pineapple, for decoration, optional

◆ Drain ½ cup of the syrup from the crushed pineapple, and put the liquid in a saucepan. Sprinkle unflavored gelatin over the syrup to soften it.

◆ Place the softened gelatin over low heat, stirring constantly. Stir in the boiling water until gelatin is dissolved.

◆ Remove from the heat and add the dissolved gelatin to the raspberry gelatin, mixing well.

◆ Stir in the remaining undrained pineapple, cranberry sauce, and wine. Chill until the mixture begins to thicken and starts to gel.

◆ Stir in the walnuts, and pour into a star mold or a 9 by 12-inch dish. Chill until firm. Unmold onto a serving plate.

◆ Mix the cream cheese with the sour cream, and spread it over the top of the salad. Decorate with sliced pineapples in the center.

PEG'S NOTES ~ I really like using the star mold for this salad. I spread the cream cheese-sour cream mixture over the top, then stack three pineapple slices right in the center of the star. It goes really well with any pork dish.

Eggnog Flan Salad

Eggnog is a must for the holidays. It is perfect for the winter season, warm and tasty and full of good cheer. I had made an eggnog dip for fruit, which was very popular, so I kept experimenting until I came up with another eggnog recipe. I was quite pleased with this dish and happy to have another salad to serve for Thanksgiving and Christmas and at the numerous holiday parties I cater. This salad is not only beautiful on a holiday table, but is also different and delicious.

12 SERVINGS

- 1 teaspoon unflavored gelatin
- ¼ cup cold water
- 1 16-ounce can pear halves, packed in juice
- 1 6-ounce package lemon gelatin
- 1 cup sour cream
- ¾ cup eggnog
- 1 11-ounce can mandarin orange sections, drained, plus additional orange sections for decoration
- Sliced kiwi, optional, for decoration
- Curly endive, for garnish

✦ Soften the unflavored gelatin in the cold water, and set aside. Drain the pear halves, saving the juice. Dice the pears, and set aside.

✦ Add enough water to the juice to measure 2 cups. Bring the juice mixture to boiling, and stir in the lemon gelatin and the unflavored gelatin mixture. Stir until the gelatin is dissolved. Cool.

✦ Blend the sour cream and eggnog, and stir into the gelatin mixture. Chill until partially set.

✦ Fold the orange sections and the diced pears into the partially set gelatin. Turn the mixture into an oiled 9½-inch flan pan or a fluted tart pan. Chill until firm.

✦ Just before serving, unmold the salad onto a serving platter and place curly endive garnish around the edge. Garnish with mandarin orange sections and kiwi slices, if using.

EGGNOG SALAD MOLD

4–6 SERVINGS

If you want to make a smaller portion of the Eggnog Flan Salad in a loaf pan, follow this recipe.

✦ Follow the recipe for Eggnog Flan Salad as directed, except:

✦ Omit the unflavored gelatin and ¼ cup cold water.

✦ Halve all the remaining ingredients, using ⅓ cup eggnog.

✦ Pour the partially set mixture into an oiled 8 by 4 by 2-inch loaf pan.

✦ Chill until firm. Unmold, and garnish with mandarin orange sections, kiwi, if using, and curly endive.

PEG'S NOTES ~ *I use a fluted tart pan and invert the mold onto the platter. This leaves a nice fluted edge with an indention on the top. I then arrange mandarin orange sections around the top edge of the indention and arrange the kiwi slices in a circle. This makes a gorgeous presentation.*

Party Dream Salad

This recipe has been in the family for decades and has made an appearance during the holidays in the South. Here is the original recipe. Alterations I have made are under Peg's Notes. For those who have ever lived in the South, I am sure this will bring back memories.

SERVES 6–8

- 8 ounces cream cheese, softened
- ¼ cup sour cream
- 2 Tablespoons powdered sugar
- 1 Tablespoon lemon juice
- ½ teaspoon sea salt
- ½ cup diced orange sections
- ½ cup halved Maraschino cherries, plus whole cherries for garnish
- ½ cup chopped pecans
- 2 cups diced bananas
- 1 cup whipping cream, whipped

- In a small mixing bowl, beat together the cream cheese, sour cream, sugar, lemon juice, and salt until light and fluffy. Fold in the remaining ingredients.
- Pour the mixture into a shallow 6-cup salad bowl that you have sprayed with non-stick cooking spray, or use a Jell-O mold. Chill until firm.
- Unmold onto a serving plate, and garnish with cherries.

PEG'S NOTES ~ My daughter Debbie does not like Maraschino cherries, but she loves mandarin oranges, so here is a good variation I created for her. Replace the diced orange sections with mandarin oranges. Omit the cherries, but add 1/2 cup coconut. I agree with Deb; this is really a delicious, refreshing salad.

PEG'S NOTES ~ This soup can be made ahead. Cool, cover, and refrigerate up to 24 hours. I serve this soup chunky, but you can purée it, if you desire. It's great with sourdough toast sprinkled with fresh grated Parmesan cheese, or you could try one of my delicious dumpling recipes. You can also substitute canned beans for dried beans. Drain them and just simmer them with the spices.

Peg's Minestrone Soup

This is a great soup with wonderful flavor, the perfect thing on a cold winter night. Feel free to add other vegetables, such as cauliflower or butternut squash, or leave out a vegetable that your family may not like.

SERVES 8

Beans

- 1 cup dried Great Northern beans, picked over and rinsed
- Water
- 1 teaspoon minced garlic
- ½ teaspoon thyme
- ½ teaspoon dried rosemary
- ½ teaspoon sea salt
- 1 bay leaf

Soup

- 2 Tablespoons olive oil
- 1 large onion, chopped
- 2 large carrots, chopped
- 1 large celery rib, chopped
- 2 teaspoons minced garlic
- 1½ teaspoons sea salt, divided
- ½ teaspoon freshly ground pepper
- ½ pound green beans, trimmed and cut into ¾-inch pieces
- 4 cups thinly sliced cabbage
- 3 14.5-ounce cans chicken stock
- 1 quart water
- 1 piece Parmesan cheese rind, 3 by 4 inches, optional
- 2 medium zucchini, quartered lengthwise and sliced
- 1 14.5-ounce can whole tomatoes in juice, drained and chopped
- ½ teaspoon dried basil
- ½ teaspoon dried oregano leaves
- ½ teaspoon dried dill weed

♦ Prepare the beans. Place the beans in a large Dutch oven with enough cold water to cover by 1 inch, and bring to a boil.

♦ Remove from the heat, cover, and let stand for 1 hour. Drain the beans, return them to the Dutch oven, and cover with 2 inches of cold water.

♦ Add the garlic, thyme, rosemary, salt, and bay leaf. Bring to a boil; reduce the heat and simmer, covered, for 30 minutes, until the beans are tender. Drain the beans; discard the bay leaf. Set aside.

♦ In the same Dutch oven, heat the olive oil over medium heat. Add the onions, carrots, celery, garlic, ½ teaspoon salt, and pepper, and cook 8 minutes, or until the garlic is golden. Add the drained beans, green beans, cabbage, broth, water, Parmesan rind, if using, and remaining 1 teaspoon salt. Bring to a boil, reduce the heat, and simmer, partially covered, for 30 minutes.

♦ Stir in the zucchini and tomatoes. Return to a boil; reduce the heat and simmer, partially covered, 15 minutes more, until the beans and vegetables are very tender.

♦ Remove the Parmesan rind and discard.

♦ Taste and adjust the salt and pepper.

♦ Stir in spices. The soup is ready to serve.

Zom's Zucchini Soup

with Cheddar Cheese Dumplings

A bounty of zucchini and tomatoes from the garden brought this soup to fruition. It is so delicious that I make gallons during the summer, and I put up the soup in quart jars for the winter months. I decided to add the dumplings to provide a more substantial meal for the grandkids. My youngest daughter, Dana, loves this soup. I ship it to her family in Kentucky.

SERVES 8

- 1 pound Italian sweet or hot sausage, casings removed
- 2 cups celery, sliced on an angle into ½-inch pieces
- 2 pounds zucchini, sliced into ½-inch pieces
- 2 green peppers, sliced into ½-inch pieces
- 3½ pounds fresh heirloom tomatoes, or 2 28-ounce cans tomatoes
- 1 cup chopped onion
- 1 teaspoon Italian seasoning
- ¼ teaspoon garlic powder
- 2 teaspoons salt
- 1 teaspoon oregano
- 1 teaspoon sugar
- ½ teaspoon basil

- ◆ In a large soup pot over medium-high heat, brown and separate the sausage.
- ◆ Add the remaining ingredients to the meat; cook and simmer until the vegetables are just barely tender.
- ◆ If serving with the dumplings, add them as soon as the soup starts a gentle boil.

Cheddar Cheese Dumplings

MAKES 10 DUMPLINGS

- 2 cups sifted all-purpose flour
- 1 teaspoon baking powder
- ½ teaspoon baking soda
- 1 teaspoon salt
- 1 Tablespoon shortening
- 1 egg, well beaten
- 1 cup buttermilk
- ¾ cup grated cheddar cheese

- ◆ Stir the dry ingredients together in a bowl. Work in the shortening with a fork.
- ◆ Combine the egg, buttermilk, and cheese, and add to the dry ingredients, mixing only enough to moisten the flour.
- ◆ Drop the dumpling batter in 2-tablespoon dollops onto the gently cooking soup. Cover and cook 20 minutes. Do not remove the cover for the first 10 minutes. Serve at once.

Turkey Tortilla Soup

with Black Bean Salsa

This is usually a seasonal soup for after Thanksgiving— another way to use up the leftover turkey. But my family wants me to make this soup all year round. I added the Black Bean Salsa because we all love black beans.

MAKES 8 CUPS

- 2 Tablespoons olive oil
- 1½ cups chopped onions
- 2 Tablespoons garlic, minced
- 3 6-inch corn tortillas, cut into 1-inch pieces
- 1 10½-ounce can diced tomatoes with green chiles
- 4 cups chicken broth
- 1½ Tablespoons chili powder
- 2 teaspoons cumin
- 1 teaspoon dried oregano
- 2 cups cooked turkey or chicken, cubed
- 1½ cups frozen corn kernels
- ½ cup heavy cream
- 1 cup Monterey Jack cheese, shredded
- 2 Tablespoons lime juice
- Sea salt and pepper
- Black Bean Salsa
- Sour cream, for topping

✦ Heat the oil in a large saucepan over medium-high heat. Add the onions and garlic, and sauté for 3 minutes.

✦ Stir in the tortilla pieces, and sauté until they are no longer crisp. Add the tomatoes, broth, and spices, and bring to a boil. Remove from the heat. Let cool 5 minutes, then purée the soup base in batches in a blender or food processor until smooth.

✦ Return the soup to the pot. Add the turkey, corn, and cream. Bring to a boil, and simmer 5 minutes or until the soup begins to thicken. Reduce the heat to medium, sprinkle in the cheese, and stir until melted. Add the lime juice, and season with salt and pepper to taste.

✦ Serve with Black Bean Salsa and sour cream.

PEG'S NOTES ~ *I use fresh corn when in season along with heirloom tomatoes, then I add a 4-ounce can of Hatch roasted green chiles.*

Black Bean Salsa

This salsa was developed to go on top of my Chicken or Turkey Tortilla Soup, but I soon started using it with any meat chili I served. When I discovered the children eating just the salsa with chips, I realized that this new dish was very versatile, and I could use it in many different ways.

MAKES 3½ CUPS

- 1 15-ounce can black beans, drained and rinsed
- 1 cup tomatoes, seeded and diced
- ½ cup shallots, slivered
- ¼ cup minced fresh cilantro
- 1 Tablespoon jalapeño pepper, seeded and minced
- ½ avocado, peeled, seeded, and diced
- 2 Tablespoons fresh lime juice
- 1 Tablespoon olive oil
- Sea salt and pepper to taste

✦ Combine all the ingredients in a bowl, tossing well to coat. Chill the salsa until ready to serve.

PEG'S NOTES ~ *You may substitute red onions for the shallots, if you prefer.*

Jalapeño peppers contain volatile oils that can burn your skin, lips, and eyes. Avoid direct contact as much as possible. Wear rubber gloves while handling the jalapeño pepper, and be careful not to touch your eyes. If you do not have rubber gloves, wash your hands with soap and warm water prior to touching your face or eyes.

Southern Pecan Soup

I discovered peanut soup when we were traveling as chaperones with Dana on a national history tour. That soup gave me the idea of trying to make a pecan soup. I always have pecans on hand, since I buy them in 50-pound boxes to meet the demands for my pecan pies. My nephew, Hardy, was coming for a visit, and I love any excuse to make something new. He was on a liquid diet due to throat surgery and needed a lot of protein. This soup would be a fantastic surprise for him!

When a new recipe passes the taste test of Pegilicious!®, I make a large batch so I can freeze it for later use without all the labor. Hardy went home with a good supply of frozen soup. He took it to the office for lunch and gave the office staff a taste. They all wanted the recipe!

This soup has the velvety smooth richness of a mushroom soup with a Southern flavor. Serve it in small bowls!

MAKES 13 CUPS

- ½ cup butter, 1 stick
- 3 celery ribs, coarsely chopped
- 2 sweet onions, chopped
- 1 large baking potato, peeled and coarsely chopped
- 4 cups chicken broth
- 3 cups heavy cream
- 1 teaspoon sea salt
- ½ teaspoon ground white pepper
- 1 pound toasted pecan halves

Garnish

- Crème fraîche—page 137
- Chopped chives
- Additional pecan halves

♦ In a Dutch oven over medium heat, melt the butter and add the celery and onion. Sauté for 20 minutes, or until translucent.

♦ Add the potato and all the other ingredients. Bring to a boil; reduce the heat and simmer on low, uncovered, for 30 minutes, or until the soup is slightly thickened and the potato is cooked. Remove from the heat, and cool slightly.

♦ Purée the soup with an immersible blender, or process in batches in a blender until smooth.

♦ Ladle into serving bowls. Garnish with crème fraîche, chives, or pecans, if using. Serve hot.

PEG'S NOTES ~ *This is the soup to bring out for a Christmas Eve dinner. I serve it with cornbread croutons or cornbread biscotti. I also use all of the garnishes; they make a beautiful presentation.*

Southern Sweet Potato Soup

All of the pureed soups in this book were created for my nephew, Hardy. When he had throat surgery, I went on a mission to create some good, healthy, flavorful soups instead of just broth. He loves sweet potatoes, so I began experimenting, creating this recipe. I sent him this one for Thanksgiving.

MAKES 1 QUART

- 2 Tablespoons butter
- 1 medium onion, chopped
- 1 celery rib, chopped
- 1 clove garlic, minced
- 2 cups chicken broth
- 1 large sweet potato, peeled and sliced
- 2 Tablespoons creamy peanut butter
- 1 1¼-inch cinnamon stick
- 1¾ cups whipping cream, divided
- ¼ teaspoon sea salt
- 2 teaspoons honey
- Pinch of salt
- Pinch of ground nutmeg

Garnish

- Chopped dry-roasted peanuts
- Fresh thyme sprigs

♦ Melt the butter in a large saucepan over medium heat. Add the onion and celery, and sauté 10 minutes, or until tender. Add the garlic and sauté 1 minute.

♦ Stir in the broth, potato, peanut butter, and cinnamon stick. Bring to a boil; reduce the heat and simmer 15 to 20 minutes, or until the potato is tender. Remove the cinnamon stick and discard.

♦ Process the sweet potato mixture in a blender or food processor until smooth. Return the mixture to the saucepan. Stir in the 1½ cups of whipping cream and ¼ teaspoon salt. Cook over medium heat, stirring constantly, until thoroughly heated.

♦ Beat the remaining ¼ cup of whipping cream, honey, salt, and nutmeg until soft peaks form. Serve a dollop on top of the soup, and garnish with peanuts and thyme, if desired.

PEG'S NOTES ~ I use my Cuisinart Smart Stick, a hand-held immersible blender, to blend the ingredients in the saucepan. This method is much safer, faster, and easier to clean up.

You can substitute 1 1/2 cups fat-free half and half for whipping cream.

You may also add more peanut butter, if you desire.

Dumplings

Here are two great dumpling recipes that I have developed over the years.

CORNBREAD DUMPLINGS

SERVES 6

- 1 cup cornmeal
- 1 cup sifted all-purpose flour
- 1 teaspoon baking powder
- ½ teaspoon baking soda
- 1 teaspoon sea salt
- ½ teaspoon poultry seasoning
- 1 Tablespoon shortening
- 1 egg, beaten well
- 1 cup buttermilk
- ¼ cup chopped parsley

✦ Stir the dry ingredients together in a bowl. Work shortening in with a fork.

✦ Combine the beaten egg with the buttermilk and parsley. Add to the dry ingredients, mixing only enough to moisten flour.

✦ Drop biscuit-size dollops into a gently cooking stew, soup, or chili. Cover and cook for 20 minutes. Do not remove the cover for the first 10 minutes of cooking.

✦ Serve at once. These dumplings are exceptionally good in bean soup.

JALAPEÑO–CHEDDAR CHEESE DUMPLINGS

MAKES 16 DUMPLINGS

- 2¼ cups all-purpose flour
- 1 teaspoon baking powder
- ½ teaspoon baking soda
- ½ teaspoon sea salt
- 3 Tablespoons oil-packed sundried tomatoes, chopped
- 1 teaspoon jalapeño pepper, seeded and minced
- 1 Tablespoon onion, minced
- 1 Tablespoon cilantro, minced
- 2 Tablespoons sour cream
- 6 ounces beer, ½ can
- ¼ cup sharp cheddar cheese, finely grated
- ¼ cup Monterey Jack cheese, finely grated

✦ Combine all the ingredients in a large bowl, stirring until just moistened.

✦ Spoon into soup or chili in biscuit-size dollops. Do not stir.

✦ Cover and simmer 18 to 20 minutes, or until the dumplings are done. Do not remove the cover for the first 10 minutes of cooking.

✦ Serve at once.

PEG'S NOTES ~ *For a Cornbread Dressing Dumpling variation, sauté 1 diced celery rib with 1/4 cup diced shallots and 1/2 teaspoon sage in 2 tablespoons of butter for 3 minutes. Add to the batter after the egg and buttermilk but before the parsley. Proceed with the same cooking instructions.*

Breakfast, Brunch, and Breads

PEG'S NOTES ~ I use several different combinations of fruit and berries, such as blackberries, blueberries, raspberries, and bananas. Peaches, strawberries, and bananas with blackberries are another good combination. Use what you like and what is in season.

I do not always use the honey. It depends on the fruit and their sweetness. I find that when I use bananas, for example, the honey makes it too sweet. When I don't use the honey, I'll sprinkle the pie with powdered sugar instead. You can also omit the honey, add sweetened whipped cream, and sprinkle with nuts for a great dessert.

Ruth Ann's favorite combination is pineapple, mango, and strawberries with chopped macadamia nuts. I found that by adding a sprinkle of coconut to that, the taste took me right back to Hawaii!

Fruit Pie for Brunch

I was in Hawaii, staying in a condo with my best friend, Ruth Ann, and we chose to cook breakfast and go out for dinner during our stay. One morning, Ruth Ann remembered a "flop pie" that her mother used to make. We had gone to the farmer's market and purchased fresh pineapple, mango, and other fruit, and we tried to recreate the dish. After I returned home from the islands, I played around with the recipe and found it to be an easy, quick, and delicious dish for family gatherings. I have always made this fruit pie for brunch, hence the name, but it can easily be served as a dessert.

FOR A 9-INCH PIE

- ¼ cup butter
- 3 eggs
- ¾ cup milk
- ¾ cup flour
- ¼ cup sugar
- 1 teaspoon vanilla

FOR A 10-INCH PIE

- ¼ cup butter
- 4 eggs
- 1 cup milk
- ¾ cup flour
- ⅓ cup sugar
- 1 teaspoon vanilla
- Fruit and berries of your choice
- ½ cup honey, heated, or powdered sugar

✦ Preheat the oven to 400 degrees.

✦ Place the butter in the pie plate, and put it into the oven to melt the butter.

✦ Whisk together the eggs, milk, flour, sugar, and vanilla, and pour the mixture into the hot pie plate with the melted butter.

✦ Bake for 20 minutes without opening the oven door. The sides of the pie will puff up. Fill the pie with fruit and berries of your choice, and then drizzle with warm honey or sprinkle with powdered sugar.

Monte Cristo Sandwich

A friend and neighbor, Mary Fermin, served this sandwich along with a lovely salad for a neighborhood luncheon on April 6, 1982, and then gave us the recipe as a parting gift. I have treasured this recipe ever since and have served the dish many times for brunch at our family reunions. One reason it's so great is that it can be prepared the day before, leaving you free to spend more time with your family or guests.

SERVES 8

One large loaf sliced sandwich bread

✦ Remove the crust from the bread. Three slices will make one sandwich.

For the first layer

2 cups lean ham, chopped
¼ cup sweet relish
½ cup mayonnaise
2 Tablespoons horseradish mustard

✦ Mix the first layer ingredients well and set aside.

For the second layer

2 cups cooked chicken, chopped
½ cup celery, minced
⅔ cup cream of chicken soup
2 Tablespoons onion, minced
⅛ teaspoon ground thyme

✦ Mix the second layer ingredients well and set aside.

To assemble

8 slices Swiss cheese
8 slices American cheese

✦ Slice 1—spread the ham mixture on a slice of bread and top it with a slice of Swiss cheese.

✦ Add slice 2—spread it with the chicken mixture, and top it with a slice of American cheese.

✦ Top with slice 3—to make the sandwich.

For the coating

3 eggs
2 cups milk
4 cups potato chips
2 cups corn flakes

✦ Dip the sandwich in the egg mixture, coating all sides. Pat on the crumb mixture. Cover and refrigerate overnight.

✦ Bake on a lightly oiled cookie sheet at 300 degrees for 20 minutes or until puffy and brown.

✦ Serve with warm preserves or fresh fruit with honey and/or syrup.

Chili Egg Puff

This recipe has a funny story behind it. Five days after moving into my new neighborhood in the Santa Ynez Valley, my back went out and I was bedridden. During this period, the wonderful ladies on my street took care of me, helping out with house chores and meals. Talk about paying it forward…they went above and beyond.

I wanted to say thanks, so I served them this dish at a morning brunch. One of the women, Mary Fermin, requested the recipe, but I did not have time to write it down. I told her to just take the recipe card but to please return it as soon as she made a copy. Well, she lost the card, and we both spent some time in the kitchen before we figured out the right proportions of ingredients again. We still share a good laugh every time we discuss this recipe.

SERVES 9

- 10 eggs
- ½ cup flour
- 1 teaspoon baking powder
- ½ teaspoon sea salt
- 2 cups small curd cottage cheese
- 1 pound Monterey Jack cheese, shredded
- 2 4-ounce cans chopped green chiles
- ½ cup butter, melted

✦ Preheat the oven to 350 degrees.

✦ Beat or whisk the eggs until light and lemony in color. Add the flour, baking powder, salt, cottage cheese, and shredded cheese. Blend until smooth.

✦ Fold in the chiles and the butter. Pour into a well-buttered 9 by 13-inch baking pan.

✦ Bake for 50 to 60 minutes, or until the center is firm.

PEG'S NOTES ~ This is a foolproof recipe that has been around for a very long time. It's great for brunch, with fresh fruit, ham, sausage, and croissants. I have also served it with a dollop of sour cream, salsa, sliced avocado, and bran muffins. It's an easy and substantial way to feed a crowd. I sometimes mix it up a little by using 1/2 Monterey Jack cheese and 1/2 cheddar cheese. You could even spice it up a little more by using pepper jack cheese. In my latest variation, I added fresh king crab, a little blue cheese, and green onions. It was superb.

The dish freezes well and reheats nicely. For a terrific on-the-go breakfast to take to work, make the recipe, and cut the baked puff into 9 pieces. Freeze the pieces in individual baggies. To serve, remove a piece from the baggie, place it on a microwavable plate, cover it with a damp paper towel, and microwave for about 3 minutes. The exact time depends on your microwave.

Deb's Stuffed French Toast

Our daughter Deb made this dish for her father and me on Mother's Day in 1988. She had invited us to brunch in her cute apartment in North Hollywood, California. She greeted us with Mimosas and served this delicious French toast with fresh strawberries. I was impressed by the meal, and she gave me the recipe. This is one of my absolute favorites; if you're inviting me for brunch, this is what I hope you'll make. I have served it myself numerous times, but nothing can replace the memory of that first bite years ago. Yum!

SERVES 6

- 12 slices sourdough bread
- 8 ounces cream cheese, softened
- 4 Tablespoons orange juice, divided
- ½ teaspoon grated orange zest
- ½ cup chopped pecans
- 8 eggs
- 2½ cups milk
- 2 Tablespoons sugar
- Powdered sugar

+ Preheat the oven to 350 degrees.
+ Spray a 13 x 9-inch pan with non-stick cooking spray. Place 6 slices of bread on the bottom of the pan.
+ In a small bowl, mix the cream cheese with 2 tablespoons of orange juice and the zest, mixing well. Stir in the pecans. Spread the mixture evenly over the bread slices in pan.
+ Place the remaining bread slices over the top of the cream cheese mixture.
+ In a medium bowl, beat the eggs, milk, sugar, and remaining 2 tablespoons of orange juice until well blended. Pour over the bread slices. Cover and refrigerate overnight.
+ Bake 1 hour. Dust with powdered sugar. Serve hot with syrup and/or fresh fruit.

PEG'S NOTES ~ This is now a family favorite and appears at all our reunions. I serve it with an array of fresh berries and bananas.

Eggs Benedict Casserole

People love traditions, and food often plays a traditional role. This eggs Benedict dish was a traditional staple at our family gatherings, and all of us expected it to be there. This dish is a wonderful way to serve a crowd without having to poach a lot of eggs at the last minute. I also often prepare it for breakfast, when my guests need to leave quickly in the morning.

SERVES 8

- 1 30-ounce bag shredded hash brown potatoes
- ½ cup chopped onion
- 2 Tablespoons chopped parsley
- ¼ cup butter
- ½ cup flour
- 1 teaspoon sea salt
- ¼ teaspoon pepper
- 1½ cups milk
- 1 cup sour cream
- 1 pound sliced Canadian bacon
- 8 eggs

- Preheat the oven to 350 degrees.
- Thaw and drain the potatoes well. Stir in the onion and parsley. Place the potatoes in a well- greased 13 by 9-inch baking dish. Sprinkle the potatoes with a little salt and pepper.
- Melt the butter in a saucepan. Whisk in the flour, salt, and pepper, and cook, whisking constantly, 2 to 3 minutes, or until flour in lightly browned.
- Whisk the milk into the butter mixture, and bring to a boil. Reduce the heat and simmer 6 minutes, or until thickened. Remove from the heat. Blend in the sour cream.
- Pour the sauce over the potatoes, lifting the potatoes lightly to permit the sauce to mix well.
- Arrange the bacon slices, overlapping them on the potatoes.
- Bake at for 45 minutes.
- Remove from the oven and break the eggs onto the dish. Bake 10 to 15 minutes longer.

PEG'S NOTES ~ I sometimes break more than 8 eggs on top, so that the Canadian bacon is completely covered. This allows you to serve more than 8 people with this dish. The baking time after you add your eggs will depend on whether you want poached or well-done eggs.

You can prepare this ahead, except for the eggs. Cover the dish and refrigerate it until ready to cook. I always make it the night before when we have a gathering at my house.

Peg's Corn Muffin Sticks

Southern cornbread is delicious, but the children had a hard time handling it because it always seemed to crumble on them. They would call out, "Gran, can you fix my bread?" Naturally I thought I could, so I made up this recipe. The grandchildren loved these "sticks" because they could dunk them into their soup or chili.

MAKES ABOUT 30 STICKS

- 2 jalapeño peppers, seeded and chopped
- 2 cloves garlic, minced
- 3 green onions, sliced
- 1 Tablespoon olive oil
- 1 cup all-purpose flour
- 2 cups cornmeal
- 2 teaspoons baking powder
- 1 teaspoon sea salt
- 1½ cups frozen white corn kernels, thawed
- 2 eggs, slightly beaten
- ¾ cup buttermilk
- ½ cup butter, melted

✦ Preheat the oven to 450 degrees.

✦ Sauté the peppers, garlic, and onions in the oil over medium heat, stirring constantly until tender. Set aside.

✦ Combine the flour, cornmeal, baking powder, and salt with the pepper mixture, making a well in the center.

✦ Stir together the eggs, milk, and butter, and add them to the well in the flour mixture, stirring just until moistened.

✦ Heat a cast-iron corn-stick pan in the oven for 5 minutes. Remove it and spray with non-stick cooking spray.

✦ Spoon the batter into the hot pan. Bake for 15 minutes.

✦ Remove the sticks from the pan immediately, and place on a wire rack. Cool slightly before serving.

Peg's Southern Cornbread

During the Depression, my mother used mayonnaise instead of eggs to make her cakes, but Deb's and Teresa's great-grandmother, Lydia Hyde Morris—born June 6, 1892; died July 1978—was the first person I ever knew who added it to her cornbread. Everyone wants to know what I put in my cornbread. Well, here is the recipe, handed down from the girls' great-grandmother, with my additions.

MAKES A 10-INCH PONE

- 1½ cups all-purpose flour
- 1 cup white cornmeal
- 1 Tablespoon baking powder
- 1 teaspoon sea salt
- ½ cup mayonnaise
- 1 large egg, slightly beaten
- 2 cups buttermilk, more if needed
- 2 Tablespoons bacon drippings or butter

✦ Preheat the oven to 425 degrees.

✦ Combine the flour, cornmeal, baking powder, and salt well. Stir in the mayonnaise; add the beaten egg and buttermilk. Stir until well blended. Use more buttermilk, if needed, to keep the mixture from being too dry.

✦ In a 10-inch cast-iron skillet, heat the bacon drippings or melt the butter over medium-high heat. When the grease is hot, pour in the batter. Bake for 20 to 25 minutes, or until a wooden toothpick inserted in the middle comes out clean.

✦ Invert immediately onto a plate, bottom side up, to preserve its crunchy crust. Serve warm with butter.

PEG'S NOTES ~ If I'm using self-rising flour and cornmeal, I still add baking powder and salt, but reduce the amounts: Use 1 teaspoon of baking powder and 1/2 teaspoon salt with self-rising flour. I do not use baking soda in my cornbread, so, no, this is not a mistake.

A well-seasoned cast-iron skillet is the key to a golden brown crust. You want your grease really hot, so that the batter sizzles a little when you put it in. This is going to create a crunchy texture on the outside of the cornbread.

If you are too busy to watch the skillet while you're heating the grease or butter, you can put the skillet with the grease or butter in the oven while it is preheating. That is the method that I use the most. Be sure to use a glove or pot holders when you remove the hot skillet to add the batter!

Zom's Monkey Bread

When my children were little, they loved to tear a piece of bread off a warm loaf. Of course this led to some of them getting bigger pieces than others, so an argument would follow. This recipe was my answer to that problem. The Monkey Bread is actually made of little biscuits cooked together, so pieces break off in equal size. It was the perfect bread for the girls.

SERVES 8

- 1 packet dry yeast
- ½ cup warm water—110 degrees
- ½ cup sugar
- 1½ cups butter, divided
- 1 teaspoon sea salt
- ½ cup warm milk
- 3½ cups flour, divided
- 2 eggs, well beaten

- ◆ Lightly coat a large smooth Bundt or tube pan with vegetable cooking spray.
- ◆ Dissolve the yeast in warm water, and set aside.
- ◆ In a large bowl, combine the sugar, 1 cup of the butter, and salt, and add the warm milk; mix until well blended.
- ◆ Add 2 cups of flour, mixing well. Then add the remaining flour, beaten eggs, and yeast. Mix well.
- ◆ Cover the dough, and let it rise in a warm place until double in size.
- ◆ Melt the remaining ½ cup butter in a saucepan. Roll out the dough on a floured surface, and use a biscuit cutter to cut out rounds. Dip the cut-out dough into the melted butter on both sides, and place the pieces in the prepared pan, overlapping layers.
- ◆ Cover and let rise for 1 hour.
- ◆ Bake at 350 degrees for 30 to 40 minutes, or until golden brown and cooked through.
- ◆ Allow the bread to cool in the pan for 5 minutes before removing. Invert it onto a serving plate, and brush with melted butter.

Sourdough Rolls

Sourdough bread is another absolute favorite, and I serve it often. Just writing about it makes me hungry! The secret to this popular bread is a leavening agent known as a starter. Some bakers prefer to purchase starter, but I always make my own, which is easily done by adding yeast to a batter of flour and water. The yeast gives rise to bacteria that flourish and create the leavening and acidity. That's what gives sourdough bread its tartness and flavor. The microbes also create a beer-like liquid that floats to the top; I always stir it back in for extra flavor, but it is fine to pour it off before using the starter.

MAKES 30 ROLLS

- 1 teaspoon active dry yeast
- ¼ cup warm water—110 degrees
- 2 cups Sourdough Starter—page 87
- 2 eggs, beaten
- ⅓ cup vegetable oil, plus more to coat bowl
- ¼ cup sugar
- 2 teaspoons sea salt
- 3½–4 cups all-purpose flour
- 1 Tablespoon melted butter

✦ In a large bowl, dissolve the yeast in water. Add the Sourdough Starter, beaten eggs, oil, sugar, and salt, whisking to mix the ingredients.

✦ Stir in 3 cups of flour. Add more flour— ¼ cup at a time—until the dough is too stiff to stir. Turn the dough out onto a floured counter. Knead the dough until smooth but still moderately soft, 10 to 12 minutes, adding 1 tablespoon of flour at a time if the dough becomes too sticky.

✦ Place the dough in a bowl brushed with oil, turning the dough to coat it. Cover the bowl with a tea towel; let the dough rise in a warm place until doubled in size, 2 to 2½ hours. How long this takes depends on the strength of the starter.

✦ Punch down the dough, and with floured hands pull off golf-ball-sized pieces of dough. Shape them into balls. Arrange the dough balls about ¼ inch apart in 2 greased cast-iron skillets. Cover the skillets with plastic wrap, and let the dough rise again until the rolls are roughly doubled in size, 1 to 1½ hours.

✦ Preheat the oven to 350 degrees. Bake the rolls 20 to 25 minutes or until golden. As soon as you remove the rolls from the oven, brush the tops with a coating of melted butter. Allow the rolls to cool slightly before serving, about 15 minutes.

Sourdough Starter

Here is something—besides your kids—that you have to remember to feed every day but only for seven days. Then you can back off and feed it only twice a week—not exactly like your kids! You will be glad you did it, though, because it's the basis of great bread and rolls. Making this starter is a seven-day process, but the results can be kept indefinitely. In fact, the King Arthur Flour Company boasts of having a starter that's more than 250 years old. Now that is old!

MAKES 3 CUPS IN 7 DAYS

- 1 package active dry yeast, or 2¼ teaspoons
- 6 cups warm water—110 degrees, divided
- 1 teaspoon honey
- 6 cups all-purpose flour, divided

✦ Dissolve the yeast in 1 cup warm water in a 1-quart container. Stir in the honey and 1 cup of flour. Cover with a towel, and set aside at room temperature for 24 hours. The starter will become foamy and smell like beer.

✦ On the second day, discard all but 1 cup of the starter, and then add 1 cup of warm water and 1 cup of flour.

✦ Repeat this process daily for four more days. The starter will be ready on the seventh day.

PEG'S NOTES ~ After you've used 2 cups of starter for the Sourdough Rolls, there will be 1 cup of starter left. To maintain it, keep the remaining starter refrigerated. Repeat the process of discarding the excess and feeding the starter with flour and warm water twice a week.

Bran Muffin Mix

A family friend named Margaret Sears was the director of the Los Angeles school district lunch program for many years. When she retired, she went to work for a catering company in Beverly Hills, and she did that until she was in her late '80s. This recipe came from her. She always told me that I needed to keep the mix in the refrigerator so I could bake hot muffins for the girls on a moment's notice. My daughters loved these muffins. So did the guests at a ladies' luncheon. When I served the muffins with tuna salad, the women all wanted the recipe.

MAKES 1 GALLON

- 2 cups boiling water
- 2 cups Kellogg's All-Bran Buds
- 2½ cups sugar
- 1 cup Crisco®
- 4 eggs
- 5 cups all-purpose flour
- 1½ teaspoons sea salt
- 5 teaspoons baking soda
- 1 quart buttermilk
- 4 cups Kellogg's All-Bran Original

✦ Pour the boiling water over the bran buds. Mix and cool.

✦ Cream the sugar with the shortening, and beat in the eggs.

✦ Sift together the flour, salt, and soda. Add the dry ingredients to the creamed mixture. Add the buttermilk and All-Bran, then add the cooled bran mixture. Mix well.

✦ Let stand in the refrigerator at least 24 hours before using. The batter keeps for a month or more.

✦ Bake, as needed, in greased muffin pans about 20 to 25 minutes at 400 degrees.

PEG'S NOTES ~ Mrs. Sears instructed me, "Do not stir in container and never take from the bottom." I found, however, that I liked to stir the mix just before using it, to keep the blend even, but I never took it from the bottom.

Since this makes a gallon of muffin mix, I create variations by adding chopped nuts, apples, cranberries, and/or raisins. I simply top each muffin with the ingredient of the day and push it down into the mixture just before baking. I especially like chopped walnuts when I plan to serve the muffins with a salad.

Sour Cream Coffee Cake

Mrs. Sears' only daughter, Shirley, became my best friend and was married to my brother for a while. Unfortunately, she died young, but she passed this recipe along to me because she knew how much I loved this dish. In her memory, I have included Aunt Shirley's coffee cake, which she always brought to family functions.

SERVES 9–12

- ½ cup butter
- 1 cup sugar
- 1 egg
- 2 egg whites
- 1 teaspoon vanilla
- 2 cups flour
- 1 teaspoon baking powder
- 1 teaspoon baking soda
- ½ teaspoon salt
- 1 cup sour cream

Filling

- 8 ounces cream cheese, softened
- 2 egg yolks
- ½ cup sugar
- ½ teaspoon vanilla
- ½ cup currants
- 2 teaspoons lemon peel

Topping

- ¼ cup crushed graham cracker crumbs
- ½ cup chopped walnuts
- 2 Tablespoons butter, melted

✦ Cream the butter. Gradually add the sugar, and beat until light and fluffy. Beat in the egg and egg whites and add the vanilla.

✦ Sift together the flour, baking powder, soda, and salt. Add the dry ingredients to the creamed mixture alternately with the sour cream.

✦ Spread half of the batter in a buttered 9-inch-square pan. Spread the filling on top—see below. Spoon the remaining batter carefully over the filling to cover it.

✦ Sprinkle the topping—see below—over the batter.

✦ Bake at 350 degrees for 50 to 55 minutes, or until the center springs back when touched lightly with a finger. Cool 30 minutes before cutting.

✦ In a small mixing bowl, beat together the cream cheese, egg yolks, sugar, and vanilla until well blended. Mix in the currants and lemon peel.

✦ In a small bowl, mix together the cracker crumbs and nuts. Stir in the butter, and mix until well blended.

PEG'S NOTES ~ *I have baked this coffee cake numerous times, but when I make it for my daughter Deb, I leave out the currants. You can also substitute raisins for the currants. The last time I made this recipe, I used dried cranberries and pistachio nuts. The coffee cake had a totally different taste but was wonderful all the same.*

Cranberry Upside-Down Coffee Cake

I started making this recipe back in 1980, and the original recipe called for canned whole cranberry sauce. When I tried fresh cranberries, I discovered what an incredible cake this really was! I decided then and there that I would never prepare this cake unless fresh cranberries were available. This is my daughter Debbie's absolute favorite—a must have on Thanksgiving morning. Yum!

SERVES 10–12

- ¾ cup butter, divided
- ½ cup firmly packed light brown sugar
- 1½ cup fresh cranberries, sliced in half—see Peg's Notes
- ¼ cup chopped walnuts
- ¾ cup sugar
- 1 egg
- 1½ cups all-purpose flour
- ½ teaspoon baking powder
- ½ teaspoon salt
- ½ cup milk

♦ Preheat the oven to 350 degrees.

♦ In an ovenproof 10-inch skillet, melt ¼ cup of the butter. Sprinkle the brown sugar evenly over the bottom. Add the cranberries and nuts, and set aside.

♦ In a small mixing bowl, cream the remaining ½ cup butter. Gradually add the sugar, and beat until light and fluffy. Add the egg and beat thoroughly.

♦ Sift together the flour, baking powder, and salt. Add the dry ingredients to the creamed mixture alternately with the milk, beginning and ending with the dry ingredients. Spread the batter evenly over the cranberries.

♦ Bake 35 to 40 minutes.

♦ Invert immediately onto a serving plate.

PEG'S NOTES ~ If fresh cranberries are not available, use 2 cans of whole cranberry sauce. In a heavy sauce pot, melt the whole cranberry sauce and drain off the whole cranberries. You should have about 1 1/2 cups.

Pumpkin Bread

My daughters and I were recycling before recycling became cool. We used empty coffee cans to bake this delicious bread, which we gave to homeless people at holiday time. They liked the fact that it was baked in cans. We also found that the bread worked well on camping trips and transported well on horseback. I even sent some to Deb when she was living in the dorm at the University of Alabama. The bread was fine for a few days without refrigeration, and when it arrived, it was always eaten very quickly!

MAKES 3 1-POUND CANS OR 6 WIDE-MOUTH PINT JARS

- 3 cups all-purpose flour
- 1½ teaspoons cinnamon
- 1½ teaspoons sea salt
- 1½ teaspoons nutmeg
- 3 cups sugar
- 4 eggs
- 2 teaspoons baking soda
- ⅔ cup water
- 1 cup salad oil
- 2 cups, or 1 15-ounce can, pumpkin

✦ Preheat the oven to 350 degrees.

✦ Mix the flour with the spices, and set aside.

✦ Beat the eggs with the sugar. Add in the flour mixture and the baking soda, water, oil, and pumpkin.

✦ Pour the batter into 3 well-greased, empty 1-pound coffee cans, filling them half full. Bake the cans for 1 hour or until a toothpick inserted into the center comes out clean. As soon as you remove the bread cans from the oven, put the lids on the cans. If the bread has risen above the rim, just push it down and seal.

✦ Serve the bread with cream cheese, whipped cream, or butter. It's good hot or cold.

PEG'S NOTES ~ I line up all 3 cans across the middle rack of the oven and bake them at the same time. Capping the bread as soon as it comes out of the oven and pushing the bread down causes the bread to sweat in the can and seals in the moisture. Today you might not have empty coffee cans on hand, so you can also bake this in wide-mouth 1-pint canning jars. Make sure the jars are hot and sterilized, and fill each jar 3/4 full. Bake following the instructions for cans. Seal the jars with the seals as soon as you remove them from the oven. If you have any jars that do not seal, you can boil them in a water bath for 15 minutes.

Fresh Pear Bread

Fresh pears are a treat when baked in fresh bread. This luscious loaf is delicious with a steaming hot cup of vanilla nut coffee. It's also great for brunch. Just pop the bread into the oven about 20 minutes before your guests arrive and have the coffee brewing when the doorbell rings. The sweet bouquet of the pears and the rich aroma of coffee will serve as a fabulous greeting!

MAKES 1 LOAF

- 1 cup chopped fresh d'Anjou or Bosc pears
- 2 cups unbleached all-purpose flour
- 1 teaspoon baking powder
- ½ teaspoon baking soda
- ½ teaspoon sea salt
- ⅓ cup butter
- 1 cup sugar
- 1 egg
- ½ cup sour cream
- ¼ cup orange juice
- 1 Tablespoon grated orange peel
- 1 cup bran flakes
- ½ cup chopped nuts
- Fresh pear slices, for garnish

Spicy topping

- 1 Tablespoon butter
- 2 Tablespoons brown sugar
- ¼ teaspoon nutmeg
- 1 Tablespoon flour
- ⅓ cup chopped nuts

- ✦ Preheat the oven to 350 degrees.
- ✦ Prepare the spicy topping. Combine the butter, sugar, nutmeg, flour, and nuts, and mix until crumbly. Set aside.
- ✦ For the batter, core the pears but do not peel them. Chop and measure 1 cup.
- ✦ Sift the flour, baking powder, soda, and salt.
- ✦ Cream the butter with the sugar and egg. Blend in the sour cream.
- ✦ Add the sifted dry ingredients and orange juice alternately to the creamed mixture.
- ✦ Fold in the chopped pears, orange peel, bran flakes, and nuts.
- ✦ Pour into a 9 by 5-inch loaf pan. Sprinkle with the spicy topping.
- ✦ Bake for 45 to 50 minutes. Cool in the pan for 10 minutes. Garnish with fresh pear slices.

PEG'S NOTES ~ Do not preheat the oven if you're using a Pyrex® loaf pan. Remove the pan as soon as a tester toothpick comes out clean. The bread will continue to cook in the hot glass pan.

Chef's Specialties

Châteaubriand

SERVED WITH PEG'S BÉARNAISE SAUCE

This elegant dinner is one I rotate with other favorite family dishes during the holidays. My daughters prefer chicken or fish, but my sons-in-law are meat-and-potatoes guys and love this dish. The Béarnaise sauce provides the perfect touch. When the guys are coming to town, I know that this must be on the table.

SERVES 8

- 2 2-pound beef tenderloins
- Snider's Prime Rib & Roast Seasoning—see Peg's Notes

◆ Preheat the broiler. Sprinkle the roasts with the seasoning. Place both roasts on a rack in a broiler pan.

◆ Broil for 30 minutes for rare beef or until the desired doneness, turning the roasts only once.

◆ Prepare the Béarnaise Sauce.

◆ Slice the tenderloins to the preferred thickness. Place a small amount of sauce on each plate, top with the sliced meat, and put additional sauce on top.

BÉARNAISE SAUCE

MAKES 1 CUP

- 2 Tablespoons red wine vinegar
- 1½ teaspoons chopped green onion
- 1½ teaspoons dried tarragon
- ⅛ teaspoon cracked black pepper
- 4 egg yolks
- ¾ cup butter—NO substitutions—softened and divided into 2-Tablespoon pieces
- 1 Tablespoon chopped parsley

◆ In the top of a double boiler, combine the vinegar, green onion, tarragon, and pepper. Place the double-boiler top directly over high heat, and heat to boiling. Boil until the vinegar is reduced to 1 tablespoon.

◆ Place the double-boiler top over the double-boiler bottom, which should contain 2 cups of hot, not boiling, water.

◆ Add the egg yolks, and cook, beating constantly with a wire whisk, until slightly thickened.

◆ Add the butter, 2 tablespoons at a time, beating constantly with a whisk, until the butter is melted and the mixture is thickened. Stir in the parsley.

◆ Serve about 1 tablespoon of warm sauce over each serving of beef tenderloin.

PEG'S NOTES ~ *You can use my Spice Rub on page 216 instead of the Snider's seasoning, or just salt. I always season the tenderloin the day before, wrap in plastic wrap, and refrigerate until ready to cook.*

Peg's Individual Beef Wellingtons
SERVED WITH MUSHROOM CREAM SAUCE

I created this recipe for Christmas Eve one year, and it was delicious. The best part for me was that I could prepare the dish ahead of time, freeze it, and then pop it in the oven at the last minute. This is a great time saver and a stress reducer during the holidays.

PEG'S NOTES ~ You can bake the Wellingtons on the same day they are assembled. After wrapping the beef filets in pastry, cover and chill the Wellingtons for 1 hour. Bake them as directed, reducing the baking time to 20 to 25 minutes.

The time stated for baking the frozen Wellingtons is correct and perfect every time.

For my Wellingtons, I purchase a whole beef tenderloin and cut my own filets, making some thicker than others. This enables me to cook all the Wellingtons for the same length of time and come out with rare, medium, and well-done servings. I mark the top of the pastry with R, M, or W so I know which is which, then I cut the slit for the herb in this mark just before serving.

SERVES 8

Beef Wellingtons

- 8 5- to 6-ounce center-cut filet mignons —1½ inch thick
- Snider's Prime Rib & Roast Seasoning or Carl's Gourmet All Natural Prime Rib & Roast Seasoning, or see Spice Rub recipe on page 216
- 1 Tablespoon olive oil
- 2 Tablespoons butter
- ½ pound fresh mushrooms, minced
- 2 shallots minced
- ½ teaspoon sea salt
- ½ teaspoon pepper
- ½ cup Madeira cooking wine
- 8 frozen puff pastry shells
- 1 large egg, lightly beaten, to seal pastry
- 2 large eggs, lightly beaten, to glaze Wellingtons
- Sprigs of fresh herbs, such as rosemary, for garnish

Mushroom cream sauce

- ¼ cup butter
- 1 pound fresh mushrooms, sliced
- 1 large shallot, thinly sliced
- ½ teaspoon sea salt
- ½ teaspoon pepper
- ½ cup Madeira cooking wine

To complete the sauce

- 2 Tablespoons butter
- 2½ Tablespoons all-purpose flour
- 2 cups beef broth
- ½ cup whipping cream
- ½ teaspoon salt

- ✦ Pat the filets dry. Coat both sides of the meat with the seasoning. Heat the oil in a large skillet over medium-high heat, until the skillet is hot. Sear the filets, in 2 batches, 1 to 1½ minutes on each side. Remove the filets from the skillet, place them on a plate, cover, and chill until ready to assemble the Wellingtons. Do not clean the skillet.

- ✦ While the filets are chilling, melt the butter in the same skillet over medium-high heat. Add the mushrooms, shallots, salt, and pepper, and sauté until all the liquid evaporates. Add the Madeira, and cook over medium-high heat, until all the liquid again evaporates. Remove from the heat, and let cool. Cover and chill, until ready to assemble the Wellingtons.

- ✦ On a lightly floured surface, roll each puff pastry shell to about a ⅛-inch-thick square. Spoon 1 heaping tablespoonful of the mushroom filling in the center of each pastry. Use all the mushroom filling by dividing any leftover amount among the eight shells.

- ✦ Top each shell with a chilled filet. Brush the edges of each pastry square with the beaten egg. Wrap 2 opposite sides of pastry over each filet, overlapping them; seal the seam with beaten egg. Wrap the remaining 2 sides of each pastry over the filet, and seal with the beaten egg. Seal any gaps with beaten egg, and press the pastry around the filet to enclose it completely.

- ✦ Wrap the Wellingtons individually in press-and-seal plastic wrap. Place the wrapped Wellingtons in a large freezer bag, and freeze them overnight or up to one month.

- ✦ To prepare the mushroom cream sauce, melt the butter in a skillet over medium-high heat. Combine the mushrooms and shallots, and add them to the butter, cooking them in batches until the mushrooms are brown. Don't crowd the mushrooms, or they will sweat and not brown properly. Season each batch with salt and pepper. After the mushrooms are brown, return the batches to the skillet, add the Madeira, and cook until all the liquid has evaporated. Remove from the heat and cool; then place the mushroom mixture in a freezer bag, and freeze until you're ready to make the sauce.

- ✦ To bake the Wellingtons, place the oven rack on the lowest oven shelf, and preheat the oven to 425 degrees. Place a broiler pan on the oven rack. Heat the pan 5 minutes. Brush the tops and sides of the frozen Wellingtons with 2 beaten eggs. Carefully place the frozen Wellingtons, seam-side down, on the preheated pan.

- ✦ Bake at 425 degrees for 36 minutes.

- ✦ Remove the frozen mushrooms from the freezer and defrost them in a microwave for 1 to 2 minutes.

- ✦ While the Wellingtons bake, complete the mushroom cream sauce. Melt the 2 tablespoons of butter in a saucepan over medium heat; add the flour, and cook, stirring constantly, for 1 minute.

- ✦ Slowly add the broth, and cook, stirring constantly, over medium heat for 6 to 8 minutes, or until slightly thickened. Add the defrosted mushrooms, and stir in the whipping cream. Simmer 5 minutes, or until the desired thickness. Add the salt, and remove from the heat.

- ✦ To serve, divide the mushroom sauce among eight plates, then arrange a baked Wellington in the center. Cut a small slit in the top of each baked pastry, and tuck a sprig of fresh herb into each slit.

Ivy Manor Chili-Coated Pork Tenderloin

WITH FRESH PEACH-AVOCADO SALSA

My dentist and his wife asked me to do a dinner party for them. His wife requested a pork roast, but only if she could have some kind of fresh salsa, as she loved salsa with a meat entrée. This is the recipe I created for her. This dish proved to be love at first bite! This spiced-rubbed pork is simple to put together and is scrumptious. Guests invariably ask for the recipe. The fresh salsa is the crowning touch.

SERVES 4–6

- 1½-2 pounds pork tenderloin, rinsed and patted dry
- 1 Tablespoon chili powder
- 1 teaspoon sea salt
- 1 teaspoon dried oregano
- ½ teaspoon freshly ground pepper
- ½ teaspoon cumin
- ¼ teaspoon ground red pepper

♦ Let the pork stand at room temperature 30 minutes. Grease a metal 13 by 9-inch baking pan.

♦ Heat the oven to 450 degrees.

♦ Combine all the spices on a sheet of wax paper. Roll the tenderloin in the spices to coat, and transfer it to the pan. Roast for 25 to 30 minutes, until an instant-read thermometer inserted into the thickest part of the tenderloin reaches 155 degrees.

♦ Remove the pork from the oven and let it stand 5 minutes. The temperature of the meat should rise upon standing.

FRESH PEACH-AVOCADO SALSA

MAKES 2¼ CUPS

- 2 small ripe fresh peaches, peeled and diced
- 1 large tomato, diced
- 1 small avocado, diced
- 1 Tablespoon minced red onion
- 1 Tablespoon lime juice
- 1 teaspoon olive oil
- ¼ teaspoon sea salt
- ¼ teaspoon ground red pepper
- ¼ cup diced jicama, optional

♦ In a large bowl, combine all the ingredients, including the jicama, if using. Cover and chill until ready to serve.

PEG'S NOTES ~ *Jicama does not have much flavor, but I like to include it because it adds crunch to the salsa. In this case, I made an exception to my own rule of always using shallots and used red onion instead, for their color.*

French Classic Poulet Périgourdine

Served With Lemon Cream Sauce

I originally came across this recipe in a newspaper way back in 1965. A close friend, Gertrude Plaza, loved chicken livers and was always asking me if I had some great recipe that incorporated them. I decided to give this one a try. I will never forget the first time I served her this dish. She could not stop talking about it.

When my daughters were little, this dish was a good way to get them to eat chicken livers without their knowing it. And when I served it to guests, I never told them that chicken livers were included. They couldn't figure out what the secret ingredient was. The original recipe said the lemon sauce was optional, but when you have someone special at the table, the sauce is a must. I also found that adding a little sauce on top of the breast while it's baking really boosts the flavor and keeps the breast moist.

Chicken breasts rolled around a delectable stuffing of chicken livers and mushrooms in the French style makes a superb dish for entertaining. You can prepare the breasts the day before and have them chilled in the refrigerator. Then you can quickly sauté the breasts and bake them while you are serving the salad course. Because this main dish is so spectacular, keep the accompaniments simple. Try glazed carrots, baby asparagus, or Brussels sprouts, with a tossed green salad. They will set off the chicken with flair.

SERVES 8

- 8 chicken breasts, boned and flattened – see Peg's Notes
- Sea salt and fresh ground black pepper
- Dried thyme leaves or ½ teaspoon powdered thyme
- ¾ cup butter, divided
- ½ pound chicken livers, chopped
- ½ pound mushrooms, chopped
- 4 shallots, chopped
- 1 teaspoon sea salt
- 1 cup grated Swiss cheese, 4 ounces
- 2 eggs, beaten
- Fine dry plain bread crumbs
- Lemon Cream Sauce
- Shaved truffles, for garnish, optional

✦ Dry the chicken breasts, and sprinkle them with salt, pepper, and thyme leaves rolled in your hands.

✦ Prepare the stuffing. Heat ¼ cup of the butter in a skillet. Add the chicken livers, mushrooms, and shallots. Sprinkle with salt. Cook slowly for about 5 minutes, until the livers are cooked. Remove from the heat and stir in the cheese.

✦ Divide the stuffing into 8 portions, and place 1 portion in the center of each chicken breast. Fold the sides of the breast over the stuffing and secure it with skewers or large toothpicks.

✦ Roll the breast first in the egg, then in the bread crumbs. Chill, uncovered, in the refrigerator for at least 2 hours to allow the coating to dry. It's best if left overnight.

✦ Heat the remaining butter in a large skillet. Add the chicken breasts, a few at a time, and brown on both sides. Remove the breasts to a shallow pan. Pour a little Lemon Cream Sauce over the top, and bake for 45 minutes in 350-degree oven.

✦ When the breasts are done, top them with more sauce. If desired, garnish with truffles. Serve the remaining sauce separately.

LEMON CREAM SAUCE

MAKES ABOUT 3 CUPS

- ¼ cup butter
- ¼ cup flour
- 2 cups chicken stock
- 1 Tablespoon fresh lemon juice
- ½ cup cream

✦ Melt the butter in a saucepan. Blend in the flour, and gradually stir in the stock. Cook, stirring constantly, until the mixture thickens and comes to a boil. Cook 3 to 5 minutes longer.

✦ Add the lemon juice, and stir in the cream. Heat, but do not allow the sauce to boil again.

PEG'S NOTES ~ To flatten the chicken breasts, place them between 2 pieces of aluminum foil and pound them with the broad side of a cleaver or a rolling pin. For the best flavor, I use whole dried thyme leaves and crush them by rubbing them in my hands over the chicken breast before adding the stuffing. Also, I use only fresh lemon juice, and I make my own chicken stock for this dish. If you buy your stock, add about a tablespoon of chicken demi-glace to boost the flavor. Taste it and add more, if needed.

Zom's Spinach-Stuffed Chicken
IN PHYLLO

Loved by both family and friends, this has become a regular at our table. A tantalizing mixture of spinach, four cheeses, nutmeg, and cumin make up the delicious filling. The recipe can be cut in half for a romantic dinner for two, or doubled to feed a gathering of sixteen.

SERVES 8

- 8 skinless, boneless chicken breasts
- 4 cups chopped fresh spinach
- 1 cup chopped onion
- 2 Tablespoons olive oil or cooking oil
- 4 ounces cream cheese, cubed and softened
- 1 cup shredded mozzarella cheese, 4 ounces
- ½ cup crumbled feta cheese, 2 ounces
- ½ cup shredded cheddar cheese, 2 ounces
- 1 beaten egg yolk
- 1 Tablespoon all-purpose flour
- ½ teaspoon ground nutmeg
- ½ teaspoon cumin
- 16 sheets phyllo dough, 18 by 14-inch rectangles
- ⅔ cup butter, melted

- ✦ Place the chicken breasts between two sheets of heavy plastic wrap or aluminum foil, and pound them with the flat side of a meat mallet or use a rolling pin to flatten them until they're ⅛ inch thick. Season with salt and pepper, and set aside.

- ✦ In a large skillet, cook the spinach and onion in hot oil until the onion is tender. Remove from the heat. Stir in the cream cheese until blended. Stir in the mozzarella, feta, cheddar cheeses, egg yolk, flour, nutmeg, and cumin.

- ✦ Place about 1/4 cup of the spinach mixture on each chicken breast half, and roll them jelly-roll style. It's not necessary to seal the ends.

- ✦ Place one sheet of phyllo on a work surface. Keep the remaining sheets covered with a damp towel to prevent their drying out. Brush the phyllo sheet with some of the melted butter. Place another phyllo sheet on top of the first, and brush with butter.

- ✦ Place one chicken roll near a short side of the phyllo. Roll the chicken and phyllo over once to cover the chicken. Fold in the long sides, and continue rolling from the short side.

- ✦ Place the roll in a shallow baking pan, and repeat with the remaining chicken, phyllo, and butter. Brush the rolls with butter.

- ✦ These can be made one day in advance. Cover the rolls with plastic wrap, and keep them refrigerated until ready to bake.

- ✦ Bake, uncovered, at 350 degrees for 30 to 35 minutes, until golden brown.

Warm Turkey Salad

TOSSED IN FRESH TARRAGON VINAIGRETTE

Ruth Ann owned and operated Posh Beauty Salon in Santa Ynez, and I would try out new recipes on her staff. When I first served this salad, they became true fans. When one of the hairdressers, Helen, became pregnant with twins, she asked me to serve this salad at her baby shower. All the clients of everyone who worked there were invited. The twins are now finishing high school, and I am still serving this salad.

It was on the menu for Ruth Ann's mother's 90th birthday in Platte, South Dakota, where the party was open to the community. Everyone loved it.

It is my most requested salad. What can I say? It's really yummy!

SERVES 8–10

- 2½ cups water
- 2 teaspoons sea salt
- 1 cup uncooked long-grain brown rice
- ¼ cup uncooked wild rice
- 1 pound turkey tenderloin
- Seasoned salt
- 2 cups frozen green peas, drained
- ¼ cup coarsely chopped red bell pepper
- ½ cup sliced green onion
- ½ cup sliced almonds, toasted

Fresh Tarragon Vinaigrette

- ½ cup peanut oil
- ¼ cup tarragon vinegar
- 2 Tablespoons Dijon mustard
- 1 Tablespoon grated fresh ginger, plus the juice from grating
- 1 teaspoon freshly ground pepper

✦ In a medium saucepan over high heat, bring the water to boil. Add the salt and the brown and wild rice. Return to a boil, reduce the heat, cover, and simmer until the water is absorbed, about 45 minutes.

✦ While the rice is cooking, season the turkey tenderloin with seasoned salt; brown, cooking until done; then cut into cubes.

✦ Measure out 2 cups green peas, rinse under cool water and set aside to drain. Do not cook them.

✦ Chop the red bell pepper and slice the green onion, and set aside.

✦ To toast the almonds, put them in a preheated 350-degree oven for about 5 minutes, stirring halfway through the cooking time.

✦ Make your vinaigrette by whisking the oil, vinegar, mustard, ginger, and pepper in a large bowl. Set aside.

✦ When the rice is done, add the turkey cubes, peas, green onion, almonds, and pepper. Combine well, then toss with the vinaigrette. Serve warm or at room temperature.

PEG'S NOTES ~ *This is a very nutritious salad, and guys love it. You can add fresh fruit and a nice roll for a complete entrée. You can also keep it warm in a crock pot if you're serving a crowd.*

Cassola de Plix

SEAFOOD CASSEROLE

If you can't beat them, I say join them. In my early years, coming from the South, I was not a great seafood fan, as I did not have cooking experience with seafood. I created this recipe so I could serve it to guests who liked it and also have a dish I enjoyed myself. In all honesty, I was trying to disguise the seafood flavor, but I ended up with something that was not only delicious but also something that I loved! This was my first introduction to the seafood world, and I've since created some outstanding seafood dishes. I like to use only fresh ingredients, and I now try to enhance the flavor, not hide it.

SERVES 4–6

- 2 Tablespoons butter
- 2 Tablespoons all-purpose flour
- ¼ teaspoon sea salt
- 1 cup milk
- 12 medium shrimp, cooked and split, or 1 4½-ounce can
- 1½ cups fresh crabmeat, or 1 7½-ounce can
- 1 cup steamed lobster meat, or 1 5½-ounce can
- 1 3-ounce can sliced mushrooms, drained
- 2 Tablespoons sherry
- 1 Tablespoon lemon juice
- Dash of bottled hot pepper sauce
- ¼ teaspoon Worcestershire sauce

Topping

- ½ cup shredded sharp cheddar cheese
- 2 Tablespoons butter
- 1 cup soft bread crumbs

♦ Preheat the oven to 375 degrees.

♦ Melt 2 tablespoons butter over low heat. Blend in the flour and salt. Add the milk all at once. Cook quickly, stirring constantly, until the sauce thickens and bubbles. Remove from the heat.

♦ Add the shrimp, crabmeat, lobster, mushrooms, sherry, lemon juice, pepper sauce, and Worcestershire sauce. Mix well. Place the mixture in a 1-quart ovenproof casserole dish.

♦ Sprinkle the cheese over the top.

♦ Melt the remaining 2 tablespoons butter and combine it with the bread crumbs. Sprinkle the bread crumbs over the cheese.

♦ Bake for 40 minutes, or until heated through.

♦ Garnish the top with mushroom caps and additional seafood, if you like.

PEG'S NOTES ~ I always garnish with mushroom caps and additional seafood, whether I'm serving family style or making individual servings. Add a salad and rolls, and you have a fantastic seafood dinner. You can easily double this recipe for more than six guests or if they have hearty appetites. Please note that I have listed canned seafood as an option, in case you are in a hurry and do not have the time to cook the seafood yourself. But fresh ingredients, even if they are more work, are always the most delicious.

Peg's Pork Chops

I am often referred to as a three P's gal—I love peanuts, popcorn, and pork chops. My sister Eloise would always serve me stuffed pork chops when I went to her house, just as I would serve her strawberry pie when she came to mine. A co-worker told me about this recipe prepared with chicken, so naturally I chose to try it with pork chops.

I have received long-distance phone calls from guests asking how to make it. The memory of the dish had lingered long after they went home, and they wanted to recreate it for their family and friends. It is not only the simplest recipe to make, but it's also truly Pegilicious!®

SERVES 6

- 6 boneless center-cut pork chops— 2 inches thick
- 1 pint sour cream
- 2–3 cups crushed Cheez-It® crackers
- Sea salt and pepper

♦ Preheat the oven to 350 degrees.

♦ Use a blender or food processor to crush enough Cheez-It® crackers to make at least 2 cups.

♦ Line a baking pan with aluminum foil. Salt and pepper each chop on both sides.

♦ Place the pork chops in the pan, and top them with dollops of sour cream, spreading the sour cream out to completely cover the chop. It needs to be at least ¼ inch thick.

♦ Spoon the crackers on top of the sour cream, so that they are about ¼ inch thick.

♦ Bake for about 1 hour and 15 minutes.

PEG'S NOTES ~ You might not need all of the sour cream, depending on how thick you make your topping. I like to be sure mine is at least 1/4 inch thick, and then I add 1/4 to 1/2 inch of the crushed crackers on top, making sure to use all the crackers I have crushed.

Cooking time can vary with ovens, so check after 1 hour. The sides of the pork chop should be browning, and the juices in the pan should be starting to brown and thicken a little. Do not overcook. You want your pork chops to be done but still moist.

Side Dishes, Entrées, and Sauces

VEGETABLES, PASTA, AND RICE

❖❖❖

ENTRÉES AND SAUCES

PEG'S NOTES ~ The trick to this dish is to swirl the pan so that the tomatoes caramelize but do not break down and the liquid becomes thick and glossy. Since the cooking time is so short, I stay with this, swirling all the time. You also want the crust to get to a **dark** golden brown. The cooking time will vary due to oven temperatures, so I always start with the least amount of time, check it, and cook longer, if needed.

If I want fresh basil leaves, I use very small ones, because the basil will bruise and turn dark if they're chopped. I've found that dried thyme and basil leaves work just as well. If you choose the dried leaves, crush them between the palms of your hands over the pan and the tart.

This is incredibly good. Just add meat and a salad, and you have a delicious meal. This is a beautiful dish that you would expect at a five-star restaurant.

Ivy Manor Tomato Tarte Tatin

One of the wonders of French cuisine is the caramelized apple tart served upside down and familiarly called Tarte Tatin. Actually, its formal name is La tarte des Demoiselles Tatin, *or the Tatin Spinsters' Apple Tart. It was created by the elder of two spinster sisters who took over the running of their deceased father's hotel. According to legend, one day in 1898 when the hotel was especially busy during the hunting season, Stephanie Tatin, absentmindedly put the peeled apple quarters, butter, and sugar in the pan without first lining it with pastry. Realizing her mistake, she then put the pastry on top of the simmering apples, popped it in the oven, inverted it and served the concoction warm. Don't you just love this story? A mistake can be a blessing. When life hands you lemons, make lemonade and enjoy!*

SERVES 6

- All-purpose flour, for dusting
- 1 sheet frozen puff pastry, thawed
- 1 Tablespoon olive oil
- 1 medium onion, chopped
- 1 large yellow pepper, chopped
- Sea salt
- Freshly ground pepper
- 1 teaspoon fresh thyme, chopped, or ½ teaspoon dried thyme leaves
- 2 Tablespoons butter—NO substitutions
- 2 Tablespoons sugar
- 7–8 firm, ripe Roma or plum tomatoes, cut in half lengthwise, seeded
- 3 ounces goat cheese, crumbled
- 8 small fresh basil leaves, or 1 teaspoon dried basil leaves

✦ Preheat the oven to 400 degrees.

✦ On a lightly floured surface, roll a 12-inch-square pastry sheet into a 12-inch round, cutting off the pointed edges to make a circle. Place the cut-off pieces of puff pastry back into the round, and roll it to blend them in. You can place the pastry on a waxed paper–lined cookie sheet and refrigerate until ready to use.

✦ In a heavy 12-inch ovenproof skillet, heat the oil over medium heat. Add the onion and pepper and sprinkle with salt and fresh ground black pepper. Cook for about 6 minutes, stirring. Stir in the thyme, and cook 1 minute. Transfer to a bowl and set aside.

✦ In the same pan, add the butter and sugar, stirring until both are melted, 1 to 2 minutes. In a single layer, add the tomatoes, cut side down, cover, and cook 2 minutes, then uncover.

✦ Swirling the pan often, cook 3 to 4 minutes longer, or until most of pan juices are reduced and thickened. Do not stir, only swirl the pan, as you do not want to break up the tomatoes. Turn the tomatoes over, sprinkle with salt and pepper, and cook for about 2 minutes more, or until most of the liquid has evaporated, continuing to swirl the pan. Any remaining liquid should be thick and glossy.

✦ Remove the pan from the heat. Sprinkle the onion and pepper mixture over and around the tomatoes. Carefully cover them by inverting the dough, still on the waxed paper, over the mixture in the pan; discard the paper. Cut six small slits in the top of the dough.

✦ Bake for 30 to 35 minutes, or until the crust is dark golden brown. Cool in the pan on a wire rack for 10 minutes.

✦ To unmold, place a platter over the top of the tart. Invert the tart by quickly and carefully turning the platter with the skillet upside down; remove the skillet. Sprinkle with salt, goat cheese, and basil.

✦ Serve immediately.

Fresh Beet Salad

with Blue Cheese and Almonds

The vegetarians were coming, and I needed to make a different salad. Since they loved beets, I decided to make a beet salad and dress it up a little. They flipped over the dish, thanks to the blue cheese and almonds. I had heard about Marcona almonds but never had them, as I really don't care for almonds. When I went looking for them, I could not find plain Marcona almonds. Instead I found them toasted with rosemary at Trader Joe's, and I knew they would be perfect for this salad. These almonds did not have a skin, were rounder, flavored with rosemary, and delicious—the real winners in this salad.

SERVES 6

- 7 medium beets
- 1 small clove garlic
- 3 Tablespoons extra-virgin olive oil
- 2 Tablespoons lemon juice
- 1 teaspoon sea salt
- ¼ teaspoon black pepper
- 8 ounces creamy blue cheese crumbles
- 2 ounces Marcona almonds toasted with rosemary, additional if desired
- 1 Tablespoon fresh flat-leaf Italian parsley, chopped

✦ Trim and peel 6 of the beets. Cut the beets into bite-size pieces. Place in a steamer, cover, and steam over boiling water for 20 to 25 minutes or until tender.

✦ In a large bowl, coarsely grate the remaining beet.

✦ For the dressing, mash the garlic with a pinch of salt into a paste. Add to the grated beet, along with the olive oil, lemon juice, salt, and pepper.

✦ When the beets are cooked, toss them with the dressing. Cool to room temperature.

✦ Sprinkle the blue cheese, almonds, and parsley over the beets just before serving.

PEG'S NOTES ~ The beets will turn everything red, so for an attractive salad add the cheese, almonds, and parsley only just before you bring it to the table.

Summertime Garden Pasta

On a hot July day, I came out of the garden dirty, sweaty, and really hungry. As I headed toward the house, I grabbed a few items from my garden to serve for dinner. I did not take the time to peel or seed the tomatoes as my energy was spent for the day. I prepared the tomato sauce, threw a pot of water on to boil for the pasta, and jumped in the shower. After my shower, I finished the dish. It was truly Pegilicious!® with all the goodness of garden-fresh taste. My family loves it when I get too tired to think and just grab whatever I can get my hands on. They say those are our best meals.

SERVES 4

- 4–6 ripe heirloom tomatoes
- ½ cup olive oil, plus 1 Tablespoon
- 2 Tablespoons chopped parsley
- 1 Tablespoon fresh chopped basil
- 2 teaspoons sea salt, divided
- 1 clove garlic, minced
- 1 pound spiral pasta
- 8 ounces mozzarella cheese, shredded
- 2 small zucchini, shredded
- ½ cup toasted walnuts, coarsely chopped
- Fresh ground black pepper

✦ Wash, stem, and chop the tomatoes. Add the ½ cup of oil, parsley, basil, 1 teaspoon of the salt, and the garlic to the chopped tomatoes. Blend, and let stand for at least 2 hours.

✦ In a large pot, bring 6 quarts of salted water to a boil, add a tablespoon of olive oil to keep the pasta from sticking together, then add the pasta and cook it until it's al dente—firm to the bite but tender. Remove from the heat and drain well. Place the pasta in a large bowl.

✦ Immediately toss the hot pasta with the shredded mozzarella, the remaining teaspoon of salt, and the shredded zucchini. The just-cooked pasta will begin to melt the cheese. Then add the tomato sauce and toss.

✦ Serve immediately, or refrigerate and serve cold. Sprinkle with the walnuts just before serving.

✦ Pass the pepper grinder for fresh ground pepper.

PEG'S NOTES ~ *You can substitute Roma tomatoes for the heirloom tomatoes or use a 35-ounce can of Italian plum tomatoes, drained. But nothing tastes like fresh tomatoes from the garden. You may also use dried herbs if you do not have fresh ones, but remember that there's a 1 to 3 ratio of dried to fresh: Use 1 teaspoon of dried basil for 1 tablespoon of fresh; the same goes for parsley.*

Calico Beans

My mentor, Margaret Sears, helped me develop this recipe for a big barbeque that I had been hired to cater. I wanted something special and different from the usual baked beans that were so commonly served. These Calico beans proved to be a big winner.

I love that I can mix up this recipe, save it in the refrigerator overnight, which enhances the flavor, and stick it in the oven to cook while we are working the grill.

FAMILY RECIPE
SERVES 8 OR MORE

- 1 medium onion
- 3 Tablespoons bacon fat or oil
- 1 31-ounce can pork and beans
- 1 15-ounce can kidney beans
- 1 15-ounce can lima beans
- 1 cup brown sugar
- 1 cup catsup
- 3 Tablespoons prepared mustard
- 2 Tablespoons vinegar
- 1 clove garlic, crushed

CROWD RECIPE
SERVES 100 OR MORE

- 12 medium onions
- 2¼ cups bacon fat or oil
- 5 gallons pork and beans, 640 ounces
- 3 gallons kidney beans, 384 ounces
- 3 gallons lima beans, 384 ounces
- 12 cups brown sugar
- 12 cups catsup
- 2¼ cups prepared mustard
- 1½ cups vinegar
- 12 cloves garlic, crushed

- Preheat the oven to 350 degrees.
- Using an ovenproof pot or pan, sauté the onion in the bacon fat or oil.
- Blend all the other ingredients together in another large pot or pan. Combine with the onion in the ovenproof pan.
- Bake for 1 hour.
- This dish can also be cooked by simmering on top of the stove in a large pot, stirring gently now and then.

PEG'S NOTES ~ Baking the beans in the oven is an easy, no-fuss way of cooking them. I've found that they do not break down or stick together that way.

If you're making the crowd recipe, you will need to simmer the beans in large stockpots on top of the stove. Adjust the cooking time to 3 to 4 hours, stirring gently now and then. However, I recommend baking the beans in the oven: Divide the recipe among large chafing dishes, and bake each pan for about 1 1/2 hours or longer. Temperatures vary in ovens, so judge your time by the look of the sauce. It needs to be thickened and look much darker, showing that it is cooked. Using the baking method, you can change out your chafing dishes as needed.

Fresh Fried White Corn

This is another one of my mother's great Southern recipes that has been handed down for generations. True Southerners frown upon serving yellow corn at the table, since they feed yellow corn to the hogs. In the South we cook only with white corn. Southerners even have trouble using the yellow cornmeal. However, since white cornmeal has been very difficult to find in Southern California, I have found myself using yellow cornmeal more and more. But I still refuse to cook and serve the yellow corn. Nothing can take the place of fresh white corn.

This recipe came about because Mother could feed more people by cutting the kernels off the cob than serving corn on the cob. With nine children in the family, we had this dish often.

SERVES 6

- 6–8 ears of fresh white corn
- 2 Tablespoons butter
- 2 Tablespoons shortening
- ¼–½ cup water
- 1–2 Tablespoons cornstarch
- Milk, to dissolve the cornstarch
- Sea salt and pepper

✦ Cut the corn off of the ears. Heat the butter and shortening in a saucepan until they're hot and bubbly.

✦ Pour the corn into the hot pan. The kernels will sizzle a little. Add just enough water so that the corn does not stick, ¼ to ½ cup. See Peg's Notes. Salt and pepper heavily.

✦ Cook for about 3 minutes, stirring often. Dissolve the cornstarch in a little milk, and add it to the corn. Continue to cook for 1 to 2 minutes, stirring so that the cornstarch is cooked, and the corn does not stick and scorch. Do not overcook. You want your kernels to still have a crunch.

✦ This will serve 6 people with seconds. And believe me, they will come back for seconds.

PEG'S NOTES ~ Some corn has more milk in the kernels than others, so the amount of water and cornstarch you need will depend on your corn. The cornstarch is used only to thicken the water, which results in a more cream-style corn.

The corn will cook quickly, so watch the pot, stirring often. The success of this dish depends on not overcooking the corn, so that it still has a fresh taste.

Fresh Vegetable Salad With Vinaigrette

This dish is a terrific way to serve fresh vegetables. This simple, beautiful dish is easy to prepare and both delicious and healthy. It is a do-ahead dish, great for any party and great for young cooks, especially at Thanksgiving. This dish solves the problem of the last-minute hassle of getting the vegetables out on time.

SERVES 12

- 1 pound fresh Brussels sprouts, cut in half
- 1 medium head cauliflower

Vinaigrette

- 1 cup salad oil
- 6 Tablespoons white wine vinegar
- 6 Tablespoons lemon juice
- 1½ teaspoons sea salt
- 1½ teaspoons dry mustard
- 1 teaspoon sugar

For salad

- Romaine lettuce leaves
- Sliced tomatoes and/or sliced green pepper rings
- 1 sieved hard-cooked egg, optional
- Snipped parsley or dill weed, optional

+ Trim the stems slightly from the Brussels sprouts. Remove any discolored leaves and wash. Halve the sprouts, and place them in a steamer rack or a basket over boiling water. Cover and steam the sprouts about 5 to 6 minutes, or until they are crisp-tender. Remove from the heat, rinse with cold water, and drain.

+ Wash the cauliflower, and remove the leaves and stems. Place the whole cauliflower head in a steamer basket over boiling water, and cook, covered, for 5 to 6 minutes, or until crisp-tender. Remove from the heat, rinse with cold water, and drain.

+ Prepare the vinaigrette. In a screw-top jar, combine the oil, vinegar, lemon juice, salt, mustard, and sugar; cover, and shake well.

+ Place the vegetables in a bowl, and pour the vinaigrette over them. Toss lightly to coat the vegetables. Cover tightly, and chill several hours or overnight.

+ To serve, line a platter with the lettuce leaves. Place sliced tomatoes and/or green pepper rings around the edge of the platter. Drain the marinade from the vegetables, and place the cauliflower head in the center of the platter. Spoon the sprouts around the cauliflower. If desired, sprinkle the egg and snipped parsley or dill atop the cauliflower.

PEG'S NOTES ~ I use both the sliced tomatoes and the green pepper rings. They add so much color to the platter. And, I always chill the vegetables overnight, so they really marinate in the dressing. I also sprinkle on the sieved hard-cooked egg and the dill weed; beautiful and delicious.

Ivy Manor Sugar Snap Peas
With Goat Cheese

People tell me that my best dishes are the ones that are created on the fly. It appears that I think and work the best when under pressure and when I am forced to concentrate on the task at hand.

I grow beautiful sugar snap peas in my garden. One evening we had friends coming to dinner, and for some reason I felt the need to dress up or change an ordinary dish into something special. Since I love shallots, tomatoes, and goat cheese, I thought it would be a good combination. It was!

Sugar Snap peas will never be the same at the Ivy Manor.

SERVES 4

- 1 pound fresh sugar snap peas
- 1 Tablespoon lemon juice
- 1 medium shallot, minced
- 1 Tablespoon olive oil
- 1–2 Tablespoons fresh dill, chopped
- 1–2 medium-size heirloom or Roma tomatoes, seeded and chopped
- 1 3-ounce goat cheese log, crumbled
- 1 teaspoon sea salt
- ½ teaspoon freshly ground black pepper

✦ Steam the peas, or cook them in just enough water to cover for 2 minutes. Plunge the peas into ice water to stop the cooking process, and drain. Drizzle lemon juice over peas.

✦ In a large skillet over medium-high heat, add the oil, and when it's hot, sauté the shallot until tender.

✦ Add the drained peas, and cook until thoroughly heated. Place the mixture in a bowl.

✦ Add the fresh dill, tomatoes, cheese, salt, and pepper, and toss gently.

✦ Serve immediately.

Fresh Herb Zucchini Pie

As a child, I remember Mother's garden as being central to our lives and an absolute necessity. I love to garden. Today, I grow my own fresh herbs and always have an abundance of zucchini. If ever there is a recipe in the making the ingredients are right here in the garden. Although I already have two zucchini recipes in this book, Zom's Zucchini Soup and the Summertime Garden Pasta, I must add one more.

This is an excellent vegetarian dish with superb flavor and, when using fresh herbs, makes a very savory pie.

Perfect companion dishes to this zucchini are Fresh Fried White Corn and sliced heirloom tomatoes. Add a little Southern fried chicken, and you have a feast!

SERVES 6–8

- 2 Tablespoons butter
- 4 cups thinly sliced zucchini
- 1 cup chopped shallots
- ½ teaspoon salt
- ½ teaspoon pepper
- 1 clove garlic, crushed
- 6 Tablespoons chopped fresh parsley
- ¾ teaspoon fresh chopped basil leaves
- ¾ teaspoon fresh chopped oregano leaves
- ½ teaspoon fresh thyme
- 2 eggs, well beaten
- 2 cups shredded mozzarella cheese, 8 ounces
- 1 sheet frozen puff-pastry, thawed
- 2 teaspoons yellow mustard

- ✦ Preheat the oven to 375 degrees.
- ✦ Melt the butter in a large skillet over medium-high heat. Add the zucchini and shallots, and cook just until the zucchini is tender, 5 to 6 minutes. Remove from heat. Stir in the salt, pepper, garlic, and fresh herbs.
- ✦ In a large bowl, mix the eggs and cheese. Add them to the cooked vegetable mixture. Stir gently to combine.
- ✦ On a slightly floured surface, roll a 12-inch-square pastry sheet into a 12-inch round, cutting off the pointed edges to make a circle. Place the cut-off pastry back into the round and roll to blend in. Fit the pastry into a pie plate, rolling the edge to form a nice border for the pie. Spread the crust with the mustard.
- ✦ Pour the vegetable mixture into the piecrust, then take the back of a spoon and evenly spread out the zucchini for a pretty pie.
- ✦ Bake 18 to 22 minutes, or until the center is set. Test by inserting a knife into the center; it should come out clean.
- ✦ If the crust is browning too fast, cover the edge with a strip of aluminum foil during the last 10 minutes.
- ✦ This serves 6 as a main dish or 8 as a side dish.

Artichokes and Potatoes Au Gratin

During the late '80s and early '90s my clients demanded my Hot Artichoke Dip—page 31—at every event that I catered. One politician in particular would call me if he was invited to a party to see if I was catering it before he accepted the invitation. If I was, he would always ask about the artichoke dip. I guess you could say that dish from the 1980s inspired this one. Since I have developed an allergy to all potatoes except for Yukon Gold and sweet potatoes, naturally I had to come up with new ideas. This is a Pegilicious!® vegetarian recipe that also goes well with any meat.

SERVES 12–16

- 2 cups grated Parmesan cheese
- 3 cups grated Gruyere cheese
- 3 pounds Yukon Gold potatoes, peeled and thinly sliced—about ⅛ inch, divided
- 1¼ teaspoons sea salt, divided
- ¾ teaspoon pepper, divided
- 2 gloves garlic, minced
- 5 cups drained Cara Mia® marinated artichoke hearts
- 1 quart heavy cream, divided

+ Preheat the oven to 350 degrees. Grease a 15 by 11-inch baking dish with butter.
+ In a medium bowl, combine the cheeses.
+ Line the bottom of the baking dish with half of the sliced potatoes, overlapping the slices to form rows and make a single layer. Season the potatoes with ¾ teaspoon salt and ½ teaspoon pepper, or to taste. Sprinkle with the garlic.
+ Add the artichoke hearts, arranging them in a single layer over the potatoes. Scatter ⅓ of the grated cheese mixture over the artichokes, and then drizzle with half of the heavy cream.
+ Arrange the remaining potatoes in a single layer over the cheese. Season with ½ teaspoon salt and ¼ teaspoon pepper. Drizzle with the remaining cream, and then sprinkle with the remaining cheese.
+ Butter the underside of a piece of foil to keep the cheese from sticking, and use it to cover the baking dish. Bake the gratin until the potatoes are softened and almost completely cooked, 45 minutes to 1 hour. A knife should easily pierce the potatoes. Uncover the gratin and continue to bake until the cheese is melted and golden brown, 15 to 20 minutes. Remove from the oven, and cool slightly on a rack before serving.

PEG'S NOTES ~ This is a great dish for a large gathering. You can halve the recipe for a small dinner party of 6 to 8 people. I spray the underside of the foil with non-stick cooking spray instead of buttering it. I have also used roasted garlic in this dish when I have leftovers from making my pizzas.

I always use Cara Mia® marinated artichokes as they are more flavorful.

Peg's Scalloped Potatoes

I am a real potato girl from the South but have become allergic to all potatoes except Yukon Gold and sweet potatoes, so I have had to go back to my test kitchen and adjust all my recipes so I could enjoy potatoes again.

I have been told that this recipe is the best and that the sauce is fabulous.

Use whatever potatoes you like. They all work for this recipe. I will tell you a secret. If you leave out the green onion, you have a great cheese sauce base for macaroni and cheese.

SERVES 8–10

- ¼ cup butter
- ¼ cup all-purpose flour
- 3 cups milk
- 1 10-ounce block cheddar cheese, shredded
- ½ cup thinly sliced green onions
- 1 teaspoon sea salt
- ¼ teaspoon freshly ground pepper
- 4 pounds Yukon Gold potatoes, peeled and thinly sliced

Topping

- 1½ cups bread crumbs
- ¼ cup butter, melted
- ¼ cup grated Parmesan cheese
- ¼ cup fresh chopped parsley

+ Melt the ¼ cup butter in a large saucepan over medium heat. Whisk in the flour and cook, whisking constantly, 2 to 3 minutes, or until the flour is lightly browned.

+ Whisk the milk into the butter mixture, and bring to a boil. Reduce the heat, and simmer 4 to 6 minutes, or until it's thickened. Stir in the cheddar cheese, green onions, salt, and pepper, stirring until the cheese melts.

+ Spread ¼ cup of the cheese sauce evenly in a lightly greased 9 by 13-inch baking dish. Layer half of the potatoes over the sauce; top with half of the remaining cheese sauce. Repeat with the remaining potatoes and cheese sauce. Cover with aluminum foil.

+ Bake at 325 degrees for 1½ to 2 hours.

+ Stir together the bread crumbs, melted butter, Parmesan cheese, and parsley, and spread the mixture evenly over the potatoes. Bake, uncovered, for 20 to 30 more minutes, or until the potatoes are tender, and the topping is browned.

PEG'S NOTES ~ When I uncover the casserole, I test for doneness by piercing the potatoes with a fork. This will determine how much longer the potatoes need to cook. If I'm in a hurry, I will parboil the potatoes in the milk, drain them, and then reuse the milk for the cheese sauce. Add more milk if you do not have 3 cups after boiling the potatoes. Boiling the potatoes in milk really adds to the flavor. Also be sure to use some of the green tops from the green onions; they add flavor and color.

New Mexico Green Rice

This recipe was created to go with Zom's Green Chili Enchiladas on page 135. I had always served Spanish rice with the enchiladas, but the family got tired of that and wanted something different. Since I was trying to find a use— besides salsa—for the tomatillos from my garden, I came up with this dish. I named it New Mexico Green Rice because my husband, Jarvis, is from that state, and he loves this recipe. I use Hatch green chiles from the Hatch Valley in New Mexico.

SERVES 9

- 3 Tablespoons butter
- 1 cup chopped onions
- 2 cloves garlic, crushed
- 2 cups uncooked white rice
- 3-4 fresh tomatillos *or*
  - 1 11- or 16-ounce can, drained
- 1 4-ounce can Hatch fire-roasted chopped green chiles
- 2 14½-ounce cans chicken broth or stock
- ¼ cup chopped fresh cilantro

+ Melt the butter in a large saucepan or skillet over medium heat. Add the onion and garlic, and cook 3 to 5 minutes, or until the onion is softened. Stir often.
+ Add the rice, and cook 3 to 4 minutes, or until lightly browned, stirring occasionally.
+ Add the tomatillos, chiles, and broth, and mix well. Bring to a boil, stirring occasionally.
+ Reduce the heat to low, cover, and simmer 20 to 25 minutes, or until the liquid is absorbed and the rice is tender, stirring occasionally.
+ Remove from the heat. Stir in the cilantro.

PEG'S NOTES ~ I always use fresh tomatillos. After the rice is browned, I put everything into my rice cooker with the remaining ingredients, except for the cilantro. This cooks nicely in the rice cooker, and the rice stays warm until it's ready to serve.

Peg's Potato Casserole

I remember coming home late at night, tired and having to come up with something for a company potluck the next day. I was at a loss for ideas, so I looked into the freezer to see what I had. Oh! My gosh! I have frozen hash browns! Thank you, Lord! Now just lead me to make something with these.

This recipe was created decades ago and was one of the very first recipes that I took to our company's monthly potlucks. How relieved I was that it was an instant hit.

I have doubled and even tripled this recipe to feed a crowd, and there are never leftovers. I serve it with my Santa Maria–style Tri-Tip. Yum!

SERVES 6–8

- 3 cups frozen hash brown potatoes
- 2 cups grated cheddar cheese, divided
- 1 10.75-ounce can cream of mushroom soup
- ½ cup sour cream
- 6 green onions, chopped

- ✦ Preheat the oven to 350 degrees.
- ✦ Mix all the ingredients together, saving 1 cup of cheddar cheese to sprinkle on top.
- ✦ Pour into a 13 by 9-inch casserole dish.
- ✦ Bake for 1 hour.

PEG'S NOTES ~ This recipe is easy to double for a crowd and can be prepared the night before. Just cover the dish and refrigerate it until you are ready to bake. If you do have any leftovers, they warm up beautifully!

Peg's Salmon and Veggie Rice

My favorite restaurant in the Santa Ynez Valley introduced me to veggie rice, and I have had a ball creating my own version. What really sets it off is that it is served on one of my lemon sauces. What's also nice is that you can use whatever vegetable you like and happen to have on hand. Even frozen corn or peas work well.

The key to this dish is advance preparation. I purchase large packages of mushrooms, red bell peppers, and shallots. Then I sauté the mushrooms and shallots in batches, so that the mushrooms brown properly, and I divide and package them for the freezer. I also cut the red peppers in half, seed them, and roast them under the broiler until they're charred. I peel them and wrap each half in press-and-seal plastic wrap and place the peppers in freezer bags for later use. This allows me to use just what I need each time. I also purchase organic brown rice bowls and have them ready when I need them. With preparations like these, you can have this dish ready to serve within 20 minutes of starting.

SERVES 2

- 1 7.4-ounce package microwavable cooked organic brown rice
- Vegetables of choice— see Peg's Notes
- 2 Tablespoons butter, divided
- Mushrooms sautéed with shallots
- Herbs that complement the vegetable of choice
- Sea salt and pepper to taste
- Roasted red pepper, chopped
- Lemon-Mustard sauce—page 138
- Toasted pine nuts, optional
- Fresh tomatoes, optional
- 2 salmon fillets, any size

- ✦ Microwave the rice for 1½ minutes, or as per the instructions.
- ✦ Steam the vegetables according to the chart in Peg's Notes, or use 1 cup frozen mixed vegetables, such as corn and peas. Do not thaw them.
- ✦ If you're using zucchini or other squash, slice them and stir-fry the pieces in the butter before adding them to the mushrooms and other vegetables.
- ✦ In a saucepan over medium heat, melt 1 tablespoon of the butter, add the prepared mushrooms and veggies of your choice, along with any herbs or spices. At this point you can add fresh spinach, if using, and it will cook just enough.
- ✦ Add the cooked rice and roasted red pepper, and stir to mix well.
- ✦ Place a spoonful of sauce on your plate. Put your veggie rice on top, add the pine nuts and fresh tomatoes, if using. The dish is now ready for the salmon or your fish of choice. Place it on top of the veggies, and serve.
- ✦ I serve salmon with this dish, but you can use any fish you like. To prepare the fillets, I pat them dry, sprinkle with seasoned salt, and cook them in a cast-iron skillet with 1 tablespoon butter. I cover the pan with a loose piece of aluminum foil, so that it holds the heat and cooks faster. Do not cover with a lid, however, as that will cause the fish to steam, and you will not get a grill effect. Cook only until the fish begins to flake, 2 to 3 minutes on each side, depending on the fillet's thickness.
- ✦ The number of servings determines how many vegetables to use or if you'll need more than 1 package of rice. One package serves 2 people with the veggies.

PEG'S NOTES ~

It takes longer to prepare the veggies than it does to cook the dish, so prior preparations are a time saver.

Time needed to steam fresh vegetables after bringing water to a full boil:

Fresh asparagus	3 minutes	Fresh cauliflower	6 minutes
Fresh broccoli	4 minutes	Fresh green beans	5 minutes
Fresh Brussels sprouts	6 minutes	Fresh petite beans	3 minutes
Fresh sliced carrots	4 minutes	Fresh sugar snap peas	3 minutes

ENTREES AND SAUCES

Peg's Meat Pie

When I was working in an office in the Los Angeles area, we had potluck lunches at least once a month, and we would exchange recipes. We often shared ideas as to how we "working gals" could have it a little easier when company came. This recipe came from those brainstorming sessions.

I always served this dish when I had to pick up out-of-town guests at the airport. It takes two hours for this pie to bake; that was just enough time for me to pick up my guests and get back home in time for dinner. No one ever believed that this could be cooking while I was picking up guests. Serve the pie with a green salad and a nice glass of wine, and you have a truly welcoming meal!

MAKES A 10-INCH DEEP-DISH PIE

- Mother Infield's Piecrust—page 163, or a Pillsbury® Pie Crust—you need 2 crusts
- 2 potatoes, sliced and divided
- Flour, for dusting
- Salt
- 2 onions, sliced and divided
- 1 teaspoon parsley
- 1 teaspoon chives
- 1 teaspoon tarragon
- 3 slices sirloin, ¼ inch thick, sliced crosswise
- 2 rutabagas, sliced
- 2 medium pork chops, cut off the bone and sliced in half
- 1 Tablespoon butter, cubed

✦ Preheat the oven to 350 degrees.

✦ Place 1 piecrust on the bottom of a 10-inch pie plate. Sprinkle with a little flour.

✦ Add a layer of potatoes, and salt it. Add a layer of onions, and salt it. Combine the parsley, chives, and tarragon. Sprinkle the pie with half the mixture of herbs.

✦ Add a layer of sirloin.

✦ Add a layer of rutabagas. Add a layer of pork chops.

✦ Add another layer of potatoes, and salt it. Add another layer of onions, and salt it. Sprinkle with the rest of the herb mixture.

✦ All these layers will result in a high pie. Put the butter on top of the last layer.

✦ Top with the second piecrust, arranging it so that you completely cover the bottom piecrust. Crimp the edges of the piecrust together to completely cover the ingredients and to keep the juices from spilling out into your oven. Make 3 slits in the top of the crust for steam to escape.

✦ Bake for about 2 hours.

PEG'S NOTES ~ I love this recipe because it has vegetables, meat, and bread all in one dish. The flour on the bottom helps thicken the meat juices, making a delicious sauce. The flour also helps keep the bottom piecrust from getting soggy. Let the pie rest for about 10 minutes before serving. This pie slices up nicely and makes a great presentation on the plate with all the layers.

Zom's Green Chili Enchiladas

I originally prepared this dish for a potluck dinner years ago and have taken it through many revisions as my family matured and could handle a little more spice. I often use what I have on hand. If I don't have garlic powder, I will use garlic salt and adjust the salt, or I will add fresh garlic.

When one of the girls is coming home for a visit, I know I will be preparing this dish.

MAKES 12 ENCHILADAS

- 1 Tablespoon olive oil
- 1 cup chopped onions
- 1 pound ground chuck
- 1 teaspoon oregano
- 1 teaspoon cumin
- 1 teaspoon seasoned salt
- 3 Tablespoons chili powder
- 1 teaspoon garlic powder
- 1 teaspoon green chili seasoning, optional
- 1 dozen corn tortillas
- Vegetable oil for frying
- ½ pound longhorn cheddar cheese, grated

Cheese sauce

- 1 10.75-ounce can cream of chicken soup
- 1 5-ounce can evaporated milk
- ½ pound Velveeta cheese
- 1 4-ounce can Hatch fire-roasted chopped green chiles
- 1 2-ounce jar pimentos, chopped

+ Preheat the oven to 350 degrees.

+ In a heavy skillet over moderate heat, add the oil and chopped onions, and sauté until opaque, 2 to 3 minutes. Add the chuck, stirring to break up the meat, and cook until it is no longer pink. Add the oregano, cumin, salt, chili powder, garlic powder, and chili seasoning, if using. Cook, stirring, until all the liquid has evaporated, and the meat is brown. Set aside.

+ In a heavy skillet, quickly fry the tortillas in oil—they need to be still pliable, and stack them on a paper sack until they're cool enough to handle.

+ Grate the longhorn cheddar cheese.

+ Prepare the cheese sauce. In a double boiler over boiling water, heat the soup, milk, and Velveeta cheese until it's melted. Stir in the green chiles and pimentos.

+ Assemble the enchiladas by placing a large spoonful of meat on a tortilla, then adding the grated cheddar. Roll up the tortilla to form an enchilada, and place the enchiladas in a buttered casserole dish as you go.

+ Top with the cheese sauce, and cover with aluminum foil.

+ Bake for 1 hour. Remove the foil and serve.

PEG'S NOTES ~ I always double this recipe, as everyone eats at least 3 enchiladas. To make the dish a little spicier, use pepper jack Velveeta, or half pepper jack and half regular Velveeta. You also can add more green chiles. If you are serving children, you can blend the pimentos and chiles in a blender before adding to the sauce and only use regular Velveeta. This really cuts down on the heat. Adjust the seasonings to suit your family, and have fun!

Chicken and Sausage Tostadas

This recipe is incredibly delicious. It has a very unique flavor that is so different from your regular tostada. Although I created this recipe years ago, I still use it when preparing a Mexican dinner and want to surprise my guests with something new and different.

MAKES 10 TOSTADAS

- 2 Tablespoons salad oil
- 1 Tablespoon lemon juice
- ¼ teaspoon dried oregano, crushed
- ⅛ teaspoon sea salt
- Dash of pepper
- 2 onions, sliced and separated into rings, plus ½ cup chopped onion
- 2 cups cooked chicken, cut into strips
- 1 pound bulk pork sausage
- 1 clove garlic, minced
- 1 15-ounce can refried beans
- 1 10-ounce can enchilada sauce
- 10 corn tortillas
- Cooking oil
- 4 cups shredded or chopped lettuce

✦ In a small bowl, combine the oil, lemon juice, oregano, salt, and pepper. Add the onion rings. Cover and marinate them in the refrigerator for at least 2 hours.

✦ In a saucepan, combine the chicken and a few tablespoons of water. Heat the chicken, and keep it warm over very low heat.

✦ In a skillet, cook the sausage, chopped onion, and garlic until the meat is browned. Drain off the excess fat. Add the refried beans and enchilada sauce, and cook, stirring frequently, until the mixture is heated through.

✦ In another skillet, cook the tortillas in hot oil until crisp, 2 to 3 minutes, turning once. Drain the tortillas on paper towels or a paper sack, and keep them warm. Spread each tortilla with the bean mixture.

✦ Drain the onion rings, reserving the marinade. Toss the lettuce with the reserved marinade, and spoon on top of the beans. Top the lettuce with the hot chicken strips and marinated onion rings.

PEG'S NOTES ~ This recipe might appear to be work intensive, but really it just seems that way. I marinate my onions overnight and shred the lettuce in advance, placing it in a plastic bag and keeping it in the crisper until ready to use. I also cook two chicken breasts the day before and have them ready to slice into strips. I warm my chicken in the microwave, but I do not recommend it unless you know how to do that without making the chicken rubbery. Microwave temperatures vary so much that it is too risky at the last minute. It is best to stay with the method in the instructions, or purchase a rotisserie chicken from the market and use only the breast. So when I'm ready to serve the dish, I just have to cook the sausage and bean mixture and fry the tortillas. Then I toss the lettuce and serve. Margaritas are the perfect drink to accompany this dish.

You can choose red or green enchilada sauce, depending on the spiciness you want in your tostadas. Choose the sausage that you love. When I do not know what my guests prefer, I always go for the milder side, putting a hot sauce on the table, in case someone wants to add some heat.

I always have my fresh avocado salsa on the table, too, in case someone wants to add it to their tostada. But this dish is so flavorful that it stands on its own. It also is a fun recipe to make when your guests want to help you in the kitchen.

Crème Fraîche

AN INCREDIBLY DECADENT TYPE OF SOUR CREAM

Crème Fraîche means fresh cream in French, but it is not fresh cream. It's a cream with a culture added. This fancy French soured cream with 28 percent butterfat is richer, thicker, and less sour than traditional American sour cream. It is sometimes difficult to find in local supermarkets, and since it is very expensive, I make my own. Crème Fraîche is fun and easy to make and is more versatile than sour cream. This is great in sauces, to top soups, and as a condiment for fresh fruit.

MAKES 1¼ CUPS

Needs 2 days

- 1 cup heavy whipping cream
- ¼ cup buttermilk
- 1 Tablespoon fresh lemon juice

✦ In a saucepan, over a low flame, warm the cream slightly. You just want to take the chill off, so it's warm to the touch. Turn off the heat.

✦ Stir in the buttermilk until well blended. The cultures in the buttermilk will turn the cream into crème fraîche, and the addition of healthy bacteria enhances the flavor.

✦ Add the lemon juice, and combine well. Pour into a glass jar, and close with a lid. Allow the crème fraîche to thicken by letting it stand at room temperature for 24 hours, stirring it occasionally.

✦ After 24 hours in a warm room, the crème fraîche is going to be pretty thick, but not quite thick enough. Stir the mixture well, and refrigerate for another 24 hours; it will continue to thicken.

PEG'S NOTES ~ I use a 1-quart mason jar so I have enough room to stir the liquid well without spilling the cream. Plan ahead, as this will take 2 days to thicken properly.

You can store the Crème Fraîche in the refrigerator for up to 2 weeks.

Crème Fraîche is very versatile and can be whipped for amazingly fluffy whipped cream.

You can add sugar if you want to use it with your desserts, or you can make it savory with a little pinch of salt and pepper, then serve it with caviar, a baked potato, or whenever a recipe calls for sour cream. I also spoon this over puddings, apple pies, or warm cobblers as an alternative to ice cream.

Lemon-Mustard Sauce

This sauce was created on the fly one night when I did not have any homemade chicken broth in the freezer. Guests were coming, and I needed a sauce to serve with my salmon. It was such a hit that I use it all the time, especially for my Salmon and Veggie Rice.

MAKES 1 CUP

- 1 packet Swanson's Flavor Boost, chicken flavor
- 1 cup water, plus additional to dissolve cornstarch
- 2 Tablespoons fresh lemon juice
- 1 Tablespoon country-style Dijon mustard
- 1½ Tablespoons cornstarch, plus additional if needed
- ½-1 teaspoon dill weed, as desired

✦ In a saucepan over low heat, whisk the Boost with the water and bring to a boil. When it's completely blended and boiling, whisk in the lemon juice and mustard.

✦ Dissolve the cornstarch in a small amount of water, and stir into the broth mixture, stirring constantly until the mixture thickens and the cornstarch has cooked, 1 to 2 minutes. Add more cornstarch, if needed, ½ tablespoon at a time, until you have the consistency that you prefer. Stir in the dill weed.

PEG'S NOTES ~ *You can use 1 cup of chicken broth, if you have it on hand. Then omit the water, whisk in the lemon juice and mustard, and continue with the recipe instructions.*

Lemon-Dill Sauce

MAKES 2 CUPS

- 2 cups chicken broth
- 2 Tablespoons lemon juice
- 2 Tablespoons cornstarch, plus additional if needed
- 2 Tablespoons capers, rinsed
- 2 teaspoons dill weed

✦ In a saucepan over low heat, bring the chicken broth and lemon juice to a boil. Dissolve the cornstarch in a small amount of water, and stir it into the broth mixture, stirring constantly until mixture thickens and cornstarch has cooked—1 to 2 minutes. If needed, add more cornstarch one tablespoon at a time, until you have the consistency that you prefer. Stir in the rinsed capers and dill weed.

PEG'S NOTES ~
I use both of these sauces with my veggie rice and fish dish, depending on the type of fish I am serving.

White Wine Sauce for Pasta

When my daughter Dana was eight, she went to a sleepover and for the first time was served spaghetti in a white sauce, instead of the traditional tomato version. She flipped over the dish and begged me to call for the recipe or create one for her. This sauce has evolved over the years. I still use it today, changing out the herbs for different dishes.

MAKES 1 CUP

- ⅓ cup white wine, such as Chardonnay
- ⅓ cup butter
- ⅓ cup olive oil
- ½ teaspoon oregano
- 1 clove garlic, crushed
- 8 ounces cooked pasta of your choice, such as spaghetti, angel hair, ravioli, etc.
- Parmesan cheese, grated
- Chopped parsley, optional

✦ Combine the butter and olive oil in a small saucepan over low heat until the butter is melted and the oil is warm. Add the wine and bring to a boil. Add the oregano and garlic.

✦ Remove from the heat, and toss with the cooked pasta of your choice.

✦ Sprinkle with the Parmesan cheese and parsley, if using.

PEG'S NOTES ~ You can also substitute sherry for wine in this recipe for a rich and flavorful sauce. Depending on the meat, fish, or poultry you serve with the pasta, accompany the dish with a white or red California table wine.

Toss cheese tortellini in this wine sauce to go with a grilled chicken breast or with shrimp, asparagus, and fresh tomatoes. If you decide on shrimp, serve it with a lemon wedge.

Change the herbs for different dishes. You can also add toasted pine nuts, along with the fresh Parmesan cheese. Serve with a green salad and garlic bread, and you really have a delicious meal. Bon appétit!

Mom's Homemade Mayonnaise

When I was growing up, we made our mayonnaise for our potato salad.

To stay true to my heritage, I felt I had to include a mayonnaise recipe, especially for our daughters. Included are ideas for variations that can be used on sandwiches or in salads. This is also very tasty when served with cold poultry and sliced meats.

If you just love homemade like I do, then use this recipe for all of your cold emulsified sauces.

MAKES 2 CUPS

- 3 egg yolks
- ½ teaspoon salt
- ½ teaspoon sugar
- ¼ teaspoon dry mustard
- 1½ cups salad oil, divided
- 3 Tablespoons cider vinegar
- 1 Tablespoon lemon juice

✦ Using a blender or food processor, blend the eggs, salt, sugar, and mustard for 2 minutes.

✦ Continue blending and gradually add ½ cup of the salad oil, ½ teaspoon at a time, until the mixture is smooth and thick. Still blending, gradually add the vinegar and lemon juice to the mixture.

✦ Blend in the remaining salad oil, 1 tablespoon at a time, until all the oil is absorbed and the mixture is smooth and creamy. Cover and refrigerate.

Variations

✦ To 1 cup of mayonnaise, add 1 teaspoon each of fresh tarragon and minced parsley.

✦ To 1 cup of mayonnaise, add ¼ cup of chopped chutney.

✦ To 1 cup of mayonnaise, add 1 teaspoon of curry powder.

PEG'S NOTES ~ If you are not comfortable using raw eggs, you can use egg substitute, but this is a safe recipe if the mayonnaise is refrigerated and used quickly. If you don't have a blender or food processor, you can use an electric mixer.

Desserts

Cookies

✦✦✦

Pies, Puddings, and Other Pastries

✦✦✦

Cakes

✦✦✦

Ice Cream and candy

Flourless Peanut Butter and Chocolate Chip Cookies

Deborah was trying not to eat gluten, yet she did not want to give up cookies. So what could be better than combining a couple of the best convenience foods of the century to create a flourless cookie? Peanut butter was first introduced at the 1904 St. Louis World Fair, and chocolate chips were first sold by Nestle in 1939. Peanut butter cookies and chocolate chip cookies are both delicious and famous. Why not combine those ingredients?

Together, the ingredients are an unbeatable team.

MAKES 2 DOZEN COOKIES

- 1 cup chunky peanut butter
- 1 cup firmly packed brown sugar
- 1 large egg
- 1 teaspoon baking soda
- ½ teaspoon vanilla
- 1 cup miniature semisweet chocolate chips

+ Preheat the oven to 350 degrees.
+ Mix the peanut butter, sugar, egg, baking soda, and vanilla in a medium bowl. Mix in the chocolate chips.
+ Using moistened hands, form a generous 1 tablespoon of dough into a ball for each cookie.
+ Arrange the cookies on 2 ungreased baking sheets, spacing them 2 inches apart.
+ Bake the cookies until puffed, golden on the bottom, and still soft to the touch in the center, about 12 minutes.
+ Cool on the baking sheets for 5 minutes. Transfer to racks, and cool completely.

Fudge Quickies

My two oldest daughters, Deborah and Teresa, brought this recipe home from elementary school. It was one of the first cookies they made, because they could do these on their own. The cookies required no baking and were ready in less than 30 minutes. We all loved these, and the girls' fudge quickies soon became the go-to choice for lunches and snacks. Deb and Teresa taught their little sister, Dana, how to make them as soon as she was old enough. And Dana wanted to make sure this recipe was included in this book so she could pass it along to her children. Quick, easy, simple, and delicious. Most of the time my girls never added the nuts, coconut, or raisins.

MAKES 4½ DOZEN COOKIES

- 2 cups sugar
- ¼ cup cocoa
- ¼ cup butter
- ½ cup milk
- 3 cups quick-cooking rolled oats
- ½ cup peanut butter
- 1 teaspoon vanilla
- ½ cup chopped nuts, coconut, or raisins, optional

✦ In a saucepan over medium heat, combine the sugar, cocoa, butter, and milk, and bring to a boil. Boil for 1 minute.

✦ Remove the pan from the heat, and add the remaining ingredients.

✦ Drop the cookies onto waxed paper. Cool and enjoy.

Irresistible Peanut Butter Cookies

Debbie loves cookies, and they fast disappear when she is around. We call her the Cookie Monster. She is constantly on the lookout for new cookie recipes to see if they pass the taste test. These certainly did!

MAKES 3 DOZEN COOKIES

- ¾ cup peanut butter
- ½ cup Crisco®
- 1¼ cups brown sugar
- 3 Tablespoons milk
- 1 Tablespoon vanilla
- 1 egg
- 1¾ cups all-purpose flour
- ¾ teaspoon baking soda
- ¾ teaspoon sea salt

◆ Preheat the oven to 375 degrees.

◆ Combine the peanut butter, Crisco®, sugar, milk, and vanilla, blending well. Add the egg and mix in well.

◆ Combine the dry ingredients and add them to the creamed mixture. Using an electric mixer, beat on low speed until blended.

◆ Place rounded tablespoons of dough 2 inches apart on a greased baking sheet. Flatten the top a little with a fork.

◆ Bake for 7 to 8 minutes.

◆ Cool on the baking sheet for 2 minutes before removing to a cooling rack.

Lemon Cherry Cookies

We moved to the Santa Ynez Valley in January of 1980. My new neighbor, Colleen Stout, brought us these cookies at Christmas time. Jarvis fell in love with them, and Colleen shared the recipe with me. The Stout family has since moved to Washington State, but we stay in touch with Christmas cards. Most of all we continue to remember and reminisce with their cookies during the holidays!

I always double this recipe, and I use both red and green cherries. These cookies are not only delicious, but they're also very pretty on a Christmas tray.

MAKES 2 DOZEN COOKIES

- ½ cup butter
- ½ cup sugar
- 1 egg yolk—save egg white, slightly beaten for dipping
- 1 teaspoon grated lemon peel
- 1 Tablespoon lemon juice
- 1 cup unsifted all-purpose flour
- ½ cup finely chopped pecans
- 24 candied red cherries

- ◆ Preheat the oven to 325 degrees.
- ◆ Using an electric mixer, on medium speed, cream the butter and sugar until light and fluffy. Add the egg yolk, lemon peel, and juice, and beat until well blended. Gradually add the flour, and beat until well mixed. Turn the dough out onto waxed paper, wrap, and chill at least 3 hours. It's best if the dough is chilled overnight.
- ◆ Take 2 to 3 teaspoons of dough to make a ball the size you want the cookies to be.
- ◆ Dip each ball into slightly beaten egg white, and then roll it in the nuts. Place the balls on an ungreased cookie sheet.
- ◆ Use a wooden spoon handle to make an indentation in the top of your ball and press a cherry lightly into the top of the cookie. Do not press down too hard with the cherries. Because the cookies flatten out during baking, it is best to start with a ball.
- ◆ Bake for 15 minutes, or until lightly brown. Cool on a wire rack.

Peg's Coconut Macaroons

My family enjoys macaroons, so, of course, I had to try my own hand at them. Here are two great variations along with the standard almond. My husband, Jarvis, prefers macaroons with an almond flavor, but I like lemon and my daughters love chocolate. Now everyone has macaroons that they love!

MAKES ABOUT 2½ DOZEN COOKIES

For lemon macaroons

- 3 cups shredded coconut
- ⅔ cup condensed milk
- 1 Tablespoon grated lemon peel
- 1 teaspoon fresh lemon juice

For chocolate macaroons

- 3 cups shredded coconut
- ⅔ cup condensed milk
- 2 Tablespoons cocoa
- 1 teaspoon vanilla

For almond macaroons

- 3 cups shredded coconut
- ⅔ cup condensed milk
- 1 teaspoon almond extract

◆ Preheat the oven to 325 degrees.

◆ Combine the coconut, condensed milk, and other ingredients, according to the flavor you are making.

◆ Drop the cookies by teaspoons onto a parchment paper–lined cookie sheet.

◆ Bake for 9 to 11 minutes, or until slightly browned around the edges. They should only begin to get brown around the edges. Remove the cookies from the cookie sheet at once to cool on a wire rack.

Teresa's Apple Drop Cookies

This recipe is my daughter Teresa's absolute favorite holiday cookie. In fact, when the supply started to get low, we had to ask her permission to nibble one. The cookies stay nice and soft and have a Christmas spice flavor. Since my daughter Deborah does not like raisins, I sometimes substitute cranberries for the raisins. I personally prefer the cranberry version, but Teresa and her dad, Jarvis, are real diehards for the original recipe.

MAKES 4 DOZEN COOKIES

- ½ cup soft shortening
- 1⅓ cups brown sugar
- ½ teaspoon sea salt
- 1 teaspoon cinnamon
- 1 teaspoon ground cloves
- ½ teaspoon nutmeg
- 1 egg
- 2 cups pre-sifted all-purpose flour
- 1 teaspoon baking soda
- 1 cup chopped nuts
- 1 cup finely chopped apples
- 1 cup seedless raisins or dried cranberries
- ¼ cup milk

♦ Preheat the oven to 400 degrees.

♦ In a mixing bowl, combine the shortening, sugar, salt, spices, and egg. Beat well.

♦ Sift together the flour and baking soda.

♦ Stir half of the flour mixture into the egg mixture. Stir in the nuts, apples, and raisins.

♦ Blend in the milk. Add the remaining flour mixture. Drop the batter by tablespoons onto a greased cookie sheet.

♦ Bake 11 to 14 minutes, until light brown. Remove from the baking sheets, and cool on a wire rack.

Fruitcake Cookies

I love fruitcake, but I cannot eat a whole slice—not even a small slice—because it is just too rich for me. I like a little taste, so I created these fruitcake cookies for a Southern supper that I catered one Christmas. They were a big hit. Everyone loved that they could just pop the small bites into their mouth! These cookies ripen just like a fruitcake, and they freeze extremely well. You can make them in advance of the holidays, store them in freezer bags, and freeze them so they're ready for cookie platters at the holidays. I bake them in Christmas holly bon-bon cups, and they look very pretty on trays.

MAKES 10 DOZEN COOKIES

- ¼ cup butter
- ½ cup brown sugar
- ¼ cup jelly, any flavor – I use apple
- 2 eggs
- 2 teaspoons baking soda
- 1½ Tablespoons milk
- 1½ cups flour, divided
- ½ teaspoon allspice
- ½ teaspoon cloves
- ½ teaspoon cinnamon
- ½ teaspoon nutmeg
- 1 pound chopped pecans – not too small, plus additional whole pecans for decoration
- 1 pound seedless raisins
- ½ pound candied cherries, chopped, plus additional sliced cherries for decoration
- ½ pound candied pineapple, chopped
- ½ pound citron, chopped

✦ Preheat the oven to 300 degrees.

✦ Cream the butter, sugar, jelly, and eggs together. Dissolve the baking soda in milk, and add that to the creamed mixture.

✦ Sift half of the flour with the spices, and gradually add it to the creamed mixture.

✦ Dredge the nuts and fruit with the remaining flour, and stir them into the batter. Mix well.

✦ Drop the dough from a spoon into small paper bon-bon cups, and decorate the tops with sliced candied cherries and/or a whole pecan. If you prefer, you can drop the cookies onto a buttered and floured cookie sheet.

✦ Bake for approximately 20 minutes.

Mexican Wedding Ring Cookies

This is a recipe that came from my sister, Eloise. I have no idea where she got the recipe, but we have been making these cookies for over 40 years. I always double this recipe, as it is a favorite at Christmas time, when they go really fast. Eloise's original recipe just called for nuts, so since I was making them for Christmas, I chose pecans since they are especially plentiful at Christmas time. The family stuck with pecans. Feel free to use whatever nut you prefer. And, yes, I know these are called Wedding Ring Cookies, but I like to make mine in a crescent shape.

MAKES 3–4 DOZEN COOKIES

- 1 cup butter, at room temperature
- ¼ cup sugar
- 2 cups flour
- 1 teaspoon vanilla
- 1 cup finely chopped pecans
- Powdered sugar, for coating

- ✦ Preheat the oven to 325 degrees.
- ✦ Cream the butter, sugar, flour, and vanilla together. Stir in the nuts. Turn the dough out onto waxed paper, and chill for a few hours before handling.
- ✦ Roll about 2 teaspoons of the mixture into small balls or oblong shapes, and place them on an ungreased cookie sheet.
- ✦ Bake for 25 minutes.
- ✦ When they're done, remove the cookies from the cookie sheet, and roll them in powdered sugar while they are hot. Be careful that they don't crumble while you handle them. You might have to roll or coat them in the powdered sugar again to coat nicely.
- ✦ The number of cookies you get depends on the shape and size of your cookie.

PEG'S NOTES ~ I prefer to shape my cookies into crescents. To coat them, I place powdered sugar on the bottom of my cookie storage tin, then slide the cookies off the cookie sheet into the powdered sugar. I then heavily dust powdered sugar on top, so I can add another layer of cookies. I've found that my cookies do not break or crumble with this method, because I do not handle them until they are cool. The normal round shape holds up well but does not cook the same way and changes the taste of the cookies.

How finely you chop your nuts also will determine how well they hold up and how quickly the cookie crumbles.

During the holidays, when I am busy and want to make a lot of cookies, I prepare the dough and store it in waxed paper in the refrigerator until I am ready to bake. Then I bake cookies all day. This is especially handy when you have to make a lot of cookies for a bake sale or other event.

Peg's Blackberry Cobbler

This is a Fourth of July favorite. After the parade, I take my grandchildren to the U-pick blackberry patch and we all pick our blackberries. We come home and make our cobbler while Granddaddy is grilling. After the barbecue, we make homemade ice cream to serve with the cobbler. It would not be Fourth of July without this cobbler. Yum, Yum!

SERVES 8

Cobbler

- 1⅓ cup sugar
- ½ cup all-purpose flour
- ½ cup butter, melted
- 2 teaspoons vanilla extract
- 8 cups fresh blackberries, or 2 14-ounce bags frozen blackberries, unthawed

Pastry

- 1¾ cups self-rising flour
- 2-3 Tablespoons sugar
- ¼ cup butter
- ⅓ cup whipping cream
- ⅓ cup buttermilk
- 2 Tablespoons butter, melted
- 1 Tablespoon sugar

- ✦ Preheat the oven to 425 degrees.
- ✦ Prepare the fruit for the cobbler. In a large bowl, stir together the sugar, flour, butter, and vanilla. Gently stir in the blackberries until the sugar mixture is crumbly.
- ✦ Spoon the fruit mixture into a lightly buttered 11 by 7-inch baking dish or a 2½-quart casserole dish.
- ✦ Prepare the pastry. Combine the flour and sugar, and add the baking powder and salt, if using—see Peg's Notes. Cut in the butter with a pastry blender, until the mixture is crumbly. Stir in the whipping cream and buttermilk.
- ✦ On a lightly floured surface, knead the dough 4 or 5 times, and roll it into a large biscuit the size of your baking dish or casserole. Place it over the fruit.
- ✦ Brush the pastry with the melted butter and sprinkle with the sugar. Line a baking sheet or large dish with foil, and place the baking dish with the cobbler on it. The foil will catch any overflow from the cobbler.
- ✦ Bake for 20 minutes, or until the pastry is golden. Cover with foil, so the pastry does not get too brown, and continue baking for 25 minutes. The total baking time is 45 minutes.

PEG'S NOTES ~

I love this recipe because you can prepare it, freeze it, and then bake it while your guests are eating dinner.

You can use all-purpose flour instead of self-rising flour, but add 2 teaspoons baking powder and 1 teaspoon salt.

Peg's Upside-Down Apple Pie

This recipe has a funny story behind it. Not only was a great dessert born, but also my new husband learned a lesson about cleaning up after himself. Jarvis and I were married in 1966, and shortly thereafter he invited his boss and his wife to dinner. I was a 22-year old who thought she was a pretty good cook, but I was still very nervous about making a meal for his boss from Proctor & Gamble.

I definitely had not mastered the art of piecrust making, but I attempted to make one for an apple pie. Wouldn't you know it? The piecrust looked awful, but I thought the bottom would be nice and smooth, so I tried to turn it over. Now it looked like I had dropped the pie! I ended up calling my mother in Alabama, crying as I told her what I'd done. Mom came to my rescue! She told me to make a caramel topping of brown sugar with pecans and put it on the pie. She promised that everyone would love it. You guessed it… the dessert was a great hit, and it's still a staple at our Thanksgiving feast, and a sought-after item at charity auctions where it brings $75. It's my absolute favorite apple pie. Serve it warm with ice cream, and you are in heaven.

It took me many, many years before I attempted another piecrust from scratch. Instead, I used Pillsbury® Pie Crusts. Now, though, I have a wonderful recipe, courtesy of Bernice Frisby in Lompoc. At 95 years old, Bernice is the pie maker of all pie makers. She taught me not to be afraid to tackle this pastry.

And my husband? We lived in a two-bedroom house with only one bathroom. After he showered, he left his underwear on the floor, thinking that I would pick up after him. Of course, I never did. He nearly died of humiliation when he found out that his boss's wife had seen his underwear where he had dropped them. He got mad at me for leaving them there, but I told him that if I had noticed them on the floor, I would have hung them on the front doorknob for the whole world to see. Nothing like that ever happened again!

PEG'S NOTES ~ A flat serving dish will not work for this pie; the pie will just fall flat. If the serving plate is indented, then the top of the pie will fit into it. I bake this pie in a 10-inch Pyrex® deep-dish pie plate, and after 45 minutes I check to make sure that the brown sugar mixture on the bottom is bubbly, making a nice caramel nut topping. You do not want to burn the nuts, so do not let it get too brown on the bottom.

I also found that if you wait too long to invert the pie, the caramel hardens and sticks on the bottom of the pie plate instead of on the top of your pie. The true trick to this pie is timing.

I place a piece of aluminum foil under the oven rack where the pie is baking to catch any caramel that boils over.

MAKES A 10-INCH PIE

Mother Infield's Piecrust—page 163 —you need 2 crusts

6 Tablespoons butter

⅔ cup firmly packed light brown sugar

1¼ cups chopped pecans

2½ pounds Rome Beauty or Fuji apples, peeled, cored, and sliced thin

1 teaspoon cinnamon

¼ cup sugar

1 Tablespoon plus 1 teaspoon flour

◆ Preheat the oven to 350 degrees.

◆ In a skillet, heat the butter over moderately low heat, until melted and hot. Stir in the brown sugar and pecans. Cook the mixture, stirring for 1 minute.

◆ Pour into a 10-inch deep-dish pie plate, and cool slightly. When the mixture is cool, arrange the larger round of pie dough over the nuts, leaving a ½-inch overhang on the plate.

◆ Combine the cinnamon, sugar, and flour, mixing well. In a large bowl, sprinkle and toss the apple slices with this mixture until well combined.

◆ Place the apple mixture on the dough in the pie plate. Arrange the second round of dough over the apple mixture, and roll the bottom layer up over the top layer, pressing the dough edges together. Trim off any excess dough, and crimp the edges as decoratively as you like.

◆ Make several incisions in the dough to allow steam to escape.

◆ Bake for 45 to 55 minutes, or until the crust is golden. Immediately invert the pie onto an indented serving dish.

◆ To invert the pie, place the serving dish over the pie. Using pot holders, hold the pie plate and the serving dish together as you turn the pie. Then take forks and very carefully lift your pie plate off the pie, trying not to disturb the topping.

Pineapple Macadamia Pie

Jarvis and I had only been married for one year, and I already wanted to prepare something different for the holidays. This pie made its first Thanksgiving appearance on my table in 1967. Macadamia nuts, with their distinctive flavor and crisp texture, replace pecans. Many years later I found out that a slightly different version of this dessert is the traditional nut pie for Thanksgiving in Hawaii.

SERVES 8

- Pastry for 9-inch pie, Mother Infield's piecrust—page 163
- 3 eggs
- ⅔ cups sugar
- 1 cup light corn syrup
- ¼ cup melted butter
- 1 teaspoon vanilla
- ½ teaspoon sea salt
- 1 cup drained pineapple tidbits
- 1 cup chopped macadamia nuts, plus additional halves for decorating
- Whipped cream, for topping

✦ Preheat the oven to 350 degrees.

✦ Place a piecrust over a 9-inch pie plate. Turn any overlap under, and flute the edges as desired. Set aside and mix the ingredients for the filling.

✦ In a mixer, beat together the eggs, sugar, syrup, butter, vanilla, and salt until thoroughly mixed.

✦ Stir in the pineapple and nuts.

✦ Pour the filling into the piecrust. Bake for 45 minutes, or until set.

✦ Cool thoroughly on a rack before cutting. Top with whipped cream when you serve.

PEG'S NOTES ~ *I save some of the halves of the macadamia nuts and place them on top of the pie filling just before baking. Take a fork and press the halves down in the syrupy mixture to coat the nuts so they brown nicely. This makes for a much prettier pie presentation.*

Be sure to drain the pineapple tidbits well so you don't have extra liquid in the pie.

Glazed Strawberry Pie

I enjoy creating special recipes for special people in my life. As I mentioned earlier, my sister Eloise loves strawberries, so I created this pie for her birthday. It immediately became her absolute favorite, so I fix it every year for her birthday. She tells people that this pie is what she wants for her last meal on earth! Quite an endorsement!

SERVES 8

- 1 baked 9-inch pie shell—you can use Mother Infield's piecrust—page 163
- 1½ quarts fresh strawberries, 6 cups
- 1¼ cups water
- 1¼ cups sugar, divided
- 4 Tablespoons cornstarch
- 1 Tablespoon butter
- 1 teaspoon red food coloring, approximately
- Whipped cream, for topping

♦ Wash, drain, and hull the strawberries, and set them aside. Crush 2 cups of the berries and combine them with the water.

♦ Mix ¼ cup of the sugar with the cornstarch. Combine both mixtures in a heavy saucepan, and bring to the boiling point. Cook until the mixture is clear and thick.

♦ Stir in the remaining cup of sugar to make a shiny glaze. Add the butter and enough food coloring to make the color bright and attractive. Cool thoroughly.

♦ Fill the baked pie shell with the remaining berries, arranging them so that the berries are standing up. Cover the berries with the glaze, making sure that all berries are covered. Chill immediately. Just before serving, top with whipped cream.

PEG'S NOTES ~ Be sure all the ingredients are thoroughly cool before assembling the pie. By adding the balance of the sugar after the mixture thickens, you create a nice shiny glaze. I glaze my strawberries as I arrange each row, making sure that every berry is covered. If your strawberries are really large, use a 10-inch deep-dish pie plate and crust.

PIES, PUDDINGS, AND OTHER PASTRIES | 159

Coconut Cream Pie

I will never forget the first time that I received a request for a coconut cream pie. A dear customer and friend asked me to make one for her birthday. I insisted that I was not a pie baker and tried desperately to talk her into a dessert that I felt I was good at, but she wanted no part of that. So I headed off to my test kitchen to see what I could come up with. After many failures, I came up with this recipe. For my friend, it was a huge success. She has ordered this pie for the last 10 years and has spread the word among her friends, so I get numerous requests. Enjoy!

SERVES 8

- 1 baked 9-inch pastry shell— see Mother Infield's piecrust — page 163
- Powdered sugar, for dusting
- ¾ cup sugar
- ¼ cup, plus 2 teaspoons cornstarch
- ⅛ teaspoon sea salt
- 3 egg yolks, beaten
- 1½ cups whipping cream
- 1½ cups fat-free milk
- 2 Tablespoons butter
- 2 teaspoons vanilla
- 1 cup flaked coconut
- 1 cup whipping cream
- ½ cup sifted powdered sugar
- ⅓ cup large organic coconut flakes, toasted, for topping

- ◆ Dust the baked piecrust with powdered sugar, which prevents it from getting soggy. Set aside until needed
- ◆ In a heavy saucepan, combine the sugar, cornstarch, and salt.
- ◆ Combine the egg yolks with the milk and whipping cream, and gradually stir the liquid into the sugar mixture. Cook over medium heat, stirring constantly, until the mixture thickens and boils. Boil for about 3 minutes, stirring constantly. Remove from the heat; stir in the butter, vanilla, and flaked coconut.
- ◆ Cover the filling with plastic wrap and cool for 30 minutes, then chill until firm.
- ◆ Fill the piecrust with chilled filling.
- ◆ With an electric mixer, beat the whipping cream at medium speed until foamy. Gradually add the powdered sugar, beating until soft peaks form. Spread the whipped cream over the chilled filling. Sprinkle with toasted coconut flakes. Keep chilled until ready to serve.

Peg's Hawaiian Cream Pie

- ◆ For Peg's Hawaiian Cream Pie, place 3 sliced ripe bananas in the bottom of the baked pie shell before adding the filling. Sprinkle toasted macadamia nuts along with the coconut on top of the whipped cream.

Peg's Double Coconut Cream Pie

- ◆ For Peg's Double Coconut Cream Pie, replace the fat-free milk with cream of coconut!

PEG'S NOTES ~ To toast your coconut flakes, place them on a cookie sheet in a 350-degree oven for about 10 minutes. Watch and stir the flakes during this time so they do not burn or get too brown. I like large organic coconut flakes for decoration because they just brown a little around the edges and are beautiful. You can substitute regular coconut for the large flakes but they will toast much faster and can burn quickly. If you prefer, forego the toasting altogether.

You can substitute Cool Whip for the whipped cream topping, especially if you have to transport the pie in the heat. Cool Whip will hold up much better. My daughters find this option quick and easy, and the pie is just as good. Some people cannot tell the difference.

Peg's Mud Pie

Mud pie has always been one of my favorite things to order in a restaurant, and when I am having guests over for dinner, I like to treat them to my own version of the dessert. After all, everybody loves ice cream. When I found out that I was allergic to coffee, I had to change out the flavors in the pie, and I discovered that this recipe could be the basis for several great versions. Take a look at my notes to see how versatile you can be.

SERVES 8

- ½ 9-ounce package Nabisco Chocolate Wafers, about 20 wafers
- ¼ cup butter, melted
- 1 quart mocha ice cream, softened
- 1 quart chocolate ice cream softened
- 1½ cups purchased fudge sauce
- Whipped cream, for topping
- Sliced almonds, for topping

✦ Crush the wafers, and mix well with the butter. Press the mixture into a 9-inch cheesecake spring-form pan.

✦ Cover with 1 quart of softened ice cream, and return it to the freezer to firm up before adding a second layer of ice cream.

✦ Remove the pie from the freezer and add the second quart of ice cream. Return it to the freezer until the ice cream is firm.

✦ Top with cold fudge sauce. Store in the freezer for at least 10 hours.

✦ Serve on a chilled dessert plate with a chilled fork. Top each slice of pie with whipped cream and sliced almonds.

PEG'S NOTES ~ It does not matter which flavor ice cream you start with. The order depends on how you want the pie to look. I found that putting the fudge sauce in the freezer for a short time to chill it helped it spread over the cold ice cream.

I have lots of flavorful variations. For the kids, I use strawberry/vanilla or banana/chocolate. I also use the chocolate candy ice creams, rocky road, or even nutty coconut along with the regular chocolate ice cream. Pineapple/coconut ice cream with lemon ice cream is also delicious.

You can make the cake higher by adding another quart of ice cream, but you will need to make the rim of your pan higher, too, by adding a band of aluminum foil—folded so that it is stiff—around the inside of the pan. The foil should stick up over the sides by 2 to 3 inches, depending on the number of ice cream layers. Feel free to mix it up with the nuts. You can substitute pistachios, walnuts, pecans, and/or peanuts. I try to match the nuts with the flavor of ice cream. I also change out the nuts for chocolate sprinkles, coconut flakes, or M&Ms.

Make your own Pegilicious!® memories!

Mother Infield's Piecrust

This piecrust recipe came from my 95-year-old friend, Bernice Frisby, of Lompoc, California, a master of pie baking, who got it from her mother. Bernice has several apple trees, and every year she brings my husband a homemade apple pie for his birthday. We can't wait to get them.

This is a tried-and true recipe for piecrust. With these instructions, you will never fail.

MAKES 3 CRUSTS

- 3 cups flour
- 1 cup chilled shortening—I use half lard and half Crisco®, or you can use 2 sticks of butter
- 1 teaspoon salt
- 1 beaten egg
- 5 Tablespoons cold water
- 1 Tablespoon white vinegar

- ✦ Mix the flour, shortening or butter, and salt until crumbly.
- ✦ Beat the egg, water, and vinegar together.
- ✦ Add the egg mixture to the flour mixture and mix.
- ✦ Divide the dough into three discs, wrap them in waxed paper, and chill them before rolling one out.

For a baked piecrust:

- ✦ Preheat the oven to 450 degrees.
- ✦ Place rolled piecrust in pie plate, fold edges under and flute. Prick bottom and side with fork.
- ✦ Bake 10 to 12 minutes or until light brown.
- ✦ Cool before filling.

PEG'S NOTES ~ This is a soft dough, so chilling is necessary. You can freeze it, too, if you aren't going to use it right away. I keep some in the freezer, so that I have homemade crust anytime I need it.

When I use butter, I freeze it, then, using a box grater, grate the butter over the flour and stir it in with a fork before adding the liquid.

PEG'S TIPS FOR A PERFECT PIECRUST

Start with cold ingredients – Chill the shortening and/or butter; you want to cut the shortening into the flour without melting it.

Handle with care – Overworking causes the dough to be tough.

Add ice water gradually – Too much water makes the crust tough; not enough and it will crack. Add any additional cold water very gradually.

Turn the dough after every few rolls of the pin – Then ease the crust into the pie plate without stretching the dough, which will cause the piecrust to shrink.

Chill the crust before baking – This will also prevent shrinkage.

Peg's Mini Cheesecakes

The recipe originated from Ruth Ann, and I believe that she got it from her mother, Wilma. I needed a dessert that was delicious and could be eaten without forks and plates. I've since found many uses for the versatile dough. It is also fun to experiment with a variety of fillings.

MAKES ABOUT 4½ DOZEN TARTS

Dough for crust

- 1 cup butter, 2 sticks
- 6 ounces cream cheese
- 2 cups all-purpose flour
- 4 Tablespoons ice water

Cheesecake filling

- 24 ounces cream cheese
- 1 cup sugar
- 4 eggs
- 1 teaspoon vanilla

Topping

- Whipped cream, or Cool Whip
- Sliced strawberries

✦ Preheat the oven to 375 degrees.

✦ Prepare the dough. In a mixing bowl, cream the butter and cream cheese.

✦ Add the flour and the ice water, one tablespoon at a time, until the dough forms. Refrigerate for 1 hour before handling.

✦ Pinch out one spoonful of dough at a time to make a small ball, then, using your thumb, press the ball into mini-tart pans, or use the end of the mini-tart tool that is pictured below, to form the crust. Add the filling before baking.

✦ For the filling, in a large mixing bowl, beat the cream cheese with the sugar until fluffy. Add the eggs one at a time, mixing slowly until well blended after each addition.

✦ Mix in the vanilla. Pour the filling into the crusts.

✦ Bake for 20 minutes. If you're baking more than two pans at a time in the same oven, you will need to add to the baking time or rotate the pans in the oven after 10 minutes.

✦ Cool the cheesecakes well before adding a topping of a sliced strawberry and whipped cream or Cool Whip.

PEG'S NOTES ~ The dough recipe can easily be doubled to make 9 1/2 dozen tarts. To fill the doubled dough recipe, you will need only 1 1/2 recipes of filling.

When baking, the filling will puff up and sometimes might crack, but that is okay since the top will be covered with the whipped cream and fruit. Mix the eggs only until well blended. Beating them too much adds a lot of air and also causes the cheesecake to crack during baking.

Other fruit can be used for the topping, but strawberries are readily available, stand up well, are tasty, and make a great presentation.

You can use this same dough for the Mini Pecan Tarts on page 166.

There is a special wooden mini-tart dough tool—if you can find it in your area—that makes it a lot easier to shape the dough in the tart pan.

Peg's Mini Pecan Tarts

I am known for my Southern Pecan Pie, which I make only at Thanksgiving. My family and clients were craving it at other times of the year, though, so I created this tart recipe. The tarts are particularly nice because you only get a bite of the rich filling. Of course, if you want a bit more sweetness, you could have more than one! These are also great for a buffet.

MAKES 20 TARTS

Pastry

- 3 ounces cream cheese
- ½ cup butter
- 1 cup unsifted all-purpose flour
- 1–2 Tablespoons ice water

Filling

- 1 egg
- ¼ cup firmly packed brown sugar
- ⅓ cup light corn syrup
- ½ teaspoon vanilla
- 1½ teaspoons bourbon, optional
- 2 Tablespoons melted butter
- ½ cup chopped pecans
- 20 whole pecans, for garnish

- Prepare the pastry. Beat the cream cheese and butter until smooth.
- Add the flour and ice water, one tablespoon at a time, mixing well until the dough forms. Shape the dough into a ball. Chill for at least 2 hours.
- Shape the dough into 20 small balls, and put each ball into a non-stick mini-tart pan. Press the dough evenly onto the bottom and sides of each tart pan to form the crust. Chill until ready to bake.
- Prepare the filling. Beat the egg, add the sugar, and beat again until well blended.
- Add the corn syrup, vanilla, bourbon, if using, and melted butter, and mix well.
- Divide the chopped pecans among the 20 tart shells. Spoon the egg-sugar mixture over the chopped nuts in the shells. Top each with a whole pecan.
- Set the oven temperature to 350 degrees, and place the tart pans into the cold oven. Bake for 25 minutes, or until golden brown. Remove the tarts from the oven, and let them stand in the pans for about 5 minutes, then remove each tart to a cooling rack.

PEG'S NOTES ~ I always use bourbon for a true Southern pecan flavor.

The recipe can be easily doubled, if needed. If you do not have non-stick mini-tart pans, then be sure to grease your pan well. If any filling runs over during cooking, loosen that tart before it cools, or the sides will stick and tear apart when you try to remove the tart.

They make a special wooden mini-tart dough tool—if you can find it in your area—that makes it a lot easier to form the crust. See the photo on page 165.

Peg's Fudgy Fudge Pudding

I worked with Margaret Sears to create this **Pegilicious!®** *pudding and perfected it over the years. It's another quick, simple, and delicious dessert. My husband loves this pudding!*

SERVES 8

Batter

- 1½ cups flour, sifted
- ¾ teaspoon sea salt
- ¾ cup sugar
- 2 teaspoons baking powder
- 3 Tablespoons cocoa
- 1 teaspoon vanilla
- 6 Tablespoons butter, softened
- 1 cup milk
- ½ cup chopped nuts, optional

Sauce

- ½ cup brown sugar, packed
- ¾ cup light corn syrup
- 3 Tablespoons cocoa
- 1 teaspoon vanilla
- 1 cup, plus 2 Tablespoons boiling water
- Whipped cream for topping

- ✦ Preheat the oven to 325 degrees.
- ✦ Prepare the batter. Combine the flour, salt, sugar, baking powder, and cocoa.
- ✦ Work in the vanilla, butter, milk, and nuts, if using.
- ✦ Place the batter into a 9 by 9-inch greased pan. Set it aside, and make the sauce.
- ✦ Prepare the sauce. Combine the sugar, syrup, cocoa, and vanilla, and mix well. Bring the measured water to a boil, and add it to the sauce mixture. Stir and mix thoroughly. Pour the sauce gently over the batter in the pan.
- ✦ Bake for 45 minutes to 1 hour. Check after 45 minutes. A toothpick placed in the center should come out clean.
- ✦ Invert onto a plate, and serve upside down with whipped cream.

Peg's Famous Cream Puffs

Cream puffs traditionally have a vanilla cream filling, but I often use these cream puffs for my Famous Crab Salad on page 50, as well as for a variety of other fillings. I make the puffs in different sizes and shapes to match the filling I am going to use.

MAKES APPROXIMATELY 40 PUFFS

- 2 cups water
- 1 cup butter
- 2 cups all-purpose flour
- ¼ teaspoon sea salt
- 8 eggs

+ Preheat the oven to 400 degrees.

+ Place the water and butter in a large saucepan, and bring to a boil. Vigorously stir in the flour and salt. Cook, beating, over low heat, for 1 to 3 minutes, or until the mixture forms a ball. Remove from the heat.

+ Place the mixture into the large bowl of an electric mixer, or use a hand-held electric mixer. Beat in the eggs, one at a time, beating well after each addition, and continue beating until smooth.

+ Drop the dough by rounded spoonfuls onto greased cookie sheets, forming mounds 2 to 3 inches apart, depending on the size of your puff.

+ Bake for 10 minutes. Lower the heat to 350 degrees, and bake for 25 minutes more.

+ The puffs are ready when they are doubled in size, golden brown, and firm to the touch. Remove the puffs from the oven, and cut partway through the side of each puff with a sharp knife. Return the puffs to the turned-off oven. Keep the oven door ajar, and let the puffs stand in the oven for another 10 minutes. Cool the puffs on racks. Fill with Vanilla Cream or your favorite filling.

PEG'S NOTES ~ *Instead of using the drop method, I use my pastry bag and different size tips and shapes to make the shape of puff I want. Just squeeze the dough through the pastry tube onto the greased cookie sheet and proceed with the cooking instructions.*

I also use a hand-held mixer and beat my eggs in the same saucepan as the flour; it saves on cleanup.

Vanilla Cream Puff Filling

MAKES APPROXIMATELY 4 CUPS

- 3½ Tablespoons cornstarch
- ⅔ cup sugar
- 2½ cups milk
- 3 egg yolks
- 1 teaspoon vanilla
- 1 cup whipping cream
- 2 Tablespoons sugar
- ½ teaspoon vanilla

✦ In a medium saucepan, combine the cornstarch and sugar. Gradually blend in the milk, and bring to a boil, stirring constantly. Cook and stir the mixture over very low heat for 1 minute, or until it thickens and the cornstarch is cooked.

✦ In a small bowl, lightly beat the egg yolks and blend in 2 tablespoons of the cooked cornstarch mixture. Blend the egg mixture into the remaining cornstarch mixture in the saucepan. Cook, stirring, over very low heat for 2 minutes, or until the egg yolks are cooked. Do not boil.

✦ Remove the mixture from the heat and stir in the vanilla. Cover the surface with waxed paper or plastic wrap, and cool.

✦ Beat the whipping cream with sugar and vanilla until stiff peaks form. Fold the whipped cream into the cool custard.

PEG'S NOTES ~ To make **Chocolate Cream Filling**, melt 3 ounces—3 squares—of unsweetened chocolate in the milk, and beat until smooth. Proceed as directed above.

I was unable to find cannoli sticks, so my husband, Jarvis, made me some by cutting 1-inch dowel rods into 5-inch lengths. They have worked so well over the years that I would not go out and buy professional cannoli sticks today. These rods do not burn, and they are so seasoned now that my shells just slide off with very little effort. You can tell I love them!

Cottone Cannoli

In 1975, Toni Cottone, age 75, told me that she wanted me to have her "old Italian family secret recipe" for cannoli. Toni told me I was the only one she knew who would go to the trouble of making them from scratch. She knew I would respect her recipe. She taught me to make these the old-fashioned way. I had to promise Toni that I would never share this recipe until I died. But the only way I know to share it is to put it in print now, so it will be here after I am long gone.

The same year that Toni gave me the recipe, she painted and signed a pair of salt and pepper shakers and a beautiful butter dish. I still put them out on my table for fancy celebrations. Toni passed away many years ago, and I cherish not only this recipe but also many other fond memories of her.

MAKES 3 DOZEN CANNOLI

Shell

- 3 cups flour
- 2 eggs yolks, beaten—save egg whites
- 3 Tablespoons sugar
- 1 teaspoon cinnamon
- 4 Tablespoons butter
- 2 teaspoons vanilla
- ⅔ cup red wine
- Oil and Crisco® for frying

Filling

- 2 pounds ricotta cheese
- ½ pound powdered sugar, 8 ounces, plus extra for dusting
- 1 bar chocolate, chopped, or mini chocolate chips
- Candied citrus fruit, or chopped nuts

- ✦ Mix the shell ingredients in the order listed, until well blended.
- ✦ Roll out the dough until thin, and cut it into 4-inch circles. Roll the circles around the cannoli sticks.
- ✦ Use the beaten egg whites to close the circle around the sticks.
- ✦ Deep-fry the shells in a mixture of oil and Crisco® until light brown. Cool them slightly. Using a pot holder to protect your hands, loosen the shell from the stick by twisting it back and forth very carefully, so that you do not break the seal or crumble the shell. Slide the cannoli shell off the stick, and cool before filling.
- ✦ Prepare the filling. Whip the cheese with the powdered sugar and mix in the rest of the ingredients.
- ✦ Pipe the filling into the cannoli shell with a pastry bag, and sprinkle with powdered sugar when ready to serve. If you don't have a pastry bag, fill a Ziploc® bag and cut off a corner to make one.

PEG'S NOTES ~ *I do not use the citrus fruit that the traditional Italians put in cannoli. I substitute chopped nuts for the fruit. And I use mini chocolate chips instead of chopping up a chocolate bar. My substitutions fit my family's taste.*

Please do not use cheap wine for the shell, as the quality will affect the taste of your final product. I always save some of the expensive wine that my guests have loved at a dinner party. That way I know they will love my cannoli, too.

PIES, PUDDINGS, AND OTHER PASTRIES | 171

Aebleskiver

We live within three miles of Solvang, sometimes called the Danish capital of the United States. My daughter belonged to local Girl Scout Troop 556—I was a troop leader—and when the girls had to earn a cooking badge, we decided to make aebleskiver, a kind of Danish doughnut. They cooked these pastries at the Little Mermaid Restaurant in town, and their picture appeared in the National Girl Scout Calendar, for August, in 1985. I am including both the girls' quick recipe and the original Danish version.

MAKES ABOUT 24 DOUGHNUTS

- 2 cups Bisquick®
- 2 eggs
- ¼ cup sugar
- 1¼ cups milk
- Oil for cooking
- Powdered sugar, for sprinkling

✦ Gently blend all the ingredients in a blender.

✦ Pour 1 teaspoon of the cooking oil into each cup of an aebleskiver pan, and get it hot over moderate heat.

✦ Fill each cup of the hot aebleskiver pan ⅔ full with the batter—about 2 tablespoons in each cup. Cook over moderate heat until the edge begins to bubble and the dough browns on the bottom. Turn each pastry a half turn with a pick.

✦ Continue to make half turns, until the aebleskiver is in a ball and completely brown and cooked. Remove to a plate and sprinkle with powder sugar.

Standing left to right: Renee Richard, Alexis Strangman, Dana Ivy, Danielle Holmstrom, Jennifer West, and Krista Jennings with the owner of the Little Mermaid, Gerd Dalby

Seated at table: Echo Benham and Jennifer Austin

PEG'S NOTES ~ The traditional aebleskiver has thick raspberry jam, a small piece of cooked apple, or a thick plum sauce pressed into each cup of batter before it's turned. You can even add chocolate chips.

We chose to serve fruit jams on the side, so that the dough was easier for the girls to handle. We also got ice picks with wooden handles for the girls to use. The wooden handles did not get hot, and the girls were able to prick and turn the doughnut without tearing up the dough. I still use wooden-handled ice picks today and often give them as gifts along with a pan.

Traditional Danish Aebleskiver

MAKES ABOUT 36 DOUGHNUTS

- 4 eggs, separated
- 1 Tablespoon sugar
- 2 cups cake flour
- ½ teaspoon sea salt
- 1 teaspoon baking powder
- ¼ cup butter, melted
- Scant 2 cups milk—just short of 2 cups
- Jam for filling, optional

✦ Beat the egg yolks until light. Add the sugar, and beat until thickened.

✦ Sift together the flour, salt, and baking powder, and add to the egg mixture, alternating with the melted butter and milk.

✦ Beat the egg whites until soft, and fold into batter.

✦ Pour 1 teaspoon of the cooking oil into each cup of an aebleskiver pan, and get it hot over moderate heat.

✦ Fill each cup of an aebleskiver pan ⅔ full with the batter—about 2 tablespoons. Cook over moderate heat until bubbly, turning with a fork, bamboo skewer, ice pick, or similar tool, making half turns until the doughnut is completely round and cooked on all sides. If you're using a jam filling, press some into each cup of batter before turning.

✦ Serve with syrup, honey, or jam.

Dana's training in Girls Scouts enabled her to continue cooking aebleskivers into adulthood. She was my pro at parties.

PEG'S NOTES ~ The very best pan to use is the traditional iron Danish aebleskiver pan. The iron keeps the heat constant, so that the doughnut browns evenly on all sides and the aebleskiver does not stick.

Use your imagination as to the fillings; savory fillings make great appetizers. I never fill my aebleskiver, however; I serve homemade fruit and berry toppings on the side. That way guests can enjoy the filling of their choice.

Peg's Walnut and Rum Baklava

Talk about being creative, this was created when I had leftover phyllo dough and was trying to figure out what to do with it. Phyllo dough cannot be easily saved or stored after you open the package. You have to use it.

This baklava is terrific when served warm with ice cream.

SERVES 8

- 1¼ cups walnut halves
- ½ cup dry plain bread crumbs
- ½ teaspoon grated lemon rind
- ½ cup sugar, plus 1 Tablespoon for topping
- ½ cup butter, melted
- ¼ cup rum
- 8 phyllo pastry sheets

- ✦ Preheat the oven to 375 degrees.
- ✦ Grind the walnuts in a food processor. Add the bread crumbs, lemon rind, and ½ cup sugar, and process until well blended.
- ✦ Mix in 2 tablespoons of the melted butter and the rum.
- ✦ Brush an 8-inch round cake pan with a bit of the remaining butter.
- ✦ Cover the bottom of the pan with one sheet of phyllo. Fit the dough into the pan, and brush lightly with butter. Layer 5 more sheets of the dough on top, brushing each layer lightly with butter and scattering each with 1/5 of the walnut mixture.
- ✦ Cover with the two remaining sheets of dough, brushing each with butter. Tuck them in around the edges. Brush the top with butter and bake for 35 to 45 minutes, or until golden in color and crisp.
- ✦ Sprinkle the remaining tablespoon of sugar on top, and let the baklava stand on a wire rack for 15 minutes.
- ✦ Cut into wedges and serve warm. Great with ice cream.

PEG'S NOTES ~ You can refrigerate the torte for 5 to 10 minutes to set the chocolate glaze prior to piping on the white chocolate. Don't leave it too long, or the butter in the glaze will chill and give your chocolate a whitish appearance.

I also use this Chocolate Glaze with nuts to make truffles at Christmas.

Southern Pecan Torte

WITH CHOCOLATE GLAZE

Here's another wonderful gluten–free dessert that was created using the Southern pecans and chocolate that I love. I have served this torte for numerous birthday celebrations and even took it to Florida for a birthday party for a friend. So I can attest that this is not only **Pegilicious!**® *but it also travels well.*

SERVES 12–16

- Flour, for dusting
- 1 cup butter – NO substitutions
- 1⅓ cups semisweet chocolate chips
- 6 eggs
- 1 cup sugar
- 1½ cups toasted pecans
- 1 cup sifted unsweetened cocoa powder
- ¼ cup Kahlúa®
- Chocolate Glaze
- 2 ounces white baking chocolate, chopped
- ¾ cup chopped toasted pecans

- ✦ Preheat the oven to 350 degrees.
- ✦ Grease a 9-inch spring-form pan. Line the bottom of the pan with parchment paper, and grease the paper.
- ✦ Dust the pan and paper with flour. In a heavy, small saucepan combine the butter and chocolate. Melt over low heat until smooth. Set the pan and chocolate mixture aside.
- ✦ Place the eggs and sugar in a food processor bowl, and process until smooth. Add the pecans, and process until nearly smooth, less than 1 minute.
- ✦ Add the melted chocolate mixture, cocoa powder, and liqueur; process just until combined, scraping down the sides as necessary.
- ✦ Spread the batter into the prepared pan.
- ✦ Bake 35 to 40 minutes, or until the sides are puffed and set about 2 inches in from edge of pan. Completely cool in the pan on a wire rack.
- ✦ Loosen the side of the pan and remove it. Invert the cake onto a wire rack placed over a baking sheet, and remove the paper.
- ✦ Pour warm Chocolate Glaze over the cake, covering the top and sides.
- ✦ Place the chopped white chocolate in a glass bowl. Microwave the chocolate, uncovered, on low for 1½ minutes, or just until melted, stirring every 30 seconds.
- ✦ Pour the melted white chocolate into a non-pleated plastic bag. Snip one corner of the bag to make a small opening. Starting at the center of the cake, pipe a spiral to the outer edge. Using a toothpick, gently swirl the white lines.
- ✦ Press the pecans onto the sides of the cake. When they're set, transfer the cake to a serving plate.
- ✦ Cover and store in the refrigerator up to 3 days.

CHOCOLATE GLAZE

- 6 Tablespoons butter, divided
- 1 Tablespoon light corn syrup
- 1 cup semisweet chocolate chips
- 2 Tablespoons Kahlúa®

- ✦ In a heavy medium saucepan, melt 3 tablespoons of the butter with the syrup over low heat, stirring occasionally.
- ✦ Stir in the chocolate chips until melted and smooth; remove from the heat.
- ✦ Add the remaining 3 tablespoons of butter and the Kahlúa®; whisk until smooth.

Japanese Fresh Fruit Cake

Aunt Vera and Uncle Olen had eight children, and when Uncle Olen and their oldest son, Johnny, were killed in an accident, Aunt Vera had to find a way to support her seven other children. Fortunately, they lived in a fairly large house in Villa Rica, Georgia, so she turned it into a boarding house. For many years, she cooked for the residents who lived there. This was one of her most popular desserts.

SERVES 12

For the first 3 layers
- 1 cup butter
- 1 Tablespoon shortening
- 3 cups sugar
- 4 cups self-rising flour
- 1½ cups milk
- 6 eggs

For 2 additional layers
- 2 cups raisins
- 1 pound ground pecans
- 1 pound ground walnuts
- 1 teaspoon cloves
- ½ teaspoon nutmeg
- ½ teaspoon cinnamon
- ½ teaspoon allspice

Filling
- 2 large fresh coconuts, flesh grated
- 2 lemons—you need the rind of 1 and the pulp of 2
- 2 oranges—you need the rind of 1 and the pulp of 2
- 3 cups sugar
- 1 8-ounce can crushed pineapple in natural juices
- 1 10-ounce jar of Maraschino cherries, juice drained and reserved
- 1½ cups milk
- 1½ teaspoons flour

- ✦ Preheat the oven to 350 degrees.
- ✦ Grease and flour 3 9-inch cake pans.
- ✦ Cream the butter, shortening, and sugar together. Alternately add in the flour and milk, ending with milk.
- ✦ Gently blend in the eggs.
- ✦ Pour just enough batter in the 3 cake pans to fill them up halfway. You are only going to bake 3 layers first, saving the remaining batter to be mixed with the ingredients for the additional two layers.
- ✦ Bake the first 3 layers for 25 to 30 minutes.
- ✦ Cool for 10 minutes. Remove from pan and place on wire rack to finish cooling. Regrease and flour 2 pans for next 2 layers.
- ✦ Mix raisins, pecans, walnuts, cloves, nutmeg, cinnamon, and allspice into the remaining batter for the additional two layers.
- ✦ Bake these 2 layers for 27 minutes.
- ✦ Prepare the filling. Grate the flesh of the fresh coconut.
- ✦ Grate the peel of 1 lemon and chop the pulp of both. Grate the peel of 1 orange and chop the pulp of both. Mix the coconut, chopped citrus with their juices, sugar, crushed pineapple, and the juice from the cherries. Save the cherries to decorate the top of the cake.
- ✦ Dissolve the flour in a little of the milk and add it to the fruit mixture. In a heavy saucepan, cook the mixture over moderate heat, stirring constantly until thick.
- ✦ Spread the filling between the cool cake layers as follows. Start with a plain layer and top with the filling. Add a nut layer and top with the filling. Add a plain layer and top with the filling. Continue alternating layers, ending with a plain layer with filling on top.
- ✦ Decorate the top with the reserved whole cherries.

Grace's Amazin' Raisin Torte

My mother loved to bake cakes, but fresh eggs were scarce during the Depression, so she experimented with using mayonnaise. She taught all her daughters how to bake with this substitution. This cake was one of mom's original recipes that I have enhanced over the years by including eggs and adjusting the spices. I bake it at Christmastime for my sister-in-law, Christa Ivy.

Although the recipe makes two layers, the layers are quite thick and way too much for a single cake. So I use each layer separately: I bake both layers, cool them, then wrap and refrigerate each one, until I am ready to frost it. Then I top it with whipping cream or Cool Whip and toasted sliced almonds for a delightful one-layer torte.

SERVES 8

- 3 cups unsifted all-purpose flour
- 2 cups sugar
- 1 cup Real Mayonnaise—do not use imitation or low-fat mayonnaise
- ⅓ cup milk
- 2 eggs
- 2 teaspoons baking soda
- 1½ teaspoons cinnamon
- ½ teaspoon nutmeg
- ½ teaspoon sea salt
- ¼ teaspoon ground cloves
- 3 cups chopped peeled apples
- 1 cup seedless raisins
- ½ cup coarsely chopped walnuts

- ✦ Preheat the oven to 350 degrees.
- ✦ Grease and flour 2 round 9-inch baking pans, and set aside.
- ✦ With an electric mixer at low speed, beat the flour, sugar, mayonnaise, milk, eggs, baking soda, cinnamon, nutmeg, salt, and cloves for 2 minutes, scraping down the bowl frequently.
- ✦ Stir in the apples, raisins, and nuts, and pour into the prepared pans.
- ✦ Bake for 45 minutes, or until a cake tester inserted into the center comes out clean.
- ✦ Cool in the pans for 10 minutes. Remove from the pans, and cool on a rack.

PEG'S NOTES ~ The mayonnaise makes this cake very moist. By using each layer separately, you get two cakes from a single recipe, and at Christmas, when you're baking for a crowd, this really helps with time and expense.

You can substitute dried cranberries for the raisins.

Peg's Brownie Torte

My daughters loved brownies and would always choose brownies over pies and cakes for dessert. This recipe came about because I wanted to jazz up the brownies to serve to guests and still satisfy the girls' desire.

SERVES 12–16

Raspberry Sauce

- 1 Tablespoon cornstarch
- 2 Tablespoons cold water
- 1 10-ounce package frozen raspberries in light syrup, thawed
- 2 Tablespoons seedless red raspberry jam
- ¼ teaspoon lemon juice
- 1 Tablespoon Amaretto, optional

Topping

- 3 ounces cream cheese, softened
- ⅓ cup powdered sugar
- ¼ teaspoon vanilla extract
- 1 1.4-ounce package Dream Whip® topping mix
- ½ cup milk

Torte

- 1 package chocolate brownie mix of your choice
- ½ pint fresh raspberries, for topping
- ½ cup fresh blueberries, for topping
- Mint leaves, for garnish, optional

♦ Prepare the raspberry sauce. In a medium saucepan, dissolve the cornstarch in water. Add the thawed raspberries, raspberry jam, and lemon juice. Cook on medium heat until the mixture comes to a boil. Remove from the heat; add Amaretto, if desired.

♦ Push the mixture through a sieve into a small bowl to remove the seeds. Refrigerate 2 to 3 hours, or until thoroughly chilled.

♦ Prepare the topping. In a large electric mixer bowl, combine the cream cheese, powdered sugar, and vanilla. Beat at medium speed until the mixture is softened and blended.

♦ Add the whipped topping mix and milk and beat at high speed for 4 minutes, until the mixture thickens and forms peaks. Cover. Refrigerate for 2 to 3 hours, or until thoroughly chilled.

♦ Preheat the oven to 350 degrees.

♦ Line a 9-inch spring-form pan with aluminum foil, and grease the foil.

♦ Prepare the brownies following the package directions for the basic recipe. Spread in the prepared pan.

♦ Bake for 35 to 37 minutes or until set. Cool completely. Remove from the pan, and peel off the aluminum foil.

♦ To assemble, place the brownie torte on a serving plate. Spread the chilled topping over the top of the brownie. Place ¼ cup of the raspberry sauce in a small, resealable plastic bag. Snip a pinpoint hole in the bottom corner of the bag. Drizzle the sauce in three concentric rings, 1 inch apart. Draw a toothpick through the topping and sauce in straight lines from the center to the edge, to form your design.

♦ Arrange fresh raspberries and blueberries in the center. Garnish with mint leaves.

♦ Serve with the remaining sauce.

Peg's Pumpkin Roll

In 1992, my daughter Debbie sent me a fax from work with a pumpkin roll recipe that she thought sounded good and that would be an alternative to the Pumpkin Bread—page 92—that I made all the time. I tried the recipe, but we didn't like it. However, it did give me the idea of creating my own pumpkin roll. I have since made hundreds of these, so I know you will enjoy this version.

SERVES 8–10

- 3 eggs
- 1 cup sugar
- ⅔ cup canned pumpkin
- ¾ cup all-purpose flour
- 1 teaspoon baking powder
- 2 teaspoons cinnamon
- 1 teaspoon ginger
- ½ teaspoon nutmeg
- ½ teaspoon sea salt
- Mint leaves, optional, for garnish
- Orange slices, optional, for garnish

Filling

- 8 ounces cream cheese, softened
- 4 Tablespoons butter or margarine
- ½ cup powdered sugar
- 1 teaspoon vanilla extract

♦ Preheat the oven to 375 degrees.

♦ In a large bowl, combine the eggs and the sugar, beating well. Add the pumpkin, mixing until blended.

♦ In a separate bowl, combine the flour, baking powder, spices, and salt. Add this to the egg mixture, and mix well.

♦ Spread the batter into a greased and waxed paper–lined 10 by 15-inch jelly-roll pan.

♦ Bake for 15 minutes. Remove the cake from the pan. Cool for 15 minutes. Place the cake on a clean tea towel. Cool 10 minutes longer.

♦ From the 10-inch side, roll the cake up in the towel. Set aside.

♦ Meanwhile, prepare the filling. Beat together the cream cheese and butter or margarine. Stir in the powdered sugar and vanilla, blending until smooth.

♦ Unroll the cake, and spread the filling evenly over it. Roll up the cake, and cover it with plastic wrap.

♦ Put the cake seam-side down on a plate, and chill for at least 2 hours. It's best if chilled overnight.

♦ When serving, cut the cake in even slices. Garnish with mint leaves and/or orange slices, if desired.

PEG'S NOTES ~ I flip the roll over onto a tea towel after it has cooled for 15 minutes, so that I can then peel off the wax paper. This also leaves the nice smooth side of the roll down on the tea towel; it will be the outside of your finished roll. These rolls freeze really well and can be shipped frozen, ready to serve upon arrival.

Eloise's Chocolate Pound Cake

My sister Eloise first served this pound cake at Christmas back in the 1970s, and I really enjoyed it. I have changed the ingredients a little to enhance the chocolate flavor and to create a moist pound cake. It can be turned into an elegant dessert by plating it with a drizzle of a fine chocolate sauce, preferably a truffle chocolate sauce, and fresh raspberries.

SERVES 10–12

- 1 cup butter
- ½ cup Crisco®
- 3 cups sugar
- 5 eggs
- 3 cups all-purpose flour
- ½ cup cocoa
- 1 teaspoon baking powder
- Pinch of salt
- 1¼ cups buttermilk
- 1 teaspoon vanilla

✦ Cream the butter, shortening, and sugar. Add the eggs, one at time, beating thoroughly after each addition.

✦ Sift the flour, then measure 3 cups, and add the cocoa, baking powder, and pinch of salt. Slowly mix the flour mixture and milk into the creamed mixture, alternating between the milk and flour mixtures and ending with the milk. Stir in the vanilla.

✦ Do not pre-heat the oven.

✦ Pour into a greased and floured tube pan. Place the cake pan in the cold oven, set the temperature to 320 degrees, and bake for about 1½ hours, or until a test toothpick comes out clean.

PEG'S NOTES ~ This is best if baked the night before and refrigerated, so it has time to settle down and thicken before serving. I always use real butter and buttermilk in this recipe. The result is a moist pound cake with good chocolate flavor. The secret is to bake it at low heat and not overcook it. You can really dress up this plain pound cake by serving it with a dollop of whipping cream and fresh fruit, especially fresh raspberries.

Frannie's Kentucky Pound Cake

When Frannie heard that I had put Eloise's Chocolate Pound Cake in my book, she immediately baked this cake for me and told me that it had to be in the book, too. She has baked this cake for years, and I love it. I asked her why it was called Kentucky Pound Cake, and she told me that a lady in Kentucky had come up with the recipe and sent it to a woman in her church.

Don't you just adore your sisters? Mine have always kept me in line with love and guidance.

SERVES 10–12

- 4 eggs, separated
- 2½ cups self-rising flour
- 1½ cups vegetable oil
- 1 8-ounce can crushed pineapple
- 2 cups sugar
- 2½ teaspoons cinnamon
- 1 cup chopped nuts

- Separate the eggs, and beat the egg whites until stiff.
- Mix the egg yolks with all the other ingredients and fold in the egg whites.
- Pour the batter into a greased and floured tube pan.
- Do not preheat the oven.
- Place the cake pan in a cold oven. Set the temperature at 300 degrees and bake for 1 hour and 20 minutes.

PEG'S NOTES ~ I always use chopped walnuts in this cake, but you can use your nut of choice. My daughter Dana lives in Kentucky now, so she thinks this pound cake is especially for her!

Peg's Dump Cake

This cake is really easy, because you just dump everything together. You can make it when you are in a hurry, need something quick, and really don't want to think too much about it.

SERVES 8

Cake

- 2 cups flour, plus additional for dusting
- 2 cups sugar
- 2 eggs
- 2 teaspoons baking soda
- 1 20-ounce can crushed pineapple in natural juices
- 1 cup chopped nuts

Icing

- 8 ounces cream cheese
- ½ cup butter
- 1 teaspoon vanilla
- 1 cup powdered sugar
- ½ cup chopped nuts

- ◆ Dump the cake ingredients into a bowl, including the juice of the canned, crushed pineapple. Stir to mix all the ingredients.
- ◆ Pour into a greased and floured 9 by 13 by 2-inch Pyrex® pan.
- ◆ Bake at 350 degrees for 35 to 40 minutes. Cool the cake before icing.
- ◆ Prepare the icing. Beat the cream cheese and butter.
- ◆ Add the vanilla and powdered sugar. Beat until smooth and fluffy.
- ◆ Frost the cooled cake. Sprinkle with chopped nuts.

PEG'S NOTES ~ If you are using a glass or Pyrex® pan, **do not preheat the oven**. Just turn on the oven when you put your cake in, as the cake will continue to cook after you remove it from the oven due to the heat that the glass holds. Easy and delicious!

Four Layer Delite

This recipe was given to me in 1975 by a sweet Italian lady named Toni Cottone. My daughter Dana was not quite one year old, and I was still working. Toni created this dessert by using instant puddings, which my girls really liked. The cake was fast, easy to make, and deliciously light and refreshing. The layers also make it very pretty, especially if you add a layer of chocolate pudding, which I do.

SERVES 8

First layer

- 1 cup flour
- ½ cup butter
- ½ cup chopped nuts

+ Preheat the oven to 375 degrees.
+ Mix all the ingredients together, and press the mixture into the bottom of a spring-form torte or cheesecake pan. You have to have a pan with removable sides
+ Bake for 15 minutes. Cool completely.

Second layer

- 1 cup Cool Whip
- 1 cup powdered sugar
- 8 ounces cream cheese, softened

+ Beat all the ingredients together until fluffy. Then spread over the cool first layer.

Third layer

- 2 3.4-ounce packages of instant vanilla pudding
- 2 cups milk

+ Beat all ingredients together and pour over the second layer.

Topping

- Cool Whip
- Chopped nuts

+ Top the assembled layers with Cool Whip, and sprinkle with chopped nuts. Refrigerate until ready to serve. Before serving, remove the side of the torte or cheesecake pan, and slice.

PEG'S NOTES ~ This is a simple but very good dessert. You can substitute any flavor pudding you like for the vanilla pudding, or you can add an additional layer of chocolate pudding on top of the vanilla. Feel free to use the nuts of your choice—walnuts, sliced almonds, chopped pecans, pistachios, etc.

Double-Chocolate Mousse Cake

This recipe was created to fill a request for a "Posh" party in 1989. The guests went crazy over it, and my daughters wanted to make sure it was included because they say this is simply the best chocolate dessert. Not only is it easy to make, it's also gluten free. If you really want to impress your guests, plate a serving of the cake over some Crème Anglaise, see recipe on page 195. The dish will look like it came from a five-star restaurant.

SERVES 16

Batter

- 2 8-ounce packages semisweet chocolate squares—16 1-ounce squares
- 2 cups butter—NO substitutions
- 1 cup sugar
- 1 cup half-and-half
- 1 Tablespoon vanilla
- ½ teaspoon sea salt
- 8 large eggs

Chocolate glaze

- 1 cup semisweet chocolate chips
- 2 Tablespoons butter
- 3 Tablespoons milk
- 2 Tablespoons white corn syrup

Topping

- 1 cup heavy whipping cream
- Candied flowers or fruit to garnish, optional

- ♦ Early in the day or a day ahead, make the cake. Preheat the oven to 350 degrees. Grease a 10 by 3-inch spring-form pan.

- ♦ In a heavy 3-quart saucepan over low heat, heat the chocolate, butter, sugar, half-and-half, vanilla, and salt, stirring constantly, until the chocolate melts and the mixture is smooth.

- ♦ In a large bowl, beat the eggs slightly. Beat the chocolate mixture into the eggs. Pour into the pan.

- ♦ Bake the cake 45 minutes, or until a toothpick inserted 2 inches from the edge comes out clean. Cool the cake completely on a wire rack. When the cake is cool, remove the side of the pan. Wrap the cake in plastic wrap and refrigerate until well chilled, at least 6 hours but preferably overnight.

- ♦ The next day or the day of the party, prepare the chocolate glaze. In a heavy 2-quart saucepan over low heat, heat the chocolate chips and butter until the chocolate melts and the mixture is smooth.

- ♦ Remove from the heat; beat in the milk and corn syrup.

- ♦ Spread the warm glaze over the top and sides of the cold cake.

- ♦ In a small mixer bowl, with the electric mixer at medium speed, beat the whipping cream until stiff peaks form.

- ♦ Pipe the whipped cream around the edge of the cake. Garnish with candied flowers and/or fruit, if using.

- ♦ Serve immediately, or refrigerate until ready to serve.

PEG'S NOTES ~ The pansies come from my garden and I candy them for this decoration. The large pansy represents me, and the three small pansies my three daughters, Deborah, Teresa, and Dana.

See's semi-sweet chocolate chips work best in this recipe. The mousse cake will last for a week in the refrigerator.

Famous Cherry Cheesecake

This recipe was created and handed down to me by Margaret Sears, who was the mother of my good friend Shirley. Mrs. Sears and my mother shared the same birthday, and they treated both of us girls as daughters. So we always called them our Southern Mother and our West Coast Mother.

SERVES 10

Graham cracker crust for a 9-inch pie

2 cups crushed graham cracker crumbs

½ cup butter, melted

Cheesecake filling

16 ounces cream cheese

½ cup sugar

2 eggs

2 Tablespoons lemon juice

Topping

1 cup sour cream

2 Tablespoons sugar

½ teaspoon vanilla

    Fresh Cherry Sauce—page 192
    —see Peg's Notes

    Cool Whip, for edging

- Preheat the oven to 350 degrees.

- Prepare the piecrust. Mix the cracker crumbs with the butter until completely mixed. Using the back of a large spoon or a measuring cup, press the crumbs onto the bottom of the pan and up the sides for about 1½ inches.

- Bake for 5 to 10 minutes. I only bake mine for 8 minutes, but the timing will depend on your oven. Cool completely before filling.

- Prepare the filling. Beat the cream cheese with the sugar until the cheese has no lumps and is fluffy.

- Add the eggs one at a time, and mix just until blended. Add the lemon juice and mix until blended. Do not over-mix, as you do not want your cheesecake to crack. Pour the filling into the cooled graham cracker crust.

- Return the cheesecake to the oven and bake for 20 minutes.

- Prepare the topping. Gently mix the sour cream, sugar, and vanilla, and set aside.

- After 20 minutes, remove from the oven, add the topping, and bake for 8 to 10 minutes more.

- Remove the cake from the oven, and cool it completely at room temperature. Run a knife around the side of the pan to loosen the cake, cover with plastic wrap, and refrigerate. When the cheesecake is chilled, pipe Cool Whip around the edge, and fill the center with Fresh Cherry Sauce, cherry pie filling, or the fruit topping of your choice. Return to the refrigerator until ready to serve.

PEG'S NOTES This cheesecake is the most requested dessert that I make. It is very light, as you only use half the cream cheese that most cheesecake recipes require. I never put sugar in a graham cracker crust as it makes the crust grainy. I think that the honey in the graham cracker is sweet enough, and I want to keep the cake light. If you prefer it sweeter, I suggest using powdered sugar in the crust so that you do not taste the grains of regular sugar. Powdered sugar is also a little sweeter so I would only add about 2 tablespoons to the crust recipe. Taste and add more, a little at a time, if needed.

If fresh cherries aren't available for the Cherry Sauce, use Comstock® Original Country Cherry Pie Filling or a fruit topping of your choice.

Fresh Cherry Sauce

I use this Cherry Sauce for my Cherry Cheesecake. When the cherries are in season, I make up this sauce and freeze it for later use. This recipe is also perfect for other types of fresh fruit, such as blueberries, raspberries, blackberries, etc.

MAKES 6 CUPS

- 2 pounds fresh cherries—Rainier or Bing
- 1 cup water
- ¼ cup sugar
- 2 Tablespoons cornstarch, more if needed

♦ Pit and stem the cherries.

♦ Place the cherries in a sauce pot; add the water and sugar. Bring to a boil over medium heat, and cook 5 minutes.

♦ Dilute the cornstarch in a small amount of water, and add it to the cherries. Cook an additional 3 minutes until the sauce thickens and the cornstarch cooks. Add additional cornstarch, 1 tablespoon at a time, diluted in water, if the sauce is not thick enough for you. Cook at least 2 minutes more to cook the cornstarch.

PEG'S NOTES ~ The 1/4 cup sugar is perfect for 2 pounds of cherries or other fruit. I normally do not use this amount of water but it is necessary to give you enough sauce to plate it under a slice of the cake. To top the cheesecake with cherries, I use a slotted spoon so I only get the cherries, leaving the sauce for plating and drizzling.

You will have extra sauce left over for topping ice cream or pound cake.

If you want a thicker sauce for other uses, you can use less water.

Carrot Cake for JarvBob

My husband, Jarvis, does not like the raisins or pineapples in a traditional carrot cake recipe, but he loves carrot cake, so I created this version for his birthday in August 1969 and gave it his Southern nickname. Our daughters are not raisin fans either, so they also liked this. Once you taste it, you will make it time and time again. It's foolproof…great for church, office potlucks, and picnics. Oh my, it is **Pegilicious!**®

SERVES 12

Batter

- 4 eggs
- 1½ cups salad oil
- 2 cups sugar
- 3 cups shredded carrots, about 9 carrots
- 2 cups flour
- 2 teaspoons baking soda
- ½ teaspoon sea salt
- 1 Tablespoon cinnamon
- 1 cup chopped walnuts

Icing

- ¾ cup butter
- 12 ounces cream cheese
- 1 16-ounce box powdered sugar, sifted
- 1 teaspoon vanilla

- With an electric mixer, beat the eggs well, and add the salad oil slowly, beating well.
- Add the sugar slowly on low speed. Add the carrots slowly.
- Mix the flour, soda, salt, and cinnamon. Add the dry mixture slowly to the eggs and sugar, mixing well. Stir in the chopped nuts.
- Pour into a greased and floured 9 by 13 by 2-inch Pyrex® pan.
- Do not preheat the oven. Bake at 350 degrees for 40 to 50 minutes.
- Cool completely before icing.
- Prepare the icing. Have the butter and cream cheese at room temperature and cream them together.
- Add the sugar and vanilla, and beat until fluffy. Make sure your cake is completely cool. Frost and refrigerate until ready to serve.

PEG'S NOTES ~ The real trick to the success of this cake is that you **do not preheat the oven** and you use a Pyrex® pan. Turn on the oven only when you are ready to put the cake in. Set your timer and cook from that point. I always start at the lowest amount of time—40 minutes—then test with a toothpick before cooking any longer. Remove the cake immediately, and let it finish cooking in the Pyrex® pan. When it's completely cool, frost it with the cream cheese icing. I also shred the carrots in my food processor with a little water, then I drain the water and squeeze out any extra and measure the carrots. This method leaves a bit of water in the carrots, making the cake more moist.

Crème Anglaise

This cream sauce is something I have played around with just to enhance the presentation of my cakes. Adding a touch of elegance to any dish is fun, and Crème Anglaise is as elegant as they come. If I am feeling especially fancy or daring, I add a little rum, Kahlúa,® or Grand Marnier.® The result is heavenly indeed!

MAKES 1 CUP

- 3 egg yolks
- 2 Tablespoons sugar
- ½ vanilla bean, or 2 teaspoons vanilla extract
- 1 cup heavy cream

- ✦ In a bowl, whisk the egg yolks and sugar until well blended.
- ✦ Put the cream into a medium-size heavy saucepan.
- ✦ Split the vanilla bean lengthwise, and, using a knife blade, scrape the seeds into the cream. Bring the cream and vanilla bean seeds just to a boil, reduce the heat, and simmer 4 minutes.
- ✦ Stir one fourth of the hot cream gradually into the yolks; add the yolk mixture to the remaining cream mixture, stirring constantly. Cook over medium-low heat, stirring constantly, for 6 minutes, or until the custard reaches 160 degrees—use a candy thermometer—or when it coats the back of a spoon.
- ✦ Remove from the heat, and set aside to cool. Store in the refrigerator until ready to serve.

PEG'S NOTES ~ This sauce is traditionally used in small amounts to plate your dessert. However, if you need more sauce, do not double the recipe. I recommend using 5 egg yolks to 2 cups heavy cream and 5 tablespoons sugar. You may add liqueur to change the flavor. Add 1 tablespoon per cup of sauce, but still use the vanilla.

Old-Fashioned Homemade Vanilla Ice Cream

This is my mother's recipe. When I was growing up, we made this ice cream every Fourth of July. And we still do! My husband, Jarvis, hand-cranks the treat using our old-fashioned White Mountain ice cream freezer. I much prefer the hand-cranked version to the new electric ones, because of the ice cream's consistency and how hard it gets by freezing it with rock salt. Plus my grandchildren always love to take their turns with the crank.

MAKES 1½ GALLONS

- 2 cups sugar
- 4 large eggs
- 1 pint whipping cream
- ½ gallon whole milk
- ½ gallon half-and-half
- 5-6 Tablespoons vanilla

✦ In a large mixing bowl on medium speed, mix the sugar and the eggs, adding the eggs one at a time until well blended.

✦ Mix in the whipping cream, but do not whip. Stir in part of the half-and-half and the milk. Your mixing bowl will be too small to stir in all of the milk.

✦ After the liquid is mixed well, pour it into a 1½-gallon container of an ice cream mixer. The paddle to the mixer should be in the container when you pour in your ice cream mixture. Add 5 tablespoons of vanilla, and the rest of the milk and half-and-half. Stir it together by twisting the paddle.

✦ Taste, and add more vanilla, if you desire. Your ice cream mixer container will be full to about 4 inches below the top. This allows for expansion of the ice cream during freezing.

✦ Place the ice cream container back into the freezer. Alternately add crushed ice and rock salt until the freezer is full. Cover with a towel, and turn the freezer handle until you are no longer able to turn it. Your ice cream will be frozen. This should take about 20 minutes.

PEG'S NOTES ~ If you want to add fresh fruit, such as peaches, do so about halfway through the freezing process, so that the fruit will be evenly distributed and will not sink to the bottom of the container. However, you will need to leave out some liquid to make up for the cups of fruit that you are adding. Just make sure the final mixture is still about 4 inches from the top of the container so that it does not overflow when frozen. I prefer to just put fresh fruit on top of the ice cream after freezing. This allows each person to top their ice cream with their preferred fruit, and the fruit does not get icy. A win-win situation!

Martha Washington Candy

MAKES 6 DOZEN BON-BONS

- 1 can flaked coconut, or you can use a 7-ounce package
- ¾ cup chopped walnuts
- 1 14-ounce can Eagle Brand® Condensed Milk
- ½ cup soft butter
- 2 16-ounce boxes powdered sugar
- 1 12-ounce, plus 1 6-ounce package chocolate chips
- ½ to ¾ cake paraffin

White chocolate drizzle, optional

- 6 ounces white chocolate
- 2 Tablespoons shortening

- ◆ Blend the coconut, walnuts, milk, butter, and sugar thoroughly, and roll by hand into small balls about ¾ of an inch in diameter.
- ◆ Chill them in the refrigerator for about 1 hour or longer.
- ◆ Prepare the chocolate. Melt the chocolate chips and paraffin over low heat 10 to 15 minutes, or until completely melted and blended.
- ◆ Insert a toothpick into each ball and dip it in the prepared chocolate. Set the balls to cool on waxed paper or aluminum foil. Remove the toothpicks after all balls are dipped, and fill each small hole with chocolate.

- ◆ If using, melt the white chocolate with shortening over warm—not hot—water.
- ◆ Pour into a Ziploc® bag, cut one corner and use as a pastry bag to drizzle over the candy.

PEG'S NOTES ~ You can substitute 4 to 6 tablespoons of shortening for the paraffin. This candy chills in the refrigerator, but putting the balls in the freezer works, too. You can also just stick the toothpick in when you get ready to dip the ball, then twist it out and reuse it, so you don't use so many toothpicks.

Peanut Butter Bon-Bons

My friend Shirley taught me how to make these bon-bons when I was only 20. I was thrilled that I could make candies that were better than store bought. At Christmastime, I fill a tin with these or with Martha Washington Candy on page 198, for a very special gift of delicious memories.

MAKES 3 DOZEN BON-BONS

- 1 cup creamy peanut butter
- 1 cup sifted powdered sugar
- 2 Tablespoons soft butter
- 1½ cups chopped nuts, optional
- 6 ounces chocolate chips
- 2 Tablespoons shortening

✦ Combine the peanut butter, powdered sugar, and butter, mixing until all is smooth. Stir in the nuts, if using. Shape into small balls on a cookie sheet. Place a toothpick in the top of each ball, and put them into the freezer to freeze.

✦ Melt the chocolate with the shortening over warm—not hot—water.

✦ Remove the balls from the freezer, and, using the toothpick as a handle, dip the balls into the chocolate. Then place them on a piece of waxed paper or aluminum foil, twisting the toothpick out to remove it.

✦ After all the bon-bons are dipped and the toothpicks removed, go back with a teaspoon of chocolate and fill each small hole that was left when you removed the toothpick.

PEG'S NOTES ~ I found that the freezer method, as opposed to just putting them in the fridge, works the best on Peanut Butter Bon-Bons. Otherwise they are too soft and fall off the toothpick. I never add the nuts to this recipe, as my family prefers plain bon-bons.

Peanut Butter-Coconut Bon-Bons

MAKES 4 DOZEN BON-BONS

- 2 cups sifted powdered sugar
- 1 cup graham cracker crumbs
- ¾ cup chopped nuts
- ½ cup flaked coconut
- ½ cup butter, softened
- ½ cup peanut butter
- 1½ cups semisweet chocolate chips
- 3 Tablespoons shortening
- Chocolate sprinkles, optional

✦ In a large bowl, combine the powdered sugar, graham cracker crumbs, nuts, and coconut.

✦ In a small saucepan, melt the butter and peanut butter, and pour over the coconut mixture. Blend until the mixture is moistened. Shape into 1-inch balls and place them on a cookie sheet. Put them into the freezer to chill.

✦ Using a double boiler over low heat, melt the chocolate chips with the shortening over warm—not hot—water. Spear the balls with wooden toothpicks, and dip them individually into the chocolate mixture to coat. Place the balls on waxed paper; chill to set.

✦ Store the candies, tightly covered, between layers of waxed paper in a cool place.

PEG'S NOTES ~ I found that the freezer method, as opposed to just putting them in the fridge, works the best. Otherwise they are too soft and fall off the toothpick. You can also just stick the toothpick in when you get ready to dip the ball, then twist it out and reuse it. That way, you're not using so many toothpicks.

The chocolate will adhere to the bon-bon quickly when the ball is chilled first.

If you don't have a double boiler, you can melt the chocolate with shortening in the microwave or in a saucepan over low heat. Make sure the butter is room temperature so as not to scorch the peanut butter when you blend it over low heat.

Candied Walnuts

By now you have read a lot about Mrs. Sears. What a great chef and caterer! She taught me how to make these candied walnuts in 1970. They have been on my Christmas dessert table ever since. Mrs. Sears' recipe is the one my girls grew up with; my version I developed later. I'm including both here. These make a great hostess gift. I put them in little Christmas bags and give them to my guests when they leave a holiday party.

PEG'S CANDIED WALNUTS

MAKES 1 POUND

- ½ cup sour cream
- 1½ cups sugar
- 1 teaspoon vanilla
- 1 pound whole walnuts

- ✦ In a large saucepan, bring the sour cream and sugar to a soft boil stage, or 240 degrees. Use a candy thermometer to check the temperature.
- ✦ Remove from heat and add the vanilla and the walnuts.
- ✦ Stir quickly to coat the nuts well, and spread them out on waxed paper. Let them cool, and break them apart. Store them in an airtight container.

MRS. SEARS' CANDIED WALNUTS

MAKES 3 CUPS

- 1 cup sugar
- 1 teaspoon cinnamon
- 6 Tablespoons milk
- Pinch of sea salt
- 1 teaspoon vanilla
- 3 cups whole walnuts, or large pieces

- ✦ In a large saucepan, bring the sugar, cinnamon, milk, and salt to a soft boil stage, or 240 degrees on a candy thermometer. Remove from the heat.
- ✦ Add the vanilla.
- ✦ Stir quickly to coat the nuts well, and spread them out on waxed paper. Let them cool, and break them apart. Store them in an airtight container.

PEG'S NOTES ~ I always double this recipe, the candy is most often given out in gift bags at Christmas. This is a great gift idea that you can prepare well in advance and is very yummy. I store the walnuts in a Christmas tin until I am ready to bag them or use them as a filler on cookie trays.

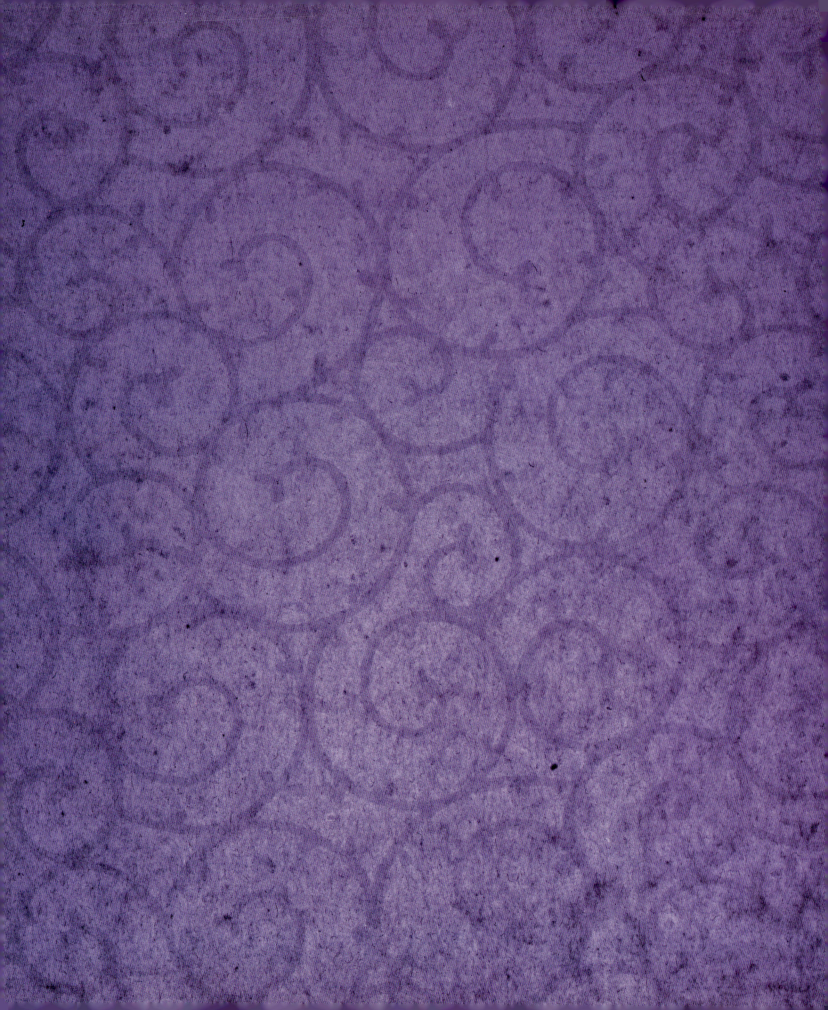

Holiday & Party Punches and Specialty Drinks

JarvBob's Famous Eggnog

Soon after we got married, I started having what we called fancy dinners for the holidays. I wanted to serve traditional eggnog on Christmas Eve, but I really did not like it because the drink was not cold enough for me. I created this recipe instead. We named it after my husband, as it is his responsibility to take care of the eggnog and keep the guests entertained while I am making final preparations for dinner.

SERVES 4–6

Eggnog ice cream—see Peg's Notes

½ cup White Bacardi® Rum, 4 1-ounce jiggers

Fresh grated nutmeg, for dusting

- Fill your blender or Vitamix with ice cream and add the rum. Blend to the thickness that you want.
- Pour the eggnog into glasses, and grate fresh nutmeg over the top. This will serve 4 to 6 people, depending on the size of glass you are using.

PEG'S NOTES ~ We like eggnog really cold, thick, and slushy, but feel free to dilute the recipe with milk, if you prefer. Purchased eggnog will retain the flavor best if you do need to dilute it. You can also add more rum if your guests like eggnog that's a little more potent. We have found, though, that this is just enough liquor to put people in a holiday mood without having them drink too much rum before dinner.

Eggnog ice cream is the safest way to have eggnog during the holidays, because you keep it in the freezer until you're ready to use it, and there's no waste. Purchased eggnog in milk cartons goes bad quickly, and sometimes has a cardboard taste.

As an alternative to eggnog ice cream, use vanilla ice cream and purchased eggnog. In that case, fill the blender with vanilla ice cream, and add 3/4 cup eggnog to start. You can add more ice cream and/or eggnog until you get the consistency and taste that you want.

Champagne Punch

Nothing says "welcome" as graciously as a table attractively set with a punch bowl and glasses. I always greet my guests with a specialty drink to let them know that we appreciated them coming.

SERVES 20, WITH ICE

- 3 fresh pineapples
- 1 16-ounce box powdered sugar
- 2 cups lemon juice
- ½ cup Leroux Curaçao
- ½ cup maraschino cherry juice
- 1 quart rum
- 4 750-milliliter bottles chilled Champagne

- ◆ Peel, core, and slice the pineapples. Crush or chop the slices.
- ◆ In a large container, dissolve the powdered sugar in the lemon juice.
- ◆ Add the pineapple, Curaçao, cherry juice, and rum. Chill 2 hours.
- ◆ Pour the punch into a punch bowl. Resting the bottles on the rim of the bowl, slowly pour the Champagne down the side of bowl, stirring with an up-and-down motion. Serve at once.

Hot Christmas Punch

Here is a tasty non-alcoholic punch for the children during the holidays.

MAKES 1½ GALLONS

- 1 gallon apple cider
- 1 quart orange juice
- 1 cup lemon juice
- 1 48-ounce can pineapple juice
- 24 cloves
- 4 sticks cinnamon
- 1 cup honey or sugar, optional

- ◆ Simmer all the ingredients in a large stockpot for 10 minutes. Remove the cloves and cinnamon, and serve hot.
- ◆ You can also use a crock pot to keep the punch warm during a party.
- ◆ For variations, you can use cranberry-apple juice instead of cider for a festive red punch. Substitute grapefruit juice for the pineapple juice, and you have a great drink for a cold or flu.

PEG'S NOTES ~ *Apple cider is non-alcoholic in the United States, and it is what makes this recipe so unique. However, if you have any concerns about the minimal alcohol content, you may substitute unsweetened apple juice.*

Peg's Party-Planning Tips

GET ORGANIZED ~ Make several lists that you can update through the planning process. Have a master to-do list that highlights every task: an all-important guest list that can be updated with RSVPs, a menu, a shopping list, and so on. Check your menu to make sure every dish gets served.

CREATE A THEME ~ Holidays and milestone birthdays are more festive when a theme sets the tone. Whether you have a Monte Carlo Night, South-of-the-Border Fiesta, or a '50s-inspired brunch with croquet on the lawn, your guests will have more memorable moments. For a bridal shower, consider having several holiday-themed tables, and ask the guests to bring gifts tied to a holiday, such as Thanksgiving, Easter, Valentine's day, Fourth of July, and so on. So much fun!

SEND OUT INVITATIONS ~ Online invitations are perfectly acceptable for last-minute get-togethers, but there's nothing quite like a mailed invitation, or one that has been created by you. Purchase theme-inspired paper, and create your own invitations, which really sets the tone for the party.

OFFER A SELF-SERVE BAR ~ Set things up so guests can make their own drinks. If you are providing margaritas or other blended drinks, pre-mix all liquid ingredients, except for liquor and ice, in plastic drinking bottles, so guests can pour them into the blender without having to measure things out. Welcome guests with a drink upon arrival by placing a tray of champagne and sparkling water near the door.

CREATE A SPECIALTY DRINK ~ It is fun to include one specialty cocktail that leaves a lasting impression with guests—it's even more impressive if it is seasonal. If you enjoyed a particular cocktail at a restaurant or bar, call the bartender, get the recipe, and recreate it. Your guests will be impressed. Serve the drink in a chic glass or incorporate creative touches, like placing little doilies over sweet tea glasses at a picnic. Don't forget that a delicious punch is nice when you are serving a crowd; it can be very festive.

HIGHLIGHT APPETIZERS ~ Consider serving dinner-by-the-bite, with trays of mouthwatering hors d'oeuvres in lieu of a sit-down dinner. Make sure that you serve a variety of appetizers, and choose your best. This less-formal approach allows guests to sample many flavors and provides more opportunities to mingle. I have provided a lot of wonderful appetizer ideas in this book.

STAY RELAXED ~ Leave yourself an hour before anyone arrives to freshen up, slip into something party-ready, and light candles for added ambiance. Don't forget that, as host, *you* set the tone, so a relaxed attitude will bring out the same in your guests. After all, you have done a great job, and it is party time…so, have fun!

DON'T FORGET THE FAVORS ~ A small token is an unforgettable way to end a celebration. Pretty boxes with candies or baked goods are sure to be appreciated. I place homemade fudge, caramels, cookies, or jam in a beribboned box or bag and add a note thanking the guests for sharing their time with us. This really is the crowning touch in making delicious memories.

FORMAL SIT-DOWN DINNERS ~ Plan your menu and your table setting. Use linens, china, crystal, and fine silverware, and always include fresh flowers. Or you can use herbs, leaves, and branches from your garden, or even fill glass vases with fresh fruit or citrus. I always type my menu out on decorative paper, roll and tie it with a ribbon, and place one at each setting. I also use place cards to arrange congenial seating. Chill your salad plates and forks and make sure that you have a hot stone in your breadbasket to keep the bread warm. If you're serving a sauce or gravy on the side, make sure that you have it in a serving piece with a tea light to keep it warm. I also like to make specialty butters and mold them into shapes for the occasion. Keep them chilled until serving time.

THINK AHEAD ~ Make everything that you can ahead of time, from salad dressings, soups, and specialty butters to pasta and rice, etc. Béarnaise, Hollandaise, and Bordelaise sauces can be kept hot for an hour in a hot thermos. Cooked pasta will keep refrigerated in a Ziploc® bag; prior to serving, just toss the pasta in hot water for 1 minute. Make and gift-wrap all party favors in advance. Homemade fudge or caramels can be made a week in advance, too.

In Measuring, Remember...

As you may recall, I learned to cook without the benefit of measuring cups or spoons. But it did not take long to realize that knowing measurements was very helpful and saved a lot of time. I made this chart and keep it in my kitchen. I've even found my husband coming in from the yard to check it when he had to mix fertilizer for our veggies, flowers, and lawn.

3 teaspoons = 1 Tablespoon

2 Tablespoons = ⅛ cup

4 Tablespoons = ¼ cup

8 Tablespoons = ½ cup

16 Tablespoons = 1 cup

5 Tablespoons + 1 teaspoon = ⅓ cup

12 Tablespoons = ¾ cup

4 ounces = ½ cup

8 ounces = 1 cup

16 ounces = 2 cups or 1 pound

1 ounce = 2 Tablespoons fat or liquid

2 cups fat = 16 ounces or 1 pound

2 cups = 1 pint

2 cups sugar = 1 pound or 16 ounces

5/8 cup = ½ cup + 2 Tablespoons

7/8 cup = ¾ cup + 2 Tablespoons

1 pound butter = 2 cups or 4 sticks

2 pints = 1 quart

1 quart = 4 cups

A few grains = less than ⅛ teaspoon

Pinch = as much as can be taken between tip of finger and thumb

Speck = less than ⅛ teaspoon

PEG'S NOTES ~ I have this posted on the refrigerator in my kitchen as an easy reference, so that I don't have to stop and calculate measurements in a hurry. This is also very helpful for anyone working in the kitchen with me, such as my grandchildren, who are learning to cook.

Peg's Decorating Ideas

Make your occasion a **FEAST FOR THE SENSES**. Your table should be attractive; your food should smell and taste heavenly. If you are going to the trouble to have a dinner party, make it special!

For a unique and decorative garnish for any dish **ADD ELEGANT SUGARED FRUIT**. Use a pastry brush to coat grape clusters, whole cranberries, lemons, and limes, for example, with lightly beaten egg whites. Then sprinkle the clusters or fruit with granulated sugar, turning them to coat, and allow the fruit to dry thoroughly on waxed paper. Because you are using raw egg whites, the fruit should not be eaten; it's for decorative purposes only. You can also purchase powdered egg whites and mix according to directions.

To **MAKE CHOCOLATE LEAVES** for your cakes, pies, and other baked goods, use camellia leaves, bay leaves, or any leaf that is strong and has definite veining on the back. Make sure that the leaf you pick is not poisonous. Wash and completely dry the leaves, then coat the backs with your chocolate. You might need to do that twice to have good coverage. Place the leaves on waxed paper or a parchment-lined baking pan and chill until set. Lift the leaves very carefully when you're ready to use them. I wear cotton gloves to handle the chocolate so that the heat of my hands does not melt it.

CRUSH PEPPERMINT CANDY CANES and mints for decorating baked goods or anything that has frosting. Process the candy in the food processor. Pulse just a few times to crush the candy for decorations, longer to have powder for baking.

Use tall clear vases or a bowl filled with fruit for a **CENTERPIECE**. A carefree bouquet of flowers from your garden is always nice. Or take autumn leaves, long twigs with berries, or pussy willow branches from your yard to add a special touch to the scene. Scatter acorns, cranberries, and colorful leaves on your table at Thanksgiving; add pinecones, holly, and ornaments for Christmas.

Napkin rings are pretty, but you can also just wrap a **BRIGHT RIBBON** around each napkin. Or tie sprigs of herbs around them, using raffia for a garden party and ribbon for a more formal party. Rosemary stands up really well for this.

Make **PLACE CARDS** for your guests to take home as keepsakes. Write the individual's name on Christmas ornaments with a metallic pen, and tie a ribbon on top. Date the ornament if you wish. You also can put glue on top of each name and sprinkle it with glitter to make the name stand out more. Place the ornament on top of the napkin on each plate.

For a final touch, include a typed, dated **MENU PRINTED ON BEAUTIFUL STATIONERY**. Roll it up, tie it with a pretty ribbon, and put one at each place setting.

Peg's Hints

Here are some of the things that I have discovered during my many years of cooking for family, friends, and clients. I have made many mistakes but learned much more in the process. I hope you find these hints helpful!

- Always use real butter, good wine, and excellent olive oil in your recipes—no substitutions. Your dish will reflect what you put in it. So if you are going to the trouble to make it, make it good. If a wine is not drinkable, don't cook with it—it will ruin the recipe. Always try the wine first.

- To eliminate uncooked bacon on bacon-wrapped appetizers, precook the strips until just done but not crispy. Drain and chill them overnight. Wrap your seafood or other appetizer with the bacon, pinning it in place with a toothpick. Bake or broil the appetizer until done. The bacon will return to its crispy cooked state, and the entire appetizer will be much more enjoyable.

- As an alternative to Snider's Prime Rib & Roast Seasoning, you can make your own Spice Rub:

    1 teaspoon sea salt
    ½ teaspoon pepper
    ½ teaspoon dried parsley
    ¼ teaspoon dried oregano
    ¼ teaspoon dried rosemary
    ¼ teaspoon garlic powder
    ¼ teaspoon onion powder
    ¼ teaspoon celery salt
    ¼ teaspoon paprika

    Mix all ingredients well, and coat the meat on both sides.

- You always have fresh salad dressings in your cupboard if you have a jar of jam: Start with ¼ cup of jam; add 1 teaspoon Dijon mustard, and equal parts of olive oil and vinegar, beginning with ½ cup. Adjust these amounts according to your taste and the amount of dressing that you need.

- You can also use your favorite jam to make an incredible condiment: Blend ½ cup of jam with 2 tablespoons of your favorite mustard.

- I always use shallots in my salad dressings: They are milder than onions, have a subtle and unique taste, and are easier to digest.

- Serve your salads on chilled plates, so that the greens remain crisp. Chilled forks are a nice touch, too.

- On fresh steamed vegetables, a splash of fresh lemon juice and a sprinkle of dill weed add to the flavor.

- To fast-cook dried beans, place picked-over, clean beans in water, and bring to a boil. Turn off the heat, and cover for 1 hour. Drain and rinse them, and you are ready to cook as usual. The result is the same as soaking them overnight.

- To have pasta on hand, you can cook it and refrigerate it in a Ziploc® bag. Before serving, toss the pasta in hot water for 1 minute. This method is great for working moms.

- You can also cook rice and refrigerate it in a Ziploc® bag. To serve it, remove the amount you want, put it on a dish, place a damp paper towel on top, and microwave it for 15 to 30 seconds. To use the whole bag, follow the same steps and microwave for 1 minute. You might have to heat it again, but it's best to do that in steps.

- Béarnaise, Hollandaise, and Bordelaise sauces will keep warm for 1 hour in a hot thermos. This is very helpful for formal dinners.

- To soften cream cheese, remove it from the wrapper, place it on a microwavable plate, and microwave on high for 15 seconds.

- Never preheat the oven when you're baking cakes or brownies with glass, Pyrex®, or non-stick pans. The baked goods continue to cook from the heat of the pans after being removed from the oven. It's ok, however, to preheat the oven if you are using the pans for casseroles or vegetables, for example.

- Puff pastry and biscuits should be baked at higher temperatures, such as 400 to 500 degrees; 425 degrees is perfect most of the time. You want these items to cook and brown quickly, so that they stay fluffy and flaky.

- The secret to making perfect flaky piecrust is using vinegar in the recipe and not working the dough too much.

- To ensure that your cheesecake does not crack, add the eggs one at a time and mix only until they're blended in. Overmixing adds extra air to the cheesecake, and it will crack during baking.

- When baking a cake during extremely warm summer months, use cold water and cold eggs. For uniform batter, be sure to scrape the bottom and sides of the bowl thoroughly during mixing. For the best results when baking a cake, use pans with 2-inch-deep sides.

- Plastic corks from wine bottles are great for making indentations for thumbprint cookies. Simply press the end into the cookie dough, and twist. Then fill the cavity with a teaspoon of jam and bake.

- Save leftover candy canes or holiday mints, and grind them to a fine powder in the food processor. You can use this year-round to jazz up cookies and cakes. It's also great for sprinkling over anything with frosting.

- **Remember:** There are five essential ingredients for the perfect balance of flavors. You always need something sweet, tart, bitter, salty, and sour.

Index

APPETIZERS

Artichoke Hearts Gratin, Deb's	31
Brie, Herb En Croute	19
Brie, Sun-Dried Tomato Pesto	21
Cheese Ball, Famous	29
Cheese Pinecones, Peg's	17
Cheesecake, Savory New Mexico	23
Crab Cakes, Peg's	34
Fondue, Three-Cheese	30
Gorgonzola Wafers	18
Jalapeño Poppers, Debbie's	24
Meatballs, Sweet and Sour	25
Mushrooms, Peg's Heavenly	26

Dips

Artichoke Dip, Hot	31
Black Bean Salsa	67
Crab Cocktail Dip, Deb's Hot	27
Fruit Salsa, Peg's Fresh	36
Mango Salsa, Peg's	37

BREADS

Bran Muffin Mix	88
Corn Muffin Sticks, Peg's	81
Cornbread, Peg's Southern	82
Pear Bread, Fresh	93
Monkey Bread, Zom's	84
Pumpkin Bread	92
Sourdough Rolls	86
Sourdough Starter	87

BREAKFAST & BRUNCH

Chili Egg Puff	77
Cranberry Upside-Down Coffee Cake	91
Eggs Benedict Casserole	80
French Toast, Deb's Stuffed	79
Fruit Pie for Brunch	75
Monte Cristo Sandwich	76
Sour Cream Coffee Cake	89

CAKES

Carrot Cake for JarvBob	194
Cherry Cheesecake, Famous	190
Chocolate Pound Cake, Eloise's	184
Cranberry Upside-Down Coffee Cake	91
Double-Chocolate Mousse Cake	189
Dump Cake, Peg's	186
Four Layer Delite	187
Fruit Cake, Japanese Fresh	178
Kentucky Pound Cake, Frannie's	185
Mini Cheesecakes, Peg's	165
Sour Cream Coffee Cake	89

CANDIES

Bon-Bons, Peanut Butter	200
Bon-Bons, Peanut Butter-Coconut	201
Candied Walnuts, Mrs. Sears' version	202
Candied Walnuts, Peg's version	202
Martha Washington Candy	198

CHEF'S SPECIALTIES

Beef

Beef Wellingtons, Peg's Individual	99
Châteaubriand with Peg's Béarnaise Sauce	97
Spice Rub	216

Pork

Pork Chops, Peg's	110
Pork Tenderloin, Ivy Manor Chili-Coated	100

Poultry

Poulet Perigourdine, French Classic	103
Spinach-Stuffed Chicken, Zom's	105
Turkey Salad, Warm	106

Seafood

Cassola de Plix, Seafood Casserole	109
Crab Cakes, Peg's	34

CONGEALED SALADS

Congealed Salad, Frannie's	57
Eggnog Flan Salad	60
Eggnog Salad Mold	60
Fruit and Cranberry Mold, Peg's	56
Orange-Pineapple Salad	54
V.I.P. Pineapple Salad	59

COOKIES

Apple Drop Cookies, Teresa's	150
Fruitcake Cookies	151
Lemon Cherry Cookies	148
Fudge Quickies	146
Macaroons, Peg's Almond	149
Macaroons, Peg's Chocolate	149
Macaroons, Peg's Coconut	149
Macaroons, Peg's Lemon	149
Mexican Wedding Ring Cookies	153
Peanut Butter Cookies, Irresistible	147
PB and Chocolate Chip Cookies, Flourless	145

DESSERTS

Aebleskiver	172
Aebleskiver, Traditional Danish	173
Amazin' Raisin Torte, Grace's	179
Baklava, Peg's Walnut and Rum	174
Blackberry Cobbler, Peg's	155
Brownie Torte, Peg's	181
Cannoli, Cottone	171
Chocolate Glaze	177
Cream Puffs, Peg's Famous	168
Cream Puff Filling, Vanilla	169
Fudgy Fudge Pudding, Peg's	167
Pecan Tarts, Peg's Mini	166
Pumpkin Roll, Peg's	182
Southern Pecan Torte	177

DUMPLINGS

Cheddar Cheese Dumplings	64
Cornbread Dumplings	71
Jalapeño-Cheddar Cheese Dumplings	71

ENTRÉES

Chicken and Sausage Tostadas	136
Green Chili Enchiladas, Zom's	135
Meat Pie, Peg's	134
Salmon and Veggie Rice, Peg's	132
Summertime Garden Pasta	118

ICE CREAM

Mud Pie, Peg's	162
Vanilla Ice Cream, Old-Fashioned Homemade	197

MISCELLANEOUS

Decorating Ideas, Peg's	215
Hints, Peg's	216
Measuring	214
Party-Planning Tips, Peg's	212
Spice Rub	216

PIE

Apple Pie, Peg's Upside-Down	156
Coconut Cream Pie	160
Double Coconut Cream Pie, Peg's	160
Hawaiian Cream Pie, Peg's	160
Mud Pie, Peg's	162
Strawberry Pie, Glazed	159
Pineapple Macadamia Pie	158
Piecrust, Mother Infield's	163

PUNCHES

Champagne Punch	211
Hot Christmas Punch	211
Southern Hot Cider	208

Index cont.

Salad Dressings

Buttermilk Dressing	45
Creamy Dill Dressing	49
Honey-Pecan Dressing	39
Orange-Poppy Seed Dressing	43
Sweet & Sour Dressing	42
Tropical Salad Dressing	46

Vinaigrettes

Cranberry Vinaigrette	52
Pomegranate-Lime Vinaigrette	53
Special Vinaigrette, Peg's	40
Tarragon Vinaigrette, Fresh	106
Vegetable Vinaigrette, Fresh	121

Salads

Beet Salad, Fresh	116
Chicken Salad, Curried	48
Christmas Eve Salad	53
Crab Salad, Peg's Famous	50
Fruit Salad, Fresh Southern	39
Gourmet Salad, Ivy Manor	40
Green Tomato Salad, Ivy Manor Fried	45
Ham and Spinach Salad	43
Organic Salad Greens	42
Party Dream Salad	61
Salmon Salad, Hawaiian	46
Shrimp and Avocado Salad	49
Turkey Salad	52
Turkey Salad, Warm	106
Vegetable Salad, Fresh	121
Watergate Salad, Frannie's	57

Salsa

Black Bean Salsa	67
Fruit Salsa, Peg's Fresh	36
Mango Salsa, Peg's	37
Mango-Pineapple Salsa	46
Peach-Avocado Salsa, Fresh	100

Sauces

Béarnaise Sauce	97
Cherry Sauce, Fresh	192
Crème Anglaise	195
Crème Fraîche	137
Lemon Cream Sauce	103
Lemon Dill Sauce	139
Lemon-Dill Mayonnaise	35
Lemon-Mustard Sauce	138
Mayonnaise, Mom's Homemade	141
Mushroom Cream Sauce	99
Red Bell Pepper Sauce, Roasted	35
White Wine Sauce for Pasta	140

Side Dishes

Artichokes and Potatoes Au Gratin	127
Beet Salad, Fresh	116
Calico Beans	119
Green Rice, New Mexico	129
Pasta, Summertime Garden	118
Peas, Ivy Manor Sugar Snap	122
Potato Casserole, Peg's	130
Potatoes, Peg's Scalloped	128
Tomato Tarte Tatin, Ivy Manor	115
Vegetable Salad, Fresh	121
White Corn, Fresh Fried	120
Zucchini Pie, Fresh Herb	124

Soups

Minestrone Soup, Peg's	63
Pecan Soup, Southern	68
Sweet Potato Soup, Southern	70
Turkey Tortilla Soup	66
Zucchini Soup, Zom's	64

Specialty Drinks

Eggnog	208
Eggnog, JarvBob's Famous	209
Tea, Southern Sweet	207

Peg's Recipe for Living

There are recipes for how we live our lives. My personal recipe includes ingredients I have needed for survival as well as recipes that have enabled me to flourish and thrive. Enjoy!

Blend equal amounts of the following:

COURAGE
to look life in the eye

STRENGTH
to move into the unknown

OPENNESS
to new ideas and to learning about those ideas

WILLINGNESS
to take responsibility for what we think or do

COMMITMENT
to personal integrity

FAITH
in the purpose and sacredness of life

Stir and simmer to blend flavors.
When cool, add humor in abundant quantities.
Serve daily and enjoy!

Acknowledgments

First, I want to thank my husband, Jarvis G. Ivy, who is not only loving and supportive but also loves good food. His appreciation of food has played a huge role in our lives together. In all that I have done, his wise guidance and steady encouragement have never faltered. Without him, this book would not be published.

To my three beautiful daughters, Deborah, Teresa, and Dana, my deep and heartfelt appreciation goes out to each of you. We have been a team. Thank you for being open to trying your mother's recipes and for your candid opinions and assistance through the years. You have been my inspiration. I am proud of you and of the women you have become.

I want to say thanks to my older sister Frannie for offering unbounded love, strong guidance and her gracious teachings — from Southern manners to how to style my hair, do my make-up, and how to put a great meal on the table.

Thanks to my very best friend, Ruth Ann Sletten, for always listening, for encouraging me to go far beyond what I thought were my limitations and for supporting me in all of my endeavors. Thanks for never being critical and accepting me for who I am—flaws and all. You have encouraged me to blossom and grow. You are what being a best friend is all about. I love you dearly and am blessed that you are in my life.

And to my sister-in-law, Christa Ivy—who is more like a sister to me—thank you for sharing recipes and cooking ideas over the years and offering "rescue" advice when something went wrong. Your assistance and ideas in preparing for the photo shoot for this book were invaluable. But most of all, thanks for being there for me!

My appreciation goes out to all of the wonderful chefs who have blazed the trail for so many of us, and to the food editors of newspapers and magazines whose work motivates and inspires us. You have certainly inspired and influenced me. Your fingerprints can be found here, and I thank you for them.

A special thanks to Dr. Lois West Bristow, from whom great words flow, for your editing and assistance with this book. Thanks for your devotion to this project and for bringing life to my stories. Words will never be sufficient to express how much you are appreciated.

This book would not have been possible without the expertise and guidance of great friends and mentors, Shukri Farhad and Mike Verbois.

And finally, an abundance of appreciation goes to all of you who believed in me and kept nudging me to finish this book. Thank you.

In memory of

My mother, Grace Lee Martin ∼ 1901-1993

My sisters, Sara Nell Bellamy ∼ 1921-2012
Opel Eloise Ware ∼ 1936-2014

My brothers, George Washington ∼ 1924-2007
Robert Lee Washington ∼ 1927-2013
Douglas Kyle Martin ∼ 1938-1999
Jerry Eugene Martin ∼ 1941-2011

The only dad I knew, John M. Plaza ∼ 1923-2012

Dr. Olaf Fisher and Peggy J. Ivy